How Humans Learn to Think Mathematically

How Humans Learn to Think Mathematically describes the development of mathematical thinking from the young child to the sophisticated adult. Professor David Tall reveals the reasons why mathematical concepts that make sense in one context may become problematic in another. For example, a child's experience of whole number arithmetic successively affects subsequent understanding of fractions, negative numbers, algebra and the introduction of definitions and proof. Tall's explanations for these developments are accessible to a general audience while encouraging specialists to relate their areas of expertise to the full range of mathematical thinking. The book offers a comprehensive framework for understanding mathematical growth, from practical beginnings through theoretical developments, to the continuing evolution of mathematical thinking at the highest level.

David Tall is Emeritus Professor of Mathematical Thinking at the University of Warwick and Visiting Professor at the Mathematics Education Centre, Loughborough University. He is internationally known for his research into long-term mathematical development at all levels, from preschool to the frontiers of research, including in-depth studies explaining mathematical success and failure.

LEARNING IN DOING: SOCIAL, COGNITIVE AND
COMPUTATIONAL PERSPECTIVES

SERIES EDITOR EMERITUS
John Seely Brown, *Xerox Palo Alto Research Center*

GENERAL EDITORS
Roy Pea, *Professor of Education and the Learning Sciences and Director, Stanford Center for Innovations in Learning, Stanford University*

Christian Heath, *The Management Centre, King's College, London*

Lucy A. Suchman, *Centre for Science Studies and Department of Sociology, Lancaster University, UK*

BOOKS IN THE SERIES

(Continued after index)

How Humans Learn to Think Mathematically

Exploring the Three Worlds of Mathematics

DAVID TALL

Emeritus Professor in Mathematical Thinking,
University of Warwick
Visiting Professor, Mathematics Education Centre,
Loughborough University

CAMBRIDGE
UNIVERSITY PRESS

CAMBRIDGE
UNIVERSITY PRESS

32 Avenue of the Americas, New York NY 10013-2473, USA

Cambridge University Press is part of the University of Cambridge.

It furthers the University's mission by disseminating knowledge in the pursuit of education, learning and research at the highest international levels of excellence.

www.cambridge.org
Information on this title: www.cambridge.org/9781107668546

First published 2013

A catalogue record for this publication is available from the British Library

Library of Congress Cataloguing in Publication data
Tall, David Orme.
How humans learn to think mathematically : exploring the three worlds of mathematics (embodiment, symbolism, formalism) / David Tall.
    pages   cm. – (Learning in doing : social, cognitive and computational
    perspectives)
Includes bibliographical references and index.
ISBN 978-1-107-03570-6 (hardback) – ISBN 978-1-107-66854-6 (paperback)
1. Mathematics – Philosophy.   2. Mathematics – Psychological aspects.
3. Mathematics – Study and teaching.   4. Thought and thinking.
5. Knowledge, Theory of.   6. Cognition.   7. Cognition in children.   I. Title.
QA8.4.T33   2013
510.1–dc23   2013002749

ISBN 978-1-107-03570-6 Hardback
ISBN 978-1-107-66854-6 Paperback

To My Family, Friends,
Teachers, Colleagues and Research Students,
Who Made this Book Possible

Contents

Series Foreword

This series for Cambridge University Press is widely known as an international forum for studies of situated learning and cognition. Innovative contributions are being made by anthropology; by cognitive, developmental and cultural psychology; by computer science; by education; and by social theory. These contributions are providing the basis for new ways of understanding the social, historical and contextual nature of learning, thinking and practice that emerges from human activity. The empirical settings of these research inquiries range from the classroom to the workplace, to the high-technology office, and to learning in the streets and in other communities of practice. The situated nature of learning and remembering through activity is a central fact. It may appear obvious that human minds develop in social situations and extend their sphere of activity and communicative competencies. But cognitive theories of knowledge representation and learning alone have not provided sufficient insight into these relationships. This series was born of the conviction that new exciting interdisciplinary syntheses are underway as scholars and practitioners from diverse fields seek to develop theory and empirical investigations adequate for characterizing the complex relations of social and mental life, and for understanding successful learning wherever it occurs. The series invites contributions that advance our understanding of these seminal issues.

Roy Pea
Christian Heath
Lucy A. Suchman

Journeys through three worlds of mathematics.

Preface

I have long been concerned with the struggle to make sense of mathematics and how it is taught and learnt in a world where a few find mathematics an enterprise of great power and beauty, many learn what to do without knowing why and many others find only anxiety and pain.

It has been my good fortune to interact with the teaching and learning of mathematics at every level from preschool to postgraduate research. As I reflected on these experiences and the insights of experts in a range of contexts, it became evident that what happens at each stage of learning is significantly affected by previous experience and has a significant effect on the development of each individual at later stages. This means that it is not sufficient to focus only on a particular level of teaching and learning, as learners at that level will already be affected by what they have met before, and what they learn now will affect future learning. This suggests the need for an overall framework for the development of mathematical thinking so that any individual participating in the enterprise may become aware of a fuller picture. This has the consequence that disputes between different viewpoints may be seen in a new revealing light.

This is, I believe, the first book to focus on the full framework of mathematical thinking as it develops from birth through to adulthood and on to the frontiers of research. It addresses very different theoretical and practical viewpoints and, though I could have decided to focus on a specific readership using technical terms related to a particular community of practice, my experience counsels me that there is a major problem in getting different communities to speak to each other. So I decided to address the book to everyone with a stake in the teaching and learning of mathematics. This includes teachers, mathematicians, educators and curriculum designers, with consequences for parents, politicians and learners, and links to other disciplines in psychology, philosophy, history, cognitive science, constructivism and so on.

This requires taking account of the differing ways in which ideas are formulated in various communities. For instance, if I speak of 'formal' mathematics, a mathematician will think of mathematics designed in terms of set-theoretic definitions and formal proof, whereas an educator following the theory of Piaget may think 'formal' refers to his notion of 'formal operational thinking'. Another reader may think of 'formal' as referring to the formal use of general principles such as 'do the same to both sides' in solving equations.

To attend to these differences I follow the lead of my late supervisor and friend, Richard Skemp, who used two words to formulate special ideas such as 'instrumental understanding' or 'relational understanding'. This juxtaposition of two familiar words in a new way signals to the reader that the terminology is intended to have a special meaning. The word 'understanding' has a general meaning, which may differ subtly for different readers, while the adjective 'instrumental' or 'relational' qualifies the meaning in a more technical way.

My friend and colleague Shlomo Vinner similarly used double-word definitions to describe 'concept definition' and 'concept image' to evoke the general idea of 'concept' in two distinct ways, one based on the definition of the concept given in mathematics, and the other based on the personal image of the concept that an individual has in mind.

I use this simple technique to formulate fundamental ideas to encourage readers from different backgrounds to reflect on the broad theoretical framework and its related empirical evidence. For instance, I need a term to encompass the richness of a meaning of a mathematical concept that becomes more sophisticated as the learner becomes more aware of subtler aspects. I term the full richness of such an idea a 'crystalline concept'. The combination of 'crystalline' and 'concept' is a signal to the reader that this term has a special use. Not only is it a concept, but it also has internal links that hold its various parts together with strong bonds that are a matter of fact within the given context. Whole numbers are crystalline concepts where 2 + 3 is 5 and cannot be 6. Likewise 5 take away 3 is 2 and cannot be otherwise. Meanwhile, in Euclidean geometry, a triangle with two equal sides must have equal angles and vice versa. In each case the relationships are an essential part of the context.

Crystalline concepts give mathematics its coherent structure. They take on their full meaning as the individual becomes attuned to more sophisticated ideas, but a young child can develop a sense of these relationships at an early stage and the learner can be encouraged to relate ideas in more coherent ways throughout the learning of mathematics.

The maturation of mathematical thinking in different individuals depends on their genetic makeup and on their successive experiences as they learn mathematics, or, more simply, in terms of nature and nurture. By analyzing how children and older students attempt to make sense of successive mathematical concepts, an overall picture of the growth of mathematical thinking emerges. It reveals how humans build ideas through *perception*, *operation* and increasingly subtle *reasoning*, using mathematical symbols and subtle developments in language.

This reveals a deep foundation that is based on what may be termed *the sensori-motor language of mathematics* that underlies three distinct forms of mathematical development, one based on the perception of objects in the world that leads to visual imagery and thought experiments, another based on operations such as counting that lead to number concepts and more sophisticated symbolic developments, and a third based on increasingly sophisticated reasoning that culminates in the formal mathematics of set-theoretic definition and formal proof.

Long-term development depends on making sense of successive levels of sophistication. Mathematics is often considered to be a logical and coherent subject, but the successive developments in mathematical thinking may involve a particular manner of working that is supportive in one context but becomes problematic in another. For example, in everyday life, and in dealing with whole numbers, taking something away always leaves less. But taking away a negative number leaves more, and strange new ideas arise, such as 'two minuses make a plus'.

This phenomenon occurs throughout the long-term development of mathematics as some supportive ways of working in one context continue to work in a subsequent context while other aspects become problematic. Emotion enters into the development as supportive aspects give pleasure and encourage generalization while problematic aspects impede progress. Some who make sense of mathematics at one level and feel confident about the future may enjoy tackling new problems, whereas others, who begin to feel that the mathematics does not make sense, may either take the alternative route to learn how to perform routines without attempting to understand them or, worse still, fall into a downward spiral of anxiety and failure.

An outline of the full theory is presented in Chapter 1. Chapters 2 to 8 are designed to be useful for teachers of mathematics at all levels and cover school mathematics and its consequences. A course for school teachers could usefully concentrate on these chapters, which include an insight into the transition to more formal axiomatic thinking.

After an interlude relating the theory to the historical development of mathematics, Chapters 10 to 14 move on to more advanced topics appropriate for university level, while allowing non-experts to gain a sense of the full range of mathematical thinking.

The final chapter reflects on the overall framework and its relationships with other theoretical frameworks. In particular, by using the observation that supportive aspects in one context may be problematic in another, it reveals new ways of blending different theories together. Rather than indulge in a polemic argument about which of various theories is to be preferred, it reflects on the use of theories being appropriate in different contexts and suggests that a range of conflicting theories have valuable aspects that can be blended together to make more coherent sense. By focusing on foundational ideas, it seeks a framework that applies not only to the personal development of differing individuals from child to adult, but also to the cultural evolution of mathematics in history, and towards the evolution of theories of mathematical thinking in the future.

Acknowledgements

This book is based on thirty years of research and development that depended on the active participation of others. My son, Nic, was my inspiration when, as a boy of five years old, he told me of his ideas on infinity that were far beyond what I expected of such a young child.[1] From then on I was always aware of the very different ways in which children develop.

I had the benefit of two of the greatest thinkers in their subjects as supervisors for my doctorates in mathematics and in the psychology of education: Sir Michael Atiyah, Order of Merit, former President of the Royal Society, awarded the Fields Medal and the Abel Prize for his distinguished research in mathematics, and Professor Richard Skemp, author of *The Psychology of Learning Mathematics* and a major force in the development of the new field of mathematics education. Both feature significantly in the text, as do my colleagues and research students, in particular Eddie Gray, who shared with me the best years of my academic life, as researcher and co-author with his rich insights into the thinking of young children, and as co-supervisor of many of our research students.

Various colleagues have shared developments with me: Professor Richard Skemp, a constant source of inspiration, with a wealth of original ideas on 'instrumental and relational understanding', the emotional affects of goals and anti-goals, and distinct modes of building and testing mathematical concepts; Professor Shlomo Vinner for his ideas on 'concept image'; Dr. Eddie Gray on the flexible idea of 'procept', dually representing process and concept; Professor Efraim Fischbein and Professor Dina Tirosh on concepts of infinity; Dr. Tony Barnard on his theory of 'cognitive units', which became the theory of 'thinkable concepts' and, more significantly, of 'crystalline concepts' in this book; Professor John Pegg, from

---

[1] Tall (2001).

whom I learnt to link van Hiele theory in geometric development with SOLO taxonomy used for analyzing qualities of learning; and Dr. Anna Poynter, with whom I discovered the three worlds of mathematics through her research on the visualization and symbolism of vectors, and her student, Joshua Payne, who explained to us his idea that 'the sum of two free vectors is the unique free vector that has the same *effect*.'

In many ways, a simple idea can trigger off a completely new train of thought. The notion of 'effect' gave rise to the link between embodied action and compressed symbolism that was the key turning point in the formation of the whole theory of 'three worlds of mathematics' – from embodiment and symbolism in school mathematics to the formal mathematics taught in universities and developed at the frontiers of research. Such ideas stimulate hypotheses that can then be tested in empirical research and built into coherent theories.

Other colleagues who had fundamental ideas that significantly changed my thinking include Rolph Schwarzenberger, Christopher Zeeman, Ian Stewart, David Fowler, Bernard Cornu, Gontran Ervynck, Walter Milner, Nicholas Herscovics, David Wheeler, Joel Hillel, James Kaput, Dick Lesh, Pat Thompson, John Mason, Tommy Dreyfus, Ted Eisenberg, Uri Leron, Keith Schwingendorf, David Feikes, Ed Dubinsky, Anna Sfard, Pessia Tsamir, Guershon Harel, Ivy Kidron, Gary Davis, Adrian Simpson, Janet Duffin, Luiz Carlos Guimarães, Gila Hanna, Bill Byers, Stephen Hegedus, Masami Isoda, Nellie Verhoef, Mikhail Katz, Boris Koichu, Walter Whiteley and many others too numerous to name.

All of my doctoral students earned their PhDs by teaching me something new: Professor John Monaghan (UK), Professor Michael Thomas (UK, now New Zealand), Dr. Norman Blackett HMI (UK), Dr. MdNor Bakar (Malaysia), Dr. Eddie Gray (UK), Dr. Yudariah binte Mohammad Yusof (Malaysia), Dr. Maselan bin Ali (Malaysia), Professor Philip DeMarois (USA), Professor Mercedes McGowen (USA), Dr. Marcia Pinto (Brazil), Dr. Richard Beare (UK, now Australia), Dr. Robin Foster (UK), Professor Lillie Crowley (USA), Dr. Soo Duck Chae (Korea), Dr. Ehr-Tsung (Abe) Chin (Taiwan), Dr. Anna Poynter (UK), Dr. Hatice Akkoç (Turkey), Dr. Nora Zakaria (Malaysia), Dr. Victor Giraldo (Brazil), Dr. Amir Asghari (Iran), Dr. Rosana Nogueira de Lima (Brazil), Dr. Juan Pablo Mejia-Ramos (Colombia, now USA), Dr. Walter Milner (UK) and Kin Eng Chin (Malaysia). Their research is the backbone of the development of the framework in this book, together with that of other Warwick University research students, in particular, Professor Demetra Pitta (Cyprus), Dr. Hazel Howat (UK), Dr. Ruslan Md Ali (Malaysia),

Dr. Eirini Geraniou (Greece), Dr. Lara Alcock (UK), Dr. Matthew Inglis (UK) and Dr. Michelle Challenger (UK).

I have also had the long-term support of my wife Sue and our children, Becki, Chris and Nic and their children, Lawrence, Zac, James, Emily and Simon, who have talked to me about mathematics over a lifetime.

I dedicate this book to all those mentioned above.

Illustration Credits

The illustrations in this book were prepared by the author with the exception of the following:

The 'three world layout' on page xii, figures 6.5, 6.6, 6.8, 7.12 and 14.1, include the figure of a child (© Rebecca Tall and Lawrence Hirst), Plato © Florida Center for Instructional Technology, and Hilbert (public domain in the USA).

Figure 2.1 © Tetsuro Matsuzawa.

Figure 2.7 © Zac Hirst.

Figure 3.1 includes pictures of a robin (© Eng 101, Dreamtime.com), penguin (© Jan Marin Will, Dreamtime.com), kiwi and platypus (© Florida Center for Instructional Technology).

Figures 3.11–3.18 © Anna Poynter and David Tall.

Figure 10.2 © Md Nor Bakar and David Tall.

Figure 10.5 © Erh-Tsung Chin and David Tall.

Figure 10.7–10.9 © Marcia Maria Fusaro Pinto.

Figure 11.31 © David Tall and Piet van Blokland.

Figures 12.3–12.5 © Juan Pablo Mejia-Ramos.

Figure 14.3 based on public domain material from
http://commons.wikimedia.org/wiki/File:Mug_and_Torus_morph.gif.

In addition, Figures 8.9, 8.10, 8.12, 8.13 and 8.16, drawn by the author, have previously appeared in *The ICME Handbook on Proof and Proving in Mathematics Education*, edited by Gila Hanna and Michael de Villiers (2012), and Figures 11.19, 11.22, 11.24 and 11.30, drawn by the author, appeared in ZDM – *The International Journal on Mathematics Education* in Tall (2009).

I
Prelude

1   About this Book

Mathematics is a subject with patterns that generate enormous pleasure for some and problems that cause impossible difficulties for others. The situation is made more complicated by different views of what mathematics is and how it should be taught. This book takes a journey from the early conceptions of a newborn child to the frontiers of mathematical research. Its purpose is to present a framework that enables everyone with an interest in mathematical thinking, at any level, to communicate with others in a manner appropriate for their needs. At its foundation is the most fundamental question of all:

> How is it that humans can learn to think mathematically in a way that is far more subtle than the possibilities available for other species?

By focusing on foundational issues and relating them to the long-term development of the subject, it becomes possible to express general ideas at all levels within a single framework, from the ways in which we make sense of the world around us through our perceptions and actions, to the development of more sophisticated ideas using language and symbolism.

Contrary to common belief, new levels of mathematical thinking are not necessarily built consistently on previous experience. Some experiences at one level may be supportive at the next but others may be problematic. For instance, number facts from whole number arithmetic continue to be supportive in fractions and decimals but the experience of multiplying whole numbers sets an expectation that the product is always larger. This becomes problematic when multiplying fractions. Everyday experience tells us that 'taking something away leaves something smaller.' This works for whole numbers and fractions, but it becomes problematic when subtracting a negative number. Over time, supportive aspects encourage progress and give pleasure, while problematic aspects may cause frustration and anxiety that can severely impede learning in new contexts. As differing individuals respond in varying ways to their experiences, there arises a wide spectrum of attitude and progress in making sense of mathematics with long-term consequences.

The foundational ideas in this framework prove to be applicable not only in the teaching and learning of mathematics, but also in the study of its historical development. Even expert mathematicians begin their lives as newborn children and need to develop their mathematical ideas to mature levels in their own cultural and professional environments.

This chapter lays out all the main ideas of the framework, which are then considered in greater detail in the remainder of the book.

1. Children Thinking about Mathematics

John, aged six, sat anxiously at the back of his class as his teacher called out the problems. His page had the numbers one to ten down the left-hand side ready for ten sums in the very first Key Stage One Test in the English National Curriculum. 'Four plus three', called the teacher firmly. Her instructions required students to respond to a question every five seconds. John held out four fingers on his left hand and three on his right and began to count them, pointing at his four left-hand fingers with his right index finger, saying silently, 'one, two, three, four', switching to his right hand, pointing with his left index finger, 'five, six, sev …'. 'Six plus two!' said the teacher. John panicked. He did not have time to write his first sum down and turned his attention to the second. Six plus two is: 'one, two, three, four, five, six, …'. Again his thought was interrupted as the teacher called: 'Four plus two!' John managed this one: the answer was six. He started to write it down, but now he didn't know which number question he was on and wrote it in the space beside the number two. 'Five take away two.' John wrote 'three' in the space beside the number three. So it went on, as he sometimes failed to complete the sum in the given five seconds and sometimes, when he completed the problem in time, he didn't know where to write the answer. He failed his Key Stage One test, feeling glumly that he would never do well in mathematics. It was just too complicated.[1]

In the same school, Peter, not yet five years old, was given a calculator that enabled him to type in a sum such as '4 + 3' on one line and then, when

---

[1] Eddie Gray and I observed and videoed this episode during a study of how young children perform arithmetic operations in Gray (1993) and Gray & Tall (1994).

he pressed the 'equals' key, the answer was printed on the next line as '7'. He and several friends were asked to use these calculators to type in a sum whose answer was '8'. His friends typed in sums such as $4 + 4$ or $7 + 1$ or $10 - 2$, all of which they could also do practically by counting fingers or objects.

Peter typed in the sum $1000000 - 999992$. He knew this was 'a million take away nine hundred and ninety nine thousand, nine hundred and ninety two'. But, of course, he had never counted a million. Just think how long it would take! He could start briskly with 'one, two, three, four, five …' and keep a moderate pace with 'one hundred and eighty seven, one hundred and eighty eight, one hundred and eighty nine, …' but he would be really struggling with 'one hundred and eleven thousand two hundred and seventy eight, one hundred and eleven thousand two hundred and seventy nine, one hundred and eleven thousand two hundred and eighty'.

Peter's ideas arose not directly from counting experiences, but from his knowledge of number relationships. He had clearly been given a great deal of support with number concepts outside of school. Even so, his knowledge was exceptional. He knew about place value: that 10 represented ten, 100 is a hundred, 1,000 a thousand and 1,000,000 a million. He knew about tens of thousands, hundreds of thousands and that a million was a thousand thousands. He knew that 9 and 1 makes 10, 39 and 1 makes 40, 99 and 1 makes a hundred and 999,999 and 1 makes a million. For him it was straightforward to see that just as the sum 92 and 8 gives 100, the sum of 992 and 8 gives a thousand and 999,992 and 8 is a million.[2]

Here we have two children in the same school at about the same age thinking very differently. Can we find a single theoretical framework that encompasses both? Do they both go through the same kind of development, but one happens to achieve more success than the other? How can we formulate a single theory that enables us to improve the teaching and learning of mathematics in a world in which some find mathematics an amazing thing of beauty while others find it a source of problematic anxiety?

To seek a unified theory of the development of mathematical thinking, this book studies the underlying development of mathematical ideas, some of which make sense and support more sophisticated mathematical thinking and some of which are problematic and impede progress.

---

[2] This episode was recorded by Eddie Gray as part of the same study in the same school.

2. The Long-Term Development of Mathematical Ideas

Mathematical thinking uses the same mental resources that are available for thinking in general. At its foundation is the stimulation of links between neurons in the brain. As these links are alerted, they change biochemically and, over time, well-used links produce more structured thinking processes and more richly connected knowledge structures.[3] The strengthening of useful links between neurons provides new and more immediate paths of thought, so that processes that occur in time – such as counting to add numbers together to get '3 + 2 is 5' – are shortened to operate without counting, so that '3 + 2' immediately outputs the result '5'. This involves a *compression* of knowledge in which lengthy operations are replaced by immediate conceptual links.

The long-term development of mathematical thinking is consequently more subtle than adding new experiences to a fixed knowledge structure. It is a continual reconstruction of mental connections that evolve to build increasingly sophisticated knowledge structures over time.

Geometry begins with the child playing with objects, recognizing their properties through the senses and describing them using language. Over time, the descriptions are made more precise and used as verbal definitions to specify figures that can be constructed by ruler and compass and eventually the properties of figures can be related in the formal framework of Euclidean geometry. For those who study mathematics at university, this may be further generalized to different forms of geometry, such as non-Euclidean geometries, differential geometry and topology. (Advanced topics featuring here, will also be given elementary explanations for the general reader in later chapters.)

The learning of arithmetic follows a different trajectory, starting not with a focus on the *properties* of physical objects, but on *actions* performed on those objects, including counting, grouping, sharing, ordering, adding, subtracting, multiplying and dividing. These actions become coherent mathematical operations and symbols are introduced that enable the operations to be performed routinely with little conscious effort. More subtly, the symbols themselves may be seen not only as operations to be performed but also compressed into mental number concepts that can be manipulated in the mind.

---

[3] The term 'knowledge structure' may have various connotations in cognitive science, philosophy and other disciplines. Here I refer broadly to the relationships that exist in a particular context or situation, including various links between concepts, processes, properties, beliefs and so on.

Young children are introduced to counting physical objects to develop the concept of number and to learn to calculate with numbers. As they learn to count, they will find that 7 + 2 calculated by counting 2 after 7 to get 'eight, *nine*' is far easier than 2 + 7 by counting 7 after 2 as 'three, four, five, six, seven, eight, *nine*'. Initially it may not be evident that addition by counting is independent of order, but when this is related to the visual layout of objects placed in various ways, properties of arithmetic emerge, such as addition and multiplication being independent of order of operation, and multiplication being distributive over addition. These observations may be formulated as the 'rules of arithmetic' offering a basis for symbolic proof. At a more advanced level, the whole numbers may be formulated as a list of axioms (the Peano Postulates) from which familiar properties of arithmetic may be proved as formal theorems.

Measurement also develops out of actions: measuring lengths, areas, volumes, weights and so on. These quantities can be calculated practically using fractions or to any desired level of accuracy using decimals. Numbers can be represented as points on a number line and formulated at university level as an axiomatic system (a complete ordered field).

Algebra builds on the generalized operations of arithmetic with symbolic manipulations following the rules observed in arithmetic. Algebraic functions may be visualized as graphs, and later algebraic structures may be formulated in various axiomatic systems (such as groups, rings and fields).

Likewise, concepts in the calculus can be expressed visually and dynamically as the changing slope of a graph and the area under a graph, which may be approximated by numerical calculations or expressed precisely through the symbolic formulae for differentiation and related techniques for integration. At university these ideas may be expressed axiomatically in the formal theory of mathematical analysis.

Vectors are introduced as physical quantities with magnitude and direction, written symbolically as column vectors and matrices, and later reformulated axiomatically as vector spaces.

Probability begins by reflecting on the repetition of physical and mental experiments to think how to predict the likely outcome, then performing specific calculations to calculate the probability numerically, and later formulating the principles axiomatically (as a probability space).

These developments incorporate three distinct forms of knowledge. The first involves the study of objects and their properties, leading to mental imagery described in language that grows increasingly subtle. The second grows out of actions that are symbolized and develop into operations in arithmetic and algebra compressed into mental objects such as numbers and algebraic expressions that can be used to formulate and solve problems using operational symbolism. Both develop initially through practical experiences at home and in school and develop through the use of more theoretical definitions and deductions in school.

The third form of mathematical knowledge flowers in the formal approach to pure mathematics encountered at university.

The full framework grows in sophistication from the activities of the child to the frontiers of mathematical research. (Figure 1.1.)

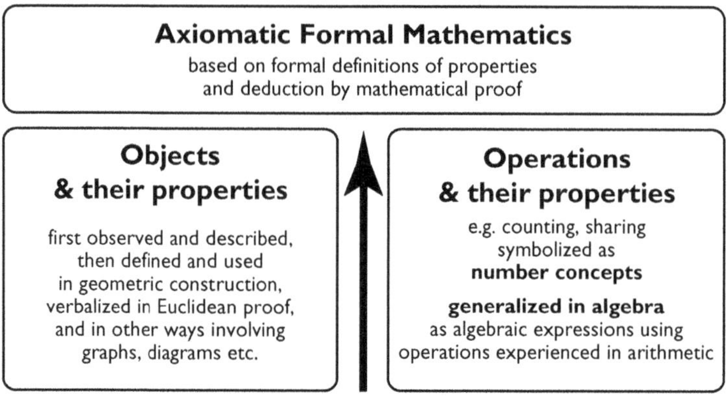

Axiomatic Formal Mathematics
based on formal definitions of properties
and deduction by mathematical proof

**Objects
& their properties**

first observed and described,
then defined and used
in geometric construction,
verbalized in Euclidean proof,
and in other ways involving
graphs, diagrams etc.

**Operations
& their properties**

e.g. counting, sharing
symbolized as
number concepts

generalized in algebra
as algebraic expressions using
operations experienced in arithmetic

Figure 1.1. An initial outline of three forms of knowledge in mathematics.

3. Existing Theoretical Frameworks

We are already privileged to have many frameworks available to provide an overview of human development in general and mathematics in particular. The father figure of modern developmental psychology, Jean Piaget[4], formulated a stage theory for the long-term development of the child through the pre-language *sensorimotor* stage, a *preoperational* stage in which children develop language and mental imagery from a personal viewpoint, a *concrete-operational* stage wherein they develop stable conceptions of the world shared with others, and a *formal-operational* stage developing the capacity for abstract thought and logical reasoning.

Jerome Bruner[5] classified three modes of human representation and communication: *enactive* (action-based, using gestures), *iconic* (image-based

---

[4] References on Piaget's Stage Theory are numerous. See, for example, Baron et al. (1995), pp. 326–9.
[5] Bruner (1966), pp. 10, 11.

using pictures and diagrams) and *symbolic* (including language and mathematical symbols).

Efraim Fischbein[6] focused on the development of mathematics and science, and formulated three different approaches, which he called *intuitive*, *algorithmic* and *formal*.

Each of these frameworks presents a long-term development from physical perception and action, through the development of symbolism and language and on to deductive reasoning. They also formulate different ways of building specific concepts. Bruner and Fischbein differ in detail, but both see a broad conceptual development in which the enaction and iconic imagery of Bruner relates to the intuition of Fischbein while Bruner's symbolic mode of operation refers not only to language, but also explicitly to two particular forms of symbolism in arithmetic and logic (relating respectively to mathematical algorithms and formal proof).

Piaget complements his global stage theory by formulating several ways in which new concepts are constructed. The first is *empirical abstraction* through playing with objects to become aware of their properties (for instance, to recognize a triangle as a three-sided figure and to distinguish this from a square or a circle).

The second is *pseudo-empirical abstraction* through focusing on *actions* on objects. This plays a major role in arithmetic where operations such as counting and sharing lead to concepts such as number and fraction.

He also formulates *reflective abstraction* where operations at one level become mental objects of thought at a higher level. This has proved to be fruitful in describing how addition becomes sum, repeated addition becomes product, and, more generally, an operation such as 'double a number and add six' becomes an algebraic expression $(2x + 6)$ that is both a process of evaluation and a thinkable algebraic object that can be manipulated to solve problems. Reflective abstraction is essentially a succession of higher-level extensions of pseudo-empirical abstraction.

By analogy, there is a fourth type of abstraction that generalizes empirical abstraction of the properties of physical objects, to imagine mental objects that can exist only in the mind, such as points that have no size and straight lines that have a length but no width. This may be termed *Platonic abstraction* as it forms Platonic mental objects by focusing on the essential properties of figures.[7] (Figure 1.2.)

---

[6] Fischbein (1987).
[7] This idea of three (or four) ways of constructing mathematical concepts was proposed in Gray & Tall (2001).

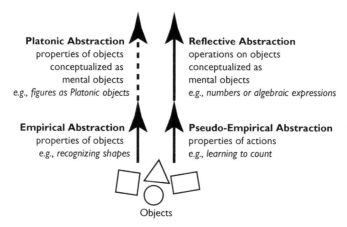

Figure 1.2. Piagetian and Platonic abstraction.

These four types of abstraction belong naturally to two long-term developments, one building from the properties of objects (empirical and Platonic abstraction), and the second from actions on objects (pseudo-empirical and reflective abstraction). These two developments relate directly to the first two forms of long-term development in mathematical thinking formulated earlier. The first focuses on the structure of objects, the second on actions that become operations that are symbolized as mental objects such as numbers and algebraic expressions. I shall refer to these as *structural abstraction* and *operational abstraction*. (Figure 1.3.)

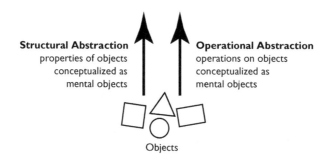

Figure 1.3. Long-term abstraction.

These ideas relate to the vision of Pierre van Hiele's *Structure and Insight*[8] in geometry, and Anna Sfard's formulation of operational and

---

[8] Van Hiele (1986).

structural conceptions[9] in general mathematical thinking, which will evolve into essential aspects of the wider framework developed in this text.

Although elementary recognition of shape and number is found in other species, only *Homo sapiens* develops sophisticated mathematical ideas such as the theorem of Pythagoras, or the proof that there are an infinite number of primes. This intellectual development arises through the development of language and symbolism, which Terence Deacon characterizes by recognizing *Homo sapiens* as *The Symbolic Species*.[10]

Mathematical thinking begins in human sensorimotor perception and action and is developed through language and symbolism. In *Philosophy in the Flesh*, George Lakoff and Mark Johnson formulate the idea of an 'embodied concept' as 'a neural structure that is actually part of, or makes use of, the sensori-motor system of our brains'.[11] This analysis is consonant with a combination of Bruner's enactive mode operating 'through action' and his iconic mode that involves not only visualization but also 'depends upon visual or other sensory organization and upon the use of summarizing images'.[12]

In *Where Mathematics Comes From*,[13] Lakoff and Núñez formulate the origins of mathematical thinking in the subtitle 'how the embodied mind brings mathematics into being'. This classification of human thought being based on embodiment can be usefully enhanced by a subdivision of embodiment into subcategories that operate in clearly different ways. The term 'sensorimotor' already refers to two different aspects of the brain: the *sensory* part relating to how we perceive the world through our senses and the *motor* part relating to how we operate on the world through our action. This relates directly to the distinction made in this text between the sensory appreciation of shape and space focusing on the structural properties of objects and the operational motor activities such as counting and sharing that lead on to arithmetic and algebra.

In his earlier book, *Women, Fire and Dangerous Things*, Lakoff refers briefly to two different aspects of embodiment that he terms *conceptual embodiment* and *functional embodiment*. The former refers to the use of mental images and the latter to 'the automatic, unconscious use of concepts without noticeable effort as part of normal functioning'.[14]

---

[9] Sfard (1991).
[10] Deacon (1997).
[11] Lakoff & Johnson (1999), p. 20.
[12] Bruner (1966), pp. 11–12.
[13] Lakoff & Núñez (2000).
[14] Lakoff (1987), pp. 12–13.

This distinction is not used, as far as I know, in any other work of Lakoff. Yet it resonates strongly with the contrast I noted previously between a *structural* focus on properties of objects and an *operational* focus on actions symbolized as mathematical operations.

I shall use the term 'conceptual embodiment' to refer to the use of mental images, both static and dynamic, that arise from physical inter-action with the world and become part of increasingly sophisticated human imagination. This includes the use of physical embodiments such as Dienes' blocks to relate to mental conceptions of numbers and arith-metic.[15] It also extends to the drawing of geometrical figures that become mental pictures described verbally in Euclidean geometry, the representa-tion of functions and graphs as static images on paper, and dynamic visual images in general, as visualized using computer graphics or solely within the mind.

Meanwhile, the manipulation of symbols in arithmetic and algebra has a functional aspect in which symbols are imagined as being shifted around mentally on the page. This functional embodiment is intimated in phrases such as 'turn upside down and multiply', 'change sides, change signs', 'put over a common denominator and add', or 'shift all the terms in x on one side and all the numbers on the other.'

This gives two different ways in which mathematical thinking grows: the use of mental images supported by language to enable us to refine and develop more sophisticated meanings, and the use of symbolism in arithmetic and algebra to formulate problems as operational equations, to solve them by calculation and symbolic manipulation. These two forms of growth occur throughout schooling before the later development of a formal axiomatic approach arises in the work of pure mathematicians. This overall development is based on three fundamental human attributes: *input through the senses* that recognizes properties of objects, *output through actions* that become routine operations, and *language* (together with symbolism) that supports both, to develop increasingly sophisticated ways of thinking and reasoning about mathematical ideas.

4. Symbols as Process and Concept

The symbols that occur in arithmetic and algebra are used in special ways. Not only do they specify operations that can be performed as a sequence of steps, they also operate as mental entities that can themselves

[15] Dienes (1960).

be operated upon. This offers a mode of operation that is different from the usual linguistic analysis for speaking about numbers.

Number words are often interpreted as adjectives or nouns, such as 'three' as an adjective in 'the three musketeers' and a noun in 'three is a prime number.' In English, words freely function as various parts of speech; for instance, the term 'abstract' can be an adjective in 'an abstract idea', a noun in 'an abstract taken from a book', or a verb 'to abstract ideas from a concrete situation'. Actions are often transformed into nouns, such as the way in which the word 'running' in 'John is running' becomes 'Running is good for your health.' The participle 'running' becomes a noun using the linguistic device that is called a 'gerund'.

However, this analysis into various parts of speech fails to capture the subtle ways in which we think about the process of counting and the concept of number. Numbers are not only used as adjectives or nouns. An expression in arithmetic such as '3 + 4' operates flexibly as an instruction to calculate the result in 'what is 3 + 4?' and also as a noun, the name of the result of the calculation, 3 + 4, which is 7. The symbol 3 + 4 operates both as a *process* (addition) and a *concept* (the sum).

Throughout the development of symbolism in arithmetic and algebra, a child learns to carry out an operation, to practice it until it becomes routine, and then to use it as a thinkable concept. A young child spends many months grasping the process of pointing and counting to find the number of elements in a set is independent of the sequence of counting and this becomes the related concept of number.

Likewise, an algebraic expression, such as $2x + 6$ may be interpreted both as a process of evaluation (twice the value of x plus 6) and also as a concept of algebraic expression that may itself be operated on. For instance, it can be factorized to give the product $2(x + 3)$. As a process, $2(x + 3)$ involves a different sequence of steps (double the result of adding the value of x and 3). However, in algebraic manipulation, the expressions $2x + 6$ and $2(x + 3)$ are interchangeable, so they may be considered as two different ways of writing the same thing. This gives a new flexibility in using symbols that occurs naturally and unconsciously for experts, but may need to be learnt explicitly by the novice.

Symbols that operate dually as both process and concept in this way give rise to a new part of speech in the language of mathematics, that Gray and Tall named a *procept*.[16] As the child relates various ways of calculating the same result, different symbols such as $7 + 3$, $3 + 7$, $13 - 3$ may then be

---

[16] Gray & Tall (1991, 1994).

reconsidered as being different ways of writing the same procept. The procept here is the number 10 and all other possible ways that an individual thinks about it to manipulate it flexibly in arithmetic. Over time it grows in richness to encompass many other connections such as 5×2, $20 \div 2$, $5 + 4 + 3 - 2$, $(-5) \times (-2)$ and even $-10i^2$. Flexible use of such symbolism to derive new relationships and to build a rich structure of flexible alternatives is called *proceptual thinking*. It manifests itself in early arithmetic as symbols are decomposed and recomposed to perform calculations. For example, the sum $7 + 6$ might be calculated by realizing that $7 + 3$ is 10 and the 6 can be seen as $3 + 3$, so that $7 + 6$ is $10 + 3$, which is 13. Later a student may factorize the expression $(2x + 3)^2 - (x + 2)^2$ by recognizing the whole expression as the difference between two squares, $A^2 - B^2$, and writing the solution $(A - B)(A + B)$ *in one operation* as $(x + 1)(3x + 5)$. A procedural thinker operating step by step is faced with a more lengthy sequence of operations, first multiplying out the expression to get

$$(2x + 3)^2 - (x + 2)^2 = 4x^2 + 12x + 9 - x^2 - 4x - 4$$

and then simplifying the expression to get

$$3x^2 + 8x + 5$$

and then factorizing this into a product of two factors using a fairly complex algorithm.

Proceptual thinking is not only important in deriving facts in arithmetic, but it is also essential in the flexible manipulation of algebra and in the long-term development of powerful mathematical thinking.[17]

5. Compression of Knowledge

The manner in which a process carried out in time may eventually be conceived as a mental concept independent of time is an example of a more general way to think of complicated situations in simple ways.

Compression of knowledge occurs when a phenomenon of some kind is conceived in the mind in a simpler or more efficient manner. This occurs through making more direct mental connections in the brain and is enhanced by using language to give the concept a name and to be able to share ideas about its properties and relationships to other concepts.

---

[17] Gray, Pitta, Pinto & Tall (1999).

Compression of knowledge occurs in several different ways. We are able to recognize things through our perception of similarities and differences, to *categorize* concepts, giving a name to identify the category, such as 'dog' or 'triangle'. This is a structural abstraction of the properties of a concept, drawing them together into a single named entity.

A second method involves the practising of a sequence of actions as a procedure so that they can be performed with little mental effort. The further compression of a process (such as addition) being compressed into a mental concept (such as sum) is an operational abstraction termed the *encapsulation* of a process as a concept.

A third method occurs as individuals use increasingly sophisticated language to specify concepts through *definition*. This is, of course, a special case of categorization. However, a definition may be used in a more formal way to *deduce* properties as a consequence of the definition.

In the framework developed in this book, mathematical thinking is seen to use categorization, encapsulation and definition in a variety of ways to compress ideas into more flexible forms.

Mathematical thinking starts with physical objects and operations on objects. In geometry objects are categorized through visual and tactile experience. Language enables this categorization to become more refined through a succession of structural abstractions as properties are recognized, described, defined and then used to deduce properties in geometry using Euclidean proof.

Symbolic thinking in arithmetic and algebra begins with operations using numbers to count objects, fractions to measure quantities, and more sophisticated representations using signed numbers, finite and infinite decimals. At each stage the operational abstraction of thinkable number concepts occurs through encapsulation. There is a growing divergence (which Gray and Tall termed 'the proceptual divide'[18]) between those who remain fixed in the procedures of counting and those who develop more flexible proceptual thinking.

Operations in arithmetic have properties that may be *recognized, described* and then *defined* as 'rules of arithmetic'. The mental number concepts also have properties that may be recognized, described and defined, such as odd numbers, even numbers, factors and prime numbers, from which further properties may be *deduced*, such as the property that every whole number can be uniquely factorized into a product of primes. In this way, arithmetic and its generalization to algebra involve both operational abstraction to

---

[18] Gray & Tall (1994).

construct number and algebraic concepts and structural abstraction of the properties of arithmetic and algebra.

At a higher level a new kind of abstraction occurs that takes mathematical thinking onto a new level. *Formal abstraction* builds from verbally defined (set-theoretic) definitions and deduces properties of the defined mathematical objects by formal proof. This is a more powerful form of structural abstraction, in which the properties are specified first and other properties are deduced from the definition. (Figure 1.4.)

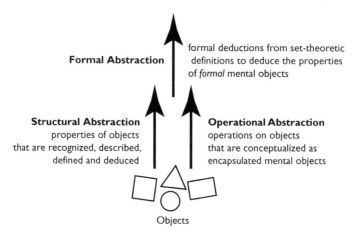

Figure 1.4. Three forms of abstraction.

The sophisticated human mind continually integrates new learning into an evolving knowledge structure. As a learner constructs each form of mathematical concept, either by categorization, encapsulation or set-theoretic definition, new developments incorporate evolving aspects of earlier forms within a single overall framework.

6. Three Worlds of Mathematics

The previous discussion highlights three essentially different ways in which mathematical thinking develops[19]:

> *Conceptual embodiment* builds on human perceptions and actions developing mental images that are verbalized in increasingly sophisticated ways and become perfect mental entities in our imagination.
>
> *Operational symbolism* grows out of physical actions into mathematical procedures. Whereas some learners may remain at a procedural level, others

---

[19] This framework has evolved from its original publication in Tall (2004).

may conceive the symbols flexibly as operations to perform and also to be operated on through calculation and manipulation.[20]

Axiomatic formalism builds formal knowledge in axiomatic systems specified by set-theoretic definition, whose properties are deduced by mathematical proof.

Each of these ways of working develops in sophistication over time, using increasingly subtle forms of language. They are more than different modes of operation. Each one has a quality of its own in a world that develops in its own special way. One is based on (conceptual) embodiment, one on (operational) symbolism and the third on (axiomatic) formalism, as each one grows from earlier experience.

The three worlds are intimately integrated within a broader framework. In school mathematics, embodiment and symbolism develop in parallel, where embodied actions give rise to symbolic operations and symbolism has embodied representations. As structural abstraction shifts to definition and deduction, this leads to the beginnings of embodied formal thinking and symbolic formal thinking, which may later translate into set-theoretic axiomatic formalism. (Figure 1.5.)

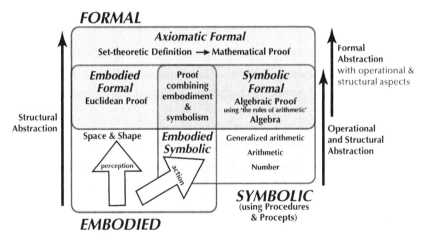

Figure 1.5. Preliminary outline of the development of the three worlds of mathematics.

---

[20] Initially the world of operational symbolism was named as 'proceptual symbolism' to represent the desirable form of flexible symbolic thinking. It is now referred to as 'operational symbolism' to include all forms of operations in arithmetic and algebra, to include both flexible (proceptual) and rote-learnt (procedural).

To be able to refer to these links between worlds, I will often compress the names to 'embodiment', 'symbolism' and 'formalism' to allow the term 'embodied symbolism' to refer to the transition between conceptual embodiment and operational symbolism, 'embodied formalism' to refer to Euclidean proof, and 'symbolic formalism' to refer to algebraic proof using the 'rules of arithmetic'.

For some time I wondered which way around I should use the pairs of words. For instance, should I speak of 'embodied formalism' or 'formal embodiment'? The answer lies in the manner in which the link is approached. Looking at embodiment becoming increasingly formal, it seemed more appropriate to use the term 'formal embodiment'; likewise, as symbolism becomes more formal, then the term 'formal symbolism' would be more appropriate. However, if one looks at the final picture, one can look from above to see formalism subdivided into three distinct forms, 'embodied formalism', 'symbolic formalism' and 'axiomatic formalism'.

There is a need for flexibility in the use of the term 'formal'. For a mathematician, 'formal mathematics' refers to mathematics presented either in terms of formal logic or in terms of set theory using formal definitions and formal proof. An educator is more likely to use the term 'formal' to refer to the 'formal operational' stage of Piaget. This tension is to be seen in Figure 1.5, where the overall term 'formal' is used to include the three forms of 'embodied formal', 'symbolic formal' and 'axiomatic formal'. We can resolve the conflict by seeing embodied and symbolic formal approaches to be the summit of school mathematics and also a basis for the applications of mathematics at higher levels. Applied mathematicians are aware of the results of formal proof, but their main task is to use the results of mathematics to study a particular situation, model it symbolically and process the symbolic model to produce a solution that can be applied to the original situation.

For higher levels of pure mathematics, the combination of embodied and symbolic mathematics can be seen as a preliminary stage to the axiomatic formal presentation of mathematics in terms of set-theoretic definitions and proof of theorems. As the story in this book shifts from school mathematics to pure mathematics in university, I will then refer to axiomatic formal mathematics simply as 'formal mathematics', provided that the context is clear.

The picture of the three-world development in Figure 1.5 applies in particular to the long-term development of reasoning and proof. This will allow three stages of development to be identified across the full range of mathematics. The initial stages involve practical experience of space and shape and calculations in arithmetic. I will refer to these as *practical mathematics*. In geometry this involves initial experiences in recognizing and describing the properties of figures that occur simultaneously without necessarily realizing that one property may imply another. In arithmetic, it involves becoming familiar with arithmetic operations and the relationships between them.

The next broad stage will be termed *theoretical mathematics*. In geometry this includes Euclidean definition and proof where the term 'theoretical' was applied by van Hiele to cover the use of definitions and Euclidean proof. In symbolic mathematics it includes the definitions and deductions of properties in arithmetic, which generalize in algebraic proof based on 'the rules of arithmetic'. Theoretical mathematics includes the more sophisticated levels of embodiment and symbolism that involve embodied and symbolic forms of definition and proof.

The third stage will be termed *formal mathematics* to refer to the development of axiomatic formal proof based on set-theoretic definitions and mathematical proof of theorems.[21] (Figure 1.6.)

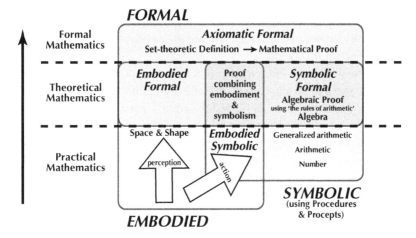

Figure 1.6. Practical, theoretical and formal mathematics.

---

[21] A viable alternative would be to call this form of mathematics 'axiomatic mathematics'. I struggled with the choice for several years and decided, in the end, to adopt the term 'formal' in line with the formalism of Hilbert.

The distinctions between practical, theoretical and formal mathematics are clearly seen in the nature of the reasoning involved. Practical mathematics involves the recognition and description of ideas in space and shape and the practical experience of arithmetic based on growing familiarity with the operations and the effects of those operations. For example, it can be seen that the order of addition of a collection of numbers does not change the final sum, nor does the order of multiplication of numbers affect the final product.

Theoretical mathematics involves the use of observed properties as definitions that can be used as the basis of deduction and proof. In geometry these include definitions of figures and ideas such as congruence of triangles to prove theorems using Euclidean proof. In arithmetic, observed properties are now recast as 'rules of arithmetic' that are then used as a basis for algebraic manipulation and proof of such relationships as algebraic identities. This leads to flexible manipulation of several symbols at a time, such as knowing that $2 + 3 + 5 + 9$ gives the same result as $5 + 3 + 9 + 2$.

Formal mathematics builds from more fundamental origins, using definitions that deal with only two elements at a time, such as the commutative law $a + b = b + a$. The associative law $(a + b) + c = a + (b + c)$ asserts that different ways of combining the elements two at a time give the same result, which may then be written as $a + b + c$. To establish the independence of order of any number of terms formally requires a proof by induction on the number of terms involved.

The transition to formal mathematics often appears overcomplicated and problematic for students who are already familiar with these general properties. The transition can be performed in a 'natural' way, building on experiences in embodiment and symbolism, or in a 'formal' way, focusing on the logic of set-theoretic definitions. However, once the idea of proving theorems in an axiomatic system is established, a new level of operation is achieved because any result proved in an axiomatic context will remain true in any new context that also satisfied those axioms.

Some formal theorems, called *structure theorems*, establish formal results that can be interpreted in terms of embodiment and symbolism. These allow higher-level mathematical thinking to combine formalism, embodiment and symbolism, blending all three worlds of mathematics into a single integrated framework. This gives an essential coherence to mathematics that offers an advantage in making sense of mathematical thinking at every level of learning.

7. Attributes that We All Share

The long-term development of mathematical thinking develops from essential human features that we all share.

The first of these is our sensory capacity for *recognition* to see patterns, similarities and differences that we express in language to categorize objects such as 'dog', 'cat' and 'triangle'.

The second builds on our motor capacity for *repetition* that enables us to practice sequences of actions until we can perform them automatically as sequential operations with little conscious thought.

The third is our fundamentally human ability for *language*. This enables us to give names to phenomena, to talk about them and refine their meaning, so that they become *thinkable concepts* that we can talk about and make mental connections to build up sophisticated *knowledge structures*. Language, including the use of mathematical symbols, raises our mathematical thinking to successively higher levels.

Language enhances recognition by enabling us to *categorize* objects and phenomena, to give them names, to talk about them and refine their meaning, to compress knowledge into thinkable concepts that we can use to build more sophisticated knowledge structures.

Language enhances repetition through the ability to give a name to the process, to *encapsulate* it as a thinkable concept that can be mentally manipulated in its own right. Now a process that is performed as a sequence of actions in time is compressed into a single entity that can operate at a higher level of thought. Complex ideas are then expressed in ways that are both sophisticated and simple.

Christopher Zeeman expressed this succinctly, saying:

> Technical skill is mastery of complexity while creativity is mastery of simplicity.[22]

Mathematical thinking requires technical skill to make calculations and manipulate symbols. It can enable the individual to solve routine problems and perform well on standardized examinations. Creative mathematical thinking requires more. It requires knowledge structures connected together in compressed ways that make complex ideas essentially simple.

---

[22] Zeeman (1977).

8. Attributes Built on Experience

Intellectual development depends on how we use our experiences to cope with new situations. Learning at one stage affects how we think at the next. A child will learn that when something is taken away, what is left is less. If you start with five apples and take away three, then only two are left. This experience serves the child well in everyday life. It is even taken as a common notion in Euclid, that 'the whole is greater than the part.' Yet this property that we all share becomes problematic in mathematics when we attempt to take away a negative number. Here, starting with 5 and taking away -2 gives 7. Taking away a negative number gives *more*. Likewise, early experience of arithmetic with whole numbers tells us that multiplication gives a bigger result, and this causes great difficulty when the product of two fractions can be smaller than either of them.

In *Metaphors We Live By*,[23] Lakoff and Johnson theorized that our thinking involves metaphors, using ideas from previous experience to refer to a new experience in a different context. This enables the biological brain to reuse existing connections to make sense of new phenomena.

The notion of metaphor is an essential part of human thinking, and its importance must be acknowledged in all situations. It allows very sophisticated analyses of the ways in which we humans think.[24] However, when we are looking at the growth of thinking of a child, it is important not just to perform a high-level metaphorical analysis of what the child may be thinking. In developing a framework for mathematical thinking from child to adult it is essential to look at the development *as it appears to the learner*, for it is this view that is directly involved in learning. I therefore sought another possible way of talking about previous experience that could be used in conversation not only from a top-down expert viewpoint, but also from a bottom-up development that could be of value to teachers and learners.

9. Set-Before and Met-Before

As I mused on the word 'metaphor', I imagined it being said as 'met-afore', using the old English word 'afore' to relate it to experiences that had been met before in the life of the child. Initially this was an amusing joke that did not raise many laughs in others. Then I changed the word to 'met-before'

---

[23] Lakoff & Johnson (1980).
[24] Lakoff & Núñez (2000); Sfard (2008).

and the new form not only sounded different, but the play on words from 'met**A**phor' to 'met**B**efore' also enabled the term to be used easily in conversation.[25] It became possible to say to a learner: 'What have you met before that makes you think that?' The term 'met-before' also proved amenable when talking to other experts, who used it easily in conversation. It operated in the way that new words operate, first as a name, with its properties to be described and then to be defined, at least in the sense of a dictionary definition. A working definition of a 'met-before' is 'a structure we have in our brains *now* as a result of experiences we have met before'.

A met-before can be *supportive* in a new situation, or it can be *problematic*.[26] For instance, the met-before '2 + 2 is 4' is supportive not only in its original context of counting objects or fingers, but throughout the development of number systems to real numbers and even complex numbers. The met-before 'take away leaves less' works for whole numbers and for (positive) fractions, but it is problematic with signed numbers, where taking away a negative number gives more. It is also problematic in the theory of infinite cardinal numbers where two sets are defined to have the same cardinal number (allowing us to say they are the same size) if their elements can be placed in one-one correspondence. The set of natural numbers and its subsets of even numbers and odd numbers all have the same cardinal number by relating n to $2n$ to $2n - 1$. Taking away the even numbers from the natural numbers leaves the subset of odd numbers with the same cardinal number as the natural numbers.

In this way, a met-before (take away leaves less) can be supportive in some contexts (whole numbers, lengths, areas) yet problematic in others (negative numbers, infinite cardinal numbers). The manner in which individuals deal with these aspects and the resulting emotional effects plays a major role in individual development of mathematical thinking.

As the term 'met-before' was used in conversation, it led naturally to the introduction of the term 'set-before' to describe the fundamental attributes that we all share. A working definition of a set-before is 'a mental structure that we are born with, which may take a little time to mature as our brains make connections in early life.'

---

[25] The term met-before is a play on words that works well in English. It translates less well in other languages where other terminology may be necessary.

[26] The idea of problematic met-before has a long history in mathematics and science education, where it has been formulated as an 'epistemological obstacle' (Bachelard, 1938). However, the earlier usage often referred to intuitive ideas that cause difficulty in later theoretical applications. Here the term met-before applies to any earlier experiences that affect current thinking and includes both supportive and problematic aspects.

At this point I realized that the capacities of *recognition* and *repetition* are set-befores that we all share, based on our human capacities for perception and action. Meanwhile *language* is the set-before specific to *Homo sapiens* that enables us to develop more sophisticated thinking.

This offers a global long-term framework for the development of mathematical thinking, based on the three set-befores of recognition, repetition and language, with three distinct ways of forming mathematical concepts through categorization, encapsulation and definition, building on met-befores.

10. Blending Knowledge Structures

The journey to develop powerful mathematical thinking involves compressing knowledge into thinkable concepts and connecting them together in knowledge structures. One further construct is required: the *blending*[27] of different knowledge structures into a new knowledge structure, perhaps leading to a newly created thinkable concept.

Our biological brains evoke thinkable concepts by a selective binding of neural structures involving a range of senses and perceptions. An apple conjures up aspects of vision, touch and smell. A red apple may offer the further promise of a sweet taste. This thinkable concept is a blend of neural structures. Likewise, a mathematical concept evokes a range of different cognitive structures, blending together different experiences to produce a single mental construct.

The real number system is a blend of embodiment, symbolism and formalism in which each contributes different aspects to our understanding of number. (Figure 1.7.)

The number line allows us to see numbers as points on a horizontal line in order from left to right. If we point at the number zero and slide a finger along to the number 1 we may imagine we are moving continuously through all the numbers from 0 to 1. However, if we think of a number as an infinite decimal, it is impossible to imagine the decimal expressions running through all the possible decimals between 0 and 1 in a finite time.

Blending ideas together from different contexts usually involves some aspects that are common and some that are in conflict. This leads to a

---

[27] See, for example, Lakoff & Núñez (2000); Fauconnier & Turner (2002). In particular, Fauconnier and Turner build a detailed theory of blending two domains of knowledge from which new elements arise in the blend that are not evident in either domain on its own, enabling the evolution of new, more comprehensive, structures.

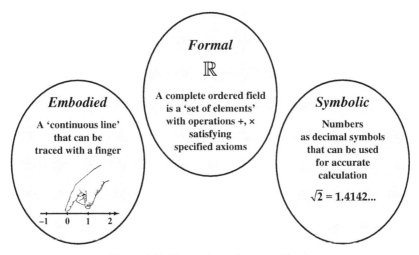

Figure 1.7. The real numbers as a blend.

divergence between those who focus on the power of the common aspects and those who are concerned about the differences.

Blending occurs when a particular context is generalized, for instance, from the counting numbers to the wider system of positive and negative integers. This will be termed an *extensional blend*. In this case the arithmetic of counting numbers is supportive, but the met-before 'takeaway makes less' becomes problematic.

The whole development of number – from whole number to fraction, to positive and negative numbers, to finite and infinite decimals represented as points on a number line – is a succession of extensional blends, broadening one number system to a larger one with richer properties. For some learners, the increasing flexibility and generality prove to be extremely powerful. For others, the subtle changes in meaning and the complications of the operations often become problematic.

Blending offers creativity as mathematical thinking develops in history as well as in the individual. By blending the arithmetic of numbers with the geometric transformations of the plane, a whole new concept of complex number was created that extended the real number system envisaged on the real line to the whole of the complex plane. Historically this took several centuries and continues to be problematic for many students, though it proves supportive for modern mathematics and applications in areas such as engineering.

11. Emotional Aspects of Mathematics Learning

Making sense of new mathematics is a challenge that blends together some aspects that are supportive and others that are problematic. A major aspect of our study of the spectrum of outcomes of mathematical learning relates to the accompanying emotional reactions.

As individuals take personal routes through their development of mathematical thinking, human emotions play a significant role in supporting or inhibiting progress. Whereas supportive met-befores encourage generalizations that give pleasure and power, problematic met-befores cause conflict in new situations, acting as a challenge to some and a source of anxiety to others.

In this way there is an intimate relationship between emotion and progress in mathematical thinking. If, at any stage, the learner encounters a new situation that is problematic, the confident learner, who has a previous record of making sense, is more likely to see the new problem as a challenge to be conquered, whereas the learner who is already feeling the strain may feel alienated and become increasingly disaffected.

This applies not only to learners but also to all of us – including teachers, mathematicians, experts who build theories and, in particular, to readers of this book. As the book is aimed at a broad audience, some topics will be unfamiliar to particular readers, be they teachers of young children with little or no experience of university mathematics, research mathematicians unfamiliar with the cognitive development of young children, or experts in other related specialties. However, the main goal of this book is to present a big picture of the whole enterprise, taking into account the supportive and problematic aspects that occur in the long-term development. To achieve this goal, readers are encouraged to see their own reactions to supportive and problematic aspects as an integral part of the whole framework.

Using the material in this book with mixed groups, I found that some primary school teachers were clearly scared of algebra or of the calculus, but they benefited from realizing how their conceptions depended on their met-befores, not on any innate stupidity. Talking about more advanced mathematics in a relaxed manner allowed them to become aware of the origins of their fears that in turn helped them empathize with the difficulties experienced by the children whom they teach.

On the other hand, expert mathematicians were often able to reflect on how different individuals make sense of formal mathematics in very different ways, to encourage them to reflect on their own thinking and the differing needs of students at university level.

Overall, the framework has helped individuals with differing forms of expertise to have a clearer grasp of their roles in the whole enterprise.

12. Crystalline Concepts

As I reflected on the increasing complication of mathematical thinking and my claim that true mathematical thinking should become not only more powerful but also more simple, I realized that the whole edifice could be integrated using a single underlying idea. The thinkable concepts of mathematics are not just compressed at the whim of the thinker, to build creations of the human mind that are totally at the behest of their creator. They are tightly organized into specific structures that are a consequence of the mathematics itself.

A thinkable concept that has a necessary structure as a consequence of its context will be said to be *crystalline*. The term does not signify that the concept necessarily has the physical features of a crystal, such as faces of a particular symmetrical shape, but that it has strong bonds within it that cause it to have inevitable properties in its given context.

This notion binds each of the developments in the three worlds of mathematics into a single overall framework. Each world builds from complicated situations, where phenomena may be imagined to have a combination of properties that are steadily linked together and seen to have necessary consequences that are implied by the context.

Even though each world constructs sophisticated mental objects in different ways, the objects themselves – as Platonic figures in geometry, numbers in arithmetic and defined concepts in formal mathematics – all grow as structures that need to be recognized and described, then defined and related through appropriate forms of reasoning and proof.

In the embodied world of Euclidean geometry, the phenomena are initially figures sketched in sand or drawn on paper. As their properties are observed and described, verbal definitions are used as a basis for constructing figures and proving theorems to develop the Platonic crystalline structures of Euclidean concepts.

Actions beginning in the embodied world are transformed into operations in the symbolic world, enshrined in the crystalline structures of an increasingly sophisticated range of procepts.

In the world of axiomatic formal mathematics, a complex structure is recognized as having properties that can be described, and then carefully defined as the basis of a formal theory whose crystalline structure is deduced by mathematical proof.

In all three worlds we see a long-term structural abstraction in mathematical thinking through recognition, description, definition and deduction. The whole development of mathematical thinking is presented as a combination of compression and blending of knowledge structures to produce crystalline concepts that can lead to imaginative new ways of thinking mathematically in new contexts.

13. A Brief Overview

This chapter has outlined the major ideas that underpin a theory of how humans learn to think mathematically.

Chapters 2 to 8 focus on the development of mathematics in school and the transition to formal mathematical thinking, beginning with the experiences of the young child involving shape and arithmetic. Chapter 3 develops the compression of knowledge into crystalline concepts. Chapters 4 and 5 study the foundational ideas of set-before and met-before and the related emotional aspects that affect long-term learning. Chapter 6 details the three worlds of mathematics and Chapter 7 focuses on the relationship between embodiment and symbolism in school mathematics. Chapter 8 studies problem solving at all levels and the long-term development of mathematical proof. These chapters offer an overview of the development of mathematical thinking, cognitively and affectively, for mathematics in school.

Chapter 9 is an interlude, using the three-world framework to analyse the historical evolution of mathematical ideas.

Chapters 10 to 14 follow the development of formal mathematical thinking and its continuing relationship with embodiment and symbolism to the frontiers of mathematical research.

Chapter 10 considers the transition from the natural mathematics of embodiment and symbolism to formal mathematical thinking in which individuals progress in a range of ways.

Chapter 11 applies the three-world framework to the calculus as a blend of dynamic visual change and operational symbolism leading to the formal ideas of the limit concept in mathematical analysis.

Chapter 12 studies the development of formal knowledge into rich crystalline concepts and the proof of 'structure theorems' that expand formalism to a various blends of embodied thought experiment, symbolic manipulation and formal proof.

Chapter 13 applies the three-world framework to the infinitely large and infinitely small, proving a structure theorem that offers a way of *seeing* infinitesimal quantities with the physical human eye, vindicating the three-world framework that blends together embodiment, symbolism and formalism as a coherent basis for mathematical thinking.

Chapter 14 carries the blending of embodiment, symbolism and formalism to the boundaries of mathematical research.

The final chapter reflects on the whole framework and its relationship with other theories.

The book closes with an appendix tracing the evolution of this theory to reveal its origins in the insights of others to whom I am forever in debt.

II

School Mathematics and Its Consequences

2   The Foundations of Mathematical Thinking

This chapter begins the quest to seek the origins of mathematical thinking by asking the fundamental question:

How does a species like *Homo sapiens* learn to think mathematically?

In particular, how do young children build ideas about space and shape on the one hand and number on the other?

Mathematical thinking occurs within a biological brain that has evolved over the millennia to enable the human species to survive and prosper in the material world. The brain is not carefully designed like a computer. Francis Crick expressed this eloquently, saying:

> Evolution is not a clean designer. ... It builds, mainly in a series of small-ish steps, on what was there before. It is opportunistic. If a new device works, in however odd a manner, evolution will try to promote it. This means that changes and improvements that can be added to the existing structures with relative ease are more likely to be selected, so the final design may not be a clean one, but rather a messy accumulation of inter-acting gadgets. Surprisingly, such a system often works better than a more straight-forward mechanism that is designed to do the job in a more direct manner.[1]

Our brains are similar to those of other great apes, with structures for perception through the senses and physical action to manipulate objects. We share many abilities with chimpanzees who can be taught to recognize numbers and put them in order, even exceeding human abilities in certain ways. For instance, the bonobo chimp Ayumu was able to remember the position of digits on a screen, flashed for only a fraction of a second,

---

[1] Crick (1994), pp.10–11.

Figure 2.1. Ayumu touching hidden numbers in sequence.

better than university students who practiced the task for six months (Figure 2.1).[2]

However, humans outstrip all other species in their creative capacity and ability to master highly complex tasks – a development that has occurred in a few thousand years after millions of years of evolutionary change. In *The Cultural Origins of Human Cognition*[3], Michael Tomasello attributes this astonishing advance to a single adaptation that uses existing cognitive skills to share and transmit advances through social collaboration. It is not simply a matter of learning to copy the activity of another person, but the realization that others think in the same way, to share and create new knowledge through cumulative social development.

There is now ample research evidence to show that a major difference between apes and humans lies in the development of socially shared skills. In a study[4] comparing human children with orangutans and chimpanzees, the apes performed as well as humans in tasks involving simple observation (such as seeing a reward placed under one of three cups on a tray and selecting the cup with the reward after the tray had been rotated). But the children were superior in tasks that required interpreting the thinking of others, such as seeing an experimenter hide three cups behind a small screen while putting a reward in one, then removing the screen and pointing at the cup with the reward. The children responded to the cue to find the reward while the apes did not.

In the wild, chimpanzees almost never point at things to draw attention to them, but in human company, they quickly learn to point without

[2] Inoue & Matsuzawa (2007).
[3] Tomasello (1999).
[4] Herrmann et al. (2007). Retrieved from http://www.sciencemag.org/cgi/reprint/317/5843/1360.pdf (Accessed August 11, 2012).

explicitly being taught, often gesturing with the whole hand towards something desired, such as unreachable food.

Pointing is essential for humans in the natural development of language. The act of pointing at something and uttering its name enables a human child to learn to name things and develop language skills. Likewise, gesturing accompanied by phrases such as 'come here', 'get up', 'sit down' and 'go over there' are linked to shared human thought and action.

From these beginnings, the human child develops socially and intellectually in ways that are far more sophisticated than his primate cousins. Language enhances social interaction and enables human children to take advantage of the knowledge accumulated in society, to develop a sophisticated personal knowledge structure that can be shared with others, developed further, and passed on through the generations.

1. Language

Children learn many words in their early years, to relate to a wide array of phenomena. From birth, a baby is usually surrounded by caring individuals who speak to him and to each other. By the end of the first year children begin to develop a vocabulary of a few individual words, which increase over the coming months. At the age of eighteen months, Emily knew:

> hello, bye, night-night, up, down, one, two, three, four, five, six, eight, nine, bath, apple, bubble, mama, dada, Emily, toes, shoes, thank-you, boo, yes, baby,

and at the same age, her brother Simon's words were:

> thank-you, another, green-man, hello-there, bye-bye, car, our-car, tractor, digger, I-get-out, I-get-down, I-get-up, nee-nah (fire engine), boo, apple, up, down, I'm-stuck (said when at the top of a slide), baa-baa (sheep), mama, Daddy, Emily, goal, gingerbread, no, yes, dog, cat, here-you-are, piggy, ball, how-are-you, woof-woof, miaow, pudding, bubble, Humpty-Dumpty, Bertie, Oh-no!, big-hug, again, OK, Peepo.[5]

Simon had more words at this stage, including several word phrases like 'I-get-down', but Emily had already started to learn counting words which made up a third of her vocabulary, in a partial sequence, strong in the first few, but still learning the later ones.

---

[5] These observations were noted down by Nicholas Tall observing his children.

Children differ greatly in the words that they learn to say, depending on their interests, the encouragement of parents and many other factors. Some of the words mentioned above were used for human communication such as hello, bye, night-night, thank-you, boo, here-you-are, peepo. Some were used to name things such as mama, dada, apple, dog, Emily, our-car, tractor, nee-nah, apple, baa-baa, Humpty-Dumpty. Others express concerns and desires – I'm-stuck, Oh-no, big-hug, again. Others deal with a variety of other aspects, including the beginnings of counting: one, two, three, four, five, six, ..., eight, nine.

At age two, Simon had an estimated vocabulary of 276 words and, within a couple of months, the list was increasing so fast that it was no longer practicable to record them. By the age of ten a child may have a vocabulary of the order of ten thousand words, continually adding new ones day by day.

2. Early Experiences of Shape

As a young child plays with toys, mental connections are made between the look and feel of various shapes. For example, at two years and ten months, Simon watched a television program with characters named Mr. Triangle, Mr. Square, Mr. Rectangle and Mr. Circle. He spontaneously put some square tablemats together to represent the characters. He called a three-by-two shape a rectangle and a two-by-two shape a square; he then rearranged the four mats into a shape with two across the bottom and two stretching above to give what he called 'a triangle'. (Figure 2.2.)

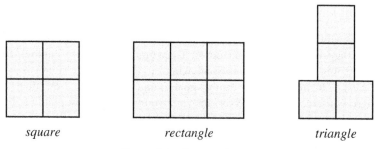

square   *rectangle*   *triangle*

Figure 2.2. Simon's shapes.

Notice that his version of a triangle does not have three sides. Yet, of the names of shapes he knows, it is closer to a triangle than to a square, a rectangle, or a circle, being wide at the bottom and narrower at the top, with a symmetry about a line through the vertical, which corresponds to the symmetry of Mr. Triangle. As his experience develops, his awareness of greater detail will lead to more precise ideas, in terms of both recognition and of reproduction of various shapes.

As children begin to draw, in the initial stages according to Piaget & Inhelder[6], children merely scribble (up to age three), Figure 2.3 (reduced from A3 size) shows eighteen-month-old Jo revelling in the power of using a crayon held in the whole hand to make a picture with large sweeps of the arm, swinging round and round, covering the page. Figure 2.4 (drawn on A4 paper) shows Nic at two years and three months with the same free expression but with greater control and finer detail using a flexible grip between finger and opposed thumb.[7]

Figure 2.3. An early drawing using a whole hand grip.

Figure 2.4. Holding the pencil with finger and thumb.

At around four years old, depending on their experiences, children begin to copy and distinguish geometric figures such as triangle and square, but it takes much greater experience to be able to perform more subtle tasks, such as copying a rhombus as opposed to copying a square.

Over the years, the coordination between hand, eye and brain becomes progressively refined and language is developed for the description of the objects and their properties. To categorize figures requires the learner to realize which aspects to focus on and which to ignore. For instance, the shapes in Figure 2.5 may be named in various ways. For a young child the

[6] Piaget & Inhelder (1958).
[7] Pictures drawn by children for the author.

first may be a square, the second a diamond and the third a rectangle. All three shapes are different. Yet shape 2 is just shape 1 turned through 45°, so it is also a square. For a mathematician, all of these are rectangles, in particular, and quadrilaterals in general.

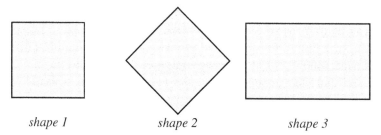

shape 1   shape 2   shape 3

Figure 2.5. Three different shapes.

3. Three Levels of Conscious Thought

The meanings of figures change as a child matures. This growing maturity is a feature of the working human brain. In his book *A Mind So Rare*[8], Merlin Donald suggests that consciousness operates at three levels. The first is 'selective binding' that operates in a fraction of a second and links together various neuronal structures to interpret what is being perceived. The second is 'short-term awareness', which links together events over a period of seconds to give a conscious flow of thought. The third level, 'extended awareness', links together events over periods of minutes or hours and extends our thought processes by reflecting upon events and conceptions that have occurred at different times. At this level, spoken and written language are used together with other forms of representation to link together various aspects at one and the same time.

It is through selective binding that we immediately attempt to make sense of what we perceive, so that a child may recognize a shape as a gestalt and see a square and a diamond as being different. By rotating the square to see a diamond, the child's short-term awareness may see the continuity of movement, revealing the square to be a diamond in a different orientation. Subsequently, through extended awareness, the child may learn to use language to say that all three shapes are rectangles with opposite sides equal and every angle a right angle.

[8] Donald (2001).

Geometrical meaning is a long journey for a child. It begins with initial perceptions of figures and talking about them to realize that the same figure may look different in different orientations. It becomes more precise through using language to describe properties of the figures. Then there is a significant development using language to specify figures by verbal definitions and the use of these definitions to infer that certain properties imply others, leading on to Euclidean geometry and beyond.

At each stage, the focus is on the *properties* of objects, which involves a *structural abstraction* of the properties (as introduced in Chapter 1). In later chapters we will see structural abstraction playing a fundamental role at successive stages of increasing sophistication not only in geometry, but also throughout the full development of mathematical thinking.

4. Early Number Concepts

A child begins to learn number names at an early age. This may involve the rhythm of nursery rhymes: 'One, two, three, four, five, once I caught a fish alive. Six, seven, eight, nine, ten, then I let it go again.'

Such rhymes have a natural rhythm that carries through to the end of a line; for example, one would not stop part way through a line such as 'Mary had a little lamb' and say, for instance, 'Mary had a.' The rhythm carries the line through to its end. Pointing at three ducks on the wall, Jessica, aged three, waved vaguely and counted 'one-two-three-four-five', completing the natural rhythm of counting.

Counting has a further complication. Pointing at something is related to naming it, but counting five objects and pointing at the last object does not mean that this last object is 'five', but that this is the number of objects in the set as a whole. Counting initially violates a basic principle, and the concept of number requires the construction of new meaning.

Counting is initially a highly complicated combination of speaking number words and pointing at objects in succession, stopping with the number at the last object pointed at. Figure 2.6 represents two different ways of counting a collection of four objects. The first starts by pointing at the disc and saying 'one', then the hexagon (two), then the square (three), then the star (*four*). The second has the same objects in a different layout and points first at the square (which here looks like a diamond), then at the disc (two), then at the star (three), and finally pointing at the hexagon and saying 'four'.

It is only when the child becomes aware that the counting process ends at the same number, no matter what order the particular collection is counted,

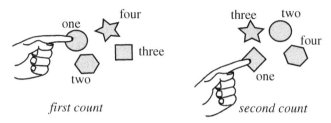

Figure 2.6. Two different counts of four.

that the concept of number begins to be formed. Now a given set has a unique number associated with it: the *number of items in the collection*. For some children, this seems to happen naturally but, as Piaget has shown, there is often a lengthy period of transition in which children believe that counting a set with a larger number of elements can give different results each time.

The words for numbers have an interesting dual function. They are used as terms in the counting sequence, 'one, two, three, …' and then have a different meaning as the number of items in a given collection. Each group of items now has its own number. Furthermore, this number is also the number of items in another set that can be paired off item by item with the first set. For instance, in setting out the table for a meal, giving each place a plate, a knife, a fork and a spoon, there is the same number of plates, knives, forks and spoons. Thus it is possible to show two sets have the same number of items by pairing off the items in one set with those in the other without specifically needing to count.

Piaget referred to this rich understanding as 'conservation of number'.[9] It includes the understanding that it does not matter how a set of objects is placed, whether the items are close together or far apart, or whether the set is counted in a different order; if two sets can have their elements placed in one-to-one correspondence then they have the same number without the need to count. These multiple mental links are necessary for the biological brain to construct the concept of number.

5. The Beginnings of Arithmetic

The learning of counting and arithmetic is long and complex. The first task is to learn to count and to do simple arithmetic by counting. For instance, to add 3 to 4, the foundational strategy is to count a collection of three

---

[9] Piaget (1952).

objects, count another collection of four objects, put the sets together and then *count all* to get seven. Those that develop conservation of number begin to realize that three separate counts are not necessary. To add 3 and 4, one might start at three and *count-on* a further four number words from three to get 'four, five, six, *seven*'. Initially this may require holding out four fingers to be counted on.[10]

Children may need to be shown how to improve their counting techniques. I well remember my own daughter Rebecca at the age of five responding to the sum '2 plus 8' by counting on eight numbers after two: 'three, four, five, six, seven, eight, nine, *ten*'. This was a complicated task, holding up eight fingers – five on one hand, three on the other – then using the fingers of one hand to point to the other, so that the role of the index finger changed from a pointing device to an item to be counted. This was performed fluently and accurately.

I separated the fingers on my left hand into three and two, then indicated that the right hand plus three left hand fingers is eight, and the remaining fingers are two. I turned my hands round the other way to show 2 and 8 had the same number of fingers as 8 and 2. Then I calculated the sum by counting on two after eight, saying 'nine, *ten*'. My daughter was *amazed*. This new technique allowed her to work out two and eight by counting-on only two, when previously she had counted-on eight! From then on she used the simpler strategy to add two numbers by *counting-on from the larger number*.

A mathematician might call this 'the commutative law'. In the time of the 'New Math' in the 1960s, an attempt was made internationally to teach children arithmetic using set theory and rules such as 'the commutative law', when they often could not pronounce the word, let alone spell it. This high-level approach to teaching mathematics from a mathematical viewpoint failed dismally. It did not allow the child's biological brain to build on its previous experiences.

For a young child, counting on eight after two is much more difficult than counting on two after eight. At this stage, counting is not commutative. A child may be shown how to 'count on from larger' to have an easier counting method. But this is not yet the full commutative law, where $8 + 2$ and $2 + 8$ are interchangeable. The child may move only in one direction, starting with $2 + 8$ and turning it round to get an easier count of $8 + 2$.

---

[10] The steady compression of counting procedures into number concepts is well established in the literature. See Gray & Tall (1994) for an analysis in terms of compression of procedures of counting into concepts of number and for a discussion of the earlier literature.

It would not make sense to replace the count-on for 8 + 2 by 2 + 8 because this makes the count more difficult.

When children learn to count, they build on their experience of counting. A child who uses 'count-all' to add a second collection to a first may solve a subtraction problem by counting out the first number as a collection of counters, then *take-away* the second number of counters and count what is left. By the same token, a child using 'count-on' may reverse the count-on procedure to *count-back* the second number from the first: to take 2 from 5, start at 5 and *count-back* two to get 'four, *three*'.

This soon gets *very* complicated. A child who attempts to calculate 18 – 16 by counting back sixteen starting from eighteen is facing an enormous task. I have seen it done, with a child counting back sixteen on his fingers, recalling part of the upward sequence to get the downward count, saying 'seventeen, sixteen, … (fourteen, fifteen), fifteen, fourteen, …' and eventually ending at the correct answer 'two'.[11]

The alternative strategy – to *count-up* from 16 to 18 by saying 'seventeen, *eighteen*' to get the difference as a count of two – is not immediately obvious. I remember when my younger son Nic, then aged about four, used to have a ten-pence piece to buy sweets at the shop and handed over his single coin only to watch with amazement as he was not only given the sweets, but he also got back more coins than he had handed over. He later developed a counting technique to take away the cost of the sweets from 10 to work out his change. He was intrigued when the shopkeeper gave him change for six pence by counting out pennies saying 'seven, eight, nine, ten', which invariably gave him the right change without doing a take-away. It was a great joy to him to learn to work out his change more easily by counting-up.

There is even a third way of counting to work out a subtraction, which is *count-back-to*. Whereas 8 – 5 can be solved by counting back five from 8 to get 'seven, six, five, four, *three*,' it can also be solved by counting back *to* the number five, saying 'seven, six, five', giving a counting back of *three* to reach five. This method of subtraction is less often used, though a calculation like 21 – 19 is easier to carry out by count-back-to 19, to get a count of 2, rather than count-back 19 numbers to get down to 2. Both of them can be replaced in this situation by the simpler counting-up in just two steps from 19 to say 20, *21*.

---

[11] This example and many others relating to children counting are taken from the research of Gray (1993) and subsequently reported in other papers such as Gray & Tall (1994).

So-called 'slow learners' often remain entrenched in their methods of count-all and count-on, using the reverse methods of take-away and count-back. Simple problems like $30 - 29$ may become a nightmare, attempting to count-back twenty-nine from thirty by going '29, 28, …' in a way that inevitably falls apart.

Speaking to young children, my colleague Eddie Gray observed a wide variety of highly inventive ways in which children attempt to cope with numbers bigger than ten.

Philip (aged 8) used his toes to supplement his fingers, though this proved problematic when attempting to move his middle toes.

Gavin (aged 9) said he *'liked counting with his fingers – that is what they are made for,'* but for problems up to twenty he assigned numbers in the teens to various parts of his body in a clockwise fashion from left shoulder, to waist, to thigh, to calf and ankle, then up his right side. *'I've only got ten fingers; I count as if I had a never-ending load.'*

Jay (aged 10) struggled with arithmetic, but did not wish to look different from other children, saying *'I'm too old for counters! My class don't use counters or fingers.'* He counted in a covert way by casually placing his fingers on the desk to count to ten and imagining a further ten fingers just off the desk to deal with numbers from eleven to twenty. He used his imaginary fingers to attempt to find a solution to $15 - 9$ by counting back. Eventually he became confused and couldn't complete the problem.

Karen (aged 11), solved the problem $15 - 9$ by holding out five fingers on her left hand and closing it completely; she then held up four fingers on her right hand closed them and opened the right thumb, then redisplayed the five fingers of her left hand at the same time and responded 'six'. The whole procedure took about three seconds. Her explanation showed a subtle understanding of number relationships (Figure 2.7).

Her highly inventive solution enabled her to solve this particular problem in her own way. She is to be complimented on her creativity. Yet this act of personal achievement proved to be a severe limitation on her future development. It worked only for calculations with small numbers that would fit on her fingers. She was unable to extend it to more sophisticated calculations.

The biological brain builds fantastic ways of performing calculations based on previous experience, but if that experience is not focused on increasingly subtle techniques of calculation, then a child may continue using old techniques that prove inadequate for more subtle problems.

Child's Hands	Child's Explanation	Interviewer's Interpretation
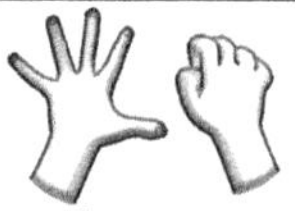	*Fifteen is ten and five. Forget the ten.*	Five fingers on left hand. (Ten in mind, not shown.)
		Nine (to take away) displayed as five and four.
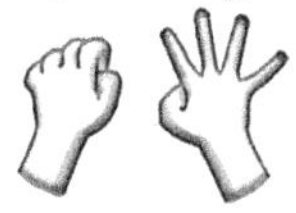		Close left hand to remove the five, leaving four in the right hand.
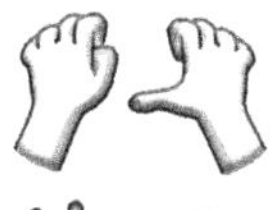	*Four, from one of the fives making ten, leaves one.*	Four in right hand taken away from a five in the mind, leaving one.
	*One and the other five from the ten makes six.*	Other five in mind now displayed to give total, 5 and 1, which is 6.

Figure 2.7. Subtracting nine from fifteen by an inventive route taking three seconds.

6. Symbols as Process and Concept

To solve increasingly complex problems, the biological brain needs to organize concepts in ways that enable them to be manipulated easily. For instance, a counting operation can be symbolized and conceived as the *result* of the operation – as the thinkable concept of number in its own right, rather than as the process of carrying out the operation.

Fields medalist William Thurston expressed this succinctly:

I remember as a child, in fifth grade, coming to the amazing (to me) realization that the answer to 134 divided by 29 is $134/29$ (and so forth). What a tremendous labor-saving device! To me, '134 divided by 29' meant a certain tedious chore, while $134/29$ was an object with no implicit work. I went excitedly to my father to explain my major discovery. He told me that of course this is so, *a/b* and *a* divided by *b* are just synonyms. To him it was just a small variation in notation.[12]

[12] Thurston (1990).

Thurston's amazing insight made me realize, in an instant, that mathematical thinking was something quite different from the viewpoint that I, as a mathematician, had ingrained in my soul. At the highest level, mathematical ideas are presented as formal definitions and deductions carried out by formal proof. This means that a definition of a mathematical concept must be clear, precise and *unambiguous*. Yet here symbolism was being used in a deliberately ambiguous way. The symbol $134/29$ is used in two different ways, to represent a *process* of division and the *concept* of fraction.

This switch from a symbol representing a process to thinking of the symbol as a concept is an instance of operational abstraction.

It is an insight that is subtly different from Thurston's father's assertion that the two symbols '*a/b*' and '*a* divided by *b*' are just a small variation in notation. While Thurston's father saw two different symbols representing *the same* underlying concept, Thurston saw the single symbol $134/29$ referring to *two entirely different things*: a process to be carried out, and a concept produced by carrying out that process.

It is generally considered that mathematicians wish to avoid ambiguity in mathematics because precision is seen to be vital. Now I see that this ambiguity and flexibility in using symbolism is *essential* to enable us to think mathematically.[13]

When we ask a child 'what is four plus three?' are we implicitly giving the child an instruction to perform a calculation, or do we simply require the answer, seven? Are we aware that the same sentence can have two very different meanings? For one child it may be an instruction to carry out a counting procedure; for another it may require only the recall of a number fact.

To describe the use of a symbol operating ambiguously as process and concept, Eddie Gray and I took the first syllable of process and the last syllable of concept and called it a 'procept'. In an attempt to be more precise, we invented a rather cumbersome 'definition' to formulate the idea, declaring that

> An *elementary procept* is the amalgam of three components: a process that produces a mathematical object, and a symbol that is used to represent either process or object.
>
> A *procept* consists of a collection of elementary procepts having the same object.[14]

---

[13] See, in particular, Byers (2007), *How Mathematicians Think*, whose working title was originally *Mathematics in the Light of Ambiguity*.
[14] Gray & Tall (1994), p. 121.

This enabled us not only to see the symbol $3 + 2$ as a process or concept (as formulated by Thurston); it also enabled us to refer to the same entity in different ways such as 5, or $3 + 2$, $1 + 4$, $4 + 1$ and so on, as formulated by Thurston's father.

We also realized that the notion of procept applied throughout arithmetic, algebra and symbolic calculus, enabling symbols to be used flexibly as process or concept, including $3 + 2$ (the process of addition, the concept of sum), $\frac{3}{4}$ (the process of sharing, the concept of fraction), $3x + 6$ (the process of evaluation, the concept of expression), showing its versatility in many areas of mathematical thinking.

The shift from process to concept is an enormous compression of knowledge allowing us to replace thinking about a process in time to thinking about a concept as a single mental entity that can be manipulated in its own right. Instead of counting, a sum like $8 + 6$ can be calculated flexibly by noting that $8 + 2$ is 10 and the 2 taken from the 6 leaves 4 to give the final answer 14.

This flexible use of number symbols leads to a powerful arithmetical engine wherein new facts can be derived from old, shifting arithmetic to a new level of sophistication. It is the first of many compressions of processes into thinkable concepts that occur throughout arithmetic, algebra and symbolic calculus.

The word 'procept' is itself a powerful compression, using a single word to describe how a symbol may be conceived as a process or a concept. The new term enables us to talk about the phenomenon and gain further insight into how children develop powerful ways of thinking in arithmetic.

7. Procepts as Crystalline Concepts

The notion of procept is our first example of a 'crystalline concept' wherein the relationships are discovered by the child. Once the child realizes that the number of items in a collection is independent of the method of counting, putting together two separate collections, say one of 5 objects and one of 4, then the total number of objects is $5 + 4$, which will always count to give 9. The result is a matter of fact, not of choice. It is part of a much richer system of relationships, where taking 5 from 9 must leave 4, or seeing that $5 + 4$ is one less than $5 + 5$, where this may be seen to be 10 (as two hands full of fingers), so $5 + 4$ is one less than 10, which is 9.

A child becomes aware of these relationships through experience and the consistency of operations. The flexible thinker can use these relationships to derive new relationships from those already known. If one seeks to add 'twelve and five', the language does not suggest any obvious short-cut, but realizing that 'twelve' is also 'ten and two' gives the result 'twelve and five' is 'ten and two and five', which is 'seventeen'. However, this flexibility may not be evident to children when they first experience the addition of numbers greater than ten. Longer-term, it is the underlying crystalline structure that makes whole number arithmetic simpler for learners who are able to derive new number facts from facts already known.

8. The Divergence in Performance in Arithmetic

While some children develop flexible ways of thinking with number concepts, others cling to procedures of counting that give them confidence operating with small numbers but are inadequate in dealing with larger numbers. A child may know a range of facts but not be able to use them flexibly to solve related problems, such as knowing 5 + 3 is 8 but not being able to use it to derive 15 + 3 is 18.

A child may even have a strategy for solving a problem by manipulating the symbols but have inadequate knowledge to carry it out. For example, Stuart (aged ten) responded to the problem 8 + 6 saying *I know 8 and 2 is ten, but I have a lot of trouble taking 2 from 6. Now 8 is 4 and 4; 6 and 4 is 10; and another 4 is 14.*[15] Stuart is to be complimented on his ingenuity, but with only partial knowledge of facts he is not able to cope with more complicated problems. At this point in time, he knows various number combinations adding to ten but has difficulty remembering 6 − 2 is 4.

Research reveals that flexible thinkers often see numbers 'flashing' into their minds, suggesting a switch to a different way of thinking about the problem[16]. For instance, a ten-year-old asked to work out 9 + 7 said he saw 10 and 6 flash through his mind and gave the answer 16. At this stage he was not counting or using images of actual objects, his focus was on the numbers themselves and the connections between them.

Children with this form of flexible knowledge have moved into a new sphere of mental operation. They have left behind the immediate need to count (though they *could* count if necessary, usually employing a more efficient method depending on the problem). Now they operate with mental number concepts, treating symbols as procepts, putting them together, seeing them in related forms and using these links to move swiftly to a conclusion. For them arithmetic is an activity rich in connections that makes it simple to perform.

[15] Gray & Tall (1994).
[16] Pitta & Gray (1997).

This flexible form of thinking is not just conceptual, it is *proceptual*, meaning that it moves easily and effortlessly between seeing expressions as operations to be performed in time and as thinkable concepts in their own right. It reveals the child having a sense of the links between numbers as crystalline concepts.

Meanwhile, other children who need to focus on the procedural steps of the counting operations have a much harder task that becomes even more difficult as the numbers increase in size.

There grows a divergence in performance wherein some develop flexible proceptual thinking that operates in more sophisticated ways compared with others who are imprisoned in limited counting procedures that become ever more complicated. While the flexible thinker develops a generative engine to construct more sophisticated methods in arithmetic with numbers of any size, the child limited to counting procedures is faced with an ever-growing mountain to climb.[17]

9. Reflections

In this chapter we have seen children grow in a supportive society, making connections to make sense of ideas, using social skills to learn from adults and taking the first steps in shape and space on the one hand and whole number arithmetic on the other. This development involves building on previous experience, compressing complicated situations into thinkable concepts and making connections between them.

Mathematical thinking emerges in two different forms: space and shape focusing on the properties of objects through structural abstraction, and number focusing on actions such as sorting and counting that lead on to the concept of number through operational abstraction.

The initial experience of figures is the beginning of a longer-term process in the development of geometry as the child steadily builds visual and tactile experiences of figures and begins to describe their properties.

The parallel development of number starts with sorting objects into collections and learning to count them, with a steady compression of counting procedures from the initial count-all to add together the number of objects in two sets through count-on and more efficient counting techniques that lead to remembered number facts and the flexible use of known facts to derive new number combinations from known ones.

[17] Gray & Tall (1994).

The arithmetic of whole numbers reveals the first examples of crystalline structure in mathematics in terms of the built-in relationships in whole number arithmetic. A spectrum of performance develops in which some children are still focusing on the step-by-step procedures of counting, while others develop a flexible proceptual knowledge structure enabling them to work fluently with larger numbers.

The ideas in the chapter also relate to the foundational ideas of Donald which specify three distinct levels of consciousness:

- *Selective binding* of neural structures (in a fraction of a second) to give thinkable concepts,
- *Short-term awareness* linking events into a conscious flow over a period of a few seconds,
- *Extended awareness* over longer periods using spoken and written language and a range of representations to build more sophisticated knowledge structures.

These will prove to be valuable in the analysis of the conceptual development of mathematical thinking in the longer term.

3   Compression, Connection and Blending
of Mathematical Ideas

In this chapter we consider the development of more sophisticated mathematical thinking through mental *compression* into *thinkable concepts* and *connection* between them to build *knowledge structures* that can be *blended* together to offer more sophisticated ways of thinking. The climax of mathematical thinking occurs with the formation of *crystalline* concepts that have a built-in structure of internal relationships.

Compression of knowledge is essential to enable us to make sense of complicated situations. We compress time and distance to a human scale. We compare events that happened years apart by recalling them and talking about them at will. We speak easily of millions of years of evolution, or of light-years of distance to another galaxy in the universe. We imagine tiny parts of matter far smaller than we can see – molecules, atoms, quarks – and we imagine tiny fractions of a second that we cannot sense in real time. All of these mysteries of our imagination use our extended awareness to take us beyond our physical confinement in time and space to enable us to think in highly sophisticated ways.

In this chapter we introduce three major methods of compression using *categorization* based on recognition, *encapsulation* based on repeating actions that are symbolized and can be manipulated as mental entities and *definition* that uses language to formulate a specific concept in a given context. We will find that definitions in mathematics occur in different ways: as Euclidean definitions of observed figures, as definitions of observed properties of numbers and arithmetic, and as more general set-theoretic definitions as the basis of more formal mathematical thinking.

1. Compression into Thinkable Concepts

I first met the idea of compression of knowledge in the writing of Fields Medalist William Thurston, who remarked:

> Mathematics is amazingly compressible: you may struggle a long time, step by step, to work through some process or idea from several approaches. But once you really understand it and have the mental perspective to see it as a whole, there is often a tremendous mental compression. You can file it away, recall it quickly and completely when you need it, and use it as just one step in some other mental process. The insight that goes with this compression is one of the real joys of mathematics.[1]

Compression of knowledge enables us to think of essential ideas, without being diverted by unnecessary detail. Language facilitates this process by enabling us to name important aspects of complicated situations and talking about them to refine their meaning. This focus gives rise to a *thinkable concept*, conceived by the biological brain as a selective binding of neuronal structures, that allows us to focus our attention on it. It will have the widest possible connotation, naming an object, a property, a relationship, an emotion, or essentially anything that the human mind can focus on. As befits the operation of the human brain evolving opportunistically over millions of years, compression into thinkable concepts occurs in a range of different ways, all of which occur through the same fundamental process of strengthening links between neurons to enable the brain to grasp a phenomenon as a single entity.

In the next three sections, we will focus on the three major forms of compression that occur in mathematics – *categorization* based on recognition of essential properties, *encapsulation* based on repeating actions that are symbolized and can be manipulated as mental objects, and *definition* that uses language to formulate specific concepts as a basis for mathematical reasoning and proof.

2. Categorization

In Chapter 2 we saw how children begin to make sense of the world by naming things such as 'apple', 'ball', 'toes'. Eleanor Rosch and her colleagues[2] noted that children first recognize 'basic' categories, which are characterized by having simple words attached to them, such as 'dog' or

---

[1] Thurston (1990), p. 847.
[2] Rosch et al. (1976).

'car'. It is only later that these are separated out into subcategories or placed together in higher categories to give successively nested categories such as 'poodle-dog-animal' or 'Ford-car-vehicle'.

Basic categories have properties that relate naturally to immediate perception. A basic category usually has prototypical mental images that can be imagined as 'representatives' of the category. The category of 'birds' includes a robin or a sparrow, which act as prototypes, even though we know of other birds that stretch the imagination. Familiar birds have wings, they can fly, they have beaks and they lay eggs. But a penguin is a bird and it can't fly, although it does have a beak and lays eggs. A kiwi is a flightless bird without visible wings. A duck-billed platypus has a beak and lays eggs, but it is not a bird. (Figure 3.1.)

Figure 3.1. Categorizing a bird.

In mathematics, basic categories often have 'typical' representatives that fully represent the properties of the whole category. For instance, in the category of products of whole numbers, any product can be represented by a specific rectangular array of counters, such as 3 rows of 2 columns. This enables us to 'see' that the total number of counters is 3×2 or 2×3 and gives a 'typical' picture in which multiplication of whole numbers is independent of the order.

This observation is independent of the number of rows and columns. It can be seen, just by looking, that all rows in Figure 3.2 have the same number of counters, as do all the columns, and the total calculated by multiplying the two together is independent of the order of operation. The picture is a genuine prototype of the concept without the need to count.

Many mathematicians are wary of visual arguments like this and assert, quite rightly, that the figure shows only a *single* example, not all possible cases. A mathematical proof requires a logical argument that does not depend on the vagaries of a specific picture. However, in this case, the

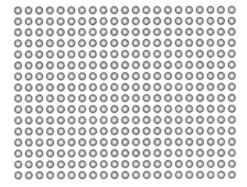

Figure 3.2. A prototypical example of a rectangular array of counters.

picture is typical of *all* pictures in the category. It is not a picture of a robin representing 'any' bird such that the robin can fly and another bird (such as an ostrich) may not. It is a picture of a rectangular array with a number of rows and a number of columns that is typical of *all* such cases, even those with so many sides that they are too big to draw. The picture may be seen as a *generic* example: a specific picture that can be imagined to represent all possible cases of the same phenomenon.

In everyday life, categorizing and grouping things into named collections can be highly complex. Various European languages categorize nouns into two or three genders – masculine, feminine and neuter – with a special form of the definite article such as 'le' and 'la' in French and 'der', 'die', 'das' in German. The reasons for some of these are related directly to gender: man is 'l'homme' (masculine) or 'der mann' and woman is 'la femme' or 'die Frau'; however, girl is 'la fille' and 'das mädchen' – a girl is classified as feminine in French and neuter in German.

The reasons for many classifications are no longer evident. The choices may even seem to be arbitrary. For instance, in French some animals have male and female counterparts: a cat is 'le chat' or 'la chatte'. Others have a specific gender for both sexes: a zebra is always 'le zèbre' and a giraffe 'la giraffe', regardless of whether it is male or female. In all such matters, our ancestors have made a choice. The reasons for these choices are often lost in the mists of time, and it is simply a case of learning the conventional form, something that the biological human brain has the resources to accomplish.

In mathematics the conventions in selecting and naming specific categories are chosen in ways that are considered appropriate for the context, but they may not always be consistent. For instance, the Greeks categorized isosceles and equilateral triangles as two distinct categories wherein an equilateral triangle has three equal sides and an isosceles triangle has precisely two. On the other hand, the modern definition of square allows it to be seen as a special case of a rectangle. Thus three-sided figures were classified separately while four-sided figures are now classified allowing inclusion. Even definitions in mathematics may involve arbitrary conventions shared within society.

2.1 *Long-term Development of Categorization in Geometry*

The learning of geometry begins with a child's experience of shape and space and develops in sophistication through structural abstraction as the child conceptualizes increasingly subtle aspects of spatial ideas. The Dutch mathematics educator Pierre van Hiele formulated this long-term development of geometric concepts as a sequence of successive levels of thinking in which each builds on the previous one, with subtle changes in meaning from one level to the next.[3]

Subsequent research has sought to refine the definitions of the levels and to show that they are broadly hierarchical. However, it is found that learners may respond at different levels on different questions in a given test.[4]

At the first level (here termed *recognition*[5]), a triangle is recognized as a basic category by its visual shape. A good example is the 'give way' traffic sign in some countries to tell vehicles to give way to others. Even though its corners are rounded, it fits the general idea of a 'triangle'. (Figure 3.3.)

At level 2 (*description*), the meaning of a figure is refined by describing its basic properties. A triangle has three straight sides (but it can have many different shapes). Rectangles and squares have four sides and all angles are right angles, but all sides of a square are equal and those of a rectangle are not. A figure is seen *as a whole*; for instance, an equilateral triangle has equal sides *and* equal angles and one is not a consequence of the other.

---

[3] Van Hiele (1986).
[4] Gutiérrez et al. (1991).
[5] The van Hiele levels have been given various different names by van Hiele himself and subsequent commentators such as Hoffer (1981) and Clements & Battista (1992). These are as follows:

Van Hiele level	Hoffer (1981)	Clements & Battista (1992)	This book
1	Recognition	Recognition	Recognition
2	Analysis	Descriptive/analytic	Description
3	Ordering	Abstract/relational	Definition
4	Deduction	Euclidean deduction	Euclidean proof
5	Rigor	Rigor	Rigor

Figure 3.3. Give way (a triangle at level 1).

At level 3 (*definition*), new figures are categorized using the definition that specifies properties to characterize it. Now a square can be a special case of a rectangle and definitions can be hierarchical.

Definitions can also be used to specify a ruler and compass construction. For instance, an isosceles triangle is defined to be a triangle with two equal sides. It may be constructed by drawing a straight line and marking two points, *A*, *B*, on it. To construct equal sides *AC* and *BC*, one then draws two arcs of circles with the same radius, one centred on *A*, the other on *B*, and if they cross in a point *C*, then *ABC* is a triangle with *AC* = *BC*. (Figure 3.4.)

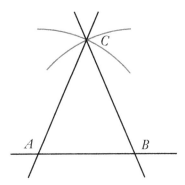

Figure 3.4. Constructing an isosceles triangle with ruler and compass.

Something profoundly new occurs here. Only the sides are involved in the construction. The angles are not mentioned. Yet the resulting figure can now be seen to have equal angles.

At level 4 (*Euclidean proof*) Euclidean geometry is used to deduce that, in the context of ruler and compass construction in the plane, if a figure has a certain property, then it also has another. The idea of congruent triangles arises through the laying of one triangle on top of the other. For instance, Euclid Book I, Proposition 4 states:

> If two triangles have two sides equal to two sides respectively, and have the angles contained by the equal straight lines equal, then they also have the

base equal to the base, the triangle equals the triangle, and the remaining angles equal the remaining angles respectively, namely those opposite the equal sides.[6]

The proof takes two triangles, *ABC* and *DEF*, where *AB* = *DE*, *DF* = *DE* (Figure 3.5) and begins as follows:

> If the triangle *ABC* is superposed on the triangle *DEF*, and if the point *A* is placed on the point *D* and the straight line *AB* on *DE*, then the point *B* also coincides with *E*, because *AB* equals *DE*.

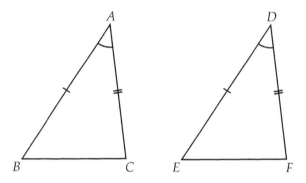

Figure 3.5. Two sides, included angle.

It continues by describing how the equality of the angles *ACB* and *DEF* causes the side *DF* to be superimposed on *AC* and so the triangle *DEF* is superimposed on *ABC* and the remaining sides and angles are equal.

Euclidean proof is a coherent organized system but it does not use the formal logic of modern axiomatic set theory. The given proof imagines a physical operation, laying one triangle on another, and uses agreed-on principles by which two triangles having specific corresponding elements equal will, as a consequence, have all other corresponding elements equal (three sides, two sides and included angle, two angles and corresponding side, or right angle, hypotenuse and one side).

Such a principle can be used to show that an isosceles triangle (with two equal sides) must, *as a consequence*, have two equal angles. For instance, if a triangle *ABC* has two equal sides, *AB* = *BC*, then, by taking *M* as the midpoint of *AC*, we can show that $\triangle ABM$ is congruent to $\triangle CBM$ and so the base angles are equal, $\angle A = \angle C$. (Figure 3.6.)

---

[6] Taken from the version given in *Euclid's Elements* on the Internet (Joyce, 1998).

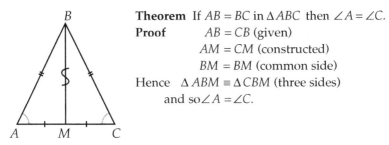

Figure 3.6. A triangle with equal sides is proved to have equal angles.

This enables the overall development formulated by van Hiele to be seen as a natural process of increasing sophistication.

1. *Recognition:* A figure is recognized by its shape and general visual appearance.
2. *Description:* The figure has various properties all of which hold simultaneously.
3. *Definition:* A figure is defined by carefully selected properties that enable it to be recognized and constructed.
4. *Euclidean proof:* The properties of figures are interrelated through relationships established by Euclidean proof.

Each of these stages involves new insights into the properties of figures. First is the categorization of the shape by its general appearance, then a focus on specific properties that can be sensed perceptually and described verbally, then as special generative properties that formulate a definition, and on to the deduction of relationships between various properties using Euclidean proof. Each of these can be seen as a new form of *structural abstraction*, focusing on properties of the structures as they are perceived in successively sophisticated ways. They give a long-term growth of sophistication through *recognition, description, definition* and *deduction* where deduction occurs using the principles of Euclidean proof.

2.2 *The Crystalline Structure of Platonic Concepts*

At levels 3 and 4, the figures in Euclidean geometry have interconnected properties, now established by Euclidean proof. For example, the isosceles triangle *ABC* drawn in Figure 3.6 now satisfies all the following:

(a) the sides *AB* and *BC* are equal;
(b) the angles *CAB* and *ACB* are equal;

(c) the line joining the vertex *B* to the midpoint of the base *AC* meets the base at right angles;

(d) the line bisecting the angle *ABC* meets the base *AC* at right angles;

(e) the line at right angles through the midpoint of the base *AC* passes through the vertex *B*.

Although it is standard practice to take (a) to be the definition of an isosceles triangle (because it is the most elementary foundation), any of the properties (a) to (e) could be used as a definition and all the others deduced from it. These properties can now be seen to be *equivalent* and interrelated within a coherent deductive system.

At this level the figure is a crystalline concept with many equivalent properties, all of which relate to the symmetry of the triangle about the line through the vertex and the midpoint of the base. (Figure 3.7.)

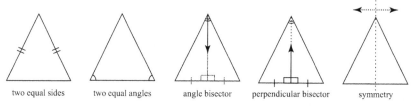

two equal sides   two equal angles   angle bisector   perpendicular bisector   symmetry

Figure 3.7. Equivalent properties of an isosceles triangle.

In addition to the figures of Euclidean geometry, other aspects are crystalline. For instance, if two straight lines in a plane never meet, then other properties necessarily follow: corresponding angles where a line cuts the two parallels are equal, alternate angles are equal, and interior angles add up to 180°. (Figure 3.8.)

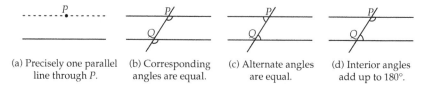

(a) Precisely one parallel   (b) Corresponding   (c) Alternate angles   (d) Interior angles
line through *P*.   angles are equal.   are equal.   add up to 180°.

Figure 3.8. Equivalent properties of parallel lines.

These various meanings for parallelism have an even more sophisticated meaning. The four given properties of parallel lines are all *equivalent*. Any one of them could be taken as the basic definition and then the others all follow. At one level they may be seen as common properties of the category of pairs of parallel lines. Any pair of lines need only satisfy one of the properties in Figure 3.8 and it then follows that they satisfy all the properties.

At a more subtle level, the concept of parallelism and its equivalent properties may be seen as simply *different aspects of the same underlying crystalline concept*: the concept of parallel lines in Euclidean geometry.

More generally, ideal Platonic concepts theorized by the Greeks can now be seen as crystalline concepts having a specific crystalline structure formulated in terms of Euclidean plane geometry.

2.3 *SOLO Taxonomy*

Another theoretical framework that has links to van Hiele theory is the SOLO taxonomy of Biggs and Collis[7] (an acronym for the Structure of Observed Learning Outcomes). This was originally designed to assign appropriate credit to successive levels of response in assessment as *unistructural* (noticing one aspect), *multistructural* (several aspects), *relational* (various aspects related together), or *extended abstract* (seen as a coherent whole). For instance, in solving a problem, a learner may recall only part of a given structure to give a unistructural response. This does not mean that the learner necessarily follows a precise trajectory, learning one fact, then several, then relating them together, then fitting them into an overall structure. Nevertheless, just as the van Hiele levels are consistent with a broad growth of connections in which thinkable concepts are linked in growing knowledge structures, SOLO taxonomy also provides a broad framework for longer-term growth.

For instance, there are relationships between SOLO taxonomy and the van Hiele levels. The first van Hiele level of recognition interprets figures as unistructural in the sense that they are recognized as whole gestalts. The second level of description involves figures with multistructural properties that occur at the same time but are not yet related to each other. The third level of definition gives rise to relational properties as definitions lead to deductions that one property implies another. This develops into the extended abstract structure of Euclidean geometry.

The development of school geometry can now be seen as one long succession of structural abstractions broadly consistent with van Hiele theory

---

[7] Biggs & Collis (1982). This book is concerned primarily with providing a template for the evaluation of learning rather than the learning process itself. However, it has been used to gain insight into how learning occurs through cycles beginning with the knowledge of individual elements of situations, moving on to several elements, relating them together, and then seeing them as part of a bigger picture.

and SOLO taxonomy. Other forms of geometry develop in different contexts, each with its own overall development of increasingly sophisticated thinkable concepts within evolving knowledge structures.

2.4 *Re-evaluating the van Hiele Levels*

In his later years, van Hiele simplified his system of levels for school mathematics to just three: *visual* (corresponding to level 1), *descriptive* (level 2) and *theoretical* (combining levels 3 and 4).[8] The difference between the descriptive level and the theoretical level is essentially the development of reason in the form 'if one property holds, then another property is also true,' as in 'if a triangle has two equal sides, then it also has two equal angles.' Using this new classification, I retain the term 'recognition' over 'visual' because it refers to the full range of senses that are appropriate for recognizing properties not only in geometry but also throughout mathematics.

I introduce the term *practical geometry* for the study of space and shape that includes the levels of recognition and description, to distinguish it from the *theoretical geometry* of definition and Euclidean proof. This gives a natural distinction between practical geometry, where properties occur simultaneously, and theoretical geometry, where one property may be seen as a consequence of another. (Figure 3.9.)

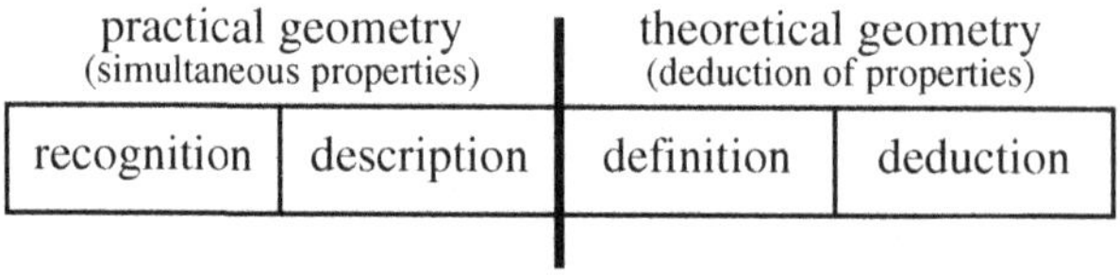

practical geometry (simultaneous properties)		theoretical geometry (deduction of properties)	
recognition	description	definition	deduction

Figure 3.9. Practical and theoretical aspects of geometric development.

This framework of structural abstraction will prove to apply equally well to the structural development of properties not only in geometry, but also in operational symbolism and axiomatic formalism.

2.5 *Long-term Development of Other Forms of Geometry*

The original fifth van Hiele level of rigor speaks of different forms of geometry from the geometry of Euclid. These take two significantly different forms. One is the recognition of other embodied forms of geometry such as projective geometry and geometry on the surface of a sphere. The

---

[8] See, for example, van Hiele (2002).

other is Hilbert's more refined logical development of Euclidean geometry as a set-theoretic axiomatic theory.

Hilbert's approach arose because he realized that, after more than two thousand years of Euclidean geometry, there were aspects being used implicitly that were not formally declared in the list of Euclidean axioms. For example, Euclidean geometry refers to the 'inside' of a figure without actually formulating a definition. Hilbert added axioms describing three points *A*, *B*, *C* on a line where *B* is said to be 'between' *A* and *C*. In doing this he shifted attention from the Platonic view of geometry as a theoretical extension of human perception and operation to a formal view of mathematics based only on set-theoretic definition and formal proof.

Projective geometry arose in Renaissance painting where the artist imagined looking at a three-dimensional scene and painting what he saw on a glass window, thus 'projecting' the three-dimensional world onto a two-dimensional plane. In this context, a pair of parallel lines going off into the distance will be represented by lines that meet at a point in the picture. If parallel lines are defined to be straight lines in a plane that never meet, then there are no parallel lines in projective geometry.

In spherical geometry, a straight line is defined to be the line of shortest distance between two points on a sphere. A straight line is now a great circle, so, once again, there are no 'parallel lines' because two different great circles always intersect.

Both projective and spherical geometry build on human perception of figures in space, where each has its own special structures that need to be recognized, described and then defined as a basis for the deduction of properties in these new contexts. Even though van Hiele formulated his theory of levels to apply to Euclidean geometry, the same framework of structural abstraction of properties through recognition, description, definition and deduction also applies to the long-term development of other geometries. I therefore continue to view spatial ideas of new forms of geometry as an extension of conceptual embodiment while the axiomatization of Hilbert moves into a more formal context of set-theoretic definition and deduction. I will later be able to show that the formal context involves the same structural 'van Hiele' cycles of recognition and description of relationships that are the basis for further development of formal definition and deduction.

3. Encapsulation

A second form of compression focuses on operations. In Chapter 2 we saw how the operation of counting is compressed into the concept of number and the symbols of arithmetic can operate dually as process or concept (procept). The shift in thinking from a process occurring in time to a thinkable concept independent of time is called *encapsulation*.

Piaget claimed that 'a physical or mental action is reconstructed and reorganized on a higher plane of thought and so comes to be understood by the knower.'[9] Dienes also saw how a process could become a thinkable concept, by explaining how the predicate of one sentence could become the subject of another.[10] For instance, the predicate in the sentence 'I *am adding three plus four*' might become the subject in the sentence '*Adding three plus four* gives seven.'

Robert Davis formulated the idea in more specific terms:

> When a procedure is first being learned, one experiences it almost one step at time; the overall patterns and continuity and flow of the entire activity are not perceived. But as the procedure is practiced, the procedure itself becomes an entity – it becomes a *thing*. It, itself, is an input or object of scrutiny. All of the full range of perception, analysis, pattern recognition and other information processing capabilities that can be used on any input data can be brought to bear on this particular procedure. Its similarities to some other procedure can be noted, and also its key points of difference. The procedure, formerly only a thing to be done – a verb – has now become an object of scrutiny and analysis; it is now, in this sense, a noun.[11]

Various other authors took up the same idea: Ed Dubinsky and his colleagues formulated APOS theory in which ACTIONS (perceived by the student as sequences of steps that are initially seen as external to themselves) are internalized as PROCESSES (perceived as internal wholes), encapsulated as thinkable OBJECTS, and are then situated within a growing SCHEMA of ideas. He later included the possibility that SCHEMAS may also be encapsulated as OBJECTS.[12]

At the same time, Anna Sfard formulated a theory relating *operational* mathematics, focusing on processes, and *structural* mathematics, focusing on objects and their properties, which alternated as mathematics becomes more refined[13]:

---

[9] Quoted from Beth & Piaget (1966), p. 247.
[10] Dienes (1960).
[11] Davis (1984), pp. 29–30.
[12] See, for example, Asiala et al. (1996),
[13] Sfard (1991).

A constant three-step pattern can be identified in the successive transitions from operational to structural conceptions: first there must be a process performed on the already familiar objects, then the idea of turning this process into a more compact, self-contained whole should emerge, and finally an ability to view this new entity as a permanent object in its own right must be acquired. These three components of concept development will be called interiorization, condensation, and reification, respectively.

Condensation means a rather technical change of approach, which expresses itself in an ability to deal with a given process in terms of input/output without necessarily considering its component steps.

Reification is the next step: in the mind of the learner, it converts the already condensed process into an object-like entity.... The fact that a process has been interiorized and condensed into a compact, self-sustained entity, does not mean, by itself, that a person has acquired the ability to think about it in a structural way. Without reification, her or his approach will remain purely operational.[14]

In Chapter 2 the development of number from the operation of counting was revealed as having more detailed development as it is steadily compressed from step-by-step counting sequences into number concepts through several possible stages including count-all, count-on, count-on-from-larger, known fact, derived fact. The operation of subtraction is more complex, with possible stages including take-away, count-back, count-back-to, count-up, known fact, derived fact. This reveals a multiprocedural stage between procedure and process in which several alternative procedures may be available from which the learner may choose the most appropriate in a given circumstance.

This already occurs in SOLO taxonomy, which speaks of:

unistructural: responding in terms of one aspect,
multistructural: responding in terms of several aspects,
relational: relating several aspects together,
extended abstract: having an overall grasp of the situation.

SOLO taxonomy interposes an extra *multistructural* stage in the development of counting and number between the ACTION and PROCESS stages of APOS theory.

---

[14] Sfard (1992), pp. 64–65.

Figure 3.10 compares various theories of compression, starting from an initial stage (o) where the learner has yet to take action. Stage (i) is a single step-by-step procedure, stage (ii) has several procedures to produce the same result, stage (iii) occurs when these procedures are seen to be equivalent to produce a single process and stage (iv) is the encapsulation of the structure into a thinkable concept that is now a flexible procept.

Stage	Procept Theory	SOLO Taxonomy	APOS Theory	Operational-Structural
(o) Initial action or actions prior to building a procedure (i) *Procedure*: A step-by-step procedure to carry out an operation	Procedure	Uni-structural	Action	Process (interiorized)
(ii) *Multi-Procedure*: Several different procedures to carry out the same operation, with a choice of the most efficient	Multi-Procedure	Multi-structural		
(iii) *A Single Input-Output Process:* Seen as a whole, performed by *equivalent* procedures	Equivalent procedures as a single Process	Relational	Process	Process (condensed)
(iv) *Procept:* A single thinkable concept represented by equivalent symbols operating dually as process or concept	Procept	Extended Abstract	Object (encapsulated)	Object (reified)

Figure 3.10. Stages in development from procedure to procept.

At stage (iv), an individual may not only think of a specific symbol as process or concept, but is also able to replace one notation for an equivalent one in a flexible manner. It includes not only the insight of Thurston, who saw the symbol for a fraction as either a division process or a fraction concept, but also the conception of his father that the same underlying concept can be symbolized in different ways. It involves a conceptual blending of different aspects into a single flexible concept that makes mathematical thinking simpler because alternative conceptions are now all available in a single crystalline form.

In practice, however, at a given time, different students may be operating at different levels of development, from level (o) through to level (iv). Figure 3.11 shows how a spectrum of performance may be expected for a particular type of problem.

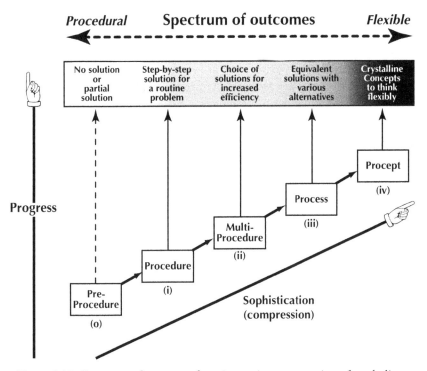

Figure 3.11. Spectrum of outcomes from increasing compression of symbolism.

At level (o), before an operational procedure has been developed for a particular problem there may be no solution or a partial solution. Procedural stage (i) is sufficient to solve a routine problem using a specific procedure. Multiprocedural stage (ii) has more than one procedure, offering the possibility of selecting a more efficient procedure for a routine problem. Process stage (iii) sees the process as an input–output operation, where the various procedures that can carry out the process are seen to be equivalent. Procept stage (iv) is the flexible stage, when it is possible to think about the symbols in the problem either as process or concept, and write them in different ways that are conceived as alternative ways of writing a single crystalline concept.

The full spectrum of outcomes suggests that routine problems can be solved by procedural methods, but more subtle problems require the greater flexibility of proceptual thinking. This broad development can be seen throughout mathematics, where operations are compressed into thinkable concepts, as can be seen from the examples that follow.

3.1 *Fractions and Rational Numbers*

In the case of fractions, several different procedures of sharing that have the same effect are called 'equivalent fractions'. In this sense, $\frac{3}{6}$ and $\frac{4}{8}$ are equivalent. But by saying they are *equivalent*, we are implicitly suggesting that they are *not the same*. As procedures, they are certainly not the same. The first divides something (say a cake) into six equal pieces and takes three; the second divides into eight pieces and takes four. They are different as a sequence of actions and they produce different results: one has three pieces, and the other has four (smaller) ones. Yet the quantity of cake that is produced is the same in both cases, and when the two equivalent fractions are marked on a number line they are marked at a single point. As *fractions* they are different but equivalent; as *rational numbers* (represented as points on the number line) they are *the same*.

3.2 *Signed Numbers*

A similar sequence of stages can be seen in the arithmetic of negative numbers. With unsigned numbers, there is a single notation for subtraction, say, $5 - 2$ is 3. With signed numbers, subtraction can be achieved by two different operations, $^{+}5 - (^{+}2)$ and $^{+}5 + (^{-}2)$ both giving $5 - 2$, which is 3. The operations $^{+}5 - (^{+}2)$ and $^{+}5 + (^{-}2)$ are different operations in stage (ii) but they are seen to be equivalent, giving the same result at stage (iii). At stage (iv), they are different ways of writing the same procept, making it simpler to replace either of them by 5.

When children are taught about the arithmetic of signed numbers, at an initial stage a distinction is usually made between the equivalent operations: $(^{+}2)$ and $+ (^{-}2)$. However, what is of longer-term importance is not that they are *different* but that they are *essentially the same* and can be represented by the simpler operation -2. When this happens, the learner is operating at a higher level where the symbols can be used flexibly and simply rather than maintaining differences in meaning that make thinking more complicated.

3.3 *Algebraic Expressions as Functions*

The same sequence of stages from procedure to procept occurs with the concept of function. First we may meet a procedure such as 'double the number and add 6', which involves a different sequence of operations in arithmetic from 'add 3 to the number and double the result'. Expressed symbolically, the first is $2x + 6$, and the second is $(x + 3) \times 2$, which is usually written as $2(x + 3)$ to satisfy the stylistic convention that, in writing products, we write numbers before algebraic expressions.

While these may be seen as two different procedures of calculation at stage (ii), they are seen as 'equivalent' at stage (iii), when, for given input, they have the same output. Written as functions, $f(x) = 2x + 6$ and $g(x) = 2(x + 3)$, they are seen as the same function at stage (iv) where both give the same output for any value of x and have the same graph.[15]

3.4 *Vectors*

A vector is usually introduced as a quantity with magnitude and direction. At stage (i), a vector may be seen as a *journey* from A to B. It may be followed by a second journey $\overrightarrow{BC}$ to give a composite journey $\overrightarrow{AB} + \overrightarrow{BC}$ starting at A and ending at C. In this way we can imagine the sum of two journeys as one journey followed by another. But this has limited application because it operates only when the second journey begins where the first one ends. It does not work for the combination $\overrightarrow{BC} + \overrightarrow{AB}$, which needs to jump across from C to A to continue the journey. The sum of journeys is not commutative: it is not even properly defined (Figure 3.12).

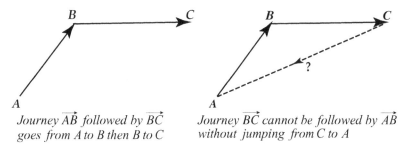

Journey $\overrightarrow{AB}$ followed by $\overrightarrow{BC}$ *Journey $\overrightarrow{BC}$ cannot be followed by $\overrightarrow{AB}$*
goes from A to B then B to C   *without jumping from C to A*

Figure 3.12. Following one journey after another.

---

[15] DeMarois (1998).

Students who think of a vector as a journey may attempt to add vectors $\overrightarrow{AB}$ and $\overrightarrow{CD}$ in Figure 3.13 by performing the journey from A to B, then jumping from B to C, to go down the second arrow from C to D to give a total journey from A to D as in solution (1). In solution (2), a student attempts to add **a** and **b** and offers two possible answers, not being sure whether to mark **a** + **b** as the journey from B to D or from A to C.[16]

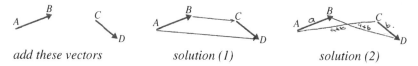

add these vectors   *solution (1)*   *solution (2)*

Figure 3.13. Adding vectors as journeys.

Figure 3.14 shows another problem in which students are asked to add two vectors that point to the same location. Solution (i) shows the student marking the vectors as **e** and **j**, and then writing **e − j** representing a journey down **e** and back along **j** in the reverse direction. Solution (ii) shows the result as the third side of the triangle, using the triangle law to fill in the third side of the triangle. The correct solution must place the two vectors nose to tail to see the true sum of the free vectors.

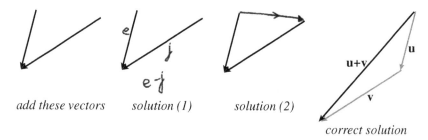

add these vectors   *solution (1)*   *solution (2)*

correct solution

Figure 3.14. Adding two vectors that point to the same location.

Anna Poynter[17] addressed these conceptual difficulties by introducing vectors as physical shifts in space to translate a flat object on a plane. At stage (i) this is an action to push a figure in a certain direction by a given magnitude. (Figure 3.15.)

[16] These results come from the PhD thesis of Anna Poynter (formerly Anna Watson) (2004). It was Anna's work on students' meanings for the concept of vector that revealed the distinctions between the different worlds of embodiment (vectors as magnitude and direction), symbolism (vectors as matrices) and formalism (vectors as elements of axiomatic vector spaces). See, for example, Watson et al. (2003).

[17] Poynter (2004).

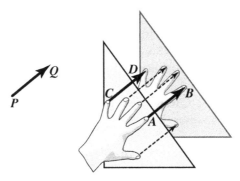

Figure 3.15. A translation of a triangle by a given magnitude and direction.

Here the first finger moves from *A* to *B* and the little finger from *C* to *D*. At stage (ii), the translation can be represented by *any one* of these vectors or by any vector $\overrightarrow{PQ}$ with the same magnitude and direction, giving a whole collection of *equivalent* vectors, $\overrightarrow{AB}$, $\overrightarrow{CD}$, $\overrightarrow{PQ}$, etc. (at stage (iii)). (Figure 3.16.)

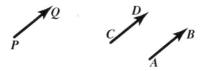

Figure 3.16. A set of equivalent vectors with the same magnitude and direction.

The final stage (iv) is a change in focus to imagine a *single vector* **u** of the given magnitude and direction that may be moved to start at any point in the plane. This moveable vector is a *free* vector that can be moved to show the translation of any particular point. (Figure 3.17.) This single free vector is an embodiment that represents the translation as a whole.

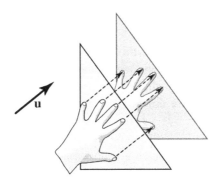

Figure 3.17. A free vector **u**.

The sum of free vectors is simply the unique single free vector that has the same effect as the two free vectors operating one after the other. This can be embodied by the simple act of moving the second free vector so that it starts where the first one ends, to give the sum using the triangle law (or parallelogram law). Figure 3.18 shows the sum of vectors **u** and **v** as $\overrightarrow{AB} + \overrightarrow{BC}$ or as $\overrightarrow{AD} + \overrightarrow{DC}$ where both give the same effect: the free vector $\overrightarrow{AC}$. Addition of free vectors is now commutative.

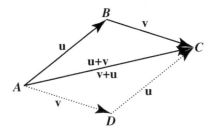

Figure 3.18. **u** + **v** = **v** + **u**.

This explanation can be performed at level (iii) using equivalent vectors, but it works much more simply at level (iv), where free vectors are added by moving them around and simply placing them end-to-end.

3.5 *Equivalence as a Transition Stage to Flexible Thinking*

In each of these four examples there is a general growth of sophistication from a single procedure, to several different procedures that give the same effect, to the *equivalence* of different procedures conceived as different ways of carrying out the same process, leading to a more flexible notion of an underlying thinkable concept.

In this development the notion of equivalence operates as a staging post, where different elements are seen as being equivalent before being compressed into a single flexible mental entity. It is the flexible entity that gives mathematical thinking its full power, becoming more powerful as it is expanded in new contexts. The procept 6 in whole number arithmetic can be thought of as a whole host of possibilities: $3 + 3, 2 \times 3, 7 - 1$, and over time it grows more sophisticated to include $\frac{12}{2}$, $(-2) \times (-3)$, $6^{(\frac{1}{2})} \times 6^{(\frac{1}{2})}$, $(\sqrt{5} + i)(\sqrt{5} - i)$ as the context shifts from whole numbers to fractions, negative numbers, rational powers and complex numbers. It is this ever-increasing sophistication of meaning of symbols as procepts that gives mathematical thinking flexibility and increasingly sophisticated computational power.

3.6 *Procepts as Crystalline Concepts*

In Chapter 2 we saw the crystalline structure of procepts in the arithmetic of whole numbers. Procepts in general are crystalline concepts that compress complicated information into manipulable mental entities. When procedures such as $7 + (^-4)$ and $7 - (^+4)$ are first encountered, they may be seen as different procedures. To maintain this difference in the long-term imposes a burden on the limited focus of attention of the human brain. When these notations are seen as interchangeable with $7 - 4$, which is 3, the cognitive strain is reduced.

Procepts have a built-in structure of relationships that enable them to be manipulated powerfully yet simply. They provide a built-in engine for manipulating symbols in the mind, deriving facts from known facts, giving a dependable flexible knowledge structure that is capable of solving problems in increasingly complex situations.

4. Definition

The third form of compression in mathematical thinking is an extension of the process of categorization. Language is used once more to specify important properties, but they are now selected to formulate a precise definition from which all other properties may be deduced. We have already seen this occur in Euclidean geometry as the focus changes from practical recognition and description to theoretical definition and deductive proof. The same structural change occurs in arithmetic and algebra as observed properties of operations and symbols are first recognized and described and then defined theoretically as a basis for symbolic proof.

Both embodied and symbolic definition and proof are later transformed into the formal mathematics of set-theoretic definition and proof.

This leads to three distinct forms of definition and proof:

- definitions of figures and Euclidean proof in geometry,
- symbolic definition and proof in arithmetic and algebra,
- set-theoretic definition and formal proof in axiomatic formalism.

4.1 *Definitions in Geometry*

Definitions in Euclidean geometry are the basis of Euclidean proof. However, they occur in two quite distinct forms. The first arises from the properties of physical figures as drawn in sand or on paper. A proof then applies to a whole category of figures where each satisfies the verbal properties stated in the theorem. At this level, a proof applies to a specific figure and the same proof can be repeated for another figure in the same category. At a higher level, these practical figures are imagined as mere shadows of perfect – yet unattainable – Platonic existence.[18] At this level a figure represents a single imagined crystalline concept.

The original books of Euclid were formulated to give an intellectual framework for mature ideas of geometry in terms of definition and Euclidean proof. Book I begins with twenty-three definitions that provide verbal formulations for geometric ideas to act as a foundation of the main framework of constructions, theorems and proofs. They include formulations such as 'a point is that which has no part,' 'a line is breadthless length,' 'the ends of lines are points' and 'a straight line is a line that lies evenly with the points on itself.' They continue with reference to surfaces, angles and figures such as circles, rectilinear figures and related ideas, ending with the definition of parallel lines.

They are followed by ten organizing principles, consisting of five 'postulates' and five conventions called 'common notions'. Postulates state what constructions are possible, such as the ability to draw a straight line from any point to any point, to extend a straight line, to draw a circle with given centre and radius, together with two more enigmatic comments: that 'all right angles are equal,' and 'if a straight line falling on two straight lines makes the interior angles on the same side less than two right angles, the two straight lines, if produced, meet on that side on which are the angles less than two right angles.' The common notions assert that 'things that equal the same thing also equal one another,' 'if equals are added to equals, then the wholes are equal,' 'if equals are subtracted from equals, then the remainders are equal,' 'things that coincide with one another equal one another,' and 'the whole is greater than the part.' These definitions can make sense only for those who have achieved a subtle level of sophistication appropriate for Euclidean definition and proof.

---

[18] This is described in Plato's allegory of the cave, in *The Republic*, Book VII, translated by Jowett (1871).

Euclid distinguished between two distinct forms of construction. The first relates to the construction of figures (based on definitions), which in Latin is followed by the mnemonic QEF (quod erat faciendum) meaning 'which was to be done'. The second relates to the proof of theorems, which are concluded with the mnemonic QED (quod erat demonstrandum) meaning 'which was to be demonstrated'. This maintains the distinction between *definition* related to constructions based on Euclidean definitions and *deduction* based on the conventions of Euclidean proof.

The formal ideas of Euclidean geometry are a natural consequence of what happens as a sophisticated learner focuses on essential properties of figures. These relate to the notion of a point as a *location* in space, or the *straightness* of a line and the ability to *extend* it as far as desired in either direction. Other aspects, such as the size of a point or the width of the line, are now irrelevant. A selective binding of the essential properties can then give rise to the conception of a perfect Platonic figure. In essence, Platonism may be seen as a natural consequence of the biological brain focusing on the essential properties and suppressing all other detail.

However, these sophisticated ideas do not arise in novice learners without considerable experience. As Dina van Hiele Geldof, the wife of Pierre van Hiele, observed:

> The deductive geometry of Euclid from which a few things have been omitted cannot produce an elementary geometry. In order to be elementary, one will have to start from a world as perceived and already partially globally known by the children. The objective should be to analyze these phenomena and to establish a logical relationship. Only through an approach modified in this way can a geometry evolve that may be called elementary according to psychological principles.[19]

Robert Recorde, the father figure of modern English Mathematics teaching, commented on the need for a practical approach in teaching in his *Pathway to Knowledge* published more than 450 years ago in 1551:

> A Poynt or Prycke is named of Geometricians that small and unsensible shape, whiche hath in it no partes, that is to say: nother length, breadth nor depth. But as this exactness of definition is more meeter for onlye Theorike speculacion, than for practise and outwarde worke (consideringe that myne intent is to applye all these whole principles to woorke) I thynke meeter for this purpose, to call a poynt or prycke, that small printe of penne, pencyle,

---

[19] van Hiele Geldof (1984), p. 16

or other instrumente, which is not moved, nor drawen from his fyrste tou-
che, and therefore hath no notable length nor bredthe.

… A great numbre of these prickes …, so if you with your pen will set in
more other prickes betweene everye two of these, then wil it be a lyne,
as here you may see – and this lyne, is called of Geometricians, Lengthe
withoute breadth.

But as they in theyr theorikes (which are only mind workes) do precisely
understand these definitions …[20]

Here we see the long history of the teaching of school geometry relating
to the practicalities of drawing with a fine pen or pencil rather than the
Platonic concepts of Euclid. (Figure 3.19.)

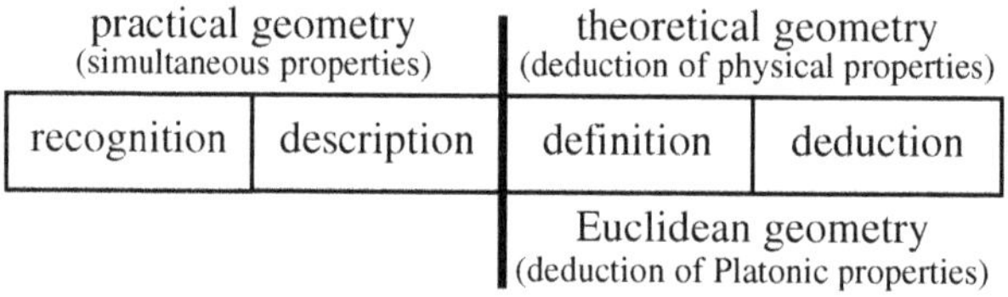

practical geometry (simultaneous properties)		theoretical geometry (deduction of physical properties)	
recognition	description	definition	deduction

Euclidean geometry (deduction of Platonic properties)

Figure 3.19. The difference between school geometry and Euclidean geometry.

It is also notable that, while Euclid saw a line as an entity on which
points could be marked, Recorde saw a line as made of 'a great number' of
points, each of which had finite size. Later Cantor would define the real
line to consist of an infinite number of points that had no size.

Although there are differences in meaning between school geometry
and Euclidean geometry, both have corresponding crystalline structures of
relationships within a framework of Euclidean proof.

---

[20] This excerpt from the book of Robert Recorde is quoted by Geoffrey Howson in *A History of Mathematics Education in England* (1982). In modern English, it translates as follows:

A Point or Prick is the name given by Geometricians to that small and non-physical shape, which has no parts, that is to say, neither length, breadth nor depth. This exactness of definition is more appropriate only for theoretical speculation than for practical work (considering that my intent is to apply all these whole principles to teaching). I think it more appropriate for this purpose, to call a point or prick, that small print of pen, pencil, or other instrument, which is not moved, nor drawn from the first touch, and therefore has no notable length nor breadth.

A great number of these pricks if you with mark in other pricks of your pen between every two of these, will be a line – as here you may see – and this line is called by Geometricians, length without breadth. But they in their theories (which are only mind works) do precisely understand these definitions.

4.2 *Definitions in Arithmetic and Algebra*

The concepts in arithmetic and algebra arise through performing operations that are symbolized and encapsulated as number concepts and algebraic expressions that can be used for calculation and manipulation.

In this development, properties that are *recognized* and *described* can be used as *definitions* of new concepts such as 'odd', 'even', 'factor', 'prime number', 'composite number'. These can be used to *deduce* theorems of arithmetic, such as the fact that there is an infinite number of prime numbers and that every whole number can be written uniquely as a product of primes.

Properties in arithmetic that are observed as being fundamental, such as the independence of order of the operations of addition and multiplication, may also be *recognized* in practice, then *described* and then reformulated, not as observed properties, but as *defined* 'rules of arithmetic' that are used as a basis to *deduce* identities in algebra and other more sophisticated ideas.

Typical rules of arithmetic that are subsequently interpreted as definitions in algebra include:

$a + b = b + a$ (the commutative law of addition),

$ab = ba$ (the commutative law of multiplication),

$a(b + c) = ab + ac$ (the distributive law).

These defined rules are then used to prove algebraic identities such as:

Algebraic identity: $(a + b)^2 = a^2 + 2ab + b^2$.

Proof: $(a + b)^2 = (a + b)(a + b)$ by definition,

$$= (a + b)a + (a + b)b \text{ using the distributive law,}$$

$$= aa + ba + ab + bb \text{ using the distributive law again,}$$

$$= a^2 + 2ab + b^2 \text{ using commutativity of addition.}$$

This gives an algebraic form of proof from specified definitions that is, once more, the culminating stage of a structural development of *recognition*, *description*, *definition* and *deduction*, now in terms of algebraic proof from defined 'rules of arithmetic'.

4.3 *Set-Theoretic Definition and Formal Proof*

A third form of definition and proof occurs at a more sophisticated level using set-theoretic definitions and formal mathematical proof. Its purpose is to free the mathematics from its particular context so that any properties proved as theorems from given verbal definitions will then apply to *any* context that satisfies the specified definitions.

Formal mathematics is not normally encountered in school. It is an enormous challenge for the learner meeting a formal approach for the first time. Any individual studying formal mathematics will already have rich knowledge structures with highly interconnected relationships. Familiar ideas may be used to *suggest* possible theorems that one may wish to prove. But the overriding formal principle is that the only ideas that can be used explicitly in proofs are those that are formulated as axioms of the theory, as definitions based on those axioms, together with any properties that have been proved as theorems.

4.4 *The Foundations of a Set-Theoretic Approach to Mathematics*

A set-theoretic approach to formal mathematics starts with the concept of a set that contains specified members. It is not necessary to say at the outset what we mean precisely by the notion of a set other than the idea that we know what its members are. For a given set S, we need to know that for any x, either x is a member of S (written $x \in S$) or it is not ($x \notin S$). For instance, if $\mathbb{N}$ is the set of whole numbers, then $5 \in \mathbb{N}$, $31 \in \mathbb{N}$, $3 \times 7 \in \mathbb{N}$, but $\frac{1}{2} \notin \mathbb{N}$ and an apple $\notin \mathbb{N}$.

In formal mathematics, a mathematical structure is given in terms of a list of properties called axioms from which all other properties must be deduced. For instance, a *group* consists of a set G where, for each pair of elements $x, y \in G$, there is an element written as $x \circ y \in G$ satisfying the axioms:

(1) The *associative* law: For all $x, y \in G$, $(x \circ y) \circ z = x \circ (y \circ z)$.
(2) *Identity*: There is an element $e \in G$ such that $e \circ x = x \circ e = x$ for all $x \in G$.
(3) *Inverse*: For every $x \in G$ there is an element $x' \in G$ such that $x \circ x' = x' \circ x = e$.

When a student encounters this idea for the first time, it is likely to be problematic because nothing like it has been met before. For instance, readers may imagine these rules applying to examples, such as addition of signed whole numbers (where the operation ∘ is +, the identity e is 0, and the inverse of x is $-x$) or multiplication of positive fractions (where the operation ∘ is ×, the identity is 1, and the inverse of m/n is n/m). If you have not experienced this approach before, imagine replacing the formal operation ∘ in (1), (2) and (3) by each of the familiar operations +, ×, to get a sense of the formal operations in a familiar context.

These examples suggest certain expectations. For example, it is clear in both cases that there is only *one* identity (0 for the integers under addition and 1 for the positive fractions under multiplication) and the inverse of each element is unique. However, axiom (2) only states there is *an* identity element e and axiom (3) only says that each element x has *an* inverse denoted by x'. Any property that is not stated explicitly must be proved from the given definitions. For instance, the fact that the identity is unique needs to be deduced from axioms (1)–(3). It may be stated as a theorem and proved as follows:

> **Theorem:** Suppose that axioms (1), (2) and (3) hold; then it follows that the identity element is unique.
> **Proof:** Suppose to the contrary that there are *two* identities e and f. Then, by using axiom (2), we know that, because e is an identity, then
> $$e \circ x = x \circ e = x \text{ for every } x \in G.$$
> Because f is an identity,
> $$f \circ x = x \circ f = x \text{ for every } x \in G.$$
> Now take $x = f$ in the first equation to get
> $$e \circ f = f \circ e = f$$
> and take $x = e$ in the second to get
> $$f \circ e = e \circ f = e.$$
> This proves that $e = f$.

A similar proof can be given to show that each element $x \in G$ has a *unique* inverse $x' \in G$.

All proofs in formal mathematics follow the same broad format. Formal set-theoretic definitions specify carefully chosen properties of the defined concepts. These definitions are used to prove additional properties as theorems, which are then used to prove more theorems, to build up a logically deduced coherent system based only on the original axiomatic definitions and the succession of formal proofs.

As the system develops, new formal concepts may be defined. For instance, in the system of group theory, we can define a *cyclic* group to consist of a single element x and its powers x, $x^2 = x \circ x$, $x^3 = x^2 \circ x$ and so on. We can also define $x^0 = e$ and $x^{-1} = x'$ where x' is the (unique) element satisfying $x \circ x' = x' \circ x = e$ specified by axiom (3). Then we may define $x^{-n} = (x^{-1})^n$ to give a full set of powers x^n for all integers n (positive or negative) so that the cyclic group consists precisely of all the powers

$$\ldots, x^{-n}, \ldots, x^{-2}, x^{-1}, e, x, x^2, \ldots, x^n, \ldots$$

With a little effort, from these definitions it is possible to prove the 'power law' that $x^m \circ x^n = x^{m+n}$ for all whole numbers, positive, negative or zero.

Once that law is established, we may consider new properties that necessarily follow from the axioms. For example, we may use the definition of a cyclic group to determine its structure so that we know what any cyclic group will look like. This can be found as follows:

Theorem: A cyclic group is either an infinite group of different powers of a single element x in the form $\ldots, x^{-2}, x^{-1}, e, x, x^2, \ldots$, or a finite set of k different elements, $e, x, x^2, \ldots x^{k-1}$ where $x^k = e$.

Proof: Either all the powers of x are different, or $x^m = x^n$, where m and n are different integers. In the second case, using the power law to deduce that $x^{m-n} = x^0 = e$, and taking k to be the smallest positive integer such that $x^k = e$, gives a succession of different terms: $e, x, x^2, \ldots, x^{k-1}$ where $x^k = e$, and then the cycle repeats: $x, x^2, \ldots, x^{k-1}, x^k = e, x^{k+1} = x, \ldots$

As an example of this theorem, we may consider the structure of the group of integers under addition with its infinite set of terms:

$$\ldots, -2, -1, 0, 1, 2, 3, \ldots$$

If we replace the normal operation of addition by recording only the remainder after dividing by 3, then we need only three elements 0, 1, 2, where $1 + 1 = 2$ and $2 + 1 = 0$, and adding 1 each time gives the recurring cycle

$$0, 1, 2, 0, 1, 2, \ldots$$

This example of deducing the structure of the formal concept of cyclic group – based only on the axioms for a group and the specific definition of a cyclic group – is typical of how formal mathematics evolves.

Prior to formulating the axiomatic definition of a group, experiences that have various aspects in common may be *recognized* and explored to *describe* various properties and to carefully select and refine axioms appropriate to *define* an appropriate structure. Then the properties of that structure are *deduced* by mathematical proof, giving a succession of theorems in a theory in which all the properties arise from deduction from the definitions. Within that axiomatic structure, more specific definitions may be made and further theorems deduced to build up formal knowledge structures. (Figure 3.20.)

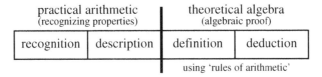

Figure 3.20. The transition to formal mathematics for students.

As mathematicians grow more sophisticated and extend their theories to new contexts, the ideas that they use to build new formal theories arise not only from practical and theoretical ideas, but also from established formal ideas, so the evolution goes on to ever widening horizons in mathematical research.

5. Thinkable Concepts and Knowledge Structures

Now we have considered three major forms of development of compressed thinkable concepts through categorization, encapsulation and definition, it is appropriate to consider the general development of these thinkable concepts within knowledge structures.

As with various other terms introduced in this book, the term *knowledge structure* is a two-word phrase. The first word refers to the knowledge of the individual and the second to the structure of the connections between pieces of knowledge.

The term 'schema' is widely used to refer to a knowledge structure in philosophy, psychology, cognitive science and other areas. It traces its lineage back to the Greek word 'schema' which literally means a shape or, more generally, a plan. The philosopher Immanuel Kant used the term in his *Critique of Pure Reason*[21] in 1781 to bridge the gap between specific perceptions and general concepts, for instance, referring to the schema for

---

[21] Kant (1781).

'dog' as a mental pattern that can 'delineate the figure of a four-footed animal in a general manner without limitation to any single determinate figure as experience or any possible image that I can present *in concreto*.'

Piaget described a 'schema' as 'the mental representation as an associated set of perceptions, ideas and/or actions'.[22] The psychologist Bartlett used the term in the nineteen-thirties in his book *Remembering*[23] to formulate the way in which individuals remembered and repeated stories that they had been told. He found that they told the story with the same basic framework while embroidering it with their own invented details.

The term 'knowledge structure' is used widely in the literature for a variety of specific technical purposes. In this book, I use the term simply to focus freely on how knowledge is linked and structured within the mind, with a particular interest in how knowledge structures develop over time. In essence, a knowledge structure is another term for schema without the additional meanings that have developed in various contexts.

5.1 *The Duality of Knowledge Structures and Thinkable Concepts*

In his book *Intelligence, Learning and Action*[24], Richard Skemp formulated the idea that schemas and concepts are essentially the same notion viewed through different lenses, where a concept can be conceived in detail as a schema and a schema can be seen, as a whole, as a concept.

After working on a theory of encapsulation of process as objects for more than a decade, Dubinsky reformulated his APOS theory to acknowledge not only that Processes could be encapsulated as Objects but also that Schemas may be conceptualized as Objects.[25] Though arising in different theoretical contexts, the duality between concept and schema is based on the same fundamental idea in which a named concept has rich internal links that reveal it to be a schema, and a schema that is sufficiently coherent may later be named and conceived as a thinkable concept.

Using Skemp's varifocal idea, a given concept starts out as some specific, possibly vague phenomenon that is recognized and explored physically and mentally to build up meanings. When it is named, it can be discussed in greater detail, both within the mind of a single individual and between individuals, to be compressed into a thinkable concept with internal richness of

---

[22] Piaget (1926).
[23] Bartlett (1932).
[24] Skemp (1979).
[25] Asiala et al. (1996).

structure and form links to other structures that build into more comprehensive schemas.

As learners meet new situations, knowledge structures develop that may be compressed into thinkable concepts. For instance, the knowledge structure of addition with its successive compressions from count-all, count-on to known fact may reach a level in which other facts can be derived from known facts to give a flexible thinkable concept of sum. The properties of arithmetic become a knowledge structure that we can speak about in a curriculum plan as 'knowledge of arithmetic operations'. At a much later stage, the knowledge structure of real number arithmetic may be formulated axiomatically to become a thinkable formal concept defined as a complete ordered field.

The ability to switch in both directions between a thinkable concept and a knowledge structure takes time to form the necessary mental links to enable the individual to change focus in a flexible manner. More than thirty years ago I was privileged to be inspired by Shlomo Vinner with his notion of *concept image*, which he introduced to formulate how we think about a concept in our mind:

> The concept image [...] is the total cognitive structure that is associated with the concept, which includes all the mental pictures and associated properties and processes. It is built up over the years through experiences of all kinds, changing as the individual meets new stimuli and matures.[26]

From the outset it was acknowledged that a concept image may not be coherent, in the sense that it can have different aspects that may be in conflict. Here we are concerned with how concept images develop over time to build new thinkable concepts and increasingly sophisticated knowledge structures.

5.2 Blending Knowledge Structures

As mathematical thinking develops in a parallel-processing biological brain, different aspects of various knowledge structures may be called to mind at the same time. A thinkable concept is conceived as a selective binding that combines links from different neural subsystems. Knowledge structures are also blended together to give new possibilities.

---

[26] Tall & Vinner (1981).

For instance, in algebra we blend together the symbolic manipulation of algebraic expressions and the visual representation of algebraic graphs. Each of these provides different information about algebraic concepts. The symbolism can be manipulated to solve linear and quadratic equations. The visual picture offers a more general vision of where graphs cross, to 'see' solutions of equations and to look at other global properties, such as where the function increases or decreases or where it has a visible maximum or minimum.

The calculus blends together our visual imagination of the changing slope of the graph and the symbolic representation of the derivative. Later formal definitions build on the embodied and symbolic ideas of the calculus to develop the formal definition of the limit concept as part of a more sophisticated formal theory.

In the visionary book *The Way We Think: Conceptual Blending and the Mind's Hidden Complexities*, Fauconnier and Turner describe how blending of different mental structures gives rise to human creativity.[27] They offer a wide variety of examples in which different knowledge structures are brought together to form a new blend with emergent aspects that are not found in either.

For example, the complex numbers may be seen as a blend of transformations in the plane and the operations of arithmetic, generalized to give the arithmetic of the complex numbers involving emergent properties, such as the new numbers having real and imaginary parts.

Such phenomena also occur in our developing students as they encounter new situations in which new ways of thinking are required, blending together new forms of embodiment and symbolism from which emerge new generalizations that extend old ideas.

6. Summary

In this chapter we have seen how mathematical thinking develops by focusing on essential aspects of a situation and compressing knowledge into thinkable concepts using language and symbolism. Three essentially different forms of compression have been described: *categorization* using language to describe properties that characterize concepts; *encapsulation* to symbolize operations as thinkable concepts; and *definition*, of observed features of geometry, arithmetic and algebra, culminating in formal set-theoretic definition as the foundation of axiomatic mathematics.

---

[27] Fauconnier & Turner (2002).

The thinkable concepts formed from categorization, encapsulation and definition all have properties that can be *recognized, described, defined* and relationships *deduced* using an appropriate form of proof, be it Euclidean proof, or proof in arithmetic and algebra based on the rules of arithmetic, or mathematical proof from axioms and set-theoretic definitions. In each case, thinkable concepts may develop an internal richness that reveals them as crystalline concepts operating within broader knowledge structures that may again become thinkable concepts at a higher level of mathematical thinking.

In Chapter 4 we see how the long-term development of the individual is affected by their previous experiences as they attempt to make sense of more sophisticated ideas.

4 Set-Befores, Met-Befores and Long-Term Learning

In this chapter, the ideas of 'set-before' and 'met-before' are employed to provide a framework for the longer-term development of mathematical thinking. A set-before is 'a mental structure that we are born with, which may take a little time to mature as our brains make connections in early life'. As such it is a fundamental structure that is shared by all. A met-before is 'a mental structure we have now as a result of experiences we have met before'. This will depend partly on the nature of the mathematics, and so there will be communalities between different individuals, and partly on the individual's cognitive growth, leading to widespread differences.

In Chapter 3 we saw how mathematical concepts arise through three forms of compression: categorization, encapsulation and definition. In this chapter we relate these developments through three major 'set-befores' based on our *sensori-motor* system and our use of *language*. These are the sensory power of *recognition* through perception, the motor power of *repetition* of actions to routinize into mathematical operations, and the use of *language* to describe increasingly sophisticated concepts.

I hypothesize that mathematical thinking is based on these three foundational set-befores that we all share, and develops in different ways as individuals build on their met-befores arising from previous experience, some of which may be supportive in a new situation, or problematic in others.

1. The Notion of Set-Before

A newborn child arrives in this world with a 'messy accumulation of interacting gadgets'. Many are related to the senses – sight, sound, touch, taste, smell, balance – and develop further through interaction with the outside world and with others.

One is the primitive notion of 'numerosity' wherein children recognize small numbers of objects such as 'two cars' without counting, based on the brain's built-in ability to distinguish and track a small number of (up to three or four) objects. Others include the sense of the vertical as we stand upright, the related sense of horizontal, and conceptions of what is heavy and what is light through the tensions in our muscles.

I hypothesize that mathematical thinking is based on three foundational set-befores:

1. *Recognition* of patterns, similarities and differences,
2. *Repetition* of actions to build into repeatable sequences,
3. *Language* to name and refine concepts encountered, including everyday language and the special symbolism of mathematics.

The first two relate to human sensory perception (input) and motor action (output) and the third enables us to formulate increasingly sophisticated mathematical concepts as we reflect on our perceptions and actions.

Recognition of patterns, similarities and differences is an evolutionary combination of mental facilities that we share with other species. It is a typical accumulation of 'interacting gadgets', combining vision, smell, touch, taste, hearing, muscle tension and spatial awareness to make sense of the world. As formulated by Donald in his three levels of consciousness[1], introduced in Chapter 2, the first level is a selective binding of different aspects of thought into a single mental entity that we can trace continuously at a second level over a period of short-term awareness and, as we do so, we are able to recognize the same entity from differing viewpoints. In the longer term, at the third level of global awareness, we can reflect on events and conceptions to make further mental connections to categorize and define concepts in more sophisticated ways.

Repetition is also a set-before that we share with other species in which a sequence of actions may be repeated until it can be performed automatically. This builds on second level short-term awareness that links together events as they happen in time and, with practice, the steps become an overall repeatable sequence. It is the basis of *procedural* thinking, where procedures can be performed automatically without being conscious of the details, except where particular decisions need to be made at critical points of the operation. This facility can also be incorporated in more flexible ways of mathematical thinking.

---

[1] Donald (2001).

Language is a human attribute that distinguishes *Homo sapiens* from all other species. Although many other species have subtle systems of signals that enable communication, the spoken and written language of *Homo sapiens* sets it apart in its ability to develop successive levels of sophisticated thinking, both in our current society and in the passing of ideas on to future generations.

Each human culture develops its own language for communication, some more sophisticated than others. This enables us to *name* a particular feature that we notice. It might be an object like 'apple' or 'dog', a feeling like 'happy' or 'warm', an adjective like 'big' or 'blue', a verb like 'walk' or 'play', or a more subtle concept such as 'love' or 'fair'.

Language is essential for mathematical thinking, not only in terms of natural language to discuss mathematical ideas, but also in combination with recognition and repetition to take us to unprecedented heights of subtlety. It enables us to categorize mathematical ideas, to say what we mean by concepts such as point, line, triangle, sine, cosine, prime number, variable, derivative, integral, algebra, calculus, infinite cardinal.

It enables us to extend our imagination beyond the confines of our physical existence. For instance, in practicing a sequence of operations until we can repeat it automatically, we have the potential to repeat it again and again. We have a first number, then a next, then a next *and so on*. The numbers go on successively, one after another, until we begin to sense that, no matter what number we have reached, we can always continue with the next. In the longer term – as a result of experiences encountered in our development – the set-before of repetition is an essential foundation for the highly sophisticated idea of *potential infinity*.

If we put together the ability to repeat actions with the facility to categorize concepts, then we can categorize the potential infinity of counting numbers in a new way. By giving the set of counting numbers a name, or a symbol, say $\mathbb{N}$, it becomes easier to think of it as a single entity. The linguistic combination of repetition and categorization may lead to the heady idea of *actual infinity*: the set $\mathbb{N}$ of *all* natural numbers.

This concept of infinity was hotly debated by the Greeks and remains a fundamental stumbling block for many today. Put simply, how can the finite mind of man contemplate the infinite? A simple response is to agree that although we certainly cannot count *all* the numbers in a finite lifetime, we can *think* of the set of numbers *as a coherent whole*.

A group of first-year undergraduate mathematicians was asked:[2]
Do you consider the following exist as coherent mathematical ideas?
Respond as follows:

1. Definitely yes   2. Fairly sure   3. Neutral/no opinion
4. Confused   5. Fairly sure not   6. Definitely not

The responses are given in Table 4.1.

Table 4.1. *Numbers as coherent mathematical ideas*

N = 42	1	2	3	4	5	6
Natural numbers	40	2	0	0	0	0
Real numbers	39	3	0	0	0	0
Complex numbers	32	8	1	0	1	0

These students had no problem thinking of the natural numbers or real numbers as coherent mathematical ideas, and most were also satisfied with the complex numbers as well. When students were asked about their concerns with complex numbers, a common problem was that they did not make sense because they violated the rule that a square must be positive, so how could $i^2 = -1$?

This brings us to the second construct in mathematical thinking: the effect of previous experience and the notion of *met-before*.

2. Met-Before

In recent years, the linguist George Lakoff and his colleagues[3] have proposed that *metaphor* is at the root of human thought and communication: a particular experience, *the target*, is spoken about in terms of another, *the source*. This enables a less familiar, possibly abstract, target to be thought about in terms of a more familiar source. For instance, 'time is money' interprets the abstract target notion of time in terms of the concrete source notion of money. The link builds a whole system of language to speak of time, not only in direct terms, such as the modern ways of paying for time in money – in hourly wages, daily hotel room rates, yearly budgets – but

[2] Tall (1980c).
[3] George Lakoff has written a series of books with colleagues on the idea of thought as metaphorical embodiment: Lakoff & Johnson (1980), Lakoff (1987), Lakoff & Johnson (1999), Lakoff & Núñez (2000).

also in situations in which money is not involved, such as '*spending* time doing an activity', '*investing* time in work', 'living on *borrowed* time' and '*paying a debt* to society in prison'.

The term 'met-before' grows out of this usage, to describe how we interpret new situations in terms of experiences we have met before, where the word 'met-before' refers not to the actual experience itself, but to the trace that it leaves in the mind that affects our current thinking. When we first meet the concept of a complex number i whose square is negative, we experience the met-before that tells us that 'a·(non-zero) square must be positive'. This 'met-before', which is true for real numbers, forms part of our selective binding of the notion of 'number' and is usually problematic for the learner meeting the notion of complex number for the first time.

As we saw in Chapter 1, some previous experiences are supportive and give pleasurable experiences in learning while others are problematic and cause initial confusion. A number fact like $5 + 2 = 7$ established through counting is supportive in subsequent learning, whether it be in decimal arithmetic where $35 + 2 = 37$ or $50 + 20 = 70$, in measurement where 5 metres plus 2 metres is 7 metres, or even in complex numbers where $5i + 3 + 2i$ is $3 + 7i$. But other experiences are problematic, such as the idea that 'after one number comes the next' or 'multiplication makes bigger', both of which are true for counting numbers but not for fractions.

We have also seen that the same met-before may be supportive in some contexts but not in others. For instance, 'take away leaves less' is true for counting numbers, and also for (positive) fractions and for finite sets, but not for negative numbers nor for infinite sets.

The philosophical notion of 'metaphor' and the cognitive notion of 'met-before' have much in common. Both link a new experience to an experience that is already familiar. However, the notion of 'metaphor' offers a high-level analogy to formulate a theory while the notion of 'met-before' is formulated to focus on the development of ideas *from the viewpoint of the learner*. In conversation with learners from young children through to adults, it is possible to say 'what have you met before that makes you think that?'. A reflective teacher can act as a mentor using this approach to address problematic aspects, such as the implicit belief that 'take-away always gives less'.

To rationalize a new problematic situation, it may be helpful to encourage the learner to recall a situation in which the ideas worked and continue to work. For instance, 'take-away gives less' always works when taking away something physical. Given confidence in an earlier situation may make it easier to see what is different in the new situation to address the issue in a position of confidence. For example, with the met-before 'take away gives less', it may be helpful to recall that taking away physical money always leaves less to spend. But an impending debt may involve putting money aside to pay for it, so that taking away the debt releases the money set aside to give more money to spend.

Supportive and problematic met-befores arise naturally in learning. However, a traditional curriculum is usually formulated in terms of supportive met-befores that need to be taught as pre-requisites to new ideas. Rarely are problematic met-befores seen as an integral part of learning, yet, as we shall see in this chapter, they can have debilitating effects in long-term learning. Our goal here is to consider the learner's encounters with more sophisticated number concepts to reveal problematic met-befores that cause difficulties that need to be addressed to encourage confident new learning. In fact, once the long-term effect of problematic met-befores has been fully realized, the teaching and learning of mathematics can never be the same again.

2.1 *Counting*

The path to learning number and arithmetic begins with counting and the transformation of the operation of counting into a flexible concept of number. When a child is secure with counting, it is usually a springboard for future success, but it may become problematic if it continues to be the dominant method of working.

Joanna, aged eight, was asked to add eight and four. She thrust up a hand with four fingers displayed and counted on from eight to get 'nine, ten, eleven, twelve'. The answer is 'twelve'. But when asked what was the original sum, she had forgotten. She was able to work out $8 + 4$ by counting on four, but she did not yet *know* that $8 + 4$ makes 12.[4]

Joanna and others like her have been taught to add by counting, and she has worked hard to develop her own method of finger counting. But counting can become problematic when the numbers become larger.

Some children imagine counters in their mind to do simple arithmetic. Amelia[5], a 'slow learner' aged eleven, saw $5 + 3$ as overleaf. (Figure 4.1.)

---

[4] This, and other individual examples come from the work of Eddie Gray (1993).
[5] Amelia is a child studied in Pitta and Gray (1999), where she was given the pseudonym Emily. She is not the same individual as Emily in Chapter 2.

Figure 4.1. 5 + 3.

She visualized the middle dot of the 5 moving to the vacant space of the three to give two rows of four, which is eight. (Figure 4.2.)

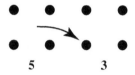

Figure 4.2. 5 + 3 is 8.

Such experiences can prove of great value in building up meaning for number relationships. But a focus on objects is limited to what can be handled by the brain's small focus of attention. Such images can become problematic when needing to deal with larger numbers where the specific images are no longer able to cope with the complexity.

A possible solution to this problem is to shift attention away from counting to focus on the relationships themselves. This may be done using a calculator that displays successive lines with the sum on one line and the answer on the next. A child using such a calculator now sees the sum and its answer *without the need to do any counting* and can focus on the relationships rather than on the ongoing processes.

Demetra Pitta used this strategy in her PhD thesis[6], working with Amelia by giving her a graphic calculator and asking her to 'find sums whose answer is 9.' Amelia's very first attempt was to try 5 + 3, which gave 8. Her next attempt was 5 + 3 + 1, which gave 9. Likewise 5 + 4 gave 9, and she was already focusing on relationships rather than counting by seeing that 5 + 3 + 1 and 5 + 4 both give 9. (Figure 4.3.)

Over a ten-week period, Amelia was seen once a week by the researcher and left a sheet of problems that grew steadily in complexity, such as 'find sums whose answer is 5, starting at 15,' building up using larger numbers. At the end of the study, she was asked what 'four' meant to her and she responded 'a hundred take away ninety six'. She had not only mastered

---

[6] Pitta (1998).

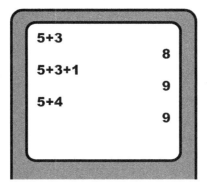

Figure 4.3. Addition on a graphic calculator.

relationships between numbers, but she also responded with a surprising degree of confidence and power.

It would be wonderful to think that such methods could tap the hidden resources in all children who struggle. However, this turned out not to be so. Another PhD student, Hazel Howat, spent a year using similar methods with a group of children with learning difficulties.[7] Some were entirely resistant to the treatment. The stumbling block seemed to be the shift from seeing ten as ten ones to a single unit of ten. The children could count past ten, going 'eight, nine, ten, eleven, twelve, …', but some did not seem to be able to grasp how ten things could be a single unit: there were *ten* things, not one. For them the number sequence went on from 'eight, nine' to 'ten, eleven', with no sense of place value in the words, even though it is visible in the symbols '8, 9, 10, 11'.

From these studies, the first shows that a child may be assisted by focusing on relationships in arithmetic to build a flexible approach to number. The second shows that in some serious cases of difficulty, the focus on counting may be so strong that it is difficult to shift from counting ten distinct objects to see it as a single unit of ten. This counsels us that, however strongly we may believe in the principle that all children have the capacity to make sense of mathematics in an appropriate manner, the wide spectrum of performance may be very resistant to our efforts to teach. The question remains as to how we may encourage *all* children to make appropriate sense of mathematics. For example, in the case of children with extreme difficulty in mathematics, it is important to find ways of helping them make sense appropriate to their own needs.

[7] Hazel Howat (2006).

2.2 *Difference and Take-Away*

The techniques of subtraction available to a child will depend on his or her current experience of addition, as discussed in Chapter 2. A child at the stage of 'count-all' (count one set, count another, put them together and count them all) is more likely to subtract by 'take-away'. To calculate $6 - 2$, count six objects, count two of these and take them away, then count those left to get '4'. Those confident with 'count-on' may subtract using 'count-back' (counting back two, to start at six and count 'five, *four*'), or, less likely, use 'count-back to' (starting at 'six' and count back to two as 'five, four, three, two' which gives a count of four numbers) or even 'count-up' (from two to six, again a count of four numbers). Those with a more flexible knowledge of number bonds many use them to subtract: if $4 + 2$ is 6, then $6 - 4$ is 2, and greater experience may lead to $56 - 4 = 52$ and perhaps even $763 - 40 = 723$. In this way, the child's development of subtraction will be enhanced or limited by the met-befores of addition available at the time.[8]

More subtly, the words 'difference' and 'take-away' are used with meanings for whole numbers that may become problematic later on. The word 'difference' is often used without a sense of direction, so that the difference between 6 and 4 and the difference between 4 and 6 are both 2. At the same time, practical take-away always starts with the larger number (often as a collection of objects) and takes away the smaller.

In all instances, the required operation is clear: the difference between two numbers is found by taking the smaller number from the larger and the result is always less than the larger number you start with.

When column arithmetic is introduced, the overall situation still involves taking a small number from a larger, for example, taking 27 from 43. But when the operation is performed column by column, for perhaps the very first time, the learner is faced with taking away a larger number from a smaller one. Now the met-before of 'taking the smaller from the larger' becomes problematic.

In the take-away

$$\begin{array}{r} 43 \\ -27 \\ \hline \end{array}$$

the units column involves taking away 7 from 3. The language used in the algorithm reflects this, saying 'seven from three won't go'. The solution is

---

[8] The links between different techniques for addition and subtraction are confirmed in the PhD thesis of Gray (1993), subsequently published in Gray and Tall (1994).

to 'borrow' from the next column or 'decompose the next column'. The new technique makes sense for some, but it is unlikely to make sense for a child having difficulties with place value, who might use the met-before of 'difference' to take the smaller from the larger. A common solution is to work out the difference between the tens (4 and 2) to get 2, and the difference between the units (3 and 7) to get 4, giving the erroneous answer 24.

The phenomenon is widespread. When my late friend Robin Foster asked ninety children aged eight and nine to calculate $14 - 7$, he found that in the form

$$14 - 7 = ?$$

89 out of 90 got it correct.[9]

When the same sum was presented in the form

$$\begin{array}{r} 14 \\ -\ 7 \\ \hline \end{array}$$

only 70 got the correct answer. Of these, 32 gave the answer 7 and 38 wrote down 07, intimating that the majority were using the algorithm rather than just writing down the result. Of the remaining twenty incorrect solutions, the most common answer was 13, arising by taking the smaller unit, 4, from the larger, 7.

The teaching of the subtraction algorithm can be highly problematic for many children. Eddie Gray found a dip in performance in arithmetic as children begin to learn column addition and subtraction at around the age of seven or eight.[10] If children feel insecure and cling to old ideas of 'difference' then they may try to cope by 'learning what to do' without understanding how the procedures work, leading to knowledge that is fragile and liable to error.

2.3 *Grouping*

Multiplication is often introduced by taking several groups of elements having the same number in each group. For instance, three groups of four give twelve in all. This carries with it a difference in meaning between the

---

[9] Robin Foster (2001).
[10] Gray (1993).

concept of 'three lots of four' and 'four lots of three'. For instance, the idea of three cats with four legs is clearly different from that of four cats with three legs.

The consequence is that some educators make a distinction between 4×3 and 3×4. In saying our tables as children, we used to say the 'four times table' as 'once four is four, two fours are eight, three fours are twelve …' and write $1 \times 4 = 4$, $2 \times 4 = 8$, $3 \times 4 = 12$, … . However, when I started as a mathematics educator in the 1970s, I was told that operations such as addition should be analyzed theoretically as 'state-operator-state', where $3 + 4$ was considered by starting at the 'initial state', 3, followed by an 'operation', +4, to give the 'final state', which is 7. Essentially this uses the technique of 'count-on'. Applying the same analysis to 3×4 gives an initial state 3, followed by an operation $\times 4$ to give the final state 12. In this interpretation 3×4 now means '3 (times 4)', which is actually 4 lots of 3.

Many curricula around the world are aware that there is a clear difference between the two different ways of interpreting the operation of multiplication and actually teach the difference in the initial stages, often maintaining the difference for some time.

My own observation shows that some children realize quite early on that the order of multiplication does not affect the result and others do not. I question whether it is a good policy to *teach* the difference.

According to Piaget, a child who has the concept of conservation of number will know that a given set will always have the same number of elements, no matter the order of counting. An array of 3 rows of 4 objects can also be seen as an array of 4 columns of 3 objects (Figure 4.4).

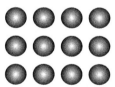

Figure 4.4. Three rows of 4 or four columns of 3.

So a child who has the concept of number should be able to *see* that 3×4 is the same as 4×3. For these it seems unhelpful to insist on maintaining a difference. For those who consider them to be different, maintaining the difference gives more detail to attend to, causing greater strain for a child already under stress.

2.4 *Sharing*

Sharing is an operation familiar to children. It can have a practical (embodied) meaning in terms of 'fair shares' long before the operations of multiplication and division are introduced, perhaps sharing sweets within a group of children. When sharing something that can be cut into equal size pieces, such as a cake, it is usually easier to cut it into halves and then quarters and then eighths, rather than cutting it into thirds, fifths, sixths or sevenths. As a result, the introduction to fractions usually focuses on the practicalities of halves, quarters and eighths. Paradoxically, this desire to begin with a practical operation can lead to fair shares without focusing on the more general idea of fraction. This in turn can cause a problematic met-before that impedes the later understanding of fractional arithmetic.

For instance, to share three cakes between four children, a practical method is to cut each cake into two, giving six halves, of which four can be given, one to each child, and the remaining two halves divided further into four quarters giving each child one half and one quarter.

Using the same technique to share three cakes between five children starts by cutting the three cakes into six halves, giving a half to each child, and then breaking the last half into five pieces. Because these pieces are small, the error is not very significant, so each child will get half a cake and a fifth of a half of a cake, which seems fair. However, it may not be apparent to the children that each share in this second case is equal to three fifths. (Figure 4.5.)

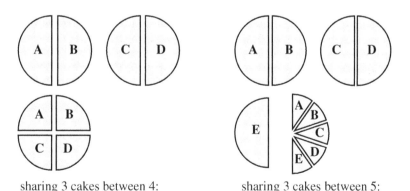

sharing 3 cakes between 4:
each has a half and a quarter

sharing 3 cakes between 5:
each has a half and a fifth

Figure 4.5. Practical sharing.

Empirical research shows that, while children and adults have strategies for practical sharing, the translation of this experience into the arithmetic of fractions is often problematic.[11]

2.5 *Fractions*

Given that many learners find fractions difficult, both in terms of the notion of equivalence and the operations of fractional arithmetic, I wrote a piece of software that enabled children to play with more general fractions, including fractions larger than one.[12] The software offered a child the picture of a disk, asking 'Into how many equal pieces should I cut this cake?' A child might type in, say, '6' and the cake would be cut successively into six equal pieces, with a counting number appearing beside each piece as it is cut in the sequence 1, 2, 3, 4, 5, 6. The request was then 'How many pieces do you want?' The pieces were then counted, 'one sixth, two sixths, three sixths ...', say up to 'four sixths', and the program responded 'I will eat the rest', leaving four sixths.

If the fraction had a smaller equivalent, the software responded saying it could give the same amount of cake, but with fewer pieces. It offered a choice in which the child could specify the equivalent form or have it provided by the computer, in each case drawing the version in lowest terms by the side of the original, showing 'two thirds' of a cake being visibly the same as 'four sixths'.

If the child had a sense of humour and asked for more pieces than were available, the software would answer, 'Greedy! I will have to cut more cake!' For instance, to give eight sixths it would draw a second cake, cut each into sixths and count eight sixths. The program would then draw the corresponding picture for four thirds. (Figure 4.6.)

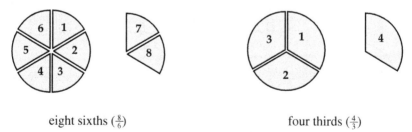

eight sixths ($\frac{8}{6}$)   four thirds ($\frac{4}{3}$)

Figure 4.6. Equivalent fractions and fractions in lowest terms.

[11] Kerslake (1986).
[12] Tall (1986c).

A child who develops a flexible grasp of whole number arithmetic and the notion of equivalence of fractions will have an unexpected bonus. The sum $\frac{2}{3} + \frac{1}{4}$ can be rewritten as $\frac{8}{12} + \frac{3}{12}$ and spoken as '8 twelfths plus 3 twelfths' where now the pieces (twelfths) are all the same size and can be added together. The flexible thinker can now relate this to familiar whole number arithmetic where '8 things plus 3 things' are 11 things, in this case 11 twelfths, which can be written as $\frac{11}{12}$. Thus the child who is already successful with arithmetic will have a much easier task with the addition of fractions.

The notion of a fraction is often introduced as an *object*, say 'half an apple'. This works well with addition, because we can add half an apple and a third of an apple by cutting them up into sixths to get '3 sixths' plus '2 sixths' to end up with '5 sixths'. But multiplication of fractions as objects is problematic. What does 'half an apple *multiplied by* half an apple' mean? It simply does not make sense.

However, if a fraction is seen flexibly as a *process*, then we can speak of the process '*half* an apple' and then take 'a *third* of half an apple' to get 'a *sixth* of an apple'. This viewpoint naturally leads to the observation '*of*' *means multiply*, in the sense that to get a fraction of a fraction of an object, we simply multiply the two fractions together. Regrettably, instead of starting from the concept of a fraction as a process to build up the meaning of taking a fraction of a fraction, the idea is often simply introduced as a rule, 'of means multiply', which can be totally opaque to a learner meeting the idea for the first time.

2.6 *The Problematic Difference between Counting and Measuring*

There is a fundamental distinction between counting and measuring that can cause endless problems for the learner. Counting involves counting *objects*. There is a natural unit involved, namely the unit representing *one* object. Measuring requires the *choice* of a unit. Do we measure length in cubits, yards or metres? Do we measure volume in gallons or litres, weight in pounds and ounces, or in kilograms and grams, or temperature in centigrade or Fahrenheit? Then there is the question of subunits. We have 3 feet in a yard, 8 pints in a gallon, 16 ounces in a pound and endless historical choices of units and subunits. Even though the metric system has attempted to select units and subunits using ten as a basic unit of subdivision, the complexity of measuring units remains.

In counting we collect individual objects into collections and count those collections. Multiplication arises from taking collections of equal size, so three times five can represent three collections each with five objects (or five collections of three objects if you so desire).

    In measurement, multiplication depends on the particular context in which it occurs. If we measure lengths, then multiplying lengths gives an area, and, more generally multiplication of measurements involving units of different kinds gives a composite unit. If one unit is a constant speed, say miles per hour and another unit is time, say hours, then the product of speed times time is a distance. All these different real world embodiments complicate the practical situation.

    As the arithmetic of measurement develops, given the complications of multiplication, if fractions are seen only as objects, it is clear that the product of fractions benefits from a flexible conception of a fraction as both a process and a concept. If the learner already has fluency dealing with the arithmetic of whole numbers, then the symbolic knowledge of whole number arithmetic is supportive in the arithmetic of fractions.

    Consider, for example, the idea of multiplying fractions where the quantities are lengths and the product is the area of a rectangle whose sides are given by the lengths. Figure 4.7 shows a rectangle in which the horizontal side is divided into five equal pieces and the vertical side is divided into three, which divides the whole into $3 \times 5 = 15$ smaller rectangles.

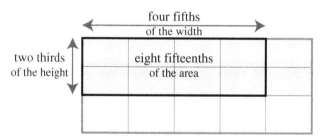

Figure 4.7. Fraction of an area.

    The shaded part has a vertical side that is two thirds of the height and so it is two thirds of the whole. From the shaded part we take a smaller rectangle with a black perimeter whose width is four fifths of the total width. The area in the black perimeter is eight smaller rectangles, which is eight fifteenths of the whole. Multiplying the lengths of the sides to obtain the area gives two thirds times four fifths is eight fifteenths, or

$$\frac{2}{3} \times \frac{4}{5} = \frac{2 \times 4}{3 \times 5} = \frac{8}{15}.$$

A child with flexible understanding of whole number arithmetic is more likely to use this knowledge to make sense of Figure 4.7. In other words, *a flexible facility with symbolism can help make sense of the embodiment.*

2.7 Negative Quantities

Arithmetic based on counting collections of objects becomes problematic when negative numbers are introduced. Although it is easy to imagine '3 apples' or '4 apples', the concept of '–3 apples' is problematic because 'you can't have less than nothing.' There are more subtle problems for the child who maintains a difference between '4 × 3' and '3 × 4' as '4 lots of 3' and '3 lots of 4'. When negative quantities are introduced, '4 lots of –3' has a very different meaning from '–3 lots of 4'. If –3 is a debt of 3, then it may be reasonable to suggest that '4 lots of –3' is a debt of 12. However, '–3 lots of 4' is quite different and is usually interpreted as 'take away three lots of 4', to be conceived as 'take away 12', written as –12.

A common strategy to help students is to use number patterns. For instance, one may begin with the product $2 \times 3 = 6$, then take one off the three to get $2 \times 2 = 4$, then repeat the action to get a pattern:

$$2 \times 3 = 6$$
$$2 \times 2 = 4$$
$$2 \times 1 = 2.$$

Each time the second number on the left is reduced by 1 and the number on the right is reduced by 2. It may seem 'reasonable' to continue the pattern, taking off one from the second factor and two off the product to get

$$2 \times 0 = 0$$
$$2 \times -1 = -2$$
$$2 \times -2 = -4.$$

A similar argument can be given by starting again with $2 \times -2 = -4$ and reducing the first number by 1 each time to give

$$2 \times -2 = -4$$
$$1 \times -2 = -2$$

$0 \times -2 = 0$

$-1 \times -2 = 2$

$-2 \times -2 = 4.$

...

In this case the pattern adds 2 to the right-hand side each time to give a sense that the product of two negatives will be *positive*.

This again leads to a spectrum of mathematical thinking, with some learners enjoying the meaningful beauty of the pattern and others finding the handling of negative numbers problematic.

A later development in measurement offers new possibilities. Multiplication by a positive number on a number line can be imagined as a scaling factor. For instance, multiplication by 3 shifts the point 1 to 3, 2 to 6, 5 to 15 and so on. Multiplying by -1 changes each positive number x into its negative $-x$, which can be seen as a reflection in the origin, swapping over the positive and negative counterparts. A multiplication by a negative number, say -2, can be thought of as a combination of a scale factor 2 and a reflection in the origin[13] (Figure 4.8).

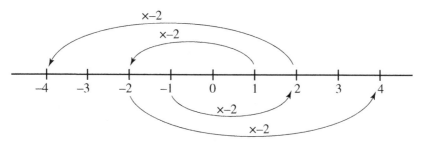

Figure 4.8. Multiplying by a negative number as a reflection and a scaling factor.

This reveals multiplication by two negative numbers as the product of the two scale factors and the double reflection returning to the original direction. Hence -2 times -3 gives a scale factor of $2 \times 3 = 6$, and the two reflections shift back to the positive direction to give the value $+6$. The success of this interpretation, of course, depends on the growing sophistication

[13] Later in development it is helpful to widen one's perspective to see not just a reflection through the origin on the line, but a *rotation* through 180° in the plane. This proves to be the key to unlock the subtle idea of multiplying complex numbers in the plane.

of the learner. A child who only counts is less likely to make sense of this conception, while a child with a flexible grasp of arithmetic and the number line may find it to be a pleasurable insight.

2.8 *The Minus Sign in Remedial College Mathematics*

The long-term development of the minus sign and the fragility of its meaning was revealed in all its glory by the research of Mercedes McGowen, who taught pre-college algebra at college level to students who had struggled with algebra in school.[14] When writing the minus symbol on the board and asking students what comes to mind, she found that the students usually first recalled the process of subtraction, then the concept of negative number, and no one ever used a term such as 'the additive inverse'. The idea from arithmetic that the minus sign referred to a negative quantity became widely problematic for these students in algebra, causing them to think that $-x$ must always be a negative, even though the numerical value of x could be positive when x has a negative value. This manifested itself in a number of subtle ways; for instance, in squaring a negative number, the rules of precedence for operations caused them great confusion and only 6 out of 26 students evaluated -3^2 as -9 and $(-3)^2$ as 9.

When given a picture of the number line with x marked as positive and y as negative, their previous experience of addition and subtraction of numbers affected their responses. (Figure 4.9.)

Figure 4.9. Three quantities on a number line.

Nearly one third of students responded that $x - y$ and $y - x$ are equal, reminiscent of the notion that the 'difference' between two numbers is the same either way. More than two thirds thought that $x + y$ is *bigger* than $x - y$, because addition makes larger and subtraction makes smaller, even though y is visibly negative. On the other hand, possibly because y is to the left of the origin and therefore negative, a fifth of the students said that $x - y = x + y$ reasoning that taking away a negative number is the same as adding a positive.

[14] McGowen (1998).

As mathematics becomes more sophisticated, the meanings of the minus sign change in subtle ways, including:

(1) The operation of 'difference' between two unsigned numbers,
(2) The operation of 'subtraction' which is possible only when taking a smaller number from a larger,
(3) The concept of 'negative number' such as -3 where subtraction is always possible and the subtraction of -3 gives the same answer as adding $+3$,
(4) The additive inverse of $-x$ which can now be negative, zero or positive for a numerical value of x that is respectively positive, zero or negative.[15]

We might go further to deal with systems that are not even ordered, such as the complex numbers, where $-z$ is the additive inverse of the complex number z. Here we still have $(-z_1)(-z_2) = z_1 z_2$ even though the terms can no longer be described as 'positive' or 'negative'. The property is not just that the product of two 'negative numbers' is a 'positive number', but that 'the product of 'two minuses' (as additive inverses) is the same as the product of the original elements, written as $(-a)(-b) = ab$.

2.9 The Transition to Algebra

The transition to algebra seems to be simple for a few but traumatic for many. There are various supportive met-befores in arithmetic that may become problematic in algebra. For example, in arithmetic, every calculation has an *answer*.[16] $2 + 2$ is 4, 2.487×23 is 80.201, and the area of a circle with radius 4.76 is 44.41 to two decimal places.

An expression in algebra such as $3 + 4x$ does not have an answer (unless x is known and the calculation can be carried out in full). Furthermore, attempts to read algebraic expressions from left to right can be quite misleading.

The expression $3 + 4x$ begins with '$3 + 4$' followed by an x. If a learner is struggling to make sense of the expression $3 + 4x$ where the value of x is not known, then a natural response may be to carry out the bit that *does* make sense, by adding $3 + 4$ to get 7 and then leaving the part that is not understood to write down the 'answer' as $7x$.

---

[15] McGowen & Tall (2012).
[16] The idea that an expression should have an answer is referred to in the literature as 'lack of closure' (Collis, 1978).

For students who are flexible with the symbolic operations in arithmetic, it may be simple and pleasing to realize that $3 + 4x$ refers to the general operation to calculate the value of 3 plus 4 times x, whatever the value of x happens to be. They may grasp an expression such as $3 + 4x$ as an entity in itself; it is then relatively simple to add $2x$ to get the expression $3 + 4x + 2x$. This now includes the terms 4 times x and 2 times x which make 6 times x, enabling the expression to be rewritten as $3 + 6x$. This may even be factorized to get $3(1 + 2x)$.

The flexible thinker with a sense of generalized patterns in arithmetic is likely to find the step from arithmetic to algebra relatively straightforward, even empowering, while the student who focuses on arithmetic only as procedures is likely to find algebra even more problematic. Once again, we see the student's previous experience and development impacting on new learning that will lead to an even greater spectrum of performance in the wider population.

2.10 *Apples and Bananas, Metres and Centimetres*

Learners will already have experiences in which letters are used to stand for units or objects. For instance, 3 m is written for 3 metres, where m is a unit of length. In this case, equations have specific meanings in which 12 m = 1200 cm translates into '12 metres equals 1200 centimetres.'

A meaning in which a letter stands for a unit or an object may be evoked when the learner encounters algebra for the first time. For instance, if a stands for 'apple' and b stands for 'banana', then $3a + 4b$ might be read as '3 apples and 4 bananas', just as 3 m + 4 cm may be read as 'three metres and 4 centimetres'. This interpretation may work in initial encounters. For example, adding $2a$ gives $3a + 4b + 2a$ and the apples can be moved together to get $5a + 4b$ (five apples and four bananas).

The interpretation even extends to allow substitutions; for instance, if an apple a costs 5p (5 English pence) and a banana b costs 10p (10 English pence), then the cost of three apples and four bananas is the cost $3a + 4b$, which can be translated into $3 \times 5p + 4 \times 10p$, which is 55p.

However, using letters to stand for objects becomes problematic in algebraic manipulation. For instance, if a stands for apple and b for banana, then what does $3a - 7b$ mean? Is it possible to have three apples and take away seven (nonexistent) bananas? What is meant by a^2? Can it be a square apple? If a is a number, then a^2 is the product $a \times a$; if a is a length, then a^2 is an area. But it has no meaning if a is an apple. Imagining a letter as the name of a unit or an object may soon become problematic.

2.11 *Students and Professors*

A problem given to college and university students in the United States gave rise to interesting data:

> Write an equation using the variables S and P to represent the following statement: 'There are six times as many students as professors at this university.' Use S for the number of students and P for the number of professors.[17]

Approximately a third of the highly educated people who answered this question wrote the equation as $6S = P$ (or $P = 6S$) and two thirds wrote $S = 6P$ (or $6P = S$). The equation $6S = P$ might be read as 'six students equal one professor,' or 'six students correspond to one professor,' relating to the interpretation of letters representing objects or units.

The correct interpretation of the task, however, is $S = 6P$. This says that *the number* of students is six times *the number* of professors.

The earlier use of letters to represent objects or units is very strong. It creates a met-before that causes individuals to reverse the algebraic meaning in the students–professors problem. Subsequent attempts to teach students the algebraic meaning of this task met with surprisingly strong resistance, consistent with them clinging to the interpretation of letters representing 'things' rather than 'the number' of things.[18]

2.12 *Procedural and Proceptual Solutions of Equations*

Initially, thinking of algebraic expressions as operations of evaluation can be helpful in solving simple equations.

For instance, an equation, such as

$$3x + 2 = 8$$

where an expression on the left equals a number on the right, may be seen as a procedural problem: '3 times a number plus 2 is 8, so what is the number?' The equation may be seen as a sequence of operations, 'multiply by 3, then add 2', which may be solved by starting with the number 8 on the right and reversing the operations 'subtract 2 and divide by 3' to end with the solution $x = 2$. This 'undoing' of an operation that gives a numeric output even works for subtraction, for example, if $4x - 3 = 5$, meaning 'four times a number take away three gives five', then the operation can be 'undone' by adding the 3 to the final 5 to get 'four times x is 8', which then easily leads to 'x is 2'.

---

[17] Clement, Lochhead & Monk (1981).
[18] Rosnick (1981).

However, an equation with operations on both sides, such as

$$3x + 2 = 6 + x$$

has a very different meaning. At a process level it is two different processes on either side giving the same result. It is not obvious how both of these can be 'undone' at the same time using arithmetic as there is no number to operate on.

The equation is usually solved by interpreting the two sides as equal quantities and 'doing the same thing to both sides' to produce a solution in a sequence of steps:

$$\begin{aligned}
\text{Start with} \quad & 3x + 2 = 6 + x, \\
\text{take 2 from both sides to get} \quad & 3x = 4 + x, \\
\text{take } x \text{ from both sides to get} \quad & 2x = 4, \\
\text{divide both sides by 2 to get} \quad & x = 2.
\end{aligned}$$

It is well known that students have much greater success in solving an equation with x only on one side.[19] Filloy and Rojano[20] named this phenomenon the 'didactic cut' between arithmetic and algebra. A simple equation of the form 'expression = number' can be solved by arithmetic operations alone while an equation with algebraic expressions on both sides requires the student to manipulate algebraic symbols.

An alternative approach is possible by thinking of the equation as a balance. (Figure 4.10).

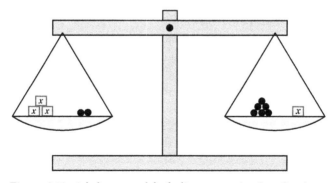

Figure 4.10. A balance model of a linear equation $3x + 2 = 6 + x$.

The problem may be solved by physical operations on the objects on the scales. Take 2 from each side, then take an x from each side (whatever

---

[19] Hart et al. (1989).
[20] Filloy & Rojano (1989).

x happens to be), and then, seeing that two x balances 6, infer that x must be 3. Research shows that such an approach makes sense to a wide range of students.[21]

However, this model again essentially represents x as an *object*. This is supportive in simple cases where the equation has positive terms and the operation of addition, but how can it be used to represent an equation involving subtraction? For instance, how on Earth is it possible to picture the equation that has an expression such as $3x - 2$ as one side when the value of x is unknown? It is even more problematic to represent the situation when x is negative.

Various possibilities have been suggested, such as imagining negative numbers using helium balloons that lift the balance up rather than weighing it down, or digging holes of a given size in a garden, producing piles of soil (positive quantities) and holes (negative). Personally, I find these examples simultaneously interesting but also problematic. They imbue the equation with all kinds of fantasy meanings that provide more fuel for confusion than enlightenment. Richard Skemp spoke of such additional meanings as 'noise'[22] that may impede understanding.

If equations are linked to embodiments that give them bizarre associations, then this may be stimulating for successful children, but it is likely to cause disillusion for those who find the ideas problematic and default to learning procedures that can become increasingly technical and fragile. In the case of using the balance as an embodiment, the increasing difficulty and fragility of such procedures is detailed by Vlassis in the prophetically titled paper: 'The Balance Model: Hindrance or Support for the Solving of Linear Equations with One Unknown?'[23]

Given the problems of the didactic cut in a symbolic approach to equations and the hindrance or support of the embodied method using a balance, an alternative method of reasoning is the general principle of 'doing the same thing to both sides'. In an experiment where this method was the chosen, Rosana de Lima found that *none* of the students mentioned the general principle in interviews after their lessons. Instead of 'adding (or subtracting) the same thing to both sides', many students said[24]:

[21] Vlassis (2002).
[22] Skemp (1971), p. 28.
[23] Vlassis (2002).
[24] Lima & Tall (2008).

(1) Move the symbol over the other side and change its sign.

Instead of dividing both sides by the same number, they said:

(2) Move the symbol over the other side *and put it underneath*.

These students seem to be imagining 'moving the symbols around' as a mental thought experiment, but just moving them is not enough. They have to apply extra 'rules' ('change signs', 'put it underneath') that are necessary to produce the desired result. These operations were often fragile and likely to become confused. For instance, in solving the equation

$$3x - 1 = 3 + x,$$

25 students out of 68 obtained the correct solution, 11 left the solution blank and 32 were unable to obtain the correct answer. Many performed the initial steps to reduce the equation to $2x = 4$ and then moved the 2 over to the other side, putting it underneath to get the desired result,

$$x = \frac{4}{2} = 2.$$

Others made different mistakes with $2x = 4$, including:

(a) $x = 4 - 2$ \qquad (b) $x = \frac{4}{-2}$ \qquad (c) $x = \frac{2}{4}$.

In case (a) the student passes the 2 over to the other side and changes its sign; in (b) correctly 'shifts the 2 over and puts it underneath' but also 'changes the sign'; and in (c) shifts the 2 over and puts the 4 underneath.

Some students tried to do several things at once, which could lead to more complicated errors. For instance, one student operated on $3x - 1 = 3 + x$ by shifting the 1 on the left to the right to give +1 on the right, at the same time shifting the $3 + x$ from the right to the left, where it was written as $3x$, with a change of sign to give:

$$3x - 3x = +1.$$

This equation is now problematic, because the left-hand side reduces to 0 and there is then no x to solve for. The student pressed forward to a solution by shifting the 0 over from the left to the right and put it underneath to get:

$$0 = \frac{1}{0}$$

and then completed the line as

$$0 = \frac{1}{0} = 0$$

to give the 'answer' as zero.

The students in this study generally operated by shifting the symbols around and adding a touch of 'magic' such as 'change signs' or 'put it underneath' to obtain the answer. If they got into difficulty, they either stopped or performed some kind of operation to 'give' a solution. Even those who responded correctly often explained their actions in terms of shifting symbols with the appropriate touch of 'magic' to get the right answer.

2.13 *Analysis of Data in Solving Linear Equations*

We here have three different approaches to solving linear equations: one embodied, using a balance, one symbolic, 'undoing an equation' and one using a general principle 'doing the same thing to both sides'. There are, of course others, for instance, drawing a graph to get a straight line and seeing where it crosses the x-axis, or using a table to work out numerical values to find where the equation is satisfied by a numerical value, interpolating values if necessary.

In all cases we have various combinations of embodiment (using a balance or drawing a graph), symbolism (numerical approximation or algebraic manipulation) or more general principles of reasoning ('do the same to both sides'). This reveals three distinct approaches, each of which offers an explanation and prediction of the causes of success and failure in solving equations:

- A symbolic approach leads to the didactic cut where the method of 'undoing' is supportive for equations of the type 'expression = number' but problematic for 'expression = another expression'.
- An embodied balance approach is supportive for simple equations involving only addition of positive terms, but increasingly problematic when signed numbers and subtraction are involved.

- The principle of 'doing the same to both sides' is supportive for students who already have a flexible (proceptual) view of arithmetic but is problematic for those who see arithmetic and algebra in terms of procedural algorithms that have to be carried out in specific ways.

This supports the idea of formulating a theoretical framework that brings together a diverse range of research studies into one overall theory bringing together embodiment, symbolism and reason.

2.14 *Quadratic Equations*

The effects of the bifurcation between those who develop a flexible sense of arithmetic and algebra and those who rely on procedural manipulation is likely to get even wider when students move to solving quadratic equations. When the students involved in the study on linear equations detailed in the previous section moved on to study quadratic equations[25], the teachers were aware that they found difficulty in manipulating symbols, so they focused mainly on the formula to solve equations of the form $ax^2 + bx + c = 0$. Some of the students, who already solved equations by shifting symbols around, interpreted an equation such as $x^2 = 9$ as an operation, to formulate a third principle for shifting symbols by 'passing the square to the other side where it becomes a square root'. This gives the solution $x = \sqrt{9}$, often giving only the positive root $x = 3$.

The students were given the problem shown in Figure 4.11.

'To solve the equation $(x–3)(x–2) = 0$ for real numbers, John answered in a single line that:

'$x = 3$ or $x = 2$.'

Is his answer correct? Analyze and comment on John's answer.

Figure 4.11. John's problem.

Only 30 out of 77 (39%) agreed that the solution was correct, even though the solutions of the equation seem to be self-evident to anyone who has learnt the technique of solution by factorization. Following their main experience of solving using the formula, most students saw the problem

---

[25] Tall, Lima & Healy (2013).

as involving multiplying out the brackets and using the formula to write down the solutions. None used the principle that if a product is zero, one of the factors must be zero, to give the solutions as $x = 3$ or $x = 2$, and only six substituted the numerical values 3, 2 into the equation to see that the equation is satisfied.

'Teaching to the test' by focusing on techniques to get answers without making sense of the ideas can have long-term adverse consequences as the fragile rules fall apart in more sophisticated circumstances.

2.15 *Further Difficulties*

The consequences of problematic met-befores continue throughout the mathematics curriculum. For example, when learning about powers, it may be meaningful to define 2^3 as 3 twos multiplied together:

$$2^3 = 2 \times 2 \times 2$$

and it is reasonable to use this idea to see that

$$2^3 \times 2^2 = (2 \times 2 \times 2) \times (2 \times 2) = 2^5$$

which may be generalized to the power rule for whole number powers:

$$2^{m+n} = 2^m \times 2^n.$$

But the experience that the power refers to the number of factors becomes problematic if one considers fractional or negative powers. How can $2^{1/2}$ mean 'half a two multiplied together'? How can the symbol 2^{-3} stand for 'minus three twos multiplied together'? The original meaning of the product of powers no longer makes sense and becomes problematic.

To generalize from whole number powers to fractional and negative powers requires the power rule to be used as a general principle, from which one must *deduce* that $2^{1/2} = \sqrt{2}$ by putting $m = n = \frac{1}{2}$ to give

$$2^{1/2} \times 2^{1/2} = 2^{1/2+1/2} = 2^1 = 2.$$

This relationship suggests that $2^{1/2}$ must be the square root of 2. Such an argument requires the learner to be comfortable making deductions from symbolism that may no longer have its original meaning. It requires a shift in approach from making meaning based on practical experience to a theoretical approach in which rules are taken as definitions and deductions are made from them. It may be highly problematic for students who do not feel comfortable dealing with ideas not based on practical experience.

The learner's long-term journey throughout arithmetic and algebra involves a succession of such transitions that challenge and empower confident students while alienating those who are in difficulty. This may result in many students, and teachers, focusing on learning rules by rote to pass the test, which may lead to a level of success, but may also fail to make flexible sense of the ideas.

2.16 *Trigonometry*

The same analysis can be applied to other areas of mathematics. For example, in trigonometry, the journey begins with the definitions of sine, cosine and tangent as ratios of sides in a right-angled triangle *ABC*. Here the sides and angles are all magnitudes, which means that they have no sign, either in the original geometry of Euclid or in the experience of today's learners encountering them for the first time. In particular, to be a triangle, none of the angles or sides can be zero because then the triangle would collapse into a straight line. Then there is the complication of so many formulae, each involving a trigonometric concept and a ratio of two sides of a right-angled triangle (Figure 4.12).

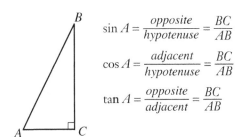

$$\sin A = \frac{opposite}{hypotenuse} = \frac{BC}{AB}$$

$$\cos A = \frac{adjacent}{hypotenuse} = \frac{BC}{AB}$$

$$\tan A = \frac{opposite}{adjacent} = \frac{BC}{AB}$$

Figure 4.12. Trigonometric ratios in a triangle.

Proofs in Euclidean geometry can be both aesthetically beautiful and also rather technical. Consider, for example, the proof of the formula for $\sin(\alpha + \beta)$ given in Figure 4.13.

I can still remember the time, more than half a century ago, when my mathematics teacher, John Butler, showed us this proof on the blackboard. I followed it at the time, but I didn't remember the detail. Even when I wrote it out for this book, I struggled to get it right. As a student,

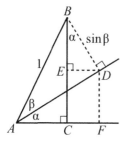

Let $AB = 1$ and $\angle A = \alpha + \beta$ as in the figure.
Then in the triangle ABC, $BC = 1 \sin(\alpha + \beta)$.
Drop the perpendicular BD from B to AD,
DE from D to BC and DF from D to AF.
Then $BC = BE + DF \ldots (*)$.
In triangle ABC, $BD = AB \sin\beta = \sin\beta$,
in BDE, $BE + BD \cos\alpha = \cos\alpha \sin\beta$.
In the same way $AD = AB \cos\beta = \cos\beta$,
And $DE + AD \sin\alpha = \sin\alpha \cos\beta$.
From $(*)$, $\sin(\alpha + \beta) = \sin\alpha \cos\beta + \cos\alpha \sin\beta$.

Figure 4.13. Proof of the formula for $\sin(\alpha + \beta)$.

when I had to use the formula in more general cases where the angles could be any size positive or negative, I could not imagine the proof as a picture in my mind; I just used the formula to solve problems. In practice, however, everything worked out nicely so that I came to accept it as part of my toolkit of useful mathematical techniques.

Researching the development of trigonometry, Michelle Challenger[26] found a huge change in meaning from 'triangle' trigonometry, which students met before they were sixteen years old, and 'circle trigonometry', where an angle could take on any value, positive or negative. Typical remarks by students studying 'circle trigonometry' included:

I hate trigonometry. There is just so much to remember: all the diagrams and formulas. I never know which one to use.

Are we talking about triangle trigonometry or circle trigonometry here?

I used to understand it when it was just triangles but now I don't know where to start.

What is sine exactly? I thought I knew but now it is so confusing.

Those who are teaching these learners may have studied even more sophisticated mathematics that may be termed 'analytic trigonometry', which includes the use of infinite power series and complex numbers that go far beyond the experience of students beginning their studies of triangle and circle trigonometry. It may also be a big leap in sophistication for readers whose main interest is in teaching mathematics relevant for young chil-

---

[26] Challenger (2009).

dren. Nevertheless, it is valuable to take a brief look into the future to see the crystalline structure that emerges in analytic trigonometry.

Here, the special number e calculated by

$$e = 1 + \frac{1}{1} + \frac{1}{1 \times 2} + \frac{1}{1 \times 2 \times 3} + \cdots + \frac{1}{1 \times 2 \times 3 \times \cdots \times n} + \cdots$$

combines with the complex number i where $i^2 = -1$ to satisfy the amazing equation

$$e^{i\theta} = \cos\theta + i\sin\theta.$$

The power law $x^{m+n} = x^m x^n$ generalizes to complex numbers, so that the equation $e^{i(\alpha + \beta)} = e^{i\alpha} e^{i\beta}$ can be rewritten as

$$\cos(\alpha + \beta) + i\sin(\alpha + \beta) = (\cos\alpha + i\sin\alpha)(\cos\beta + i\sin\beta).$$

Multiplying out the brackets gives

$$\cos(\alpha + \beta) + i\sin(\alpha + \beta) = \cos\alpha\cos\beta - \sin\alpha\sin\beta + i(\sin\alpha\cos\beta + \cos\alpha\sin\beta)$$

and, by 'comparing real and imaginary parts', in a single stroke we get *both* trigonometric identities:

$$\cos(\alpha + \beta) = \cos\alpha\cos\beta - \sin\alpha\sin\beta,$$

$$\sin(\alpha + \beta) = \sin\alpha\cos\beta + \cos\alpha\sin\beta.$$

This is an amazing example of the way in which mathematics not only gets more sophisticated, but it also becomes much simpler, *for those who can come to terms with the more sophisticated ideas*.

The reason for speaking about the fuller development at this point is to show that, even if one wishes to encourage learners to make sense of mathematics at every stage, the full crystalline structure of mathematics may lie in a later level that is not available to the learner at the time.

To reach the level of analytic trigonometry, a learner must pass through a minefield of problematic met-befores, from the arithmetic of unsigned numbers to the arithmetic of signed numbers, from the Euclidean geometry of the triangle to circle trigonometry and on to analytic trigonometry involving infinite series and unsettling ideas of complex numbers. It is clear that such a path is littered with danger, which can be challenging and exciting for those who are able to make sense of successive ideas, but is a formidable task for anyone suffering from the adverse effects of problematic met-befores.

3. Supportive and Problematic Conceptions

This long-term change in meaning has consequences for university students who have just finished mathematics degrees and are preparing to teach mathematics in school. Kin Eng Chin, whom I have the privilege of supervising for his doctorate, researched the conceptions of trigonometry held by newly qualified mathematicians training to be teachers. He found examples of students who saw triangles as Euclidean figures with angles and sides that *must* have non-zero positive values and consequently did not have a fully coherent link between triangle trigonometry and circle trigonometry. There were those who spoke of sine and cosine being defined as power series but were unable to link this knowledge to triangle and circle trigonometry. There were others who had immense emotional hang-ups about infinite series or complex numbers.[27] It is evident that 'knowing' more advanced mathematics does not fully prepare future teachers to be aware of how students learn.

As Kin Eng described his data, he looked at me intently and said, 'there is a difference between *knowing*,' at which point he touched his head, 'and *grasping*', as he held out his hand and closed it around an imagined object. In a sentence, using fundamental gestures, he touched the heart of the secret of the evolution of human thinking, from having ideas about some phenomenon to being able to hold it and manipulate it within the mind. He suggested that we use Anna Sfard's idea of 'conception'[28], meaning the interpretation that an individual has of a concept, so that we may speak about 'supportive conceptions' and 'problematic conceptions'.

As we looked at his data, it became absolutely clear that different individuals had some 'supportive aspects' of a given concept and some 'problematic aspects'. Indeed, students with first-class degrees, who felt very confident about mathematics, had problematic aspects that they suppressed to focus on supportive aspects that worked and enabled them to solve problems. Meanwhile, it is also clear that other individuals have conceptions

---

[27] Chin & Tall (2012).
[28] Sfard (1991).

that include supportive aspects, yet their overall feeling is one of lack of understanding because of dominant problematic aspects.[29]

Students who have travelled the full mathematical path from childhood to a mathematics degree are likely to have personal conceptions of mathematics that need further reflection to enable them to be fully aware of the needs of children that they will teach in school.

Their later experience gives them a new view of mathematics that may be described as a 'met-after'.[30] This refers to the effect of an experience that was met later in development that profoundly changes the way in which earlier ideas are considered. In particular, it refers to ideas held by experts that mean a great deal *to them* but have no meaning for those who have yet to experience them.

A good example of a 'met-after' is the proof using complex numbers to give the trigonometric identities for $\sin(A + B)$ and $\cos(A + B)$. This offers incredible insight to those who can make sense of the more advanced ideas required, but it cannot be used to teach the identity in triangle and circle trigonometry. Instead, the learner is required to accept a theoretical approach in which the identities may be given a proof using triangle trigonometry and, based on the assumption that the formula continues to work in more general cases, security and pleasure may follow from the coherent use of the formulae in applications such as differentiation of trigonometric functions in the calculus. This will be addressed by relating dynamic visual ideas of the changing slope of the graph of trigonometric functions to the symbolic use of trigonometric formulae. It will play a major role in our studies of calculus and formal mathematics in the latter stages of this book.

3.1 *Met-Befores Affect Us All*

Met-befores (and met-afters) are features of the development of human knowledge structures that are highly significant in attempting to grasp

---

[29] I thank Kin Eng Chin for his permission to speak of ideas that he is currently working on for his thesis. His analysis of supportive and problematic conceptions, both of which can include supportive and problematic aspects, has proved to be most helpful in the theoretical refinement of ideas in this book.

[30] The concept of 'met-after' was first coined by Australian student Glenda Ashleigh in a conversation when we were talking about her PhD thesis. It has also been used by others and is part of the ongoing evolution of theoretical ideas about cognitive growth that are still under development.

how humans learn to think mathematically. Curriculum designers focus mainly on supportive met-befores that are intended to form a basis for future development, for instance, the largely American use of the term 'pre-calculus' to describe courses intended to lay the foundation of a theory that students will meet in the future. The evidence of this chapter reveals the many problematic aspects that arise when learners encounter new situations. A sensible approach to learning requires not only the building towards powerful ideas that will be encountered in the future but also addressing problematic issues in the present that may have long-term consequences.

There needs to be a balance between the supportive aspects that encourage generalization and the problematic aspects that impede progress. Ideas that are supportive at one stage may become problematic in another. This applies not only to students, but also to experts, who may develop a particular view that prevents them from grasping new avenues of progress. Because they are experts, they may defend their position, vigorously opposing a possible change in paradigm.

Our language is full of such instances in history. We speak of rational and *irrational* numbers, of fractions and *surds* (that are ab*surd*), positive numbers and *negative* numbers, real numbers and *complex* numbers with real and *imaginary* parts. This desire to stay with the familiar rather than face revolutionary change is well documented in Thomas Kuhn's influential work, *The Structure of Scientific Revolutions*.[31]

As the story in this book develops, I regard it as a duty to expose readers to ideas that may be problematic. If I avoid problematic ideas (as happens in the design of most modern curricula) then these problems may never be addressed. The moral of this story is that we should realize that we are not simply *observers* of the drama, seeing how students deal with the joys and trials of mathematics: we are *participants* in the story ourselves. While we should maintain stable ways of operating that work in practice, we should also question our theoretical frameworks, to seek further insights in the evolution of mathematical thinking.

4. Summary

In this chapter I have addressed the development of mathematical thinking, beginning with the fundamental facilities of the sensori-motor human brain and our special ability for communication using language and symbolism. I

---

[31] Kuhn (1962).

hypothesize that mathematical thinking builds on these facilities set-before birth in our genes and develops through successive experiences where new situations are interpreted using knowledge structures based on experiences that the individual has met before.

The chapter reveals that the long-term development of mathematical thinking involves changes of meaning where some supportive experiences met-before remain supportive in a new context and encourage generalization but other previously supportive aspects become problematic and impede progress.

In Chapter 5 we will consider the wider aspects of the relationship between the cognitive growth of mathematical thinking and related emotional responses that affect the long-term development of increasing confidence or the downward spiral of anxiety.

5   Mathematics and Emotion

This chapter considers how mathematical thinking affects and is affected by the emotions. At one extreme is the delight of having the power to solve a tricky problem, and at the other is the anxiety of being unable to do mathematics under pressure or even being unable to do mathematics at all. In this chapter we consider the possible sources of this range of emotions, both in terms of the general literature and in terms of the theoretical framework formulated in this book.

Extensive research into mathematics anxiety, particularly in the United States, reveals a range of possible sources, including personal attributes of confidence or insecurity; the attitudes of parents, teachers and peers; inadequate teaching; or poor preparation for examinations. These are all taken into account in the discussion that follows, with the main focus on the individual's relationship with the mathematics itself.

The path to long-term development of flexible thinking is not the same for everyone. We saw in Chapter 2 that there is already a 'proceptual divide' between those who remain fixed in the rigid procedures of counting while others remember known facts and use them to derive other facts with greater fluency. In Chapter 4 we saw how successive experiences in mathematics involve both supportive aspects that encourage generalization and problematic aspects that impede progress. At each stage individual children will have already built personal ways of making sense of previous experience and are likely to react differently to new topics. I take the view that this underlying reaction to new ideas encountered in mathematics plays a major role in both the joy of mathematics and the negative feelings of anxiety. In turn, the emotional reactions have long-term effects on learners' personal development, encouraging some to build on their confidence to enjoy the challenge of more sophisticated ideas while others are impeded in their progress and may resort to rote-learning procedures without meaning, or become disaffected and develop mathematical anxiety.

1. Instrumental and Relational Understanding

Richard Skemp formulated two distinct forms of understanding: *instrumental understanding* (*knowing how* to perform mathematical operations) and *relational understanding* (which also involves *knowing why*).[1] He reasoned that both types of understanding have their roles to play. Instrumental understanding is often quicker to acquire and gives immediate results in timed examinations. Relational understanding has longer-term consequences in building richly connected knowledge structures, but may involve dealing with more subtle concepts. For instance, in handling the multiplication of two negative numbers it may be easier to learn that 'two minuses make a plus' than to consider all the ramifications involved in making sense of the operation in general.

It can also happen that a simple understanding of a concept may not be feasible at a given stage because necessary ideas require a higher level of development than is currently available to the learner. For instance, we saw in Chapter 4 that the proof of the general formula for $\sin(A + B)$ requires sophisticated techniques that may not be available when the formula is used in the initial stages of calculus, yet it can be *used* in pragmatic ways, and lead to coherent results so that students can gain pleasure and confidence in the successful use of the formula, even though they do not regard its proof as a priority. As a consequence, relational understanding does not require total understanding of all elements involved, but it does require fitting ideas together in a supportive way that works coherently for the individual learner.

Both instrumental and relational understanding can give pleasure. For example, instrumental mathematics is pleasurable when it enables the learner to succeed in performing well in mathematical calculations; relational mathematics is pleasurable when ideas fit together in meaningful ways. On the other hand, both can also cause emotional problems: instrumental learning may cause anxiety or fear of failure when the calculations become too complicated; relational understanding may involve confusion or frustration when the mathematics fails to make sense.

2. Skemp's Theory of Goals and Anti-Goals

The analysis of the relationship between mathematical thinking and the emotions requires an appropriate theoretical framework to organize the

---

[1] Skemp (1976).

discussion. Richard Skemp built on fundamental ideas in psychology to formulate a framework that not only involved goals that a learner may wish to achieve, but also anti-goals that a learner wishes to avoid.[2] The combination of the two gives a broader sense of coherence to the overall picture in the same way as supportive and problematic met-befores clarify the pleasures and problems of the full range of learners.

A goal or anti-goal can be short-term, such as the goal of adding two numbers together, or long-term, for example, the overall goal to succeed in mathematics. An anti-goal may involve a short-term wish to avoid being asked a question in class for fear of looking foolish, or a longer-term desire to avoid mathematics altogether.

Children are usually born with a positive attitude to learning. They explore the world spontaneously, often with great pleasure. But unpleasant experiences are likely to lead to the desire to avoid the unpleasantness, leading to the development of anti-goals.

Skemp theorized that there are very different emotions related to goals and anti-goals. He distinguished between the emotions sensed as one moves towards, or away from, a goal or anti-goal (represented by arrows in Figure 5.1). He also considered the individual's overall sense of being able to achieve a goal, or to avoid an anti-goal (which I represent here by the smiling faces for a positive sense and frowning faces for a negative).

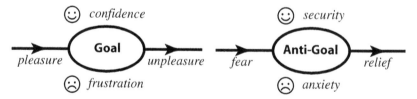

Figure 5.1. Emotions associated with goals and anti-goals.

The diagram makes explicit the different emotions related to approaching or moving away from a goal or anti-goal. A goal that one believes is achievable is suffused with a feeling of confidence, which may change to frustration if it proves subsequently to be difficult to achieve. Frustration sensed by a confident person is likely to act as a positive encouragement to redouble the effort to achieve the goal. Moving towards a goal gives pleasure and moving away from it gives unpleasure – a term used in Freudian analysis to denote the opposite of pleasure.

---

[2] Skemp (1979).

Coping with an anti-goal is quite different. According to Skemp, an anti-goal that one believes one can avoid gives a sense of security but, when it cannot be avoided, the emotion turns to anxiety. Moving towards a goal instills a sense of fear, while moving away gives relief.

This reveals the vast difference between the positive emotions relating to goals that are considered achievable and the negative emotions relating to anti-goals that offer, at best, a sense of security and relief and, at worst, a sense of anxiety and fear.

The difference is seen in the mathematics classroom where some learners build a positive attitude, related to the long-term confidence that they can solve problems, coupled with a sense of security that they can avoid difficulties. Richard Skemp insightfully claimed that 'pleasure is a signpost, not a destination'[3], stating a principle that pleasure is not something that one should seek in itself, but a state of being aware of making progress towards a desired goal. For him, mathematical learning becomes pleasurable by making sense of the mathematics and tackling interesting problems that are within the grasp of the pupil willing to accept a challenge. The idea of 'making mathematics fun' may be an important ingredient in learning to think mathematically but it is only a partial solution, for the main goal should be to improve the power of one's mathematical thinking.

Pleasure that arises from relational understanding comes from growing more powerful through being able to make sense of the ideas and build them into rich flexible knowledge structures. A learner who builds confidence through success will not be pleased if a particular problem proves more difficult than expected, but the frustration experienced is more likely to provoke a determination to find a way of resolving the difficulty rather than any initial fear of failure.

If the frustration is unresolved, there are two distinct possibilities. One is to replace the now frustrated goal of relational understanding by the more pragmatic goal of rote-learning the procedures to pass the examination. This can lead to its own sense of success, particularly for those who may have little interest in mathematics itself but need a qualification in mathematics for something else. However, if the learner then has difficulty in performing the mathematical calculations, the situation can change dramatically from the goal of success to the anti-goal of avoiding failure.

Writing an editorial in a journal for teachers, John Pegg once commented:

> I was interviewing a number of students about how they worked through their mathematics. What became very clear was the desire of the students

---

[3] Skemp (1979).

to 'know the rule' or 'the way to do it'. Any attempt on my part to provide some background development or some context was greeted with polite indifference – 'Don't worry about that stuff; just tell me how it goes.'[4]

Until recently, I had always seen this as a desire for instrumental understanding over relational understanding. However, using Skemp's theory of goals and anti-goals, it is not one phenomenon, but two. One is the goal of wishing to 'know the rule' or 'the way to do it.' The other is the anti-goal of avoiding any 'explanations' that the student may believe will cause confusion.

3. Mathematics Anxiety

Mathematics anxiety has been described as 'feelings of tension and anxiety that interfere with the manipulation of mathematical problems in a wide variety of ordinary life and academic situations'.[5] Research carried out in the United States reveals that it occurs at all levels of learning from elementary school, through high school and on to college mathematics.[6] It is manifested by physiological factors such as increased heart rate and sweaty palms, as well as a horrendous inability to recall facts under pressure and a genuine antipathy to mathematics. Mathematics anxiety appears to be so widespread that the author Marilyn Burns was able to claim that almost two-thirds of all American adults had a hatred and deep fear of mathematics.[7] Even at college level, a study of more than 9,000 American students found that one in four had a moderate to high need for help with their mathematical anxieties.[8]

To seek factors relating to mathematics anxiety, it first needs to be identified and its extent measured in a consistent way. This has been traditionally studied and measured by questionnaires that request respondents to rate their reaction to a number of statements such as 'being able to explain how you arrived at a particular answer for a problem', 'being asked to remember the telephone numbers of three people you have met', or 'counting a pile of change'.[9]

The first such questionnaire to obtain broad currency was the 'Mathematics Anxiety Rating Scale' (MARS)[10] with 98 items, and this has

---

[4] Pegg (1991), p. 70.
[5] Richardson and Suin (1972), p. 551.
[6] See, for example, Steele & Arth (1998); Jackson & Leffingwell (1999); Hembree (1990); Bitner, Austin & Wadlington (1994); Tobias (1990).
[7] Burns (1998).
[8] Jones (2001).
[9] Sheffield & Hunt (2006).
[10] Richardson & Suin (1972).

since formed the basis of other shorter questionnaires modified for specific use.[11] Such questionnaires can then be used in conjunction with other data to seek correlation between mathematics anxiety (as measured by the test) and other factors. These include the correlation between students finding mathematics difficult and the tendency to be anxious[12], a growing incidence of anxiety in older learners[13], and evidence of older females having increased anxiety compared to males.[14]

The many diverse factors related to mathematics anxiety include negative images of mathematics from teachers, parents and others; social deprivation; disturbing previous experiences in mathematics classes; poor teaching based on learning rules that are not understood; poor preparation for tests; anxiety at being asked to do mathematical problems in front of the class; fear of failure; poor self-image; poor memory and so on.[15]

Few of these explicitly relate to the nature of mathematics itself, but more to the effects of inadequate teaching, negative attitudes or anxiety arising from being put under pressure in front of others, or in a timed test. Furthermore, whatever the source of the difficulty, a cycle can build up in which anxious students begin to avoid mathematics or put in little effort, leaving significant gaps in their knowledge, causing increasing difficulties in more advanced topics, reinforcing their anxiety and deepening their problems. This develops a cycle in which 'unreasonable beliefs can lead to anxiety, anxiety can lead to protective behavior, and the long-term disadvantage of protective behavior can reinforce unreasonable beliefs.'[16]

Mathematics anxiety is therefore a complex issue with diverse sources that can increase in cycles of intensity as difficulties cause anxiety and anxiety causes difficulties.

To combat the problem, the National Council of Teachers of Mathematics (NCTM) focused a positive emphasis on:

- confidence in using math to solve problems, to communicate ideas and to reason;
- flexibility in exploring mathematical ideas and trying alternative methods in solving problems;

---

[11] For instance, the shortened 25-item test sMARS (Alexander & Martray 1989), the Revised Mathematics Anxiety Rating Scale [R-MARS] (Plake & Parker 1982).

[12] Betz (1978); Ma (1999a).

[13] See, for example, Betz (1978); Bitner, Austin & Wadlington (1994); Hembree (1990); Jackson & Leffingwell (1999); Tobias (1990).

[14] Campbell & Evans (1997).

[15] Furner & Berman (2003).

[16] Baroody & Costlick (1998).

- willingness to persevere in mathematical tasks;
- interest, curiosity, and inventiveness in doing mathematics;
- valuing of the application of mathematics to situations arising in other disciplines and everyday experiences;
- appreciation of the role of mathematics in our culture and its value as a tool and as a language.[17]

These suggestions all involve developing positive attitudes in mathematical thinking – there is no mention of mathematical thinking itself being a cause of anxiety. Yet, if we consider the various factors that are related to anxiety such as parents and teachers passing on to students their own anxieties, we find that many factors that are identified are *symptoms* of anxiety, not the original source. Where do parents and teachers get their negative empathy? Is it an infinite regression of negative empathy from others before them? Or does it trace back to one of the other sources of anxiety such as the individual's fear of being asked to do mathematical problems in front of the class, or a fear of forgetting everything in an exam?

Although general sources of anxiety may be involved, mathematics anxiety is a problem that in some way must relate to *mathematics* itself and to the individual's relationship with mathematics.

The solution proposed by the NCTM is to produce a positive approach to mathematics that increases confidence, flexibility, willingness, interest, reflection and appreciation of mathematics in its applications. In a nation founded on the belief that anyone can do anything if he or she only works hard and has personal belief, it is natural to focus on the positive side of mathematical thinking and seek relational understanding that can come from the involvement of learners in their own learning. This concentrates on gaining confidence in solving problems, communicating ideas, learning to reason, developing flexibility in problem solving, willingness to persevere and so on. It is in distinct contrast from the instrumental learning of mathematical routines for column arithmetic, long division, adding fractions, solving linear equations, with the goal of performing well in timed tests that puts pressure on the individual and has the potential to cause anxiety.

However, engendering a positive attitude without seeking the source of the problem is not the full solution. Mathematics as a subject has the distinction of having its own form of anxiety, suggesting that there are specific aspects of mathematics and how it is perceived in society that cause individuals to feel anxious about it.

---

[17] NCTM (1989), p. 233.

In the earlier chapters of this book we have seen several possible sources of anxiety: in the complication of the situations that are encountered in mathematics, in the possible lack of compression of operations into flexible thinkable concepts, in the transitions to new mathematical concepts that involve problematic met-befores, and in the blending of different knowledge structures that on the one hand give the possibility of creating new knowledge and on the other the conflict between problematic aspects of the blend that can cause confusion.

The quest to understand the fundamental sources of mathematical anxiety – and its complement, mathematical confidence – benefits from a consideration of the nature of mathematics itself and how ideas mature in the learner as new possibilities are encountered.

3.1 *Limitations in Short-term Memory*

Ashcraft and Kirk[18] highlighted a correlation between mathematics anxiety (measured by a questionnaire) and performance on a test involving two simultaneous activities – remembering a sequence of letters while the subject performed a simple arithmetical task, and was then asked to recall the letters. They found a significant correlation between smaller working memory and higher mathematics anxiety.

Short-term memory limitation is consistent with difficulties in handling more complicated aspects of mathematics at all levels. Arithmetic involves subtle operations that become more manageable when they are compressed into remembered facts and processed more efficiently.

At one extreme is the child who has difficulty holding sufficient information in short-term memory to even be able to grasp the problem, let alone solve it. At other extreme is the gifted child who has a sense of ideas that enable him or her to grasp overall principles that make mathematical thinking essentially simple. We saw this divergence in the opening example of Chapter 1 where young John was unable to carry out the simplest number tasks in a timed test while the even younger Peter could imagine relationships involving numbers in the millions.

3.2 *Problematic Aspects Related to Lack of Compression*

In Chapter 2 we saw the growing 'proceptual divide' between those who remain fixed in lengthy counting procedures and those that develop more

---

[18] Ashcraft & Kirk (2001).

efficient knowledge structures in arithmetic. This involves a second source of anxiety caused by the failure to compress mathematical operations into thinkable concepts that enable flexible calculations in arithmetic and flexible manipulation of symbols in algebra.

As problems require more extended calculations, learners who continue to be engaged in long-winded counting procedures will find the arithmetic more difficult than those who learn to use more flexible methods. The difficulties are therefore compounded as the struggling student is confronted with more complicated solution processes than those available to the flexible thinker.

Process-object theories such as Dubinsky's APOS[19] and Sfard's operational-structural theory[20] imply that lack of compression of process into object causes difficulties. Sfard theorized that students who fail to reify processes as mental objects cope by using procedural techniques. Dubinsky proposed a method of encouraging long-term encapsulation of process as mental objects by constructing a 'genetic decomposition' of mathematical objects to structure learning to encourage the necessary constructions. This is done in a positive sense, encouraging cooperative learning in which students share ideas as they construct meanings for themselves, in a manner consistent with the aforementioned NCTM principles.

Accentuating the positive is a helpful objective, but it does not necessarily eliminate the negative. On the contrary, to comprehend the full nature of success and failure, it is essential to take into account not only positive aspects that support mathematical thinking but also problematic met-befores that may cause disaffection. This is the main thrust of the argument in this book: that problematic met-befores cause negative emotional reactions that impede learning. It is not enough to say that students suffer mathematical anxiety and attempt to lessen it by a friendly, supportive approach. It is important to be aware of *why* such problems occur.

3.3 *Problematic Aspects Related to Met-Befores*

Problematic met-befores interfere in learning when students meet generalizations of old ideas in new contexts. Well-known instances discussed in Chapter 3 include the introduction of fractions, the subtle notion of

---

[19] Asiala et al. (1996).
[20] Sfard (1991).

negative numbers, the transition from arithmetic to algebra, fractional and negative powers, real numbers and limits, complex numbers and the square root of −1.

In each case the *mathematics* changes in meaning to apply in a broader context that conflicts with previous experience. Some students see the power of the more general ideas and embrace them with pleasure. Others sense an underlying difficulty but manage to carry out the necessary procedures, perhaps with a lingering sense of doubt.

Uri Wilensky referred to this as 'epistemological anxiety', which he described as 'a feeling, often in the background, that one does not comprehend the meanings, purposes, source or legitimacy of the mathematical objects one is manipulating and using'.[21] He illustrated this with the following excerpt from an interview:

> *Interviewer:* So, what was math like for you in school?
> *Student:* Well, I was always good at math. But, I didn't really like it.
> *Interviewer:* Why was that?
> *Student:* Why? I don't know. I guess I always felt like I was getting away with something, you know, like I was cheating. I could do the problems and I did well on the tests, but I didn't really know what was going on.[22]

Epistemological anxiety is a sign of inability to achieve the goal of relational understanding of mathematics. To relieve the frustration, the goal may switch to the instrumental understanding of being able to perform the requisite procedures, as happened here with a level of success but a sense of underlying doubt.

The alternative goal of seeking to learn the procedures occurred in the study reported in Chapter 4[23] where teachers, realizing that students were having difficulty with algebra, resorted to teaching students to solve algebraic equations using rules for shifting symbols around. For a few, the method led to successful solutions, but others found the methods stressful and likely to lead to error. The teacher encouraged the students to work hard and concentrate on doing the problems without attempting to make sense of the process. The emotions roused were recalled by a fifteen-year-old in a later interview:

> When I saw the teacher coming into the room shouting 'get out your calculators' and writing 'Equation' on the board, the whole class was silenced

---

[21] Wilensky (1993b), p. 172.
[22] Wilensky (1993b), p. 184.
[23] See Chapter 4, Section 2.12, page 104.

and I thought 'My God, what is this?' Then, she started to write signs, brackets, and other abstract symbols. I was in panic, no exaggeration; all feelings from mathematics came through. When she saw that I wasn't doing the exercises in the book, she shouted 'Fabiooooo, get your book and find the solutions to the problems!' I thought that I should stop, but she started to talk about the various qualities a student should have, like dedication and endeavor. I was scared. Every time I heard her say 'quadratic formula', 'tangent', 'cosine', my mind was full of doubts; while she was talking about the unknown, I had a knot in my head. So, I made an exception and thought, 'it is better to stop this.' I remembered my reasoning capacity, got the pencil, the rubber and other instruments and started to do the exercises.[24]

This illustrates the general problem. The student is already in a situation where the mathematics is complicated and disconnected, with all kinds of ideas in 'a knot in my head'. The strategy adopted in the given quotation is to appeal to qualities such as dedication and endeavor and to focus on doing the exercises. The frustration of not being able to achieve the goal of relational understanding is replaced by the instrumental goal to practice the procedures to pass the test. However, in the reported study[25], the procedural goal proved to be totally inadequate.

Successful instrumental learning can generate a new attitude with new goals. If instrumental learning has been successful in the past and the goal of relational learning seems not to be possible, then learning 'what to do' can become the main goal for the future. Once a level of success has been achieved by learning procedures by rote, this in itself becomes a met-before that affects future learning and may lead to a cycle of rote-learning in the future.

4. Generalization and Extensional Blends

Many of the examples of generalization involve an extensional blend in which one system is generalized to a larger one, for example, when whole number arithmetic is generalized to fractional arithmetic, counting numbers to signed numbers, arithmetic to algebra.

Such extensional blends are vital developments of the growth of mathematical thinking. Some mathematically-inclined individuals find such extensions to offer great pleasure and delight. For instance, to show that the sum of two odd numbers is even, one may begin by looking at individual

---

[24] Lima & Tall (2006), p. 234.
[25] Lima & Tall (2008).

cases, such as $5 + 3$ is 8 or $9 + 3$ is 12. However, to write two odd numbers algebraically as $2m - 1$ and $2n - 1$, where m and n now represent general whole numbers and to add them to get $2(m + n - 1)$ as a multiple of 2, clearly represents the general case without any need for further argument.

The extensional generalization from arithmetic to algebra is problematic and many find algebra difficult to understand. It is part of the folklore that even appears in the columns of newspapers, such as the following by staff writer Deb Kollar, in the *Sacramento Bee*.

> For some, audits and root canals hurt less than algebra. Brian White hated it. It made Julie Beall cry. Tim Broneck got an F-minus. Tina Casale failed seven times. And Mollie Burrows just never saw the point. This is not a collection of wayward students, of unproductive losers in life. They are regular people [...] with jobs and families, hobbies and homes. And a common nightmare in their past.[26]

Generalization is inevitably a blend of ideas that focuses on certain essentials and suppresses others so that the essentials can operate in a wider domain. The essentials take the form of supportive met-befores that will continue to operate in the new situation. But there are other problematic aspects that may impede the generalization, as in the case of students encountering algebra and being bewildered by new ideas that do not fit their previous experiences in arithmetic.

A whole range of examples have already been given in Chapter 4 that confirm that the phenomenon occurs throughout the development of mathematical thinking, where specific embodiments help in initial cases but may prove problematic in new situations. Some learners may grasp the essential power of an extensional blend but others, who find the blend to be problematic, may turn to the goal of being able to perform the necessary procedures to pass the test. Some may be successful and sense the pleasure of achievement, while others may remain in conflict, leading to alienation and anxiety.

Even the most able, who succeed in the International Mathematics Olympiad for gifted mathematicians, are aware of the distinction between conceptual insight and procedural power. Boris Koichu, who studies the problem-solving skills of gifted students, sees what he calls 'the principle of parsimony' in which the best solutions are those that take a minimal path to the answer.[27] However, he finds that successful students are aware of two

---

[26] Kollar (2000).
[27] Olympiad problem solvers that experience a conflict between different types of parsimony are described in Koichu & Berman (2005). See also Koichu (2008).

distinct kinds of parsimony. One, which they regard as the greater of the two, involves reflecting deeply and seeing links that reduce the problem to its essence. The other, in a time-limited test with little room for reflection, involves attacking the problem with a barrage of powerful algorithms to crack it as quickly as possible.

This illustrates the subtle nature of mathematical thinking that builds over the long-term by compressing complicated ideas into subtle knowledge structures. In a new problem-solving situation, making the connections to build a satisfying crystalline structure requires deep reflection on the relationships. Although this may eventually yield a solution that is both insightful and elegant, when under pressure, gifted mathematicians often use well-rehearsed procedural methods to crush a problem by brute force.

5. Supportive and Problematic Conceptions

This highlights the significance of the notions of supportive and problematic personal conceptions that are a fundamental feature of learning. As we go through life learning mathematics, we are faced with changes of meaning that incorporate both supportive and problematic aspects. It is not a case of developing fully coherent concepts at all times. Successful mathematical thinkers will have problematic aspects in their knowledge that they may push to the back of their mind to focus on the supportive aspects that allow them to solve problems and sense the sweet taste of success. As human beings we do not enjoy exposing our weaknesses, so many experts do not admit their personal difficulties. On the other hand, for those who are struggling, the problematic aspects may overwhelm supportive aspects to swamp their feelings, leading either to the need to learn by rote or even to fall into dysfunctional anxiety. By considering both the positive and negative aspects of emotion in mathematics we have a better opportunity to understand *why* students develop mathematical anxiety and to find ways of encouraging them to seek success.

6. Goals and Success

An individual who builds knowledge in an increasingly confident way with a history of conquering difficulties will still encounter challenges in new learning. Previous experiences of resolving frustration can enhance the pleasure that is sensed when a solution is finally achieved. The constant search for the sweet smell of success leads to the desire to overcome even greater challenges, just as a mountain-climber seeks to conquer the most difficult routes up a mountain. Hard-won successes act as a spur to confident, successful individuals, who come alive when faced with adversity and revel in seeking new ways to achieve even higher levels of accomplishment and delight.

Consider the legendary case of Andrew Wiles, who solved the 300-year-old problem known as Fermat's Last Theorem. His was an exceptional intellect that built richly connected mental structures, enabling him to bring together many resources to reconsider the centuries-old problem from new viewpoints. After many years of secret work, in 1994 he announced a solution to the problem that had defeated all attempts by mathematicians for more than three centuries. At the apparent apex of his achievement, other mathematicians carefully analyzed his proof and a gap was found. In the *Scientific American*, André Weil remarked scathingly:[28]

> I am willing to believe he has had some good ideas in trying to construct the proof, but the proof is not there. To some extent, proving Fermat's Theorem is like climbing Everest. If a man wants to climb Everest and falls short of it by 100 yards, he has not climbed Everest.

Now in the glare of worldwide publicity, Wiles worked to plug the gap. The possibility of failure and the negative emotions that this may generate were overcome by his frustrated desire to achieve the ultimate goal. A year later, he produced the proof that was accepted by the mathematical community as definitive. Triumph was sweet.

In the aftermath of the turbulent final stages that led to the accepted proof, we may still ask whether the theorem is proved absolutely for all time, or only proven to the satisfaction of today's mathematicians, so that perhaps an even subtler flaw might be found by a future generation. The complexity is such that we can never be absolutely sure. As the biological brain strives to gain success over its sensory perceptions to move towards the desired certainty of perfection, it remains an enigma in two quite different ways. On the one hand, the biological brain cannot, of itself, entirely throw off the shackles of its evolutionary origins. On the other, the miracle of its ingenious creativity is a testament to the amazing human capacity for mathematical thinking.

7. Summary

In the long-term development of a mathematical mind, the journey is not always easy. Learners may encounter serious obstacles on the way, just

---

[28] Horgan (1994) in an interview with Weil.

as mathematicians face difficulties in solving new problems with current knowledge. As we consider mathematical growth from child to mathematician, we see that, far from being a simple logical development, the cognitive growth of mathematical ideas in the individual is punctuated by changes in context that require serious cognitive reconstruction of knowledge. Whereas a confident thinker with a history of making sense of mathematics may see the challenge that is faced and attempt to find a solution, an individual who begins to fear failure may develop a level of anxiety that makes it far more difficult to cope in stressful situations.

The consequence is that individuals develop different ways of responding to the challenges presented. Some will resolve the stress by shifting to the goal of memorizing routines to pass the tests, a natural consequence of the fundamental set-before of repetition to routinize operations to solve routine problems. Teachers faced with the problems of preparing students to pass tests may also see this route as a way of resolving the problems that students have in addressing the complexities of mathematics. However, the choice of teaching strategy is not an alternative between conceptual understanding *or* operational fluency. Powerful mathematical thinking requires both. Its long-term development is enhanced by making sense of generative ideas that act as a foundation for the compression of rich structures into thinkable concepts linked together flexibly in coherently related knowledge structures. The cognitive growth of mathematical knowledge enhances, and is enhanced by, the development of confidence through making personal sense of new ideas.

6 The Three Worlds of Mathematics

We now have the constructs to formulate the development of mathematical thinking in terms of 'three worlds of mathematics' arising from a sensori-motor-linguistic foundation building on the set-befores of *recognition*, *repetition* and *language* and the met-befores from previous experience that may be supportive or problematic in new situations.

Mathematical thinking involves the *compression* of mathematical structures into *thinkable concepts* connected into *knowledge structures* that are *blended* together, leading to sophisticated *crystalline concepts* that have an inevitable mathematical structure.

1. The Three Worlds

The three set-befores common to us all are foundational in the development of three mental worlds of mathematics:

> A world of (conceptual) *embodiment* building on human perceptions and actions developing mental images verbalized in increasingly sophisticated ways to become perfect mental entities in our imagination;
>
> A world of (operational) *symbolism* developing from embodied human actions into symbolic procedures of calculation and manipulation that may be compressed into procepts to enable flexible operational thinking;
>
> A world of (axiomatic) *formalism* building formal knowledge in axiomatic systems specified by set-theoretic definition, whose properties are deduced by mathematical proof.

In each world of mathematics, recognition, repetition and language all play their part. Thinkable concepts are formulated initially through recognition and *categorization* in the world of conceptual embodiment. The symbolic world is built through repetition of sequences of actions to construct mathematical operations either as routine procedures or, through *encapsulation*, as flexible procepts. Later language comes into its own in the *definition* of concepts – of geometric figures in Euclidean geometry, of properties in arithmetic that are formulated as rules of operation in algebra, and subsequently the seismic shift to set-theoretic definition in axiomatic mathematics.

In Euclidean geometry, the properties of figures are conceptualized through structural abstraction in four stages: practical *recognition* and *description*, then theoretical Euclidean *definition* and *proof*. In arithmetic and algebra, operations are encapsulated as mental objects through *operational abstraction*, and in axiomatic formal mathematics concepts are constructed through *formal abstraction*, based on set-theoretic *definition* and *proof*. In all three worlds, concepts are refined through structural abstraction involving *recognition*, *description*, *definition* and *deduction* in forms appropriate for each context.

2. Embodiment

The term 'embodiment' has a range of subtly different meanings. In everyday language an embodiment can refer to a concrete representation of an abstract concept, such as 'Mother Theresa is the embodiment of Christian Charity.'

The mathematics educator Zoltan Dienes used the term 'embodiment' in this sense, producing physical equipment to represent abstract mathematical concepts, including his 'multi-base arithmetic blocks' to represent place value and 'logic blocks' to represent logical relationships.[1] Figure 6.1 shows his multi-base arithmetic blocks in base ten.

To encourage children to conceptualize the idea of place value he used blocks with different bases (say, 2, 3 or 5) and embodiments with different structures (such as grouping straws into tens, then grouping ten of these into hundreds). His aim was to enable learners to appreciate the underlying mathematics common to them all and filter out properties of specific embodiments that are irrelevant to the general concept.

However, there is a huge difference between what a mature adult may see in an embodiment and what may be noticed by a child. For instance, multiplication by 10 using Dienes' blocks involves replacing 10 units by one long, or 10 longs by one flat, or 10 flats by a big cube. Written in

---

[1] Dienes (1960).

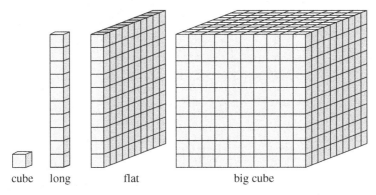

cube　long　　　flat　　　　　　big cube

Figure 6.1. Dienes' blocks.

decimal notation, this gives the principle that multiplying a decimal by 10 shifts all digits one place to the left. This idea of shifting symbols to represent multiplying and dividing by 10, if understood meaningfully, is far simpler than that of replacing one kind of unit by another.

An interesting possibility arises in which the embodiment of place value may be represented not by physical materials such as Dienes' blocks, but by embodied actions shifting the symbols themselves. One might begin with three zeros drawn in a row to represent the positions of hundreds, tens and units and use strips of paper with a single digit at the right-hand end to place over the zeros. (Figure 6.2 overleaf.)

Picture (1) shows the basic page, (2) shows a digit 2 placed over the units value to represent 2 units, and in picture (3) this is shifted one place to the left to expose the zero units to represent 2 tens as 20. Picture (4) starts with 7 units and picture (5) superimposes a 2 covering the tens place. This offers an opportunity to 'see' the numbers flexibly as 2 tens and 7 units or as 27 units. A shift one place to the left in picture (6) gives 270, which can be seen flexibly as 270 units, or as 27 tens, or as 2 hundreds and 7 tens. The last of these corresponds to the usual name 'two hundred and seventy'.

The physical act of shifting the digits one place to the left multiplies by 10. By the same token, a shift to the right takes 27 tens (270) to 27 units (27), a division by a factor 10.

The embodiment can be taken further to introduce larger numbers in thousands, millions and billions by placing extra groups of three more zeros to the left. Placing strips over these extra zeros gives larger units of a thousand, with successive places to the left repeating the earlier pattern: *one* thousand, *ten* thousand, a *hundred* thousand. Another three zeros to the right repeats the pattern to give millions, the next billions and so on.

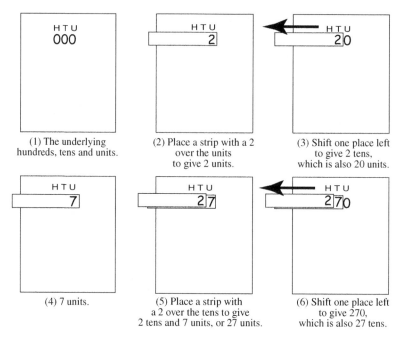

(1) The underlying hundreds, tens and units.

(2) Place a strip with a 2 over the units to give 2 units.

(3) Shift one place left to give 2 tens, which is also 20 units.

(4) 7 units.

(5) Place a strip with a 2 over the tens to give 2 tens and 7 units, or 27 units.

(6) Shift one place left to give 270, which is also 27 tens.

Figure 6.2. Embodying place value.

Figure 6.3 shows the underlying zeros in picture (1), then 27 thousand (27,000) is represented in picture (2) and shifted one place to the left in picture (3) to give 270 thousand.

The essential idea is to see the decimal places as being fixed and the digits being shifted, to see the shift to the left multiplying by 10 and to the right dividing by 10.

Once a child can 'see' the placing of the digits, a strip with a digit on the right may be replaced by a smaller piece of paper with a single digit on it. All that is required is to ignore the zeros to the left to read 027 as 27.

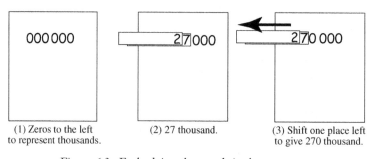

(1) Zeros to the left to represent thousands.

(2) 27 thousand.

(3) Shift one place left to give 270 thousand.

Figure 6.3. Embodying thousands in the same way.

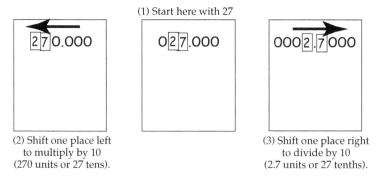

(1) Start here with 27

(2) Shift one place left
to multiply by 10
(270 units or 27 tens).

(3) Shift one place right
to divide by 10
(2.7 units or 27 tenths).

Figure 6.4. Move one place left to multiply by 10, one place right to divide by 10.

Figure 6.4 shows the number 27 in the middle picture being shifted one place to the left to give 270 units or 27 tens, or shifting it one place to the right interprets 2.7 as 2 units and 7 tenths or even 27 tenths.

This can also help the child see all the digits in a number as a whole rather than the commonly held view that 12.53 consists of two numbers: a 12 on the left hand of the decimal point and 53 on the right. The latter view is supported by the met-before arising from using money to introduce place value that can play havoc with the general meaning of decimal notation. $12.53 is 12 dollars and 53 cents, but $12.5 is not 12 dollars 5 cents; it is 12 dollars 50. No wonder many children become confused.

For instance, ten-year-old Harry experienced difficulty with arithmetic and took private lessons after school using the Kumon approach to practice routine skills. His ability to cope with the operations of column arithmetic increased significantly. But he continued to have difficulties with decimals. When asked the decimal for a half, he responded firmly 'nought point five' but when asked about a third he seemed to sense that it was less than a half (point five) and guessed a smaller number to suggest 'point one'.

A few minutes playing with a row of zeros on a piece of paper and strips of paper with digits on the end, shifting digits to the left and right, led to the idea of shifting a digit from the units place of the decimal point. He immediately recognized the result as 5 tenths. When shown 0.1, a great smile of recognition came across his face as he said '0.1 is a tenth!' There followed a beautiful conversation about 0.5, 0.50, 0.05 and money in pounds and pence. He was quite definite in seeing 0.5 as five tenths, which is a half, 0.50 as fifty hundredths, which is also a half, while 0.05 is five hundredths so it is much less.

As he explained the idea of moving the digits over fixed place values, he gestured to the left and right to represent multiplying and dividing by 10. This occurred in a few minutes of embodiment when several months practicing symbolic calculations had given him fluency without meaning.

Nor was it necessary to continue with the physical embodiment; once he could *see* the symbols moving to the left and right, he was able to proceed by mentally shifting the symbols in his mind.

2.1 *Ideas from Philosophy and Cognitive Science*

The term 'embodiment' carries with it a number of subtle refinements of meaning that have developed over the years in classical philosophy and in modern cognitive science.

As the Greeks grappled with ideas in science and philosophy, they realized that what we sense in the physical world leads to mental conceptions that can no longer be represented in physical terms. Plato asserted that there was a perfect world beyond our human existence that could only be dimly imagined in terms of physical reality.[2] In mathematics, in particular, there is a perfect world of geometry with points that have no size, lines with length and no breadth, and perfect circles that have properties that are deduced through proof in Euclidean geometry. This led to a distinction between what the physical body senses and what the spiritual mind and soul conceive on a higher conceptual level.

The philosopher Descartes took this further by making a clear distinction between the brain with its human limitations and the mind with its awareness of the human soul. His 'Cartesian dualism', separating body and mind, led to centuries of fundamental debate on the true nature of the mind and its relationship with the biological brain.[3]

As our knowledge of neurophysiology has progressed, Cartesian dualism has been challenged by the increasing evidence that higher-level human thought is no more and no less than a product of the activity of the human brain.

In 1990, President Bush Senior declared the last decade of the twentieth century to be 'the decade of the brain.'[4] The enormous research efforts at the time led to new information and new ways of interpreting this information.

---

[2] See 'the allegory of the cave', Book VII of *The Republic* by Plato (360 BC) trans. Jowett (1871).

[3] Descartes (1641), vol. 2, pp. 1–62.

[4] See http://www.loc.gov/loc/brain/. (Accessed March 10, 2013).

In 1992, Nobel Prize Winner Gerald Edelman published *Bright Air, Brilliant Fire: On the Matter of the Mind*[5] in which he proposed the thesis that the individual brain develops in a manner according to Darwinian evolution: the connections in the brain are made and strengthened by 'survival of the fittest', with useful links being enhanced and used in preference to less appropriate ones.

In 1994, Nobel Prize Winner Francis Crick published *The Astonishing Hypothesis: The Search for the Soul*[6] – the 'astonishing hypothesis' being that the soul is simply the product of the processes of the biological brain. Meanwhile, linguist George Lakoff and his colleagues[7] proposed that all thought is embodied and based on our sensori-motor operations.

In 2002, Merlin Donald produced *A Mind So Rare*[8], analysing the maturation of various levels of consciousness in evolving species that focused in humans on three successive levels: selective binding in fraction of a second; its dynamic continuation in short-term awareness over a few seconds; and its intellectual flowering through the extended awareness of human language, representation and communication.

The framework proposed in this book builds from sensori-motor operations into conceptual embodiment focusing on the properties of objects and operational embodiment focusing on operations, using language to describe and define more subtle forms of reasoning.

2.2 Operations in Embodiment and Symbolism

Mathematical thinking builds initially through making sense of our perceptions and actions. An action performed with a specific purpose will be called an *operation*.

Often the notion of operation is linked to the operations that we perform in arithmetic or algebra. However, an action with a specific purpose can also include a construction in geometry. Such operations may differ in their purpose. On some occasions we focus on the effects of the operations and sometimes we focus on the operation itself. For instance, if we count the sides of a figure made out of straight lines, we can confirm that it is a triangle with three sides, a quadrilateral with four, a pentagon with five and so on. This tells us *a property of the object*. If we take a compass and draw a

---

[5] Edelmann (1992).
[6] Crick (1994).
[7] Lakoff & Johnson (1980); Lakoff (1987); Lakoff & Johnson (1999); Lakoff & Núñez (2000).
[8] Donald (2001).

circle, we *construct* the circle as an object, but we may also reflect on what we have done and realize a *property* of this object: a circle is the locus of points a fixed distance from the centre.

In Chapter 3 we observed a triangle with two equal sides, $AB = BC$, and operated by drawing the perpendicular bisector BM from the vertex B to the base AC, to construct new objects, the triangles ABM and CBM. (Figure 3.6.) By seeing that these triangles are congruent, we may deduce that the angles A and C are equal, thus proving a new property of the original triangle ABC – that a triangle with two equal sides must also have equal angles. This enables us to focus on the structural property of the original equilateral triangle: that *if* it has equal sides *then* it also has equal angles. This reasoning about structure I refer to as *structural abstraction*.

On the other hand, if we operate on a set of objects by counting, on repeating the count in different ways we find the count always results in the same output, namely the number of objects in the set. Operating in more subtle ways such as putting sets together and adding the number of elements, we begin to find properties that are independent of the particular sets and are seen to be properties of the numbers themselves. This involves a shift to a new way of thinking, focusing not on the properties of the objects, but through a process of *operational abstraction* to determine the properties of the *operations* themselves.

This gives a fundamental distinction between the world of conceptual embodiment that arises from a focus on objects, and the world of operational symbolism that arises from a focus on operations and their representation as manipulable symbols.

3. The World of Conceptual Embodiment

Conceptual embodiment grows from a child's experience of everyday perception and action. Figure 6.5 shows a young child playing with several shapes as he begins his lifetime's journey through the mathematics bequeathed to him through many generations of human thought. At first we can imagine him playing with the shapes, feeling the roundness of the circle and the corners of the other objects, as he begins to learn about two-dimensional figures such as triangles, circles, squares, rectangles, and three-dimensional solids such as spheres and cubes.

The journey through geometry in school builds on the set-before of recognition of similarities and differences to categorize shapes, analyzed

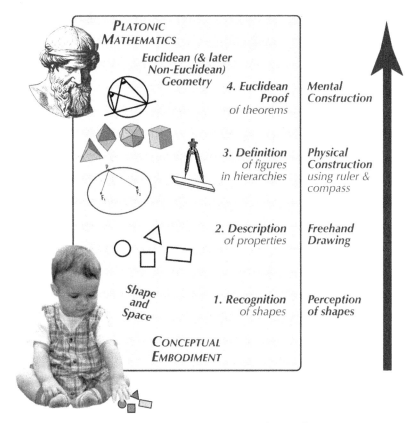

Figure 6.5. The child's development of conceptual embodiment in geometry.

in Chapter 4 as a succession of structural abstractions through the practical mathematics of *recognition* and *description*, then on to the theoretical mathematics of *definition* and *Euclidean proof*. It moves through Euclidean geometry referring either to physical pictures representing the theorems or to imagined Platonic concepts representing crystalline geometric concepts and perhaps on to non-Euclidean geometries built from new forms of embodied perception and thought experiment.

4. The Transition from Embodiment to Operational Symbolism

In the framework of three worlds of mathematics, the world of operational symbolism grows out of embodiment by focusing on actions on objects rather than on the objects themselves.

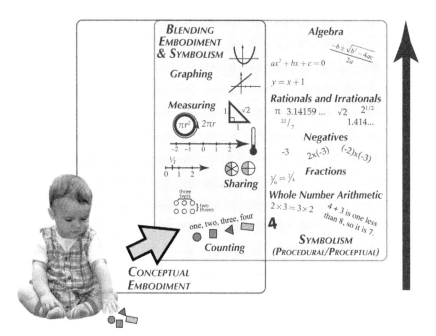

Figure 6.6. From embodiment to symbolism.

In Figure 6.6 the child is playing with the same four shapes as before, but now his attention is not on the shapes, but on the operation of counting them: one, two, three, *four*, which, over time, leads to the concept of number.

The relationship between embodiment and operational symbolism in arithmetic and algebra is more complex that the structural embodiment of geometry. It involves the blending of embodied operations such as counting, sharing, measuring, graphing, with increasingly sophisticated number systems such as whole numbers, fractions, negatives, rationals, irrationals, and the generalization of arithmetical operations to algebraic manipulation. At every stage there is the compression of operations to number concepts and extensional blends that involve both supportive aspects that generalize and problematic aspects that do not.

To an expert, the successive number systems may be seen embedded one within another from the natural numbers $\mathbb{N}$, fractions $\mathbb{F}$, integers $\mathbb{Z}$, rational numbers $\mathbb{Q}$ and real numbers $\mathbb{R}$ as points on the number line and then on to complex numbers $\mathbb{C}$ in the plane. As sets we have the inclusions shown in Figure 6.7.

$$\text{N} \underset{\subset \text{ F} \subset}{\overset{\subset \text{ Z} \subset}{}} \text{Q} \subset \mathbb{R} \subset \mathbb{C}$$

Figure 6.7. Number systems as extensional blends.

The curriculum is often designed to build up this sequence, starting with the natural numbers, steadily expanding to the rationals, negative numbers, rational numbers, real numbers and even to the complex numbers. This is possible in a visual way by seeing the numbers marked on a number line, and later situating the number line within the plane to represent the larger set of complex numbers. It makes sense to a curriculum designer.

However, to the learner, these are not just sets of numbers; they also have operations that behave in different ways that we have seen can be problematic. Natural numbers form a succession, starting with 1 and going on, 2, 3, ... with each one being followed by the next. Fractions can be subdivided as much as is desired, and between two fractions there are many others. Natural numbers are added by putting sets together and counting the total, building up a host of 'known facts' related together in a crystalline structure. On the other hand, fractions are encountered as embodied operations of sharing that involve new symbolic properties of equivalence and new procedures of addition and multiplication.

Later experiences introduce new kinds of numbers. For example, trigonometry begins with operations to calculate the ratio of sides in a right-angled triangle as a practical approximation, but some angles such as 30°, 45° and 60° have trigonometric ratios involving irrationals such as $\sqrt{2}$ and $\sqrt{3}$ that are infinite decimals that do not repeat. Then the measurement of the area and circumference of a circle leads to a new mystery number called π. Each extended number system is an extensional blend that involves supportive aspects that enable generalization and problematic aspects that are potential impediments to progress.

4.1 *Theoretical Aspects of Arithmetic*

In Chapter 3 we saw how the regularities of operations in arithmetic may be sensed by some learners, so that not only do they realize that addition and multiplication are independent of order, but that the same principles apply to adding or multiplying several numbers together.

However, when operations are combined, it becomes necessary to use brackets to specify the order of operation. For instance, $3 + 4 \times 5$ is ambiguous unless brackets are used because $(3 + 4) \times 5$ is $7 \times 5 = 35$ and

$3 + (4 \times 5) = 3 + 20 = 23$. This proves to be significant with calculators, some of which perform the operation always in order of input, left to right, where $3 + 4 \times 5$ is 35, and some perform multiplication before addition to give $3 + 4 \times 5$ is 23.

As more complicated operations are considered, it becomes necessary to make a choice as to how they should be written and interpreted. This is no longer a simple matter. Conventions that have been agreed upon in the past are presented to the learner to operate in a manner that is shared by the community. Traditionally the convention is to read the operations from left to right, and take account of the order of precedence in which one first perform operations in **B**rackets, then take powers (or **I**ndexes), then perform **M**ultiplication and **D**ivision before **A**ddition and **S**ubtraction, compressed into the mnemonic **BIDMAS** currently used in the English National Curriculum. A similar mnemonic is used in the United States where **PEMDAS** refers to the order **P**arentheses, **E**xponents, **M**ultiplication, **D**ivision, **A**ddition, **S**ubtraction (often remembered as the initial letters of the sentence 'Please Excuse My Dear Aunt Sally'). These rules add a level of complexity that can make arithmetic more complicated for procedural learners while the flexible thinker may find them supportive in making sense of complicated symbolism.

4.2 *The Transition from Arithmetic to Algebra*

Algebra involves a switch from the embodiment of real-world problems to the manipulation of algebraic symbolism. Consider the following problem:

> Amy's older brother Ben is now three times as old as her. In four years he will only be twice as old. How old is Amy now?

An algebraic solution is to let Amy be x years old now; then Ben is $3x$ years old. In 4 years Amy will be $x + 4$ years old, and Ben will be $3x + 4$. Ben is then twice as old as Amy, so

$$3x + 4 = 2(x + 4).$$

This equation can be seen to represent the information: the left-hand side is Ben's age now ($3x$) plus 4, so it is Ben's age in 4 years. The right-hand side is twice Amy's age in 4 years' time.

However, as soon as the brackets are expanded, we get

$$3x + 4 = 2x + 8.$$

Now what does the right-hand side represent? Do we conceive it as the age of someone in 8 years' time who is now twice Amy's age? As we continue to operate algebraically, to subtract 4 from both sides to get

$$3x = 2x + 4$$

do we see the left-hand side as Ben's age now and the right-hand side as the age of someone in 4 years who is twice Amy's age now? Of course not. As we proceed through the algebraic manipulation, we no longer treat algebraic expressions as real-world embodiments of the ages at different times but simply as symbols to be manipulated.

In this way, the process of solving the equation does not depend consciously on the underlying embodiment, but operates in the symbolic world using the relationships between the symbols themselves.

This reveals that sense making in mathematics shifts from embodiment to symbolism. Initially making sense means precisely that – using our human senses to make links between our perceptions and actions. But in the symbolic world we begin to shift to a new way of making sense of the symbols themselves and the coherent ways in which they operate, without consciously referring back to their earlier meanings.

Applied mathematicians use embodiment and symbolism in these complementary ways. Faced with a real-world problem, the solution process starts by modeling the situation in terms of symbolic equations, solving the equations using algebra or calculus and then translating the solution back to the real-world context to interpret the result.

The changing focus of attention – from embodiment to symbolism, to manipulate the symbols, then back to embodiment to interpret the solution – may be a natural consequence of the limited focus of attention of the human brain. At each stage, the focus of attention is concentrated on the essential detail to make decisions. This begins with a focus on the original problem to model it symbolically, but once the symbolism is formulated, the focus of attention shifts to operating with the symbols to obtain a symbolic solution. There is thus a *switch* in attention from embodiment to symbolism and back again. This clearly exhibits the complementary roles of conceptual embodiment and operational symbolism that blend together to give more powerful ways of thinking mathematically. As the use of algebra becomes more sophisticated, operational symbolism takes on a role of its own that no longer needs to be permanently linked to embodiment.

4.3 *Theoretical Aspects of Algebra*

The generalization from arithmetic to algebra uses observed properties of operations in arithmetic, reformulated as theoretical 'rules of arithmetic'. These include the commutative laws

$$a + b = b + a \quad \text{and} \quad ab = ba$$

associative laws

$$a + (b + c) = (a + b) + c \quad \text{and} \quad (ab)c = a(bc)$$

and the distributive law

$$a(b + c) = ab + ac.$$

Combining these all together to deal with general algebraic operations requires a genuine 'feel' for the ideas and how they operate. For instance, using these rules in Chapter 3, we saw how to justify that the square $(a + b)^2$ gives $a^2 + 2ab + b^2$ by multiplying out the brackets and using the conventional rules of arithmetic.

However, these rules may be used in two essentially different ways. One is to observe the rules as guides for the manipulation of algebraic symbols, following the same sense of operations encountered in arithmetic. This allows the terms in a sequence of operations such as $3 + 2x - 4 + 5x$ to be shifted around to get $3 - 4 + 2x + 5x$, which simplifies to $7x - 1$.

The other is to adopt a far more severe *formal* approach to deduce the properties of algebraic manipulation in full detail using *only* the stated rules. Even to calculate $2x + 5x$ as $7x$ actually uses the distributive law in the form $2x + 5x = 7x$, which is in the form $ba + ca = (b + c)a$ for $b = 2, c = 5$, $a = x$ and requires three applications of the commutative law to replace $a(b + c)$ by $(b + c)a$, ab by ba and ac by ca.

In school mathematics it is more natural to build on a flexible sense of operations with symbols than attempt a formal approach too early. This can be illustrated by a classroom experience in which I, as a mathematician, attempted to explain the ideas of negative and fractional powers using a formal approach that assumed the rule $x^{m + n} = x^m x^n$ applied to numerical powers in general.

Using the rule for $m = n = \frac{1}{2}$ gives $x^{\frac{1}{2}} \times x^{\frac{1}{2}} = x^{\frac{1}{2} + \frac{1}{2}} = x^1 = x$, and this infers that $x^{\frac{1}{2}}$ must be the square root of x. Using $x^m \times x^0 = x^{m + 0} = x^m$ shows that $x^0 = 1$ and, because $x \times x^{-1} = x^{1 - 1} = x^0 = 1$, then $x^{-1} = 1/x$. This seemed so simple ... to me! The same feeling of sense making may occur to other teachers and curriculum designers who attempt to explain their own sophisticated ideas to their pupils.

However, when I presented this formal argument to a class of eighteen-year-olds studying mathematics, there was a general consensus that the law was proven only for whole number powers, so the implication was invalid. No one objected to accepting the idea *as a rule to be committed to memory*, but the majority protested that the rule was being applied in an inappropriate context, so it failed to be convincing.

The day was saved by a student who explained that he saw x^3/x^2 as

$$\frac{x \times x \times x}{x \times x}$$

and he could cancel this to get

$$\frac{x \times \cancel{x} \times \cancel{x}}{\cancel{x} \times \cancel{x}}$$

so it was natural to think of $1/x^2$ as x^{-2} and see x^3/x^2 as $x^3 \times x^{-2} = x$. He could then combine the powers x^3 and x^{-2} to obtain $x^{3-2} = x^1$. This helped the students realize that $1/x^n$ could be replaced by x^{-n} and then to use this in algebra to write $x^m \times x^{-n} = x^{m-n}$.[9]

This generalization to fractional and negative powers is a significant step in sophistication from using the symbol to *describe* the power law for whole numbers to *define* the power law to make deductions in a more general case. It signals the significant change from the practical mathematics based on natural experiences to theoretical mathematics based on definition and proof.

4.4 *Structural Aspects of Operational Symbolism*

Over the long term, the development of operational symbolism involves encounters with whole numbers, fractions, negatives, as well as the generalization of arithmetic to algebra.

This involves both operational compression of operations to thinkable concepts and the structural properties of the concepts that arise from the operations. For example, whole numbers may be even or odd, or more generally, prime or composite, and it can be proved that they have a unique factorization into prime factors. The long-term development of

[9] This conversation took place in a class taught by Anna Poynter.

these properties again follows the broad sequence of structural abstraction discussed in Chapter 3:

1. *Recognition* of properties of operations in arithmetic, such as independence of order of addition and multiplication.
2. *Description* of properties such as commutativity (e.g., 3 + 4 is the same as 4 + 3), based on experience.
3. *Definition* of rules of operation, which are now to be obeyed in general, such as $a + b = b + a$, $ab = ba$, $a(b + c) = ab + ac$.
4. *Deduction* of identities such as $(a + b)^2 = a^2 + 2ab + b^2$, using the 'rules of arithmetic' as a basis for reasoning.

The development of arithmetic and algebra is then revealed as a blend of operational abstraction, in which generalized operations are conceived as manipulable algebraic expressions, and structural abstraction of properties that are recognized, described and defined for use in symbolic forms of proof.

The terms 'operational' and 'structural' were originally used by Anna Sfard[10] to specify the alternation of operational compression into concepts that then have structure. This offers a broad view of the development of operational symbolism in which it was hypothesized that operational thinking invariably precedes structural thinking. Practical evidence reveals that the development is more complex. While the development of geometry in the conceptual embodied world focuses mainly on structural thinking, the operational symbolic world blends together both operational and structural thinking as new forms of number are introduced as extensional blends and generalized in algebra.

4.5 *Real Numbers, Limits and the Calculus*

In the later stages of schooling or the first year of college, mathematics students are introduced to the ideas of the calculus. The traditional approach is a blend of geometry, arithmetic and algebra, to find the slope of a function $y = f(x)$ from x to $x + h$ as

$$\frac{f(x+h) - f(x)}{h}$$

and then to calculate 'the limit' as h gets small. The idea of a quantity becoming arbitrarily small is problematic. It was problematic in history

---

[10] Sfard (1991).

when Newton and Leibniz were criticized for failing to give a logical meaning to the limit concept. It is problematic for students in school today, who imagine the process of a sequence of numbers tending to zero giving a limit that is almost zero, but not quite.[11] A full analysis of this phenomenon requires the formal idea of the limit concept and will be postponed until this has been studied in detail. Here we consider the shift from embodiment and symbolism to the formal level of axiomatic thinking available to mathematicians.

5. The Axiomatic Formal World

Even though mathematical thinking developed into a Platonic framework in the Euclidean geometry of the ancient Greeks, until the mid-nineteenth century, mathematics was regarded as a natural extension of perception and operation formulated in more general theoretical ways. It was considered as a major part of the 'natural sciences', where the term 'natural' arises from the study of nature and 'science' arises from the Latin term for knowledge. Hilbert realized that reason could be applied to an axiomatic structure given only in terms of formal set-theoretic axioms and definitions that did not depend on the underlying nature of the phenomena involved.

This involves a total reversal of meaning. Instead of studying objects or operations that *have* (natural) properties, the chosen properties (axioms) are specified first and the structure is shown to have other properties that can be *deduced* from the axioms.

Previously the operation of addition arose from natural experiences, such as putting together two collections and counting the result. Initially a young child might sense that the sum of $8 + 2$ by counting on two to say 'nine', '*ten*', is clearly different from $2 + 8$ with its longer count-on of eight. But then, natural experience revealed that the order of operation does not affect the result, leading to the 'commutative property' of addition.

In the formal world, the statement '$x + y = y + x$' is assumed as an axiom, and how it is performed is now irrelevant. What matters is that the axiom is satisfied. The purpose of such a drastic change in strategy is dramatic. On the one hand it increases the cognitive strain on the learner; on the other hand, proofs no longer depend on the context. If a system satisfies the axioms for a particular formal structure, then it also has all the properties deduced formally from those axioms.

---

[11] See, for example, Cornu (1991).

5.1 *Various Meanings of the Term 'Formal'*

The word 'formal' is used in different ways in mathematics and mathematics education. In mathematics it is used to describe the approach advocated by Hilbert, which I will formulate using the two-word phrase *axiomatic formalism*. In mathematics education, the term 'formal' often refers to the formal operational stage of Piaget's theory, which occurs when thought becomes hypothetical and no longer needs to involve physical referents. This may be called *Piagetian formalism*. In his research, Piaget found his subjects shifting to formal operations as early as eleven or twelve years old, but later research suggested that many students in college had not reached this formal operational stage.[12] Axiomatic formalism occurs as a much later development in mathematical thinking.

In the framework proposed in this book, I have sympathy with both meanings, so I decided to use the term 'formal' to apply in general to the theoretical mathematics of embodied formalism in geometry, symbolic formalism in arithmetic and algebra, and the axiomatic formal mathematics of Hilbert. But in the later stages of the book, which focuses on mathematics at university level, I will refer to axiomatic formalism simply as 'formal mathematics'. I did consider using the term 'axiomatic mathematics' instead of 'formal mathematics', but this would also conflict with the use of axioms in Euclidean geometry. The decision was fortified by the use of the names 'natural philosophy' and 'natural sciences' that included the study of mathematics prior to the set-theoretic change in meaning. This also allows me to speak of a 'natural' approach to mathematical thinking in mathematics incorporating both practical and theoretical mathematics and a 'formal' approach to mathematics using set-theoretic definition and formal proof.

Figure 6.8 is a broad outline of some of the aspects of the full development of mathematical thinking, from the practical mathematics of shape and number to the theoretical mathematics of definition and deduction and on to formal mathematics of set-theoretic definition and formal proof.

The shift from the Platonic world represented by the figure of Plato to the formal world of Hilbert is immense. The inhabitants of Plato's mental world are perfect crystalline concepts that can be defined verbally: perfect straight lines, perfect circles, perfect spheres in geometry and perfect

---

[12] Ausubel et al. (1978).

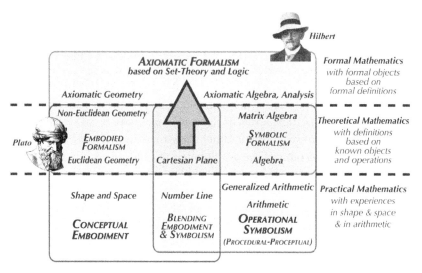

Figure 6.8. Practical, theoretical and formal mathematics.

number concepts in arithmetic. The formal objects in Hilbert's world are expressed only in terms of set-theoretic definitions with properties deduced by formal proof.

Many modern mathematicians see their creations as perfect Platonic objects that have an existence of their own, independent of the mind that constructed them. However, Hilbert's concepts are built *from* the definitions and their properties are *only* those properties that can be deduced from the definitions.

Although Hilbert emphasized the use of formal mathematics focusing on axiomatic definitions and proof, he readily acknowledged that formal definitions and formal proof develop from ideas that are suggested by prior experience.[13] In this way, mathematical ideas developed from practical and theoretical experiences are later translated to formal mathematics and subjected to far higher standards of rigor.

Mathematicians are often suspicious of intuitive ideas precisely because they consider them subject to hidden assumptions that may invalidate their arguments. They have good reason to do so. It took more than two thousand years to spot the subtle fact that the proofs in Euclid were based on

---

[13] Hilbert emphasized the role of previous experience in his famous lecture in 1900 when he formulated the 23 Hilbert problems that taxed the minds of mathematicians for the next century.

properties that were not explicitly specified in Euclid's axioms. It was in this spirit that André Weil criticized Wiles' first proof of Fermat's last theorem that I quoted at the end of Chapter 5, in which he said, 'If a man wants to climb Everest and falls short of it by 100 yards, he has not climbed Everest.'

To grasp the full extent of mathematical thinking, from the early ideas of the child to the highest levels of rigor, it is necessary to take account of the full landscape of mathematics, including the views of mathematicians while also taking account of the developmental needs of each individual as they follow their personal journeys through mathematics.

Research mathematicians will focus attention on the higher demands of research and assert professional standards appropriate at that level. Teachers and educators on the other hand are wise to take account of the developmental needs of the learner. But this does not mean that different communities should remain separated from each other and not attempt to communicate about different views of mathematics. Even at university where mathematicians teach their subject to undergraduates, there is a need to understand how students attempt to make sense of the mathematics in their courses rather than presenting mathematics in a way that appeals only to a few who may become research mathematicians.

At the same time, the axiomatic formal approach initiated by Hilbert should not be seen as being relevant only for experts. All participants in mathematical thinking should be aware of its importance in the total framework of mathematical thinking.

As we have seen, formal mathematics is more powerful than the mathematics of embodiment and symbolism, which are constrained by the context in which the mathematics is used. Formal mathematics is *future-proofed* in the sense that any system met in the future that satisfies the definitions of a given axiomatic structure will also satisfy all the theorems proved in that structure.

Later in this book we will study how formal mathematics has an interesting outcome. Some theorems proved from formal definitions and proof will reveal properties that lead to new visual and symbolic ways of interpreting formal mathematics. Such *structure theorems* return formal mathematics to embodiment and symbolism, but now integrated with formal proof. The full picture of the development of mathematical thinking will therefore bring us back to a blend of embodiment, symbolism and formalism.

This underlines the central importance of structural abstraction. Although mathematical objects can be constructed in various ways, through categorization, encapsulation or definition, there is a broad sequence of development in four stages:

1. *Recognition* of properties of thinkable concepts.
2. *Description* of properties perceived in the given context.
3. *Definition* of properties that are now used as a basis for identification and construction of thinkable concepts.
4. *Deduction* of properties from definitions using specified methods of proof (Euclidean, algebraic and formal) to build up integrated knowledge structures.

Even though the three worlds build on different foundations, they all culminate in knowledge structures that feature relationships within and between crystalline concepts. Each has its own form of crystalline concept: Platonic objects in geometry, procepts in arithmetic and algebra, and axiomatically defined concepts in formal mathematics.

As we reconsider the whole framework of development of mathematical thinking, we see a prescient meaning in the title of van Hiele's book *Structure and Insight*.[14] Even though he saw his theoretical development of levels of structure applying only to geometry and not to algebra[15], his broad development, interpreted as structural abstraction through *recognition*, *description*, *definition* and *deduction*, can now be extended to apply throughout the whole of mathematics.

7. The Story So Far

At this point, the overall framework for the development of mathematical thinking has been established through the blending of three mental worlds of mathematics, based on human recognition, repetition and language to evolve through perception, operation and reason. It begins in the practical mathematics of shape and number and progresses through increasing sophistication of theoretical mathematics in Euclidean geometry and algebra. While geometry builds through increasing structural sophistication, symbolism develops through operational compression from embodied operations to manipulable symbolism that then has structural properties that develop its own forms of definition and proof. A third world of axiomatic formal mathematics builds a formal stage of mathematics based on set-theoretic definition and formal proof.

In shifting to new contexts, aspects that are supportive in one situation may be supportive or problematic in another. Supportive aspects

[14] Van Hiele (1986).
[15] Van Hiele (2002).

encourage generalization whereas problematic aspects impede progress. Related emotions affect the long-term development with supportive aspects encouraging confidence, and problematic aspects being seen either as a challenge by those who are confident, or as a source of concern for those who may attempt to gain success by rote-learning or descend into a spiral of mathematical anxiety.

Chapter 7 considers a more detailed analysis of the relationship between embodiment and symbolism. Chapter 8 moves on to wider issues of problem solving and the development of proof. We can then use the framework of three worlds of mathematics to analyze the historical development of the subject in Chapter 9, ready to move on to formal mathematics in university, and on to the frontiers of research.

7 Journeys through Embodiment and Symbolism

In this chapter we make a more detailed analysis of the parallel development of embodiment and symbolism as children learn to count collections of objects, to operate with whole numbers, and move on to fractions, signed numbers and the generalized arithmetic of algebra.

Following the vision of Bruner, one would expect a steady growth from enactive and iconic representations to symbolic representations in a transition from the actions and perceptions of the embodied world to the operations in the symbolic world. A closer analysis of the relationship between embodiment to symbolism reveals a more subtle story.

When performing operations on objects, the attention may focus on the objects, on how to perform the operations, or both. The operational compression from process to mental object has two aspects, which I term *embodied compression*, focusing on the objects and *symbolic compression* focusing on the symbols. Focusing on the objects offers the possibility of sensing what happens as a consequence of the operation. It has an *effect* that can be *seen*.

For instance, once the child realizes that counting a set is independent of the order of counting then the positioning of the objects doesn't matter and counting a set of 'two' and 'four' to give 'six' can be seen to give the same result as rearranging the objects and counting 'four' and 'two'. Shifting one of the four objects over to the other collection gives 'three and three', which is also 'six'. Lining them up in rows gives 'two lots of three' or 'three lots of two'. Focusing on the embodied effect of an operation encourages a general sense of the relationships between operations and numbers.

On the other hand, focusing on the operation of counting, say, 'two' after 'four' to give 'five, *six*', gives a shorter count than counting 'four' after 'two' to get 'three, four, five, *six*', so the procedures are initially sensed to be different.

Thus embodied compression, focusing on the effects of the operation, has the potential to encourage the child to sense more general properties of arithmetic that may not be so apparent when only practicing procedures, while symbolic compression focuses on being able to perform the routines.

This simple observation supports Bruner's initial focus on enactive and iconic representations to encourage meaningful relationships between operations on the symbols in arithmetic. It suggests that embodied compression focusing on the effects of operations offers more initial insight into the flexible properties of arithmetic than operational compression focusing on counting procedures.

However, the distinction between embodied and symbolic compression is not a dichotomy. Some children may prefer embodied counting while others may learn symbolic operations procedurally, but there is also a more flexible approach that blends both to develop a flexible sense of relationships and fluency in arithmetic.

In this chapter we consider the long-term development of mathematical thinking to consider how the relationship between embodiment and symbolism may change as operational symbolism becomes more sophisticated. Is it always the case that enactive and iconic embodied ideas are a good introduction to symbolism, or are there other possibilities as mathematics becomes more sophisticated?

1. Compression of Knowledge Structures

1.1 *Embodied and Symbolic Compression*

The long-term growth of arithmetic and algebra was presented in Chapter 3 in terms of symbolic compression – from Action to Process to Object, or alternatively labeled as procedure through process to procept. Such process–object theories focus first on an action or operation that is performed by the individual. However, the child is initially operating on physical objects and these are also part of the activity. It is therefore important to take account of what learners focus on when they perform operations on objects. Do they focus on the operations, or do they focus on the effect of those operations on the objects, or are they aware of both?

To formulate these ideas theoretically, I use the term *base object* (or base objects) to denote the object or objects that are operated on. The actions performed on the base objects will have a recognizable *effect*. Equivalent actions are different actions that have the same effect.

The symbolic compression from procedure through multiprocedure, process and precept, then has an embodied expression in terms of the physical operation. For instance, Figure 7.1 shows the counting of five base objects, first with a single procedure, then with other equivalent procedures that all have the same effect 'five'. The effect can be embodied as a generic array of five counters.

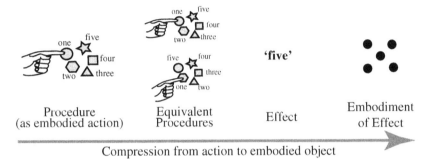

Figure 7.1. Compression from counting to the number five.

The same embodiment can be separated into subsets of two counters and three counters, whose sum can be calculated by various equivalent procedures, each of which gives the same effect that is embodied in the layout of the counters. (Figure 7.2.)

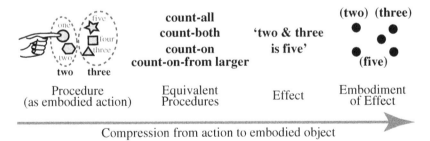

Figure 7.2. Compression from addition to sum represented by the sum 2 + 3 = 5.

The same five objects can be arranged in various ways as 3 + 2, 2 + 3, 4 + 1, 1 + 4 and even as 7 − 2 (if embedded in a larger array of seven items). The focus on the various layouts of the objects *embodies* the notion of 5 as a single entity that may be seen in various ways as a precept.

A corresponding phenomenon occurs sharing a continuous quantity such as a cake as a base object. In Figure 7.3, the cake is first divided into six equal pieces and three are selected. Equivalently the cake may be divided

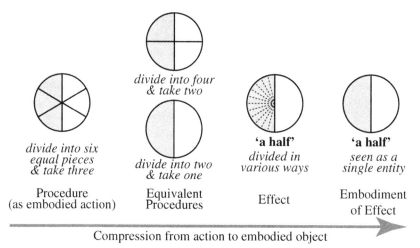

Figure 7.3. Compression of sharing into fraction as an embodied object.

into four equal pieces to take two, or into two equal pieces to take one. Each has the same effect in terms of the *quantity* of cake selected, giving the effect of producing a half in total. The embodiment of the effect is the quantity 'a half', which is now represented by many equivalent procedures of sharing. Furthermore, the embodiment of 'a half' as a single entity can also be seen by imagining the same quantity to be expressed in different ways as equivalent fractions, $\frac{1}{2}, \frac{2}{4}, \frac{3}{6}, \ldots$ or embodied as a single entity.

This representation of a fraction as an object works well for addition of fractions. To add a half and a third, subdivide the parts into sixths, to see the sum as three sixths plus two sixths, to get five sixths.

The case of vectors under addition, given in Chapter 4, fits the same framework. It is the embodied action of translating a (base) object, such as a triangle, on a plane. The shift of a point on the object may be seen as an arrow. All these arrows are *equivalent* in the sense that they have the same magnitude and direction. The *effect* of the translation is the shift of the object from its starting point to its finishing point, which can be embodied by the *free vector* of that given magnitude and direction (Figure 7.4).

The effect is simply the shift from start to finish: what happens in between is irrelevant. The effect of one translation followed by another is the unique translation from the starting point of the first to the end of the second. Free vectors can be moved around and placed end to end so that the sum of two free vectors can be embodied using the triangle law.

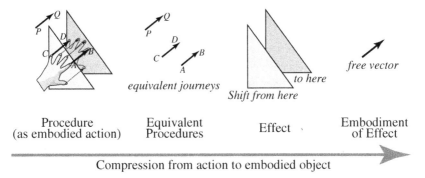

Procedure
(as embodied action)   Equivalent Procedures   Effect   Embodiment of Effect

Compression from action to embodied object

Figure 7.4. Compression of a translation into a free vector as an embodied object.

1.2 *Flexible Compression of Operation into Thinkable Concept*

All the aforementioned examples embody the operation of addition and reveal its properties in a flexible way. However, thinking of a symbol only as an object has already been shown to be problematic in Chapter 4. To be fully functional, operational compression requires the symbols to operate dually as process or concept. For example, if a fraction is an object, say half an apple or a third of an apple, then these can be added to get five sixths of an apple. But the product of half an apple times a third of an apple makes no sense. It is therefore essential to see a fraction also as an operation, so that we may compute half *of* an apple, then a third *of* half an apple to get one-sixth of an apple.

Embodied compression focusing on the effect of an operation is a double-edged sword. It is supportive in being able to visualize many relationships but it may also be problematic to think of symbols *only* as objects.

Focusing only on embodied objects or only on symbolic operations each has strengths and limitations. In Chapter 4, we saw how Amelia progressed by using mental images of counters that she moved around in her mind. This allowed her to perform calculations with numbers small enough to imagine but prevented her from coping with larger numbers. Her problem was solved by giving her a graphic calculator that performed the operations in arithmetic to allow her to see the results without having to count so that she could refocus her attention on the relationships that occur in arithmetic. This method failed with other eleven-year-olds who were in difficulty because they could not make the step from seeing ten as ten separate objects to seeing it as a single entity in a way that enabled them to grasp the concept of place value.

In Chapter 4, we saw children solving the problem of sharing cakes using practical methods of operation without developing a full arithmetic of fractions. This was just one of many instances in which particular embodiments involve aspects that work well in the given situation but may become problematic if they do not evolve into more appropriate ways of symbolic thinking in more sophisticated contexts.

1.3 *Practicing Routine Operations*

A strong focus on the symbolic operations can improve fluency but it may at the same time not lead to full flexibility.

For example, as part of the Malaysian Vision for 2020 to develop the country's economy to the highest standards by that date, the Malaysian curriculum is designed to teach fractions to emphasize flexibility. For instance, to calculate 'two-fifths of twenty-five' is taught both by working out a fifth of twenty-five and multiplying by two, or by multiplying two by twenty-five and dividing by five. (Figure 7.5.)

Figure 7.5. Fraction multiplication.

To ensure that all children can accomplish both procedures, the teacher encourages the pupils to remember them by reciting successive parts of the procedure and inviting the children to fill in missing words. The teacher might say (in Bahasa Malay), 'How do we work out two-fifths of twenty five?' and draw three circles on the board one above the other for numerator and denominator of the fraction, the other for the whole number. 'What do we put in the top circle? The nu...' to which the class gleefully says 'the numerator'. 'What do we put in the bottom circle? The de...' – 'denominator'. 'Of means mul...' – 'multiply'. And so the lesson continues, building up the ritual of the two different procedures of multiplication by a fraction.

The consequence was that children improved on standardized tests.[1] However, using the four-stage compression introduced in Chapter 3 from procedure to flexible procepts, the method focuses more on the equivalence

---

[1] The data is from the PhD study of Md Ali (2006). Interviews with teachers revealed that although the teachers subscribed to the aspirations of Vision 2020 to help children 'really

of specific multistructural thinking rather than the flexibility required for thinking mathematically in more sophisticated situations.

Around the world children are being encouraged to do well on tests, often focusing on detailed practice to solve routine problems. This may give short-term success, but what happens in the long term?

1.4 *The Case of Dillon*

Learning procedures can give success in routine tests but may have other long-term consequences.

Dillon[2] (a pseudonym) was a committed and vital eighteen-year-old who had succeeded at every stage by learning the formulae necessary to solve routine problems and practicing their use to prepare for examinations. As he met successive modules of work, he concentrated on the new procedures and did not attempt to link them to what he had learnt before.

For example, he was allowed to use a calculator to get a numerical solution for a problem such as 1/0.08. But when asked in class to perform the calculation without a calculator, he had no idea how to proceed.

When the teacher wrote the calculation as

$$\frac{1}{0.08}$$

Dillon did not remember that 0.08 is 8/100, and even when the teacher wrote the calculation as

$$\frac{1}{\frac{8}{100}}$$

he did not recall that he could multiply numerator and denominator by 100 to translate this into the equivalent problem

$$\frac{100}{8}.$$

Even when this simplification was suggested he was unable to perform the division without a calculator.

This illustrates the manner in which a learner who focuses only on learning procedures to pass immediate tests may continue to have a measure of

---

understand mathematics', the general consensus was that they felt constrained by the teaching schedule and the need for success in the National UPSR Examination.

[2] Dillon was a student I observed in a class taught by Anna Poynter.

success in later years while failing to build a flexible knowledge structure. This problem may be related to the use of calculators and the consequent lack of technique in arithmetic, but there is also a problem in relating visual meaning to symbolic calculation.

Dillon rejected the need for visual meaning in a problem that he could answer by routine computation. For instance, in a course in probability and statistics, his teacher began by considering a problem that involved finding the ratio between the areas of two rectangles under a horizontal graph $y = k$, where one is half the width of the other. (Figure 7.6.)

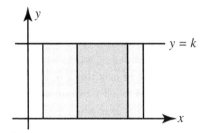

Figure 7.6. Two rectangles with the same height k where the darker one is half the width of the other.

The areas of the two rectangles are in the same proportion as the width, so the darker rectangle is visibly one-half of the larger one. However, the information was presented numerically and Dillon preferred to calculate the areas using a calculus formula learned by rote, finding the answer using his calculator. When the teacher attempted to show him a picture, to see the relationship between areas, he rejected it, asserting that he had calculated the right answer in his own way.

One may sympathize with Dillon. He was studying a module that would be tested soon after it ended. Time was at a premium with little opportunity for reflection. The examination syllabus advised him to practice problems from the textbook and, if he was not sure what to do, he should look through the book, find a similar-looking question and work through the given solution to practice the method required.

Dillon believed that he could maximize his mark on the examination by practicing routines to solve routine questions and he succeeded. He passed the module, and went on to use the same techniques to pass successive examinations, learning *what* to do without ever feeling the need to understand *why*. He was pleased with his success and was confident he had the necessary qualifications to pursue his chosen career. His parents were pleased, his teachers were satisfied and politicians could claim that standards had been maintained. Everyone seemed to be happy. But such a development would not be suitable for anyone hoping to take mathematical thinking to higher formal levels in university.

2. Growing Complications in Embodiment

To gain insight into the longer-term growth of the relationship between embodiment and symbolism, we turn to the example of the factorization of $a^2 - b^2$ and its longer-term generalization to the factorization of $a^n - b^n$ for a general whole number n. This reveals a developing pattern in the long-term development of mathematical thinking.

The algebraic identity

$$a^2 - b^2 = (a - b)(a + b)$$

can be embodied by drawing a square of side length a, taking away a smaller square of side length b, and reorganizing the pieces left (Figure 7.7).

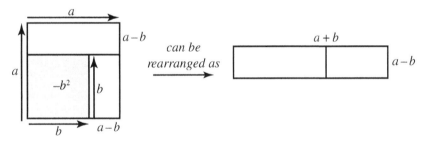

Figure 7.7. $a^2 - b^2 = (a - b)(a + b)$ for positive a and b with $a > b$.

This picture represents the case when a and b are *positive* and $a > b$. What happens in other cases, for example, when $b < a$ or if a or b is negative? In Figure 7.7 the lengths are marked with arrows to show the direction, with a positive direction for a being vertically up the page and b being in the horizontal direction to the right, as in the standard directions of the axes in the Cartesian plane. We can imagine that a change in sign turns a directed line in the opposite direction. This may be applied not only to signed lengths, but also to their product, which is represented as a signed area where one side is considered positive and coloured white and the other side considered negative and coloured grey.

If a rectangular area is turned over by turning one side in the opposite direction, then the opposite side of the rectangle is revealed. For instance, if a and b are positive, we might start with a rectangle with sides a and b in the first quadrant facing upwards and coloured white. Turning the side a over the y-axis to face in the opposite direction to represent $-a$, we turn over the rectangle and represent $(-a)b$ as the reverse side of the rectangle, shaded grey. (Figure 7.8.) Further turns over the negative x-axis to switch b to $-b$ reveals $(-a)(-b)$ turned over to see the white side, while $a(-b)$ turned over to the fourth quadrant reveals the reverse grey side once more.

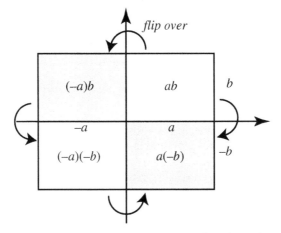

Figure 7.8. Turning areas over to see the other side.

The case for $a^2 - b^2$ where a is positive and b is negative and $|b| < a$ is shown in Figure 7.9. Now a is positive and points upwards, but b is negative and points downwards. For negative b, the square b^2 is positive, so $-b^2$ is negative and shaded grey. Removing the square $-b^2$ from the larger square a^2 leaves two white rectangles that can be placed side by side. Because b is negative, the rearranged rectangle has side lengths $a + |b|$ and $a - |b|$ where

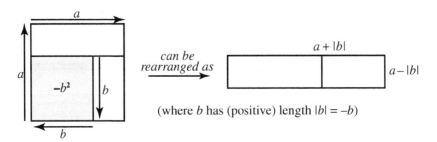

Figure 7.9. $a^2 - b^2 = (a - b)(a + b)$ where a is positive, b is negative and $a > |b|$.

$|b|$ is the absolute value of b. Other possibilities, depending on the relative size and sign of a and b, need to be considered to visualize all possibilities.

Such pictures may be insightful and very pleasing for some, but they are likely to be problematic for those who are used to seeing lengths only as unsigned quantities.

The situation becomes even more complicated with the formula

$$a^3 - b^3 = (a-b)(a^2 + ab + b^2).$$

Figure 7.10 shows the difference between two cubes a^3 and b^3 in the case where a, b are positive and $a > b$.

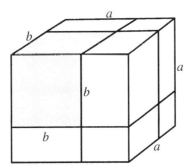

Figure 7.10. The difference between two cubes $a^3 - b^3$.

It is possible with physical materials to derive the symbolic relation by identifying the different blocks in Figure 7.11.

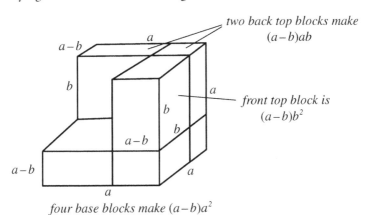

two back top blocks make $(a-b)ab$

front top block is $(a-b)b^2$

four base blocks make $(a-b)a^2$

Figure 7.11. The remaining blocks make $(a-b)a^2 + (a-b)ab + (a-b)b^2$.

This visualization in three dimensions is already more difficult to comprehend than the two-dimensional case. It becomes even more complicated when $a < b$ or when one or both of a, b is negative. (Changing the sign of a side involves a reflection of the block in a mirror, which cannot be performed physically but may be imagined mentally with some effort.)

2.1 *The Shift to Flexible Symbolism*

Generalizing to $a^4 - b^4$ in four dimensions takes us beyond our practical real-world experience. Even though professional geometers develop ways of imagining higher dimensions, ordinary mortals cannot 'see' the embodied picture for powers greater than three.

As we saw earlier, this algebraic manipulation becomes unexpectedly simple by writing $a^4 = (a^2)^2$, $b^4 = (b^2)^2$ and using the formula twice to get

$$a^4 - b^4 = (a^2 - b^2)(a^2 + b^2) = (a - b)(a + b)(a^2 + b^2).$$

The symbolic factorization is pleasingly insightful, suggesting that symbolism is becoming steadily preferable to embodiment. For this reason it is natural to believe that it is easier to progress to more complicated situations by shifting from blending embodiment and symbolism to working with the symbolism only.

However, if we generalize further, the symbolism also becomes more complicated. For instance, how do we factorize $a^5 - b^5$ or $a^{101} - b^{101}$?

2.2 *Unexpected New Uses of Embodiment*

The factorization of $a^n - b^n$ for larger values of n can be performed by combining embodiment and symbolism; however, this requires the introduction of complex numbers involving a quantity i whose square is -1. Previous experience tells us that the square of any non-zero number on the number line is always positive. This continues to be true for real numbers marked on the horizontal x-axis. However, complex numbers are not restricted to the x-axis; they can be anywhere in the whole plane.

A real number x is now visualized as the point $(x, 0)$ on the horizontal axis, the complex number i lies on the y-axis as the point $(0, 1)$ and a general complex number $x + iy$ is the point (x, y) in the plane (Figure 7.12).

The arithmetic of complex numbers may be performed symbolically by algebraic manipulation where i is initially regarded as an unknown. For instance:

$$(3 + 4i)(3 - 4i) = 3^2 - 4^2 i^2.$$

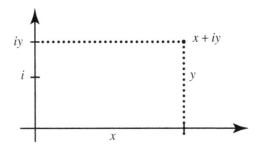

Figure 7.12. A complex number $x + iy$.

The result as a complex number can then be found by replacing i^2 by -1 to give $3^2 + 4^2 = 25$, so $(3 + 4i)(3 - 4i) = 25$. This procedural operation often feels uncomfortable for learners experienced in working with real numbers. However, the multiplication of complex numbers proves to have a very beautiful new embodied meaning in the geometry of the plane. For example, the product of i and $x + iy$ has the symbolic result $i(x + iy) = ix + i^2 y = -y + ix$. In Figure 7.13, it can be seen that this multiplication by i rotates (x, y) around the origin through 90° to $(-y, x)$.

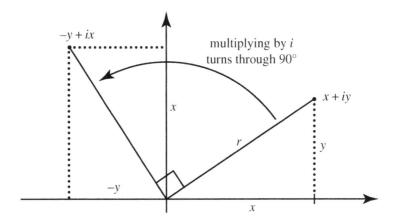

Figure 7.13. Multiplying by i turns the plane through 90°.

Multiplication of complex numbers is more easily expressed using polar coordinates r, θ for the point (x, y) related by the equations

$$x = r\cos\theta, \quad y = r\sin\theta.$$

More generally, it can be shown that multiplying by a complex number $x + iy$ can be expressed geometrically by scaling by a factor r and rotating through an angle θ.[3] (Figure 7.14.)

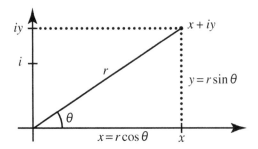

Figure 7.14. A complex number in Cartesian and polar coordinates.

Once again, we find that multiplication has a significantly different meaning from addition. In the case of complex numbers, addition involves the addition of Cartesian coordinates, but multiplication is formulated in terms of polar coordinates where the product of numbers with polar coordinates, r, θ and s, ϕ has polar coordinates rs, $\theta + \phi$. Such a complication took many generations to come to terms with in history, and it remains problematic for many students today.

2.3 Visualizing the Complex Roots of Unity

The geometric idea of multiplication has a particularly simple application when applied to the complex number i with polar coordinates $r = 1, \theta = 90°$. As shown in Figure 7.13, multiplication by i is a rotation through $90°$, and so the powers of the complex number i rotate around the unit circle (for $r = 1$) where $i^2 = -1$, $i^3 = -i$ and $i^4 = 1$. (Figure 7.15.)

The four values all satisfy the equation $z^4 = 1$ and the factorization of the expression $z^4 - 1$ can now be written in terms of these roots as

$$z^4 - 1 = (z - i)(z - i^2)(z - i^3)(z - i^4) = (z - i)(z + 1)(z - i)(z - 1).$$

Substituting $z = a / b$ into this equation gives

$$(a / b)^4 - 1 = (a / b - i)(a / b + 1)(a / b + i)(a / b - 1)$$

---

[3] Here I indulge in the mathematician's ploy of stating the general principle without detailed explanation so that I can move on with the argument without it becoming too complicated.

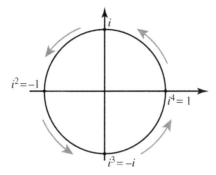

Figure 7.15. Roots of the equation $z^4 = 1$.

and multiplying through by b^4 gives the factorization

$$a^4 - b^4 = (a - ib)(a + b)(a + ib)(a - b)$$
$$= (a + b)(a - b)(a + ib)(a - ib)$$
$$= (a + b)(a - b)(a^2 + b^2)$$

as found earlier by algebraic factorization.

2.4 *Factorizing $a^n - b^n$*

More generally, if we begin with the complex number ω with polar coordinates $r = 1$, $\theta = 360°/n$, then the powers $\omega, \omega^2, ..., \omega^k, ...$ lie equally spread around the circle, turning successively through the angle $\theta = 360°/n$, returning to the starting point with $\omega^n = 1$. (Figure 7.16.)

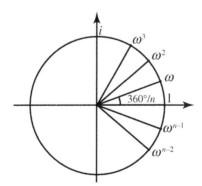

Figure 7.16. Roots of unity.

The elements $\omega, \omega^2, ..., \omega^n = 1$ are precisely the full set of n roots of the equation $z^n = 1$ and the equation $z^n - 1 = 0$ factorizes into

$$(z - \omega)(z - \omega^2) \ldots (z - \omega^{n-1})(z - 1) = 0.$$

Substituting $z = a/b$, and simplifying as before, gives the factorization

$$a^n - b^n = (a - \omega b)(a - \omega^2 b) \ldots (a - \omega^{n-1} b)(a - b).$$

The factorization of $a^4 - b^4$ has two of the complex factors $(a - ib)$ and $(a + ib)$ that can be grouped together to give the real quadratic factor $(a^2 + b^2)$. The factorization of $a^n - b^n$ also involves terms ω^k and ω^{n-k} that (apart from the special cases where $\omega^k = 1$ or $\omega^k = -1$) are mirror images in the horizontal axis and can be paired together. (Figure 7.17.)

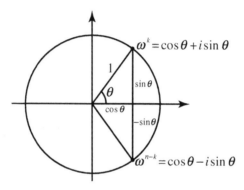

Figure 7.17. Roots as mirror images where $\theta = 360° \times k/n$.

Adding $\omega^k = \cos \theta + i \sin \theta$ to $\omega^{n-k} = \cos \theta - i \sin \theta$ gives $\omega^k + \omega^{n-k} = 2 \cos \theta$, so that

$$(a - \omega^k b)(a - \omega^{n-k} b) = a^2 - (\omega^k + \omega^{n-k})ab + b^2$$
$$= a^2 - 2\cos(360°/n)ab + b^2.$$

This allows $a^n - b^n$ to be written as a combination of real factors. For instance, for $n = 5$:

$$\begin{aligned}
a^5 - b^5 &= (a - \omega b)(a - \omega^2 b)(a - \omega^3 b)(a - \omega^4 b)(a - b)\\
&= \big((a - \omega b)(a - \omega^4 b)\big)\big((a - \omega^2 b)(a - \omega^3 b)\big)(a - b)\\
&= \big(a^2 - 2\cos(360°/5)ab + b^2\big)\\
&\quad \times \big(a^2 - 2\cos(2 \times 360°/5)ab + b^2\big)(a - b)\\
&= \big(a^2 - 2\cos(72°)ab + b^2\big)\big(a^2 - 2\cos(144°)ab + b^2\big)(a - b)
\end{aligned}$$

When $n = 7$, the factorization of $a^7 - b^7$ follows the same pattern with angle $360° / 7 = 51\tfrac{3}{7}°$ to give

$$(a - b)\left(a^2 - 2\cos(51\tfrac{3}{7}°)ab + b^2\right)\left(a^2 - 2\cos(102\tfrac{6}{7}°)ab + b^2\right)\left(a^2 - 2\cos(154\tfrac{1}{7}°)ab + b^2\right).$$

This factorization would not be found easily using symbolic algebra alone, and it certainly cannot be seen by imagining a picture in seven-dimensional space, yet this complicated formula can be visualized simply in terms of seven points spaced equally around a unit circle. As mathematics becomes more sophisticated, seen in a new light, complicated ideas may suddenly become much simpler.

3. Consequences

The consequences of this one example are highly significant for the long-term simplification of mathematical ideas. It shows that an initial embodiment may give meaningful insight but as the ideas are generalized then the more sophisticated embodiment may become problematic while the symbolism becomes more powerful.

In school algebra, this leads to the tendency to switch from embodiment to algebraic manipulation. But the example shows that at a new level of sophistication (here the introduction of complex numbers), a new form of embodiment enables us to see things in simple ways that lead on to even more powerful symbolic methods.

From a higher viewpoint looking at the whole known development of mathematical thinking, we see a new vision. As practical mathematics shifts to theoretical mathematics, it moves away from familiar ideas in the everyday world to new contexts that involve new embodiments with their own sense of structure and operations that may be symbolized in new ways. But once the basic ideas of symbolism in the new context become familiar, the relationships between the symbols may take on a life of their own to give enormous power of calculation and manipulation that far exceeds the capacity of the initial embodied ideas.

The longer-term development of mathematical thinking begins with practical mathematics involving the recognition and description of shapes and operations of arithmetic. At this stage, making sense occurs through human perceptions and actions. Then, as the operations make sense in themselves, mathematical sense making shifts to the coherence of the operations. Over the longer term our capacity for reason is encouraged to develop in more insightful ways to make sense of mathematics through increasingly sophisticated *perception, operation* and *reason*. However, as mathematics shifts to more sophisticated contexts, it is also necessary to take account of the supportive and problematic aspects that encourage or impede generalization and contribute to a widening spectrum of success throughout school mathematics and beyond.

4. Long-term Development of Embodiment, Symbolism and Formalism

The analysis of embodied and symbolic development in this chapter confirms that the theory of Bruner has a significant role to play, not only in the long-term development, but also in each new context encountered along the way. In this chapter we have seen that, at successive stages, the balance between embodiment and symbolism changes.

Bruner revisited his original theoretical framework in the preface of the second edition of *The Process of Education*[4], emphasizing that teaching must start *somewhere*, which is where the student is at the time. He was fully aware of the advantages of the symbolic compression of knowledge:

> I should also mention one other property of a symbolic system – its compactibility – a property that permits condensations of the order $F = MA$ or $s = \frac{1}{2} gt^2$. In each case [...] the semantic squeeze is quite enormous.[5]

The details of different forms of compression in Chapter 3 need to be blended with the supportive and problematic aspects that arise in shifting to more sophisticated contexts, described in Chapter 4.

4.1 *Possible Routes through Embodiment and Symbolism*

As learners travel on their journey through practical and theoretical mathematics, their paths may diverge as a result of the way that they make sense of new ideas and develop fluency in operation in varying degrees. We have seen that some learners operate meaningfully with simple practical examples that do not extend to more sophisticated situations, while some learn

---

[4] Bruner (1977).
[5] Bruner (1966), p. 12.

to operate procedurally but lack the flexibility to operate in non-routine problems. Others learn to use various blends of embodiment and symbolism to develop personal ways of working that allow them to reason about mathematical ideas in more successful ways.

Focusing on the most successful mathematical thinkers, Krutetskii produced significant evidence that gifted children are much more likely to develop a strong verbal-logical basis to mathematical thinking than a visual-pictorial foundation. The nine most gifted students, selected from a population of more than a thousand that he studied, consisted of five analytic thinkers (verbal-logical), one geometric thinker (visual-pictorial), two harmonic thinkers combining the two (one more verbal, the other more visual) and one who was not classified.[6] Norma Presmeg found that the most outstanding senior school mathematics students (7 pupils, out of 277) were almost always non-visualizers. Of 27 'very good' students (10% of the sample), eighteen were non-visualizers and five were visualizers.[7] Gifted students who are shifting towards verbal-logical thinking will benefit from their increasing powers of reasoning in the verbal-logical world of formal mathematical thinking. Those with harmonic qualities will have a different viewpoint that may build up formal thinking by blending together embodied thought experiments putting together relationships and verbal-logical reasoning that leads from embodied inspiration to formal proof.

In the long term, mathematical thinking combines embodiment and symbolism in a range of different ways. A focus on real-world embodiment can make sense for early learners, giving embodied meaning to symbolic operations. But, as the mathematics becomes more sophisticated and new situations demand new ways of thinking, there is a widening spectrum of ways of thinking mathematically.

Some learners find mathematics complicated and fail to build coherent knowledge structures, and some are confused by problematic met-befores in more sophisticated contexts and may default to procedural learning.

In Chapter 8, we complete our journey through school mathematics, focusing on how flexibility may be developed through problem solving, and how mathematical proof develops from the natural embodiment and symbolism and theoretical proof in school mathematics and its applications, to

[6] Krutetskii (1976).
[7] Presmeg (1986), p. 297.

formal proof in university pure mathematics. In later chapters, we will see that those who go on to study formal mathematics develop personal ways of making sense, some building 'naturally' on experiences in embodiment and symbolism or 'formally' on the verbal-logical language of axiomatic mathematics, whereas others seek to survive by procedural learning.

8   Problem Solving and Proof

So far in this book we have considered the building of knowledge structures over the long term as mathematical thinking becomes more sophisticated. At any stage the individual may meet a situation that does not appear to have an available method of solution. The activity that the individual pursues to reach a solution is termed *problem solving*.

The immediate problem is to characterize the meaning of 'problem solving'. In many traditional curricula it means a sequence of exercises following a new piece of learning, starting with simple reproduction of learnt procedures and then shifting to slightly more complicated situations that require more than a simple reproduction of a learned algorithm.

Many curricula speak of 'word problems', meaning problems involving simple arithmetic that are formulated in words, such as 'if Mary has three more apples than John and Mary has five apples, how many apples does John have?' Here the arithmetic is simple: Mary has five and John has three less, which is two. However, cue words such as 'three' and 'more' in a moderately complicated sentence lead some children to respond with the incorrect solution 'eight'. Hence, for some children, this question is a problem.

At the opposite extreme are problem-solving situations in which the solver needs first to clarify precisely what the problem is before attempting to solve it. Then, having found a possible solution, the student needs to reconsider it to see if it is an appropriate solution, whether other solutions are possible, and even whether, in some sense, it is possible to *prove* that the solution is the correct and only solution.

In this chapter the intention is to consider the nature of problem solving within the developmental framework of three worlds of mathematics and then to relate this to the development of various kinds of mathematical proof.

1. Problem Solving

Given the widely differing meanings for the term 'problem solving', I offer the following working definition:

> Problem solving is the activity that occurs when the individual (or individuals) concerned is (or are) faced with a problem situation for which the precise nature of the problem and its solution are not initially evident.[1]

Because the solution is not immediately evident, it is necessary to clarify precisely what the problem is, to explore the knowledge structures the solver already has that might help to resolve the problem, and to see what is required to bridge the gap between the two. In his inspiring book *How to Solve It*[2], Polya suggested four stages:

1. Understand the problem.
2. Make a plan.
3. Carry out the plan.
4. Look back on your work. How could it be better?

The principles are sound but the idea of 'making a plan' to then 'carry it out' can be daunting. The principles were reformulated in *Thinking Mathematically* by John Mason, working with Leone Burton and Kay Stacey. Their approach begins with three stages: 'What do I *want*?', 'What do I *know*?', and 'What do I *introduce*?'[3] I used this approach with undergraduates in the United Kingdom and the United States over the years, together with references to Skemp's ideas of goals and anti-goals expressed in Chapter 5, which encouraged students to reflect with growing confidence on their own emotional reactions to problems.

The need to make sense of a problem occurs at many stages of development. For instance, Stuart in Chapter 2 had the problem of calculating $8 + 6$. He already knew a strategy to add such numbers by using number pairs that make 10 and he knew $8 + 2$ is 10. However, the solution was not immediately evident because he could not take 2 from 6. So he thought about what he could introduce and realized that he knew $4 + 4$ is 8 and recalled that 6 and 4 is 10, so he used one 4 from the 8 to add to 6 to get 10 and the other 4 to make 14.

---

[1] This formulation is based on general principle inspired, in particular, by Nunokawa (2005).
[2] Pólya (1945).
[3] Mason, Burton & Stacey (1982).

To focus on problem solving in a way that will be helpful at all levels of development, I will begin by considering a specific problem whose solution illustrates many of the commonly occurring aspects of good problem-solving practice.

1.1 *An Example*

The first problem in problem solving is often the need to find out *precisely* what the problem is, and to formulate it clearly. A typical problem from *Thinking Mathematically* is

'Into how many squares can I cut a square?'

In my experience, over more than twenty years working with undergraduate classes, initial suggestions are often 'four, nine, sixteen, ...' recognizing the pattern of square numbers. Then someone may provide a different viewpoint, perhaps taking the case of nine equal squares and putting four together to get a larger square, giving one large and five small, a total of six squares of different sizes. (Figure 8.1.)

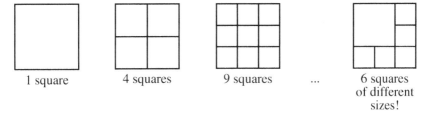

1 square   4 squares   9 squares   ...   6 squares
of different
sizes!

Figure 8.1. Cutting a square into squares.

Now we have a clarification of the problem: it does not require the squares to have equal size.

At this point I have seen students focus on this notion of putting four squares together to make a bigger square, taking away four and adding one, to take away three. This may then be formulated as a conjecture that if a square can be cut into n squares, then it can be cut into $n - 3$.

This is very promising, because it works for all the cases involving any square number n, such as 4, 9, 16, 25, 36. However, it fails for the case $n = 6$ in Figure 8.1 because this has no array of four small squares making a larger square that can be put together to be replaced by the larger one. This shows that problem solving can include making conjectures that may fail. However, the conjecture that if a square can be cut into n squares, then it can be cut into $n + 3$ squares *is* true, because one can take always take any one of the n squares and divide it into four, to get four smaller squares to replace it, giving three more.

Exploring various possibilities, it is relatively straightforward to find the cases $n = 6, 7, 8$. (Figure 8.2.)

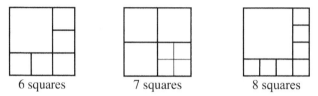

6 squares   7 squares   8 squares

Figure 8.2. Cutting a square into six, seven or eight squares.

The general step, to start with these three examples and deduce that it is possible to get all cases of $n - 6$, is less evident for many students. It requires starting with any one of the three and adding on three at a time, to get the sequences $n = 6, 9, 12, \dots, n = 7, 10, 13, \dots, n = 8, 11, 14, \dots$, which cover all cases $n - 6$. As the cases $n = 1, 4$ are also possible, these show that one can cut a square into n squares, except possibly $n = 2, 3, 5$.

The new problem now turns to the investigation, 'is it possible to *prove* that $n = 2, 4, 5$ are not possible?' This is a lot messier. As I observed successive groups attempt to solve this problem over the years, I never saw a really exquisite solution. On many occasions, the problem-solvers, all of whom were undergraduates studying mathematics, simply felt it was 'obvious' but rarely offered any coherent reasons. One argument put forward on occasion is that, apart from the trivial case with one square, there must be a square in each corner (Figure 8.3). This shows that if there is more than one square, there must be at least four, so there cannot be two or three.

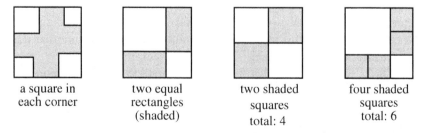

a square in   two equal   two shaded   four shaded
each corner   rectangles   squares   squares
                     (shaded)   total: 4   total: 6

Figure 8.3. There must be at least four squares and two possibilities
are 4, 6, but not 5.

With a square in each corner, if the squares do not meet, the remaining shaded shape is visibly not a square, so 5 is not possible. However, if the two squares have a common vertex, the remaining shape is two equal rectangles (shaded in the figure) and, by imagining the shaded rectangles being stretched appropriately (which can be done in the mind's eye, but not with non-elastic pieces of paper), it is possible for each to be a square, to give four squares in total, or for each to be divided into two equal squares to give six. In general, this strategy gives a new sequence 4, 6, 8, … with an even number of shaded squares either side of two changing white squares. The gap between 4 and 6 suggests that it is not possible to cut the large square into 5.

This is an *embodied* proof, carried out by physical experiment accompanied by mental imagination. It gives an explanation and sheds light onto why the numbers 2, 3, 5 are not possible.

Thinking Mathematically suggests three levels of operation:

1. Convince yourself.
2. Convince a friend.
3. Convince an enemy.

To convince yourself at least requires some kind of argument that makes the problem solution look plausible. To convince a friend means being able to express the solution in a way that can convince someone else who is not being too critical. To convince an enemy means to produce evidence that will stand the test of serious scrutiny.

So is the visual proof in Figure 8.3 good enough to convince an enemy? There are some mathematicians who will not accept a pictorial proof (even in this case, which is about a pictorial problem). Over the years I rarely saw a proof expressed in a way that was fully convincing. So I offered a prize of a bottle of Auslese German wine for the undergraduate who produced the 'sweetest' proof. None of the proofs offered really satisfied me, but I gave the prize to a competition entry from a young undergraduate by the name of Adrian Simpson who produced a proof printed on paper with sugar stuck all over it. Problems can mean different things and have different solutions, even a sweet one.

A sequel to this story occurred some years later when I gave the problem to an audience of 200 gifted young people aged eleven to sixteen. When they had had time to investigate the problem, I opened up the discussion to take suggestions from the audience. We came to the point where it seemed not possible to get $n = 2, 3$ and 5 when there was an objection from a thirteen-year-old girl. She insisted that she could achieve them all! Given my long experience of the problem, I was intrigued to see her solution, which I had never seen before in many occasions working with university mathematics students. For two squares, she cut the original squares down the diagonals to get four right-angled triangles, putting them together in pairs to give two squares. With a new way of looking at the problem by allowing squares to be reassembled from parts, new possibilities arise as to how to cut a square to produce three or five squares. This is left as a problem for the reader. (Try it now!)

The moral of this story is that a problem situation may be interpreted in different ways, so the first thing to do is to clarify precisely what the problem is and to be aware that it might be interpreted in different ways to give essentially different problems with different solutions.

As I wrote this chapter, I realized that I had been working under a mental limitation for the last quarter of a century! Even the insight to cope in a different way with the cases $n = 2, 3$ and 5 had not affected my fundamental thinking about the problem. I had always interpreted it to say that the square must be cut to give complete squares and had not considered the possibility that four separate squares could be moved around and put together to build a larger square. If this were allowed, then I *can* take the case $n = 6$ and reorganize it as three squares of different sizes! (Figure 8.4.)

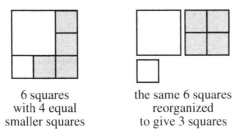

6 squares   the same 6 squares
with 4 equal   reorganized
smaller squares   to give 3 squares

Figure 8.4. Reorganizing six squares into three squares.

This new method refers to a different problem. It is not 'Into how many squares can I cut a square?' It is 'Into how many squares can I cut a square if I am allowed to reassemble the cut pieces?' The original problem and its solution are still valid, but the new version shows that problem solving can incorporate a wide range of flexibility and interpretation.

1.2 *Problem-Solving Strategies*

To be truly open-ended in the posing and solving of problems, *Thinking Mathematically* suggests a strategy in three phases: *Entry,*

Attack, and *Review*. The Entry Phase is when the solver attempts to come to grips with the problem by asking 'What do I want?', 'What do I know?', and 'What do I introduce?'. When a possible way of moving to a solution arises, a period of intense activity may follow in the Attack Phase, leading either to the pleasure of a possible solution, which may be accompanied by an 'Aha!' experience, or to the realization that the attack has failed, leading to a less pleasant feeling of being 'stuck'.

What is important is to retain the problem as a positive goal rather than becoming disenchanted and seeing the problem as an anti-goal where failure is to be avoided.

After finding a possible solution or becoming 'stuck' it is time to enter the Review Phase. When the solver is 'stuck', the review should look at what has been done so far, to see if there are alternative ways of attack, and, if possible, to re-enter the problem to attack it again. Being 'stuck' need not be a negative experience; it is an opportunity to think carefully about the attempted solution so far, to use the experiences in a positive way to attack the problem again. When a possible solution is found, first it should be enjoyed, and then it requires checking, to confirm that the solution applies to the original problem, to check that the argument is sound, to reflect on whether there is anything more to be learnt from the solution, and whether a better solution is possible. Then there is an opportunity to see if the solution can be extended to a wider class of problems to develop new insights.

As with the example of cutting squares into squares, problems usually have a general content, so two major complementary strategies are to *specialize* to look at particular cases and to *generalize* from specific examples to broader solutions. In the squares problem, there are specializations to look at specific cases to get a feel for the problem and specific techniques, such as cutting a square into four smaller squares, which can be generalized to say 'if I can cut a square into n squares (of possible different sizes), then I can cut it into $n + 3$ squares.'

Specialization can be performed in different ways, depending on the stage of the development of the solution. Initially, it may be a case of using *any* specialization to get a feel for the problem itself. When a pattern has been spotted, it might be helpful to specialize *systematically* to get a sense of the pattern. Later, when the problem seems to have been solved, it may be useful to specialize *artfully*, by choosing an example to test specific aspects of the final solution, to refine the precise conditions under which the problem is solved.

1.3 *Problem Solving in Three Worlds of Mathematics*

The way in which an individual recognizes and solves a problem clearly depends on that individual's current knowledge structure. This includes the thinkable concepts that are appropriate and the connections between them. Problems are situated in different contexts that may suggest certain kinds of attack. For instance, the squares problem is an embodied problem involving physical drawing and testing of ideas through pictures. But it also has a numerical element, for instance, in showing that if n is possible, so is $n + 3$, and an argument to show that the starting values $n = 6, 7, 8$ enable solutions for all $n - 6$.

In my experience, problem-solvers often become fixated on the context in which the problem is presented. For instance, if it is formulated in a numerical way, then the solution may initially be numerical rather than algebraic, or if it is geometric, then the first attack may be through exploring geometric examples. The specifics of the problem and the way it is attacked may also lead to mental fixations that act as impediments.

For example, another well-known problem is to draw straight lines across a square to cut it into a number of pieces and to seek the minimum number of colours required to colour each piece so that adjoining pieces are given different colours. (This requires a decision as to what happens when pieces meet only at a point, and it is usual to declare that pieces are adjoining only if they have a common edge.) Some undergraduate problem-solvers may have met the four-colour theorem before and suggest 'four' but then explore the problem by drawing random examples. (Figure 8.5.)

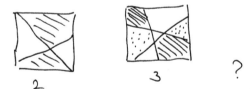

Figure 8.5. Colouring pieces of a square cut with straight lines.

Unbeknown to the solvers, this method of shading can block the eventual solution. As the shading is in pencil or pen, having drawn one picture, it is not possible to draw an extra line, as in Figure 8.6, and swap the colours on one side of the line. This would show, immediately, that only two colours are required for any number of lines. But the physical colouring is an impediment to this insight.

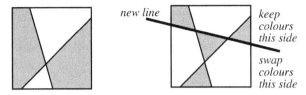

Figure 8.6. Adding a new line allows a shading again using two colours.

My purpose here is not to spoil the surprise by showing solutions, because my greatest pleasure working with students on problem solving comes from my *not* knowing the solution. If I don't know the solution then this encourages them to tackle it on their own or in collaborative groups. However, the example does show how easy it is to get fixated on a particular way of tackling the problem and the ever-present need to be aware that flexibility is required to seek a successful solution strategy.

My own view is that, in the long term, children develop greater sophistication by making connections and compressing processes into thinkable concepts that are more easily manipulated. The teacher, *as a mentor*, can use problem-solving situations to help guide learners towards greater sophistication by being aware of their current knowledge structures and their long-term needs. The problem is to find strategies that encourage learners to develop their own powers within an organized strategy without falling back to *telling* them what to do. The latter may lead to procedural thinking, following instructions rather than flexible thinking that develops increasingly sophisticated knowledge structures.

2. Lesson Study

One way forward is a technique used in primary schools in Japan. This involves a highly structured development in which children are exposed to various ways of dealing with a situation and helped to develop strategies to compress knowledge and build knowledge structures in their own way. One widely used strategy involves the Japanese word *Ha-Ka-Se*, which means 'Doctor' or 'Professor'. Each syllable also links to a separate meaning. The Japanese word *ha*yai means fast, *ka*ntan means both easy and understandable, and *se*ikaku means accurate and logical. *Fast*, *easy* and *accurate* are useable words for primary school children to compare various processes. Using Ha-Ka-Se in the classroom, especially in whole class discussion, helps children become accustomed to comparing alternative procedures to seek those that are faster, easier and accurate.

In many countries around the world, a standard procedure such as column addition, subtraction or long multiplication and division is taught as an explicit sequence of actions and decisions. Not so in lesson study. As an example, I recall with pleasure a class I observed as the teacher introduced the concept of multi-digit multiplication in a mixed-ability class of forty children. This was part of a sequence of lessons in which the children had earlier learnt how to multiply any two single-digit numbers to get the answer. Now it was time to move on to multi-digit multiplication.

The particular lesson that I describe here is one of a series of lessons, building the children's knowledge structures in a highly organized way. In previous weeks the children's activities had included learning all the products of single-digit numbers from 1×1 to 9×9. In the previous lesson the teacher had moved on to multi-digit multiplication and presented the class with the problem of finding out how many counters were in the array shown in Figure 8.7, using what they already knew.

Figure 8.7. How many counters?

The lesson had begun with a class discussion to focus on the nature of the problem, including the counting of the discs in each row to find the problem was to multiply 20 by 3. The children then worked on the problem and wrote down the solutions in their workbooks, and in class discussion they suggested various strategies such as breaking the 20 into $10 + 10$ or $5 + 5 + 5 + 5$ or $9 + 2 + 9$. The general strategy was to break 20 into parts, multiplying each part number by 3 and adding the results.

This laid the groundwork for the next lesson. Here the children were presented with the problem of calculating 3 rows of 23. It began with an air of expectancy as the teacher revealed the picture row by row and individual children called out comments as the problem was uncovered. The discussion then focused on the new problem, confirming that it was 23 times 3 as the children were given individual copies of the problem and spent a few minutes in private work and discussion with their classmates. As this happened, the teacher walked around the class, talking to different groups of children. His objective was more than simply interacting with the children, and his strategy became clearer as the class discussion progressed. He asked for solutions and orchestrated the lesson to consider solutions of increasing sophistication. Because he had walked around the class conversing with individual children, he had a good idea what solutions were available. He began by soliciting solutions from children who used the technique of breaking each row into 20 + 3 or 10 + 10 + 3. Then a solution using 10 + 3 + 10 was met with gasps of amazement from many of the children, astonished by its symmetry. As each solution was presented, it was placed on the board from left to right, building up a complete picture of the development of the lesson. The next child suggested thinking of the problem as two 10-yen coins and three 1-yen coins. The teacher wrote the answer on the board. Then a child stood up and observed that so far everyone had added 60 and 9; no one had calculated, say, 39 and 30.

The discussion broadened as further solutions were presented, such as subdividing 23 into 11 + 12, 9 + 9 + 5 and 11 + 11 + 1. Of these, 9 + 9 + 5 was particularly complicated as the child calculated 9×3 and 5×3 and had to add 27 + 27 + 15. This was done by breaking down the 27 into 20 + 7, adding the two 20s to get 40, the two 7s to get 14 and adding these to get 54, to which the 15 was added by a separation into tens and units.

The teacher wrote this calculation on the board, following the instructions from the child. It was so *complicated!* Some children may have found it fascinating, but others did not find it to be fast or easy, and the complication makes it more likely to fail.

The class then moved on to the method of column multiplication, which was used by some children in the class who had already encountered the technique. They explained the method as the teacher wrote it up, following their instructions.

$$\begin{array}{r} 23 \\ \times\ 3 \\ \hline 69 \\ \hline \end{array}$$

The column multiplication was then discussed with the class and linked to the idea of two 10-yen coins and three 1-yen coins. Then the teacher took the earliest picture breaking 23 into 2 tens and a 3 and placed it beside the column multiplication to display the link between the physical problem and the symbolic layout of the multiplication algorithm, clarifying matters by asking more questions as he worked. (Figure 8.8.)

There followed a discussion on the relative merits of the various methods and the children wrote down what they had learnt in the lesson, aided by the whole development laid out on the board from the problem on the left through its successive solutions moving to the right.

The lesson was an exemplary demonstration of a flexible route, blending embodiment with symbolism. It began with the embodied layout of the

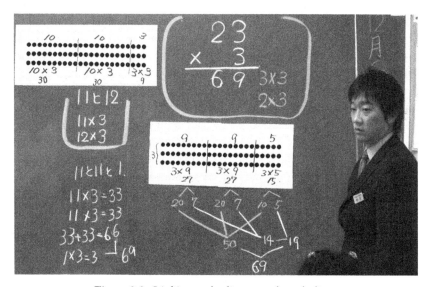

Figure 8.8. Linking embodiment and symbolism.

problem as 3 rows of 23. The children could *see* the set and so would know that it has a specific number of disks, which they use known techniques to build up the total in a range of different ways. It therefore started at a multistructural level of several possible procedures and moved towards finding a fast, easy and accurate way of performing the calculation. Of all the possible techniques, the standard algorithm emerged as a good way of performing the operation. It was not taught as the one and only method. The children worked individually and corporately to seek various ways of making the calculation, and the column method was revealed as having a meaningful link to the embodiment of the original problem, yet in an organized form ready to build the next stage of column arithmetic in general.

The class was mixed in its ability. There were children who were advanced and confident with their calculations who produced solutions such as breaking 23 into $9 + 9 + 5$ and multiplying each term by 3. There were other children who were still struggling with their number bonds. While the more advanced children could luxuriate in their powerful flexibility, the less advanced were encouraged to see that the column method is easier to perform and everyone in the class can focus on the column method as offering a solution that is faster, easier and more likely to be accurate compared with alternative methods. They experienced the flexibility of the use of symbolism and were encouraged to see the standard algorithm as the most suitable way ahead instead of being presented with it as a routine to be learnt by rote.

3. Thinking about Proof

As solving problems progresses, the question arises as to the *proof* of a solution. Interestingly, the book *Thinking Mathematically* does not contain the word 'proof' anywhere. I understand that John Mason found that the term provoked anxiety when mentioned in summer schools with students and so the topic was replaced by the beautiful idea of 'developing an *internal enemy*'. This empowers individuals to think about the structure of the mathematics themselves and to subject their own thinking to critical appraisal. It is not just a matter of explaining the idea to oneself, or to a supportive friend, or to a critical enemy; it is a matter of putting the ideas together in a coherent mathematical way that makes sense to the individual in a suitable mathematical framework.

Richard Skemp[4] analyzed mathematical concept building in a way consistent with this view. He saw three distinct modes of building and testing mathematical concepts. One is by personal experience and experiment, testing through prediction followed by action to see if the prediction is realized. A second is through communication and discussion with others. The third is through personal creativity and the search for internal consistency within one's own knowledge and beliefs.

Although these frameworks are different in detail, they share the growth from personal exploration, sharing ideas with others to get feedback, and moving on to a higher level of insight, seeking consistency within mathematics itself.

This consistency develops first at a practical level, in the embodied world of space and shape where simultaneous properties of figures can be perceived and described. Geometric proof then evolves at the theoretical level of definition and deduction in Euclidean geometry and (for a minority) may lead to more general embodied forms of geometry and on to the formal world of axiomatic geometry.

Meanwhile the symbolic world of practical arithmetic develops out of operations that are compressed into number concepts that are sensed as having generic properties that apply not just to specific examples, but operate as more general principles. These principles are then used as 'rules of arithmetic' in the theoretical level of the symbolic world as foundations for algebraic proof. This can later evolve into the axiomatic formal world of pure mathematics in university.

---

[4] Skemp (1979).

3.1 *Development of Proof in Geometry*

Proof in geometry begins from the practical activities of the child. For example, a triangle may be drawn on a piece of paper and cut out with scissors. Tearing off two corners to fit them on either side of the third corner reveals a straight line and suggests that the sum of the angles of the triangle is 180°. (Figure 8.9.)

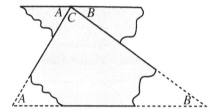

Figure 8.9. The angles of a triangle make a straight line.

This is certainly not a formal proof in the sense expected by a mathematician. It applies only to a specific triangle; it *looks* like a straight line, but is it really straight? If it is measured using a protractor, then a child may measure it as 179° or something else near 180°. However, it has many embodied elements: *picking up* the corners A and C, *turning the pieces round* to fit either side of the third angle. It is therefore a precursor of a formal Euclidean proof in which a line DE is drawn through C parallel to AB, revealing alternating angles BAC and ACD, ABC and BCE, between the parallel lines. (Figure 8.10.)

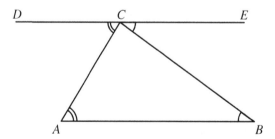

Figure 8.10. A Euclidean proof using parallel lines.

In this instance the conceptions change, from a specific experiment with a specific triangle, to a generic experience typical of all triangles and, later, a proof based on the definitions and techniques of Euclidean geometry.

Embodied proofs continue to be of value at higher levels of operation. For instance, how do we prove that there are only five Platonic solids (with all faces being made of a specific regular polygon)? This can be shown by a thought experiment playing with regular polygons. A triangle is a flat figure. If we have a supply of equilateral triangles, what kind of three-dimensional figures can we make out of them by sticking them together? Playing about with the triangles, we may see that we need to put at least three triangles together to meet at a vertex with each pair meeting along a side. We can also do this with four or five triangles, but six is too many to make a vertex (six equilateral triangles fit to lie in a plane).

In Figure 8.11 we see that we can make three regular figures with triangular faces: a tetrahedron with four faces, an octahedron with eight faces and an icosahedron with twenty. In the same way, making a regular three-dimensional figure with squares or pentagons allows just one in each case: the cube with six faces and the dodecahedron with twelve. No other cases can be made.

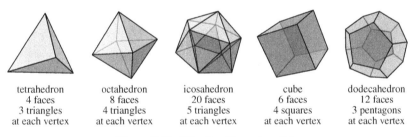

tetrahedron	octahedron	icosahedron	cube	dodecahedron
4 faces	8 faces	20 faces	6 faces	12 faces
3 triangles	4 triangles	5 triangles	4 squares	3 pentagons
at each vertex	at each vertex	at each vertex	at each vertex	at each vertex

Figure 8.11. The five Platonic solids.

Embodied proofs can also operate in other forms of geometry, such as projective geometry with figures projected onto a fixed plane and non-Euclidean geometries such as Poincaré's hyperbolic geometry that we will consider in Chapter 9.

Hilbert took the major step from embodiment to formalism by translating Euclidean geometry into a set-theoretic axiomatic format, proving theorems from verbal axioms without any dependence on implicit properties of pictures.

This development of embodied proof in geometry, based on the analysis from Chapter 6, is outlined in Figure 8.12.

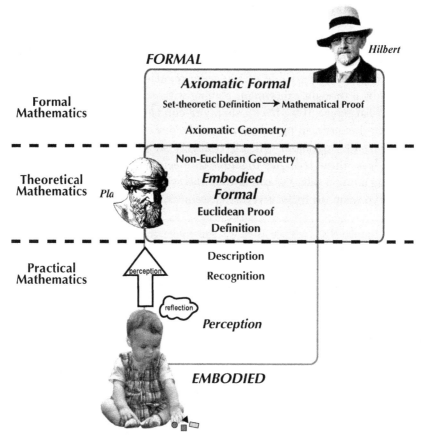

Figure 8.12. The embodied and formal development of proof in geometry.

3.2 *Blending Embodiment and Symbolism*

As soon as geometry involves measurement, mathematical thinking requires the blending of embodiment and symbolism. For example, to prove the formula for the area of a spherical triangle now involves both the embodiment of figures on the surface of a sphere and the symbolism of trigonometry. A spherical triangle has sides that are parts of three great circles and the area can be calculated as a proportion of the symbolic surface area $4\pi r^2$.

In Figure 8.13 the spherical triangle *ABC* has sides lying on great circles with a mirror image *A'B'C'* on the opposite side of the sphere.

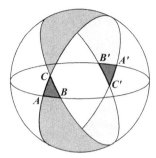

Figure 8.13. A spherical triangle *ABC* and its mirror image *A'B'C'*.

The great circles cut the surface of the sphere into three parts each consisting of two sectors of area S_A, S_B, S_C. (Figure 8.14.)

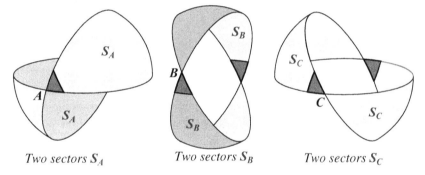

Two sectors S_A   *Two sectors S_B*   *Two sectors S_C*

Figure 8.14. Cutting the surface into pairs of sectors along the great circles.

Add these together and note that the three pairs of sectors precisely cover the whole surface but that the spherical triangle is repeated six times when only two are required to make up the area. This gives:

$$2S_A + 2S_B + 2S_C = 4\pi r^2 + 4\Delta$$

where Δ is the area of the spherical triangle.

Measuring angles in radians rather than degrees gives a full turn as 2π radians, so the sector S_A is A/π times the surface area $2\pi r^2$ of a hemisphere. (Figure 8.15.)

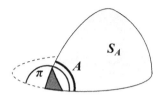

Figure 8.15. The area of a sector is A/π times the area of a hemisphere.

This gives

$$S_A = 2\pi r^2 \times A/\pi = 2Ar^2,$$

so that substituting the three values of the areas of the sectors into the previous equation gives

$$4Ar^2 + 4Br^2 + 4Cr^2 = 4\pi r^2 + 4\Delta$$

with the result

$$A + B + C = \pi + \Delta/r^2.$$

While the sum of the angles of a triangle in the plane is – radians (180°), the sum of the angles of a spherical triangle is $\pi + \Delta/r^2$, which is always greater than π and, for fixed r, grows bigger as the area Δ grows bigger.

This blend of embodiment and symbolism illustrates how spherical geometry has different properties from Euclidean geometry, yet these properties can be deduced using a blend of embodiment and symbolism.

3.3 *Development of Proof in Arithmetic and Algebra*

The long-term development of symbolic proof is more complicated than embodied proof because it begins with operations such as counting that have properties that are observed and later lead to properties of numbers. Proof in practical arithmetic begins by performing specific calculations and seeing the general patterns that occur as generic proof. Theoretical proofs occur in arithmetic based on definitions of concepts such as 'prime numbers' that lead to unique factorization of whole numbers into primes, and also in algebra, performing algebraic manipulations based on 'the rules of arithmetic.' At a more advanced level, formal algebraic structures are defined based on axioms and set-theoretic deductions that lead to formal proof.

The increasing sophistication of techniques of proof can be illustrated by the 'Little Theorem of Gauss'[5], said to have been given to a class including the fourteen-year-old Gauss in the following form:

Find the sum of the first 100 numbers.

The teacher expected his pupils to do the calculation by starting with 1, adding 2, then 3, and then so on up to 100. It was clearly a long chore that would occupy them for the rest of the lesson. Gauss thought a moment, then wrote the answer 5050 on his slate. The teacher was amazed at his speed. Gauss explained that he broke up the sum

$$1+2+3+\cdots+50+51+\cdots+98+99+100$$

into the terms up to 50 plus the terms from 51 to 100, reversing the second sequence and adding them term by term to get each pair of terms adding to 101 and, with 50 pairs, the total is then 50×101 which is 5050. (Figure 8.16.)

$$
\begin{array}{l}
1 + 2 + 3 + \cdots + 50 \\
+ 100 + 99 + 98 + \cdots + 51 \\
\hline
\underbrace{101 + 101 + 101 + \cdots + 101}_{\text{50 terms}} \;=\; 50 \times 101 = 5050
\end{array}
$$

Figure 8.16. Calculating the sum of the first 100 whole numbers.

A variant of this problem was given every year in a university course for student teachers who were asked to find the sum of the first few whole numbers, and, in true problem-solving style, it was suggested that they look at some specific examples to get a sense of the pattern.[6]

It was expected that they would find the formula for the sum of the first n whole numbers as $\frac{1}{2}n(n+1)$. However, they found not *one* formula, but *two*. For even values of n, such as 6, they were able to split the sum into two halves following the Gaussian argument to get 1, 2, 3 and 6, 5, 4 which add up in pairs to get $1 + 6$, $2 + 5$, $3 + 5$, giving 3 times 7. This is a half of 6 times 7. However, when n is odd, this method does not work. For an odd

---

[5] The development of proof based on the theorem of Gauss also appears in Tall, Yevdokimov et al. (2012).

[6] This lesson was taken at Warwick University by Robin Foster, who showed me the distinct solutions given by his student teachers.

number, such as 5, there are pairs $1 + 5$, $2 + 4$, and a middle term 3. The two pairs give 2×6, leaving the remaining term 3. This is more complicated. It requires some insight to see 3 as $\frac{1}{2} \times 6$ to give the total as 2×6 plus $\frac{1}{2} \times 6$ which is $\frac{1}{2} \times 5 \times 6$. In both cases the sum of the first n whole numbers is $\frac{1}{2} n(n+1)$.

The two distinct cases occur because when n is even, it is divisible by 2 and when n is odd, then $n + 1$ is divisible by 2. This cautions the teacher designing a lesson to be aware that considering special cases of a general problem may lead to unexpected complications. As in lesson study, it is helpful to prepare a carefully organized lesson that has been tested to reveal different possible ways in which a problem may be posed.

A careful choice of an alternative approach may give a better learning experience. For example, the sum of the first 100 numbers may take a second copy of $1 + \cdots + 100$, turn it round and add $1 + \cdots + 100$ to $100 + \cdots + 1$ to get twice the sum as $101 + \cdots + 101$ (a hundred times) and divide by two to get $\frac{1}{2} \times 100 \times 101$. This works for *any* whole number, so it applies generically to *all* whole numbers. The argument can be presented in generalized arithmetic using n to stand for any whole number to give the algebraic formula as:

$$1 + \cdots + n = \frac{1}{2} n(n+1).$$

The same proof may be embodied in a picture by putting objects in successive rows of length 1, 2, 3, ... This gives a triangular set of objects (darker in Figure 8.17) and when a second set of the same shape is rotated and placed with it (the lighter set), the result is a rectangular array with sides n and $n + 1$ giving a visual argument for

$$1 + \cdots + n = \frac{1}{2} n(n+1).$$

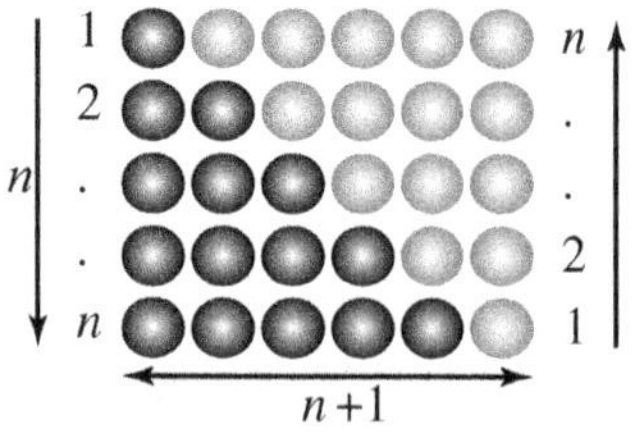

Figure 8.17. The sum $1 + \ldots + n$ is half of $n(n + 1)$.

Technically, the pictorial proof may be declared unsatisfactory because it shows not a general value of n but only a specific value, 5. However, if we look at Figure 8.18, we see that the argument is visually satisfying even when the number of items is so large that it is not easy to count them.

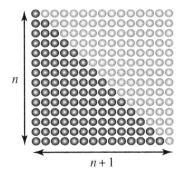

Figure 8.18. A generic pictorial proof.

The array is visibly rectangular. There are n rows and an extra column as the bottom row has an additional lighter object at the end, making $n + 1$ columns. Most importantly, all of this can be *seen* without counting the actual number of objects involved. Hence this visual image gives a generic proof in which the picture for a specific case can be seen to operate in general.

3.4 *A Potentially Infinite Proof by Induction*

The formula can also be proved by induction in two similar-looking but subtly different ways. The first is a potentially infinite proof:

Theorem: $1 + \cdots + n = \frac{1}{2} n(n + 1)$.

Proof: The formula is true for $n = 1$, because $1 = \frac{1}{2} \times 1 \times (1 + 1)$.

If it is true for $n = k$, then $1 + \cdots + k = \frac{1}{2} k(k + 1)$ and add $k + 1$ to both sides to deduce the formula for $n = k + 1$.

Repeat this general step as often as is required:

It is true for $n = 1$, hence it is true for $n = 2$,
hence for $n = 3$, hence for $n = 4$, ...
and so on for any specific whole number .... (*ad infinitum*).

This proof is often given in school, but may cause confusion as it requires knowledge of the formula from the beginning and then apparently uses the formula at one stage to deduce the next. The distinction between knowing the truth for a specific *n* before knowing it *for all n* is subtle.

This proof, which mathematicians often consider more rigorous than an embodied proof, is less helpful to students as it does not *explain* anything. The embodied proof shows *why* the formula is true.[7]

3.5 *A Finite Formal Proof by Induction*

In the axiomatic formal world, the induction proof can be recast as a *finite* proof, by introducing an axiomatic definition of the natural numbers $\mathbb{N}$. The Peano axioms express the properties that there is a starting number 1, and each number *n* has a successor $s(n)$ that is different from all those that came before. This can be formulated in terms of a set $\mathbb{N}$ and a function $s : \mathbb{N} \rightarrow \mathbb{N}$ where $s(n)$ is thought of as 'the successor of *n*'. The structure satisfies:

> *Axiom I: s* is one-one (meaning if $m \neq n$ then $s(m) \neq s(n)$) but not onto (meaning there is an element not equal to $s(n)$ for any $n \in \mathbb{N}$).

This first axiom declares there is at least one element not of the form $s(n)$. Call such an element 1. Then $1 \in \mathbb{N}$, and $s(n) \neq 1$ for any *n*. Now, for each *n*, define $n + 1$ to be $s(n)$. To say that these successors make up the whole of $\mathbb{N}$ requires a second axiom saying that any subset containing 1 and all the successors of its elements must be the whole of $\mathbb{N}$:

> *Axiom II*: If *A* is a subset of $\mathbb{N}$ with $1 \in A$,
>   and, for all $k \in \mathbb{N}, k \in A$ implies $s(k) \in A$,
>   then $A = \mathbb{N}$.

Axiom II is usually called 'the axiom of induction'.

From these two minimal axioms we can generate the usual arithmetic of the natural numbers! For instance, we might begin by showing that there is only *one* element that is not a successor.

Theorem: Given Axioms I and II, the element 1 is unique.

Proof: Suppose another element $a \in \mathbb{N}$ satisfies $a \neq s(k)$ for all $k \in \mathbb{N}$. Consider the set *A* consisting of all elements of $\mathbb{N}$ except *a*. Because $a \neq 1$, we have $1 \in A$. For any $k \in A$, by the definition of *a*, $s(k) \neq a$, so $s(k) \in A$. By Axiom II, *A* is the whole of $\mathbb{N}$, which contradicts $a \in A$. Hence there is only *one* element not a successor of another element.

---

[7] Rodd (2000).

The element 1 starts the set, with successors that can be written as $2 = s(1) = 1 + 1$, $3 = s(2) = 2 + 1$, and so on. Addition and multiplication can be defined by induction:

Definition: Define $m + 1 = s(m)$ and, if $m + k$ is defined, define $m + s(k)$ to be $s(m + k)$.

The set S of elements k for which the sum $m + k$ is defined contains 1 (because $m + 1 = s(m)$) and, if it contains k it contains the successor $s(k)$ (because $m + s(k)$ is $s(m + k)$). Hence, by the induction axiom, the set S equals $\mathbb{N}$.

Multiplication can be similarly defined by defining $m \times 1 = m$, and, in general, when $m \times k$ has been defined, then $m \times s(k) = m \times k + k$. The usual rules of whole number arithmetic can be derived by similar techniques. These formal proofs are again both tedious and routine, but once established they provide a foundation for axiomatic formal proof of properties of the formally defined natural numbers $\mathbb{N}$.

Once this formal approach using the Peano axioms I and II is established, it becomes possible to give a new formal proof of the sum of the first n whole numbers:

Proof: Let A be the subset of $n \in \mathbb{N}$ such that $1 + \cdots + n = \frac{1}{2}n(n+1)$.

1. By substitution in the formula, $1 \in A$.
2. If $k \in A$ then use the formula for k as above to show that $k + 1 \in A$.
3. Use Axiom II to deduce that A is the whole of $\mathbb{N}$.

This is a proof with just *three* steps (1, 2, 3 above). The first establishes the formula for $n = 1$, the second establishes the general step, and the third quotes the induction axiom.

It reveals an *enormous* compression from a potentially infinite proof with the same step carried out time and time again and again, *ad infinitum*, to a *finite* proof with just three steps. The infinite part of the structure is now subsumed in the axioms themselves, because any set with a map s satisfying Axiom I *must be infinite*.

As a mathematician, I was delighted that the axioms allowed a three-step proof for a potentially infinite formula and presented this in lectures, praising its wonderful compression. It fell on deaf ears.

Why? The symbolic and pictorial proofs show *why* the argument is meaningful based on well-established knowledge structures. The students' knowledge structures already have connections built up over the years.

They attempt to make sense of the well-connected old ideas and the new set-theoretic definitions. The blend is often problematic as the student may be unsure of which connection to be made – the implicit, strong connections made over the years, or the new connections demanded by the formal theory. Superficially, the induction proof uses the result to prove the result. The subtlety of the quantifiers – that one wishes to prove it true *for all n*, while using the result *for any n so far* – is usually problematic.

The finite proof by induction shifts to the formal mathematics of the axiomatic formal world. It requires a transition from a blend of embodied and symbolic experiences in theoretical mathematics to a knowledge structure based on formal definition and proof. (Figure 8.19.)

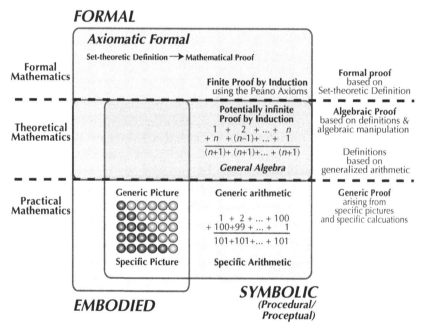

Figure 8.19. The Little Gauss Theorem presented in increasing sophistication.

3.6 *Proof in Life and in Mathematics*

The steady development of proof in mathematics involves subtle changes in meaning as the mathematics becomes more sophisticated. Inferences in the practical language of everyday life operate in implicit ways that are different from proofs in theoretical and formal mathematics. If a parent says to a child 'If you are good, then I will buy you an ice cream', then the child infers that, not only is it true that if he is good he will be rewarded, but if he is not then he will not have the ice cream. Having the ice cream is synonymous with being good and not having the ice cream with not being good. In this context the two concepts of 'being good' and 'having an ice cream' occur together.

In everyday practical language we often say 'if A then B' to also mean 'if B then A'. This does not happen in mathematics. We say 'if n is a prime number bigger than 2, then it is odd.' It is not true to say 'if n is odd, then it is a prime number bigger than 2.'

We also use other words with subtle distinctions in meaning. A simple example is the use of the word 'some', which has subtly different meanings in everyday life and in mathematics.

I gave a questionnaire[8] to students who had just arrived at university asking them to say whether certain statements are true or false[9]. The statement:

'Some rational numbers are real'

was adjudged by the majority of students to be false. In mathematical formulation, the statement 'some A are B' includes the possibility that '*all* A are B.' The statement is true in mathematical language, but not for students who see that *all* rational numbers are real, not just 'some'.

A follow-up questionnaire tried the following:

Let S be the set of numbers 19, 3677, 601, 2, 257, 11119, 7559, 12653, 11177.

Without doing any calculations, say whether the following statements are true or false:

(1) Some numbers in the set S are prime,
(2) Some numbers in the set S are even.

Statement (1) was universally adjudged true (some are visibly prime but the rest are, to the student, unknown). In fact *all* the numbers are prime. Statement (2) was considered false by most, (probably) because of the plurality of the verb, but some students were happy to consider it true. A

---

[8] Tall (1977).
[9] Tall (1979).

colloquial interpretation of the word 'some' in many cases seems to be that it means 'more than one of a given set, but without the certain knowledge that it is all of the set.' Shades of meaning may vary from person to person. In formal mathematics, the word 'some' simply means 'at least one'.

3.7 *Proof by Contradiction*

Proof by contradiction is a fundamental watershed for many students. It involves assuming that a statement is either true or false, and that assuming it to be false leads to a contradiction, so it must be true. During the proof, the prover is under stress because it involves assuming something that is true is regarded as being false.

The major example in school mathematics is the proof that $\sqrt{2}$ is irrational. The usual proof is to suppose it is false and that $\sqrt{2}$ is rational and in the form

$$\sqrt{2} = \frac{p}{q} \quad \text{for whole numbers } p \text{ and } q \text{ in lowest terms}$$

so that only one of p and q can be even, for if not, we could cancel the factor 2. Now square the equation to get

$$p^2 = 2q^2.$$

This shows that p^2 is even and it follows that p also must be even (for if p were odd, then p^2 would be odd – another proof by contradiction). Hence $p = 2r$ for some whole number r, and substituting this into the earlier equation gives $(2r)^2 = 2q^2$, so $r^2 = 2q^2$ and by the same argument, r is also even, which is a contradiction.

One student, Alan[10], was questioned about the deduction that 'if p^2 is even then it follows that p also must be even.' He responded quoting the authority of the lecturer: 'He [the lecturer] said, "the root of an even number is even – he just assumed it".' Alan supported his answer with examples, saying 'the square root of 4 and the square root of 16 are both even.' He could recognize and describe that a whole number and its square were simultaneously even, in the sense of practical mathematics, but he had not yet grasped the use of the properties as *definitions* at a theoretical level so that they may be used as a basis for deduction.

---

[10] Alan (a pseudonym) was one of the students I interviewed on five occasions as he took a first course on mathematical analysis.

For a student operating at a practical level, it may be more profitable to offer a generic proof to give a sense of the ideas through suitably typical examples. I presented a class of first-year university students with the standard proof by contradiction that √2 is irrational and also a generic proof starting with a typical fraction, say 5/8 and squaring it (say $5^2/2^6$) to reveal that it has an *even* number of prime factors in its numerator and denominator. This illustrates the generic principle that squaring a factored fraction doubles the number of each prime factor, so the number 2 (which, as 2/1, has just one factor 2) cannot be the square of a fraction.[11]

Most students preferred the generic proof to the contradiction proof, and most of those initially preferring the proof by contradiction shifted to preferring the generic proof two days later. Generic proofs work much better for students requiring theoretical mathematics based on practical experience than the greater demands of formal mathematics.

However, in formal mathematics, proof by contradiction becomes a standard proving technique for theorems that apply to an infinite number of cases. It is then far simpler to assume that a statement is false in a single case and derive a contradiction. This is consistent with the observation that generic proofs may be appropriate for students studying practical and theoretical applications of mathematics requiring mainly calculation and symbolic manipulation, but for those travelling further into formal mathematics, contradiction proofs become essential.

4. Formal Proof

Formal axiomatic proof is the current ideal form of proof desired by most pure mathematicians. It involves making formal definitions and deducing all consequent properties by mathematical proof. Although the theorems that we formulate may arise from our experiences in embodiment and symbolism, the proof itself must follow only by deduction from the formal definitions without the implicit use of any extraneous ideas.

As biological creatures, however, we all recycle what we know. As our knowledge structures mature to incorporate formal elements, we continue to use connections made in our brain when we learnt simple arithmetic. For instance, despite the formal claim that the real numbers are defined as a complete ordered field, they remain, in all of us, as a subtle multi-blend of embodiment as a number line that we trace with a finger, a decimal number

[11] Tall (1979).

system that we use for calculation, and a complete ordered field that is used in formal proof.

In *Where Mathematics Comes From*, Lakoff and Núñez perform a top-down intellectual 'idea analysis' of the real numbers and arrive at a dual structure, one of which is a 'space-set' blend of a naturally continuous line and a set of points, and the other is the symbolism of the decimal numbers.[12] This blends the embodied line as a set of points on the one hand and the operational symbolism on the other. A bottom-up analysis reveals the various aspects of the blend arising in a different sequence, as a blend of the embodied number line with points marked on it representing decimal numbers arising in school mathematics and the later formal definition of the real numbers as a complete ordered field. This follows the parallel development of practical and theoretical mathematics and the later transition to formal mathematics that is problematic for most students.

4.1 *Axiomatic Systems*

The student being introduced to axiomatic systems does not yet share the richer formal knowledge structures available to the expert mathematician. The initial stages for a student to make sense of an axiomatic system build on previous experience. Earlier examples of number systems include their earlier experiences with the integers (positive and negative) $\mathbb{Z}$, the rational numbers (positive and negative) $\mathbb{Q}$, the real numbers $\mathbb{R}$ and the complex numbers $\mathbb{C}$.

All these systems have two operations – addition and multiplication – where the operation of addition takes two elements a and b and gives a third element written as $a + b$ (called the *sum*) and the operation of multiplication gives an element written as ab or $a \times b$ (called the *product*). The notation also uses brackets to indicate the order in which the operations are carried out, for instance $(a + b) + c$ means 'first operate with a and b to get the sum $a + b$ and then operate with this and c to get the sum $(a + b) + c$.

In the formal world what matters is not how these operations are performed, only what properties they are required to satisfy. The plan is to write down a list of properties that function as axioms from which all other properties can be deduced.

This is not an easy process for a novice as it involves a long list of axioms that look familiar and are linked together with multiple previous experiences in the mind. This means that the novice reader will not be

---

[12] Lakoff & Núñez (2000), p. 281.

able to read the axioms without making implicit mental associations with previous mathematical ideas. It is 'natural' to attempt to make sense of formal mathematics building on previous experience of embodiment and symbolism experienced in school mathematics. An alternative is a 'formal' approach in which one takes the written definitions as they are given and seeks to make sense of the formal deductions without reference to particular previous experiences.

The transition from natural experience to formal proof is likely to have problematic aspects for a reader who does not have previous experience of formalism. However, it is important for all participants in mathematical thinking to be aware of the power of the formal approach that frees mathematics of its specific connections to specific contexts. Once a theorem is proven formally, its consequences will apply to situations already known and to any that arise in the future in a context that satisfies the given axioms and definitions.

We introduce a formal approach to number systems that builds on ideas that will be familiar in a natural form to readers, but also generalize formally to a wide range of structures in later developments. We begin with a set D having two operations that satisfy the following:

(0)　For each pair of elements $a, b \in D$ there are unique elements $a + b$, $ab \in D$.

(A1)　$a + b = b + a$ for all $a, b \in D$ (addition is *commutative*).

(A2)　$(a + b) + c = a + (b + c)$ for all $a, b, c \in D$ (addition is *associative*).

(A3)　There exists a unique element $0 \in D$ such that $a + 0 = a$ for all $a \in D$ (where 0 is called *zero*).

(A4)　For each $a \in D$ there is a unique element written as $-a \in D$ such that $a + (-a) = 0$ (called the *additive inverse* of a).

(M1)　$ab = ba$ for all $a, b \in D$ (multiplication is *commutative*),

(M2)　$(ab)c = a(bc)$ for all $a, b, c \in D$ (multiplication is *associative*).

(M3)　There exists a unique element $1 \in D$ (different from zero) such that $a1 = 0$ for all $a \in D$ (where 1 is called the *additive identity* or *one*).

(M4)　For each $a \in D$ where $a \neq 0$, there is a unique element $b \in D$ called its *multiplicative inverse* such that $ab = 1$. This unique multiplicative inverse is written as a^{-1}.

(D)　$a(b + c) = ab + ac$ for all $a, b, c \in D$ (the distributive law).

A system satisfying these axioms is called a *field*. Examples include the rational numbers $\mathbb{Q}$, the real numbers $\mathbb{R}$ and the complex numbers $\mathbb{C}$. The system of signed integers $\mathbb{Z}$ is not a field because it fails to satisfy (M4); for instance, $2 \in \mathbb{Z}$ has no multiplicative inverse in $\mathbb{Z}$. A system satisfying axioms for a field except perhaps (M4) is called a *commutative ring*. All the systems $\mathbb{Z}, \mathbb{Q}, \mathbb{R}, \mathbb{C}$ are commutative rings.

The systems of natural numbers $\mathbb{N}$ and positive fractions $\mathbb{F}$ fail to be commutative rings because they do not have additive inverses specified in axiom (A4). However, they can be characterized as being the positive elements in the commutative rings $\mathbb{Z}$ and $\mathbb{Q}$.

The idea of an element being 'positive' can be made formal by saying that a commutative ring D is *ordered* if it has a subset D^+ satisfying the following properties:

(O1) For $x \in D$, precisely one of the following three properties holds: $x \in D^+$, or $-x \in D^+$, or $x = 0$.

(O2) If $x, y \in D^+$ then $x + y, xy \in D^+$.

Familiar ideas of arithmetic can now be formalized by saying that an element x in D^+ is defined to be *positive*, and its additive inverse $-x$ is *negative*. Axiom (O1) (called 'the law of trichotomy') says that every element is either *positive*, or *negative* or *zero* and the three are mutually exclusive. These two axioms characterize the positive elements of $\mathbb{Z}$ as $\mathbb{N}$ and the positive elements of $\mathbb{Q}$ as (positive) fractions $\mathbb{F}$.

Our human brain naturally blends the formal definition with our experience of embodiment and symbolism in working with natural numbers and fractions. However, the formal world involves a fundamentally different mode of operation. The symbols are not assumed to have any properties other than those specified in the axioms. Any other properties, even those we believe to be true from our vast experience with numbers, must be proved, once and for all, *directly from the axioms*.

For instance, if we were to attempt to prove that 'two minuses make a plus' in the form $(-a)(-b) = ab$, then this must be proven from the axioms alone. This is a difficult task for learners as it involves working only with the axioms and making sure that every step follows without introducing any other ideas, however self-evident they may seem.

In the next section I will use a problem-solving approach to seek a formal proof of this elusive idea. Readers with mathematical expertise will consider this exercise to be routine, but those with little experience of formal proof are very likely to find it problematic, because intuitive links in the mind must not be used without precisely specifying how they follow directly from the axioms. Simultaneously 'knowing' something intuitively and needing to prove it formally can be very perplexing.

Moreover, a formal proof steps back to more fundamental properties. Whereas theoretical experience in school means that a learner realizes that adding several numbers together can be performed in any order and always gives the same result, a formal approach is based only on operations performed two elements at a time. So an axiom might affirm that $a + b = b + a$ but it says nothing about the flexibility of adding three elements. Instead, another axiom is introduced to add elements only two at a time and use brackets to denote which additions are performed first and to assert that $(a + b) + c = a + (b + c)$. To return to the flexibility of being able to add any number of terms in any order and get the same result needs to be *proved* carefully from the axioms. This requires proof by induction on the number of terms. It is tedious and often seems problematic.

By considering the proof that 'two minuses makes a plus', it will be possible to reveal the considerable challenges that face a learner in making the transition from school mathematics to formal proof. Also, by carefully noting what axioms are actually used, it will be possible to specify more precisely under what conditions the theorem is true. This reveals a gigantic leap in meaning. The relationship $(-a)(-b) = ab$ seems to be saying something about negative numbers and how they operate under multiplication. We will find that the axioms required to prove this do not involve order. The proof applies in any commutative ring. This illustrates how formal proof is more powerful and more general than a theoretical proof formulated in a specific context.

4.2 *Two Minuses Make a Plus*

As we journeyed through the embodied and symbolic worlds in earlier chapters, we saw how to embody the idea that two minuses make a plus in various ways, for instance, when operating on a number line, multiplying by a number stretches the number line by the given factor and a minus sign reverses the direction, so two minus signs reverse the direction twice and return to the original direction. In imagining the product of two signed lengths as an area, we envisaged a negative area in terms of turning the area over to see the other side. Turning it over twice returns it to its original direction.

But what happens when we want to prove the relationship for complex numbers, or for other systems in which it might also be true? We could perhaps continue to invent new ways of embodying new situations.

The formal world changes all this. It only requires the theorem to be proved from the given axioms and definitions. That's all. There is no need to appeal to any of the earlier meanings of embodiment and symbolism.

The search for a formal proof considered here uses a problem-solving approach in which we are given the axioms (0), (A1)–(A4), (M1)–(M4), (D) and (O1), (O2) and we investigate which axioms are required to prove the identity $(-a)(-b) = ab$.

Working directly from the axioms as they stand can be quite daunting as each axiom is given only in a minimal form. For example, the distributive law is given only in the form $a(b + c) = ab + ac$. To use it in the form $(b + c)a = ba + ca$ requires a combination of (D) $(a(b + c) = ab + ac)$ and three applications of (M1) to change $a(b + c)$ to $(b + c)a$, ab to ba and ac to ca. Similarly, the rule $0 + a = a$ requires a combination of (A3) that $a + 0 = 0$ and (A1) that $0 + a = a + 0$.

Initially a few auxiliary results need to be proved to allow the axioms to operate in flexible ways that are already familiar to the learner from school algebra. For instance, axiom (0) is more powerful that it may seem at first sight. By specifying that for given a, b, there are *unique* elements $a + b$ and ab, it allows us to assert that, if we replace a or b by different symbols for the same elements, then the results remain the same.

For instance, the axiom $c + (-c) = 0$ says that $c + (-c)$ and 0 are different names for the same element. Therefore replacing a in the expression $a + b$ by either of these expressions tells us that $(c + (-c)) + b = 0 + b$. In effect, Axiom (0) allows us to substitute expressions into any statement that is either an axiom or has been proved from the axioms as a theorem.

We will assume that these auxiliary results have been established so that we can use the axioms in a more expert, flexible manner.

We begin, in true problem-solving tradition, by thinking about 'what we want to know' – which is the required identity $(-a)(-b) = ab$ – and consider 'what we can introduce' that may be relevant to move towards a proof.

Looking at the axioms we have been given, we can see from (A4) that the element $-a$ is the *unique* additive inverse that satisfies $a + (-a) = 0$. We can use (A1) to write this as

$$(-a) + a = 0.$$

But $(-a)$ has its own unique inverse written as $-(-a)$ and this satisfies

$$(-a) + (-(-a)) = 0.$$

By the *uniqueness* of the inverse, the two inverses are the same, namely

$$(-(-a)) = a$$

so *two minuses make a plus*, as required.

At this stage, we should pause and reflect on what we have done. As we check the argument carefully, we can see that we have only proved that 'the negative of the negative of an element' returns us to the original element. The proof is not yet finished. What we want to prove relates to the *product* of two such inverses $(-a)(-b)$.

Looking back at the axioms, to see what we can introduce into the argument, the only axiom relating addition and multiplication is the distributive law (D). Using this with the term $-a$ outside the bracket and axiom (A4) in the form $b + (-b) = 0$ inside, then we see that

$$(-a)b + (-a)(-b) = (-a)(b + (-b)) = (-a)0.$$

This looks really promising, because if we knew that $(-a)0 = 0$, then we would have

$$(-a)b + (-a)(-b) = 0,$$

which reveals that $(-a)(-b)$ is the unique additive inverse of $(-a)b$.

Focusing on the term $(-a)b$ reveals it as part of $((-a) + a)b$ in the distributive axiom (D) that can be flexibly rewritten by changing the order of multiplication to give

$$(-a)b + ab = ((-a) + a)b = 0b.$$

Assuming that $0b = 0$ gives

$$(-a)b + ab = 0.$$

AHA! Now both ab and $(-a)(-b)$ are additive inverses of $(-a)b$ and, because the additive inverse is unique, we have $(-a)(-b) = ab$.

This completes the proof.

Enjoy the moment. The desired conclusion has been reached. But before we celebrate, the proof should be reviewed to make sure it is watertight.

Reflecting very deeply, there is still a step that remains unproven from the axioms. It remains to show that $0x = x0 = 0$ in general. This seems obvious, *but it is not part of the axioms!* Stuck! How can this be proved?

A possible attack is to introduce Axiom (A3) in the argument to get $0 + 0 = 0$ and multiply by x to get

$$x(0 + 0) = x0.$$

The distributive axiom (D) shows

$$x0 + x0 = x0.$$

Using Axiom (A4) and adding $-x0$ to both sides gives

$$(x0 + x0) + (-x0) = x0 + (-x0).$$

The right-hand side is 0 by (A4). Using the associative law (A2) on the left gives

$$x0 + (x0 + (-x0)) = 0.$$

Using the definition of the additive inverse $-x0$, this simplifies to

$$x0 + 0 = 0$$

and using the definition of 0, this simplifies further to

$$x0 = 0$$

as required.

After a struggle, the journey is finished.

4.3 *Organizing a Formal Proof*

On reflection this proof is rather messy. A mathematics professor giving a formal lecture course might rearrange it into a more organized sequence of steps. This will now be done. As we proceed formally, step-by-step, we will keep an account of what information is used in each step of the proof to see what properties are required to prove the relationship.

To write the proof out in a neater fashion, start with a little preliminary result (called a lemma):

Lemma 1: If $a + a = a$ for an element a in a system satisfying the given axioms, then $a = 0$.

Proof: By (A4) there is an element $-a$ such that $a + (-a) = 0$. (A4)

Since $a + a = a$ is given, we have $(a + a) + (-a) = a + (-a)$. (0)

Use the associative law (A2) to rewrite this as $a + (a + (-a)) = a + (-a)$. (A2)

then substitute $a + (-a) = 0$ in the left hand side and the right-hand side to get $a + 0 = 0$. (A4)

Now use commutativity of addition (A1) to get $0 + a = 0$ and then the property of 0 (A3) to simplify this to $a = 0$ as required. (A1)(A3)

Now set out a second lemma:

Lemma 2: If x is any element in a system satisfying the given axioms then
   $x0 = 0x = 0$.

Proof: Use the distributive law to get $x0 + x0 = x(0 + 0) = x0$.   (D)
and then use Lemma 1 to deduce that $x0 = 0$.
Multiplication is commutative (M2), so $0x = 0$.   (M2)

We are then ready to write out the main argument:

Theorem: If a, b are elements of system satisfying the given
   axioms, then $(-a)(-b) = ab$.

Proof: Use the distributive law (D) to show that   (D) (M1)
   $(-a)b + (-a)(-b) = (-a)0$ and $(-a)b + ab = 0b$,

and then use lemma 2 in the form $(-a)0 = 0$ and $0b = 0$ to   Lemma 2 using
   deduce that: $(-a)b + (-a)(-b) = 0$ and $(-a)(-b) = 0$.   (D)(M2)
Finally, use the uniqueness of the additive inverse proved   (A4)
   earlier to deduce that $(-a)(-b) = ab$.

The proof is now part of a well-organized sequence of theorems stated and proved from earlier deductions that can be traced back to the axioms.

You can see from this how technical such proofs are in their construction and presentation. A university professor may present only the final stage of the proof to make it more palatable for students. It is no wonder that many students see their task is to rote learn the proof with its two lemmas to reproduce in an examination. However, being able to produce formal proofs has an enormous payoff, as we will now see.

4.4 *A Wider Vista of Meaning*

Looking closely at the proof reveals that the only axioms used to prove $(-a)(-b) = ab$ are (0), (A1)–(A4), (M1)–(M3) and (D). The order axioms (O1), (O2) are not used at all! In other words, *the result is true in any commutative ring* where $-x$ denotes the additive inverse of x satisfying $x + (-x) = 0$.

Now we can extend the idea that 'two minuses make a plus' to further number systems that may not be ordered and may not even have elements that can be classified as 'positive' or 'negative', provided that they satisfy the axioms for a commutative ring.

This applies to the field $\mathbb{C}$ of complex numbers, and the commutative ring $\mathbb{Z}_n$ ('clock arithmetic' with remainders $0, 1, 2, \ldots, n - 1$ after division by n). It also applies to polynomials in one or more variables whose coefficients can be rational numbers, real numbers, complex numbers, integers modulo n, or even elements from any specified commutative ring.

In the cases of the ring $\mathbb{Z}_n$ of integers modulo n and the field $\mathbb{C}$ of complex numbers, the negatives of given elements may be embodied by symmetry. For instance, the negative of the complex number $z = x + iy$ $z = x + iy$ is $-z = -x - iy$, which may be seen as a reflection of the point in a straight line through the origin. (Figure 8.20.)

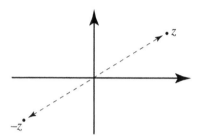

Figure 8.20. The additive inverse in $\mathbb{C}$.

For Z_n, with its elements evenly spaced around a circle, the inverse of x is found by reflecting in the vertical axis. (Figure 8.21.)

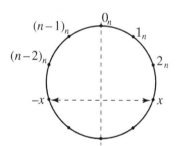

Figure 8.21. The additive inverse in $\mathbb{Z}_n$.

In these two examples, we still have a visual representation that reveals the relationship between x and $-x$ as a symmetry. But we do not need to appeal to a visual symmetry to prove the relationship $(-a)(-b) = ab$. We now know that it is true for any elements in any commutative ring.[13]

---

[13] More generally, the multiplication does not need to be commutative. If the distributive law (D) is broadened to include both $a(b + c) = ab + ac$ and $(b + c)a = ba + ca$, then the commutative axiom (M2) can be removed and the theorem is still true in a general ring. An example is the ring of $n - n$ matrices.

4.5 *The Power of Axiomatic Proof*

This reveals the ultimate power of the axiomatic formal world. Once a formal structure has been framed as an axiomatic system and theorems have been proved within that system, then all the theorems apply in any system that obeys the axioms. While the embodied and symbolic world grow in generality through extensional blends that change the meanings of the embodiment and symbolism, the axiomatic formal world consists of formal deductions that hold in *any* structure that satisfies the axioms, including those known now and any encountered in the future.

The deductions in an axiomatic system give the ultimate form of crystalline concept with properties deduced from axioms and definitions. The rescarch mathematician can select axioms of his or her own choice to formulate required properties in any interesting context and, provided that the axioms are consistent, then all the properties deduced from axioms and subsequent definitions remain true in any more general context that also satisfies the given axioms and definitions. Mathematics can now be extended to new, previously unchartered territory, to solve old problems in new ways and to find solutions of new problems that arise in the exploration of new realms of thought.

For this reason, mathematicians value formal proof as the final test of validity above all other kinds of specific embodiment or symbolism. Yet mathematicians continue to have human qualities that are more than the application of formal logic. The world of axiomatic formalism is a new world in which problem-solving activities ask new questions, formulate new hypotheses, and seek new proofs that are then organized into theorem-proof structures.

The product of research, once formally proved, may then be used by wider communities to apply to new contexts, so that the full range of mathematical thinking may be of benefit to the whole community in ways that allow society to evolve into the future.

This brings us to a point in our journey where we have formulated the cognitive growth of mathematical thinking from embodiment and symbolism to formalism. Chapter 9 will study the historical development of mathematics using the three-world framework that led to the modern view of mathematical proof. We will then be in a position to return to the journeys faced by our students as they make the transition from the embodiment and symbolism of school mathematics to the formalism of pure mathematics.

III
Interlude

9   The Historical Evolution of Mathematics

The mathematics we use today is part of the ongoing evolution of ideas as succeeding generations build on the progress of their predecessors. At this current time in history, we can see the mathematical landscape changing before our eyes as computers allow us to operate mathematically in ways that were unimaginable a generation ago.

In each generation, children are introduced to the concepts currently available in their culture, and as adults they may blend ideas together to create new forms of mathematics to pass on to subsequent generations. The history of mathematics is the story of these successive advances.

This chapter focuses on events that trace the evolution of mathematics over the centuries, to illustrate that historical development also follows a sequence formulated in the three worlds of mathematics from practical embodiment and symbolism, to the development of theoretical mathematics in geometry and algebra, with their blending in the Cartesian plane and the problematic issues of negative and complex numbers in the solution of equations. The development of the calculus offers a new blending of perception of change and the power of symbolism accompanied by the problematic notion of infinitesimal. The advances of the nineteenth century addressed problematic aspects in a range of areas, leading to the formalism of the twentieth century, which continues to develop increasing power while supportive and problematic issues continue as the boundaries of mathematical thinking extend into the future.

1. The Development of Number Notations and Arithmetic

As humans developed from being hunter-gatherers, whose main preoccupation was travelling to find food, they joined together to form stable communities that required mathematics to organize their lives. Their new way of life farming the land and keeping domestic animals required methods of measuring and valuing commodities and an understanding of the calendar to predict the changing seasons. In the great river basins between the Tigris and Euphrates in Mesopotamia and the Nile delta in Egypt, two civilizations developed their own ways of operating with whole numbers and fractions.

In Mesopotamia, around 2 millennia BC, the Babylonians had long used clay tablets to record information with a stylus shaped to provide a thin line (⟋) to represent one unit and a triangular shaped wedge (➤) to represent ten units. The division of the year into approximately 360 days suggested a sexagesimal system in which 10 units made a ten and 6 tens made 60. Successive groups of up to 60 were written from left to right, from largest to smallest. (Figure 9.1.)

23   83 (60+23)

Figure 9.1. Babylonian positional value in base 60.

The notation was used flexibly depending on the context to represent different size units; for instance, the representation of 83 could also be read as 83 sixtieths to represent the number $1 + \frac{23}{60}$. This led to a flexible arithmetic of numbers typified by the drawing on a tablet in the Yale Babylonian Collection showing a square with side 30 and the diagonal numbered by symbols representing 42, 25, 35. Translating this into fractions gives $42 + \frac{25}{60} + \frac{35}{60^2}$, which is 30 times 1.414213: an excellent approximation of $\sqrt{2}$ accurate to five decimal places. The same approximation continued to be used by Ptolemy in his mathematical tables more than two thousand years later.[1]

The Egyptians developed a base ten system, using I to represent one, ∩ for ten, ϑ for 100 and so on. This system could unambiguously represent small whole numbers, such as ∩ I I I (a ten and three ones) for 13. The order is not critical as I I I ∩ or ∩ ∩ I both clearly represent 13, unlike modern symbols where 13 and 31 stand for different numbers. In practice the symbols were written in groups for easy scanning.

Egyptian symbols are easily added, for instance, thirteen and eight is

∩ I I I   I I I I I I I I I

and ten of the units can be grouped like this:

∩ | I I I   I I I I I I I | I

---

[1] Neugebauer (1969), p. 35.

to be replaced by a ten symbol ∩ to give the result:

∩∩|

which is 21.

Multiplication was performed by a procedure of repeated addition using an efficient doubling technique. To multiply, say, 13 times 21, rather than add thirteen lots of ∩∩| together, an Egyptian scribe would perform a succession of doublings, with multiplier 2, to calculate two lots of 21, then four lots, then eight lots; then (seeing that 13 is $8 + 4 + 1$) would use the rows containing 1, 4 and 8 to add together $21 + 84 + 168$ to get the required product (Figure 9.2).

multiplier		*duplication*		*calculations required*
I	(1)	∩∩ I		✓
II	(2)	∩∩∩∩ II		
IIII	(4)	∩∩∩∩∩∩∩ IIII		✓
IIIIIIII	(8)	ϑ∩∩∩∩∩ IIIIIIII		✓
∩III	(13)	ϑϑ∩∩∩∩∩∩∩ III	(273)	*(adding rows 1, 3, 4)*

Figure 9.2. Calculating 13 times 21 by successive doubling and adding selected results.

Division used the reverse procedure. To divide 65 by 13, the scribe would write a column beginning with 13 and then double and redouble, stopping at $4 \times 13 = 52$, before the result exceeds 65. (Figure 9.3.) Taking 52 from 65 gives 13, which is in row 1, and adding the multipliers in rows 1 and 4 gives the answer 5.

multiplier		*duplication*		*calculations required*
I	(1)	∩∩ III	(13)	✓
II	(2)	∩∩ IIIIII	(26)	
IIII	(4)	∩∩∩∩∩∩ IIII	(52)	✓
IIIII	(5)	∩∩∩∩∩∩ IIIII	(65)	*(adding rows 1, 4)*

Figure 9.3. Dividing 65 by 13 by successive doubling of 13.

If the division is not exact, the Egyptians represented fractions by writing the reciprocal of a number (say 1 over 21) with an oval shape over the original. So 'one twenty-first' is written as

Other fractions (with the exception of two thirds, which has its own symbol) were written as a combination of unitary fractions, for instance, $\frac{3}{4}$ is written as $\frac{1}{2} + \frac{1}{4}$ (⌒⌒⌒ ⌒⌒⌒⌒) and $\frac{2}{13}$ as $\frac{1}{8} + \frac{1}{52} + \frac{1}{104}$. As a rule, different unitary fractions were used, so $\frac{2}{7}$ was not written as $\frac{1}{7} + \frac{1}{7}$ but as $\frac{1}{4} + \frac{1}{28}$. This made the arithmetic of fractions highly complicated.

In the Rhind Papyrus (c. 1650 BC), preserved in the British Museum[2], a scribe had written a table of values of fractions of the form one tenth, two tenths, up to nine tenths as sums of unitary fractions. He uses this information to solve six successive problems to divide a number of loaves between ten men.

Dividing one loaf among ten clearly gives each man $\frac{1}{10}$. However, the scribe has to use the available methods of arithmetic to show that the ten parts make up a whole loaf. To calculate ten times $\frac{1}{10}$ he uses the standard duplicating technique together with the list of unitary fractions to calculate the result, so he needs to calculate twice $\frac{1}{10}$, then four times $\frac{1}{10}$, then eight times $\frac{1}{10}$. Because 2 and 8 makes 10, the value of 10 times $\frac{1}{10}$ is calculated by adding the values for twice $\frac{1}{10}$ plus eight times $\frac{1}{10}$. From the table of tenths represented as unitary fractions, he knows that twice $\frac{1}{10}$ is $\frac{1}{5}$, four times $\frac{1}{10}$ is $\frac{1}{3} + \frac{1}{15}$ and eight times $\frac{1}{10}\frac{1}{5}$ is $\frac{2}{3} + \frac{1}{10} + \frac{1}{30}$. Two men plus eight men therefore have plus $\frac{2}{3} + \frac{1}{10} + \frac{1}{30}$, which simplifies to give 1! Other problems show how to share 2, 6, 7, 8 and 9 loaves between ten men using the same techniques in detail.

It would be incredible to think that Ahmes, the scribe who wrote this text, was not aware directly that ten times a tenth is one. The Rhind papyrus is a set of textbook exercises for drilling students in practical arithmetic and it works relentlessly through the customary techniques. Nevertheless, it illustrates the complication of the arithmetic of ancient Egyptian fractions.

Around 450 BC, the ancient Greeks developed an alphabetic numbering system, using their 24-letter alphabet together with three Phoenician letters to give a total of 27 symbols. These were used to represent $1, 2, 3, \ldots, 9$, then $10, 20, 30, \ldots, 90$ and $100, 200, 300, \ldots, 900$. For instance, α (alpha), β (beta), γ (gamma) stood for 1, 2, 3 respectively, ι (iota), κ (kappa), λ (lambda) for 10, 20, 30 and ρ (rho), σ (sigma), τ (tau) for 100, 200, 300. This allowed numbers less than a thousand to be written as a combination of at most three symbols, for instance, κ for 20, $\kappa\alpha$ for 21 and $\tau\kappa\alpha$ for 321.

It is a compact notation and has some of the patterns of our modern system, for instance, just as $1 + 2 = 3$ is related to $21 + 2 = 23$, so the addition

[2] Chace (1927–1929).

of ι and β gives λ and addition of $\kappa\iota$ and β gives $\kappa\lambda$. However, patterns such as those relating

$$1 + 2 = 3, \quad 10 + 20 = 30, \quad 100 + 200 = 300$$

in our modern notation are not evident in the Greek equivalents:

α plus β makes λ, ι plus κ makes λ, ρ plus σ equals τ.

Mental arithmetic in this Greek system is therefore more complicated than in our modern decimal system.

The Greeks embodied properties of whole number by laying out pebbles. For instance, an even number allowed the pebbles to be paired together in twos, while an odd number had two equal sets of pebbles, with one pebble over. By arranging an odd number of pebbles around two sides of a square starting with a pebble in the upper left corner, successive odd numbers could be added together to see that their sum is a square. (Figure 9.4.)

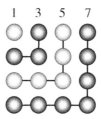

Figure 9.4. The sum of the first four odd numbers is embodied as the square of 4.

In a similar manner, if a number is a product of two whole numbers then that number of pebbles can be laid out as a rectangle of pebbles whose sides are given by the two numbers. Such a number is called a *rectangular* number and those that are not rectangular are *prime*, leading to a study of prime numbers and Euclid's famous proof that the number of primes is potentially infinite.

The Romans built their number system on fives and tens. There are various suggestions for the meanings of this symbolism. One that I like is the idea that five is a handful, represented by a V, which is what you see when you hold your hand up and look sideways on with a thumb open and fingers together (Figure 9.5). Two Vs, one upon another inverted, make an X representing ten. This, together with a vertical stroke representing a one, gives a ready notation for small numbers, for instance XVII for ten plus five

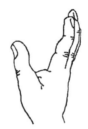

Figure 9.5. Five as a handful.

plus two, which is seventeen. The number of symbols used is minimized by using a subtractive mechanism, so that when a smaller unit is placed before a larger, it is to be subtracted: IV being one from five, namely four, using only two symbols instead of the four required by the notation IIII. But now the order of the symbols does matter: XIX is nineteen, XXI is twenty-one and IXX is not used.

The Roman number system is satisfactory for representing numbers but not practical for operating with them. Instead, Roman civilization used a physical abacus to perform whole number arithmetic. Fractions of a quantity were handled by having smaller subunits, just as today we have a hundred centimetres in a metre, and speak of 75 centimetres instead of three-quarters of a metre.

The Chinese number system has words for the nine digits and for ten, a hundred, a thousand and so on (Figure 9.6). These are used in a highly efficient way. A short monosyllabic word suffices for each of the numbers from one to ten, then eleven is 'shi yi' (ten one), twelve is 'shi er' (ten two) and so on. Twenty is 'er shi' (two-ten), twenty-one is 'er shi yi' (two-ten one), eighty-seven is 'ba shi qi' (eight-ten seven). Larger numbers are expressed as a sum of digits times powers of ten, for instance, 356 is 'san-bai wu-shi lai' (three-hundred five-ten six). Because the powers of ten are mentioned explicitly, there is no problem with zero digits such as in 203, which may be called 'er-bai san' (two-hundred three).

Chinese number symbolism is a highly efficient representation that also lends itself to systematic arithmetic. Its explicit base ten system makes it easier for young children to learn than our English spoken version, which has irregular word patterns between ten and twenty. Unlike modern decimal numbers in which there are repetitions every thousand, the Chinese system uses repetitions every ten thousand, so that 'shi-yi wan' is eleven 'ten thousands' and bai wan is a hundred ten-thousands (a million).

1	一	*yi*
2	二	*er*
3	三	*san*
4	四	*si*
5	五	*wu*
6	六	*liu*
7	七	*qi*
8	八	*ba*
9	九	*jiu*
10	十	*shi*
100	百	*bai*
1000	千	*qian*
10000	萬	*wan*

Figure 9.6. Chinese numerals.

The Chinese notation requires a new symbol to be introduced for each power of ten million. The modern Hindu-Arabic decimal notation has no such weakness. It uses just ten digits 0, 1, 2, 3, 4, 5, 6, 7, 8, 9 and a simple but extremely sophisticated place-value system to represent whole numbers that can be arbitrarily large. In the decimal notation 343, the two threes refer to different things. The first is 3 hundreds, the second is 3 units. By using successive places from right to left to represent units, tens, hundreds, thousands and so on, any whole number can be represented, no matter how large. The original Arabic language reads from right to left, so a number like 925367884 would be read first as 4 units, then 8 tens, 8 hundreds and so on. Our modern Western languages read from left to right have the additional need to scan the whole number to see that the first 9 is nine hundred million to start saying the number name.

The positional notation is useful for highlighting patterns in number operations that help in performing mental arithmetic. For instance, $53 + 4 = 57$, $130 + 40 = 170$, $300 + 400 = 700$ are all manifestations of the operation $3 + 4 = 7$ on single digits. The decimal system is not only an efficient method of *representation*, but it is also highly appropriate for *calculation*. It enables operations of addition, subtraction, multiplication and division to be performed in flexible ways once one has learnt the relevant number facts for working with single-digit numbers.

Mathematicians in China and India developed secure algorithms for the arithmetic of whole numbers based on remembering the basic number facts for single-digit arithmetic, including all products from 1×1 to 9×9.

Both civilizations introduced fractions in their arithmetic long before the Europeans. In the first century AD, the Chinese wrote fractions verbally in terms of dividing into a certain number of equal parts and selecting a number of these; for instance, ¾ is formulated as 'divide into four equal parts and take three'. They had a full arithmetic of fractions using the lowest common denominator for addition. A similar system was used in India.

When Simon Stevin extended the Hindu-Arabic decimal notation for whole numbers to include decimal fractions in 1585,[3] the result was a system that can represent any number – no matter how large or small – to any desired accuracy. Even this passed through a subtle process of compression. Stevin's notation originally used additional symbols to denote the successive positions of tenths, hundredths, thousandths, as in the symbol 327①5②4③2. It took a further small compression to denote the concept in its modern compact form as 327.542. Now the arithmetic of numbers of any size can be performed using operations on highly compressed symbols requiring only ten digits and a decimal point. This gives the flexible system of arithmetic that we use to this day.

The spoken language for numbers still involves many features of our cultural heritage. In English the term 'eleven' comes from the old English *ein leifon*, meaning 'one left over' and 'twelve' is from *twe lif* (two left). This old meaning links the number words to the embodied configuration of our hands. The phenomenon still persists in our children today, where five (a handful) and six (one more than a handful) are added together to give ten and 'one left over'.

After this, the 'teen' numbers repeat the single-digit words with minor irregularities for thirteen and fifteen before regularity sets in with six-teen, seven-teen, eigh(t)-teen and nine-teen. The word twenty comes from the Old English *twe ty* or *twain ty* for 'two tens' and the following numbers have the regular pattern 'twenty-one', 'twenty-two' to 'twenty-nine' with a repeating pattern for successive groups of ten based on the same pattern as the teens (thirty, forty, fifty, sixty, seventy, eighty, ninety). A clearer regularity appears in counting in hundreds – one hundred, two hundred, and on up to nine hundred – then one thousand, one thousand one hundred, one thousand two hundred. Larger numbers, such as 1212 (one thousand

---

[3] See http://en.wikipedia.org/wiki/Simon_Stevin. (Accessed August 29, 2012).

two hundred and twelve) are read by putting together the old words and the later regularity.

Other Western verbal number systems have their own idiosyncrasies. The German system reverses units and tens in three-digit numbers to say 135 as 'ein hundert, fünf und dreisig' (one hundred, five and thirty). A vestige of this system was around in English when I was a child, saying the time '1.25' as 'five and twenty past one.' Now digital watches have produced a more uniform 'one twenty-five'.

The French language has even greater variants, with 'quatre-vingt' (four twenties) to represent 80 and 'quatre vingt dix-neuf' (four twenties and nineteen) to represent 99. The Belgians have simplified this by using their own terms 'octant' and 'nonant' for eighty and ninety. The French usage goes back to an earlier age when the Celts and then the Normans counted in twenties, with 40 described as 'two twenties', 60 as 'three twenties' and 80 as 'four twenties'. The Académie Français in 1694 advocated a change to regularize counting in tens, but this was resisted, especially in Paris, and overall, while numbers up to 69 changed to counting in tens, 70 remained as soixant-dix (sixty-ten), 80 as quatre-vingts (four twenties), and the numbers from 70 to 99 retained their older forms. Such terms have their English equivalents in the use of the word 'score' for twenty and the biblical life span of man being 70 or 'three score years and ten'.

These various examples illustrate that the symbols we use in mathematics are chosen in different forms in different societies and, though they may be good for certain purposes, they can be poor in others. The decimal number notation is extremely powerful, but there are underlying linguistic idiosyncrasies and subtleties that can cause children great difficulties in learning. For instance, the irregularities in language disguise the relationship between single-digit numbers and the corresponding numbers in the range 11 to 19. Children who learn arithmetic in English have far more difficulty with place value than children learning in Chinese. While the English child is using the words 'nine, ten, eleven, twelve, thirteen, ...' as a continuing number sequence, the Chinese child is saying 'nine, ten, ten-one, ten-two, ten-three, ...', which explicitly reveals the distinct roles of tens and units. Evidence shows that whilst few American children have a grasp of place value at age five or six, it occurs with far greater regularity amongst Chinese children of the same age.[4]

---

[4] Ma (1999b).

2. The Development of Geometry and Proof

Practical geometrical constructions were widely used in Babylon and Egypt. For instance, the 'rope-stretchers' of Egypt knew that a rope tied into a triangle with side lengths 3, 4, 5 would make a right-angled triangle, valuable as a practical construction in surveying and building. The concept of proof, however, does not appear to be necessary.

The inquisitive Greeks built a coherent theory of geometry that not only constructed figures, but also deduced consequences of those constructions, leading eventually to the Platonic imagination of figures and the verbal formulation of Euclidean proof.

The Greeks inherited mathematical ideas from both Mesopotamia and Egypt and these differed in some respects. For example, the Babylonian approximation of π was $3\frac{1}{8}$ (3.125) and the Egyptians used $4 \times \left(\frac{8}{9}\right)^2$ (approximately 3.16). So one problem addressed by the Greeks was to calculate a better approximation using a regular polygon with an increasing number of sides. Archimedes visualized the perimeter of a circle lying between the perimeters of two regular polygons inscribed and circumscribed round the circle. Using a polygon with 96 sides, he computed the perimeter to lie between $3\frac{1}{7}$ and $3\frac{10}{71}$.

In ancient Greece there was also a separation between the aristocratic art of geometry and the pragmatic use of arithmetic. For instance, arithmetic may be used to calculate lengths, areas and volumes using appropriate units, but in Euclidean geometry, constructions used a ruler without any subdivisions, so lengths, areas and volumes were not computed, they were compared.

Euclid Book II, Proposition 2, states:

If a straight line is drawn parallel to one of the sides of a triangle, then it cuts the sides of the triangle proportionally; and, if the sides of the triangle are cut proportionally, then the line joining the points of section is parallel to the remaining side of the triangle.

BD is to *AD* also as *CE* is to *AE*, which is written *BD* : *AD* :: *CE* : *AE*. (Figure 9.7.)

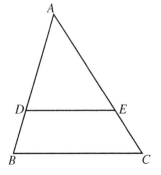

Figure 9.7. Parallel lines and proportionality.

Throughout Euclid, ratios are compared between magnitudes of the same kind. For instance, Euclid proves that 'triangles with the same height are to one another as their bases' equating a ratio between areas to a ratio between lengths.

In blending together ideas of whole numbers and Platonic figures, the Greeks faced the dilemma that the hypotenuse of a right-angled isosceles triangle is not represented as the ratio of two whole numbers. In addition, while the system of whole numbers has a natural unit, namely 1, and all other whole numbers arise from successively adding 1 to the previous number, the geometry of space and distance has no natural unit. Instead one must *choose* a unit of length, as we choose a foot or a metre.

The Greeks did not choose a specific unit in geometry. Their straight edge and compass constructions had no units on the straight edge. Instead, they compared a length *AB* with a shorter length *CD*, by removing successive lengths equal to *CD* from *AB* and counting how many were removed before the remainder *EB* became smaller than *CD*. This approximates the ratio by a whole number and a remainder *EB*. (Figure 9.8.)

Figure 9.8. Dividing one length by another to give a quotient and a remainder.

As *EB* is now smaller than *CD*, it is either zero and reveals *AB* as a precise multiple of *CD*, or one can repeat the process to see how many times *EB* fits into *CD* and so on. This gives a sequence of whole numbers that can be used to give a better and better approximation for the ratio and leads to the concept of *continued fraction*.

In modern notation, we may compare the hypotenuse of an isosceles right triangle to one of its other sides by seeing how often a length 1 can be fitted into a length $\sqrt{2}$. It fits just once, with remainder $r = \sqrt{2} - 1$. Now we must see how often r fits into the length 1, by calculating the ratio of 1 to r to get:

$$\frac{1}{r} = \frac{1}{\sqrt{2} - 1} = \frac{\sqrt{2} + 1}{(\sqrt{2} - 1)(\sqrt{2} + 1)} = 2 + (\sqrt{2} - 1) = 2 + r.$$

This gives

$$\sqrt{2} = 1 + r = 1 + \cfrac{1}{2+r}$$

and we can repeatedly replace r by $\cfrac{1}{2+r}$ to get the continued fraction

$$\sqrt{2} = 1 + r = 1 + \cfrac{1}{2+r} = \cfrac{1}{2+\cfrac{1}{2+r}} = \cfrac{1}{2+\cfrac{1}{2+\cfrac{1}{2+\cdots}}}$$

The Greeks calculated this formula using a geometric argument and wrote down the continued fraction as the sequence consisting of the first whole number 1, and the repeating sequence 2, 2, 2, ... to get the notation [1; 2, 2, 2, ...]. The great benefit is that the square root of 2 is now represented by a sequence of whole numbers. This aesthetic solution to the problem of the irrationality of $\sqrt{2}$ led to the subtle development of ratio and proportion using continued fractions, which took the Greeks in a new direction in the arithmetic of lengths, areas and volumes.

The Greeks were able to calculate approximations for other irrational numbers, such as π, which can be written initially as [3;7,16] in the form:

$$\pi = 3 + \cfrac{1}{7+\cfrac{1}{16+\cdots}}$$

This corresponds to fractional approximations to π in the form

$$3 + \frac{1}{7} = \frac{22}{7} \quad \text{and} \quad 3 + \cfrac{1}{7+\frac{1}{16}} = 3 + \frac{16}{113} = \frac{355}{113}.$$

2.1 Greek Concepts of Infinity and Infinitesimal

The Greeks conceived the sequence of whole numbers as a *potential infinity* rather than an actual infinity, in the sense that, although one could not contemplate the collection of *all* numbers, for any given number, one could always imagine a larger one, potentially imagining as many numbers as desired.

In the opposite direction halving a line segment again and again, gives an ever-smaller length that is never zero. On reflection, this phenomenon can be seen as a natural operation of the human brain. If the brain contemplates a sequence of terms that get smaller at every stage, while never being zero, the natural selective binding is to imagine a variable quantity that is arbitrarily small but non-zero. This suggests that the concept of infinitesimal is a natural product of the biological brain.

On the other hand, there is also the practical fact that if one cuts a physical length in half again and again, it can be done only a relatively small number of times before it is too small to be cut in half again. Try it by folding an A4 piece of paper. How many times can it be folded and cut in half before further halving is impossible? Each division halves the size, and $2^{10} = 1024$, so twenty subdivisions reduces the size to less than $1/1,000,000$ of the original. Even 20 times is a physical impossibility.

The clear difference between theory and practice led the Greeks to dispute which conclusion is correct. Is it possible to subdivide again and again, ad infinitum, to produce an arbitrarily small *infinitesimal* quantity, or does there come a point where the subdivisions can be performed no more to give an *indivisible* quantity?

In the light of this unresolved dispute, the Greeks chose to publish their calculations of area using proofs by 'exhaustion'. They showed that the area could not be smaller or larger than a specified value by a contradiction argument using a close polygonal approximation inside or outside the boundary.

For instance, Archimedes calculated the area inside a parabola cut off by the line *AB* in Figure 9.9 by finding the point *C* on the graph where the tangent is parallel to *AB* and declaring the area to be $\frac{4}{3}$ the area of triangle *ABC*.

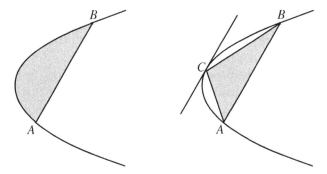

Figure 9.9. The area of the segment of the parabola cut off by *AB* is $\frac{4}{3}$ triangle *ABC*.

His published proof was by exhaustion, using polygonal approximations inside and outside the parabola to show that if the area was different
from that proposed, then it would be possible to fit in a polygon that was
even closer. The result was correct, but how was it conceived in the first
place? More than two millennia later, in 1906, a parchment was found written over another document. The hidden document proved to be a copy of a
translation of a previously unknown work of Archimedes, his *Method*.[5]

This revealed that he considered the two areas as being composed of
straight lines or thin strips with an inspired use of geometry to compare
them. The details are not important. What is significant is that, though the
Greeks offered public proofs of areas formally using the method of exhaustion, in private, Archimedes found the area by an embodied thought experiment in which he imagined the area made up of lines or thin strips. The
distinction between insightful, but problematic, embodied intuition and
the rigor of formal proof was already deeply embedded in Greek thought
more than two thousand years ago.

3. The Development of Algebra

The generalization of arithmetic to algebra began in ancient times. The
Egyptian solution to the problem 'heap plus its seventh is 19' involved
performing the calculation 'heap plus its seventh' in the simple case where
heap equals 7 to get 'heap plus its seventh' is 8, then multiplying the estimate 7 by 19 and dividing by 8 to get the precise solution.

Greek mathematics proved geometrical versions of various algebraic
identities. For instance, Euclid Book II, proposition 4, is a geometric version of the algebraic identity $(a + b)^2 = a^2 + b^2 + 2ab$ in the form: 'if a straight
line is cut at random, then the square on the whole equals the sum of the
squares on the segments plus twice the rectangle contained by the segments.' The objective was to give meanings to constructions in geometry
rather than any attempt at developing symbolic algebra.

The Persian mathematician Al-Khwarizmi, who was familiar with
Euclid Book II, developed a significant new approach in c. 820 AD. He was
an amazing character who wrote a book to introduce the Indian decimal
notation to the West and corrected the calculations of Ptolemy to draw a
more accurate map of the known world.

His major work introduced techniques for solving linear and quadratic equations. These involved 'adding the same quantity to both sides'

---

[5] Archimedes, translated by Heath (1912).

(*al-jabra*) and 'shifting all like terms to one side' (*muqābala*). It is from the Arabic word *al-jabra* that we get the name 'algebra'.

His equations were written in Arabic script, so that what we now write as $x^2 + 10x = 39$ he wrote as a sentence that translates to 'a square and ten roots is equal to 39 units.'[6] His solution was an embodied picture in which he drew a square side x and then arranged an area $10x$ as four rectangles with one side equal to x and the other equal to 10/4 (Figure 9.10).

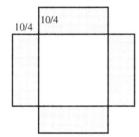 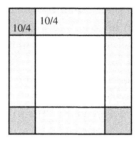

This figure has total area 39.

Adding four squares of side 10/4 to 'complete the square' gives a total area of 39 + 25 = 64.

Figure 9.10. Completing the square.

He then added four squares with sides equal to 10/4, one in each corner, so that the total area is now $39 + 25 = 64$, which gives the side length as $\sqrt{64}$, which is 8. But it is also $x + 2 \times (10/4)$, which is $x + 5$. Subtracting 5 from 8 gives the single solution, $x = 3$.

Similar embodied methods dealt with other types of equation such as $ax^2 = bx$, $ax^2 = c$, $bx = c$, $ax^2 + bx = c$, $ax^2 + c = bx$ and $ax^2 = bx + c$.

In the sixteenth century, Italian mathematicians expressed such equations in Latin. The quadratic equation to find a number such that 'its square equals twice the number plus 8' (which we would write as $x^2 = 2x + 8$) would be written in Latin as 'census equales 2 rebus et 8.' Here 'rebus' ('thing') stands for a number and 'census' for its square. Each form of equation now had a Latin verbal form for its solution. For instance, the only root of the equation written in modern notation as $px + q = x^2$ was expressed as a verbal equivalent of our modern formula:

$$\tfrac{1}{2} p + \sqrt{\tfrac{1}{4} p^2 + q}.$$

[6] Van der Waerden (1980), p. 8.

The search for formulae to solve cubic equations now involved imagining situations in three dimensions or attempting to extend what was known about quadratic equations to generalize to the solution of the cubic. This was more complicated because there are more categories required to express all possible cubics as equations with positive coefficients.

In 1530, the Italian mathematician Tartaglia claimed to have found a method for solving equations of the form $x^3 + px = q$ that he kept secret, but was able to support his case by competing against other mathematicians to produce solutions, defeating all comers. His methods (revealed by Cardan in his *Ars Magna* of 1545[7]) used ingenious symbol manipulation. His method was subtle and quite complicated, but it is useful to consider it in outline to understand how he was able to reduce the problem of solving a cubic equation to the solution of a related quadratic equation for which he already had a solution.

In modern notation, the solution of an equation in the form

$$x^3 + px = q$$

was found by considering the result x to be the difference between the sides of two cubes, so that $x = r - s$ where $r = \sqrt[3]{u}$, $s = \sqrt[3]{v}$. Then

$$\begin{aligned} x^3 &= (r - s)^3 \\ &= r^3 - 3r^2 s + 3rs^2 - s^3 \\ &= r^3 - s^3 - 3rsx. \end{aligned}$$

Substituting this into the equation $x^3 + px = q$ gives

$$r^3 - s^3 - 3rsx + px = q.$$

Looking at this as an identity in x, of the form $a + bx = q$, the equation is satisfied if $a = q$ and $b = 0$, so

$$r^3 - s^3 = q \quad \text{and} \quad 3rs = p.$$

$$r^3 - s^3 = q \quad \text{and} \quad 3rs = p.$$

Rewriting these in terms of $u = r^3$, $v = s^3$ gives

$$u - v = q \quad \text{and} \quad 27uv = p^3.$$

---

[7] Cardano (1545).

Substituting $v = u - q$ from the first into the second gives a *quadratic* equation in u:

$$u^2 = qu + \frac{p^3}{27}.$$

This quadratic is of a form already known and (from the preceding) has the solution

$$u = \sqrt{\left(\tfrac{1}{4}q^2 + \frac{p^3}{27}\right)} + \tfrac{1}{2}q.$$

Because $v = u - q$, this gives

$$u = \sqrt{\left(\tfrac{1}{4}q^2 + \frac{p^3}{27}\right)} - \tfrac{1}{2}q.$$

Finally, and triumphantly(!), this gives the formula for the solution of the cubic equation $x + px = q$ as $x = \sqrt[3]{u} - \sqrt[3]{v}$, or:

$$x = \sqrt[3]{\sqrt{\left(\tfrac{1}{4}q^2 + \frac{p^3}{27}\right)} + \tfrac{1}{2}q} - \sqrt[3]{\sqrt{\left(\tfrac{1}{4}q^2 + \frac{p^3}{27}\right)} - \tfrac{1}{2}q}.$$

Cardan illustrated this by showing that a solution of $x^3 + 6x = 20$ is

$$x = \sqrt[3]{\sqrt{108} + 10} - \sqrt[3]{\sqrt{108} - 10}.$$

He then turned his attention to an equation of the form $x^3 = px + q$ using a similar approach, replacing x by $\sqrt[3]{u} + \sqrt[3]{v}$ to obtain a similar formula, in which a root of $x^3 = 15x + 4$ turned out to be

$$x = \sqrt[3]{2 + \sqrt{-121}} + \sqrt[3]{2 - \sqrt{-121}}.$$

This was problematic. He knew that the square of a non-zero number is positive, so a negative number cannot have a square root.

At first this seemed a dead end. But then, a few years later, the Italian Bombelli attacked the problem by manipulating $\sqrt{-1}$ *as if it satisfied the usual rules of arithmetic*. He found that

$$\left(2 \pm \sqrt{-1}\right)^3 = 2 \pm \sqrt{-121}$$

and so

$$\sqrt[3]{2+\sqrt{-121}} + \sqrt[3]{2-\sqrt{-121}} = \left(2-\sqrt{-1}\right) + \left(2-\sqrt{-1}\right) = 4.$$

The strange root is just the number 4 in disguise! Now it was possible to use these mysterious square roots of negative numbers and end up with a genuine solution! But still, the solution process involved manipulating symbols in a way that does not have a corresponding embodiment.

The French philosopher René Descartes (1596–1650) rejected the idea of square roots of negative numbers and called them 'imaginary'. However, he was also to make important advances that moved mathematical thinking into a new realm of flexibility.

4. Linking Algebra and Geometry

Descartes made significant progress in both mathematics and philosophy. He theorized a dualism between mind and body, identifying the mind with consciousness and self-awareness and distinguishing it from the physical apparatus of the brain. He also introduced algebraic notation and took the Greek idea of ratio and proportion as a basis for calculating the product of two lengths as a length rather than as an area.

In *La Géométrie* (1635) he began by selecting a particular length to be unity 'in order to relate it as close as possible to numbers' and then used geometric constructions to multiply and divide lengths to give answers that are also lengths.

The breakthrough was as profound as it was simple. He simply chose a particular length in the picture to represent a unit and used Greek theorems of proportion to perform calculations.

To multiply two lengths, say *BD* and *BC* in Figure 9.11, he said:

> Let *AB* be taken as unity and let it be required to multiply *BD* by *BC*. I have only to join the points *A* and *C* and draw *DE* parallel to *CA*; then *BE* is the product of *BD* and *BC*.[8]

He also divided one length by another to give a length, saying:

> to divide *BE* by *BD*, I join *E* and *D* and draw *AC* parallel to *DE*, then *BC* is the result of the division.

[8] Descartes, ed. Smith & Latham (1954), pp. 2–4.

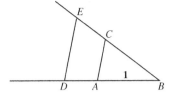

Figure 9.11. Multiplying *BD* by *BC* taking *AB* as unity to get *BE*.

At a stroke he changed the landscape by allowing a full arithmetic of lengths in which the product of two numbers was a number of the same kind, not two lengths multiplied together to give an area.

As if this were not enough, he also went on to introduce the representation of relationships between algebra and geometry in what became known as the Cartesian plane.

In his early twenties, the story goes, he was a soldier, billeted in a peasant house in Bavaria. There was no war and he had little to do, spending much of his spare time in a room with a stove that warmed the ceiling where flies congregated. As he lay staring at them, he thought how he could describe the position of a particular fly. In a flash of inspiration he realized he could relate its position to a corner of the room, measuring a distance, say *x* along one wall, then a distance *y* at right angles to meet the fly. (Figure 9.12.)

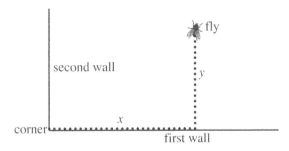

Figure 9.12. The fly on the ceiling.

This simple observation of flies moving about a ceiling proved to be the key that related geometry to algebra and allowed geometric problems to be investigated by algebraic means and vice versa, bringing together the worlds of embodiment and symbolism. The physical position of the fly could be specified by two numbers (x, y). Geometrical figures such as circles, ellipses, parabolas and so on could now be described by writing down an algebraic relationship between *x* and *y*.

For instance, the algebraic relationship $y = x^2$ could now be plotted geometrically by computing corresponding values such as $x = 0$, $y = 0$; $x = 1$, $y = 1$; $x = 2$, $y = 4$; $x = 3$, $y = 9$; and plotting the points $(0, 0)$, $(1, 1)$, $(2, 4)$, $(3, 9)$. Intermediate points can also be plotted and connected to represent the relationship for a range of values of x and y (Figure 9.13).

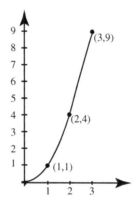

Figure 9.13. $y = x^2$ expressed geometrically.

This link between algebra and geometry is one of the defining moments of mathematical evolution. It enables the two strands of mathematics, one based on visual embodiment and the other on symbolic calculations, to come together and complement each other. The consequences were phenomenal. In the years that followed, there was an explosion of new mathematical ideas.

5. Calculus

By relating algebra and geometry in the manner of Descartes, Isaac Newton (1642–1727) was able to investigate the movement of the planets and produce an entirely new theory that described the motion of the universe. He and Leibniz (1646–1716) independently produced theories of how to calculate the rate of change using the ratio of very small quantities and areas by adding together a large number of very thin strips. Their methods gave powerful ways of calculating rates of change, lengths of curves, areas and volumes. Yet it proved difficult to explain them in logical terms. The struggle to understand and explain the infinitely large and infinitely small continued in the centuries that followed and is taken up in detail in Chapter 11.

Armed with the techniques of the calculus, successive generations developed previously inconceivable tools for modelling, computation and prediction, enabling them to plan the paths of communication satellites above the earth, spaceships travelling to the moon and back and probes travelling to the outermost reaches of the solar system.

6. Giving Meaning to Complex Numbers

In the latter half of the sixteenth century, as calculus was flowering, the arithmetic of imaginary numbers continued to be a mystery. Newton rejected complex roots because they failed to have a physical or geometric meaning. Leibniz referred to $\sqrt{-1}$ as 'that portent of the ideal world, that amphibian between being and not being'. Even though Wallis in his 1685 book on algebra suggested a geometric meaning for $x + y\sqrt{-1}$ as a step x along the horizontal axis and a step y at right angles, the idea was not generally accepted. Instead algebraic methods that worked with positive numbers were applied to negative numbers to obtain symbolic solutions of equations with no embodied meaning.

Euler introduced the symbol i for $\sqrt{-1}$ and manipulated it as one might manipulate any other algebraic symbol, except that whenever a calculation produced the term i^2, this was replaced by -1. Any 'imaginary number' of the form $\sqrt{-c}$ could be written as $i\sqrt{c}$ and any 'complex' number could be written as $x + iy$. Complex numbers revealed undreamt of relationships through calculation. For instance, the calculus gave methods of calculating functions by power series to give the exponential function as

$$e^x = 1 + \frac{x}{1!} + \frac{x^2}{2!} + \cdots + \frac{x^n}{n!} + \cdots$$

where $n!$ (n factorial) denotes $1 \times 2 \times 3 \times \cdots \times n$.

Measuring angles in radians rather than in degrees, he was able to express the trigonometric functions in series as:

$$\sin x = x - \frac{x^3}{3!} + \frac{x^5}{5!} + \cdots$$

$$\cos x = 1 - \frac{x^2}{2!} + \frac{x^4}{4!} + \cdots$$

He then used these three series, replacing x by ix, and manipulated the symbols as if they obeyed the usual rules of arithmetic to give the remarkable identity:

$$e^{ix} = \cos x + i \sin x.$$

Putting $x = \pi$ gives

$$e^{i\pi} = \cos \pi + i \sin \pi = -1$$

and multiplying by −1 gives

$$-e^{i\pi} = 1.$$

This remarkable result combines four problematic symbols of mathematics – the minus sign, the irrational numbers e and π, and the imaginary number i – to give the simplest number of all: 1.

For a mathematician seeking beauty in simplicity, this solution is the sweetest possible result. All the complications of symbolism reduce to an elemental expression of unity.

Furthermore, as intimated in Chapters 4[9] and 7[10], complex numbers give new insights into the properties of trigonometric functions using the equation $e^{ix} = \cos x + i \sin x$ with $x = \theta + \varphi$ to expand the identity

$$e^{i(\theta + \varphi)} = e^{i\theta} e^{i\varphi}$$

to give

$$\cos(\theta + \varphi) + i \sin(\theta + \varphi) = (\cos \theta + i \sin \theta)(\cos \varphi + i \sin \varphi)$$
$$= \cos \theta \cos \varphi - \cos \theta \cos \varphi$$
$$+ i(\sin \theta \cos \varphi + \cos \theta \sin \varphi)$$

and compare real and imaginary parts to give the trigonometric formulae:

$$\cos(\theta + \varphi) = \cos \theta \cos \varphi - \cos \theta \cos \varphi$$
$$\sin(\theta + \varphi) = \sin \theta \cos \varphi + \cos \theta \sin \varphi$$

Unlike the proof in triangle trigonometry (Figure 3.14), which refers only to angles in a triangle, this holds generally in analytic trigonometry.

Today, mathematicians are able to conceive such calculations with complex numbers in the complex plane. To reach this level, however, took a long time in history as the problematic meaning of complex numbers remained firmly in the consciousness of mathematicians as 'useful

---

[9] See Chapter 4, Section 2.16, pp. 111–113.
[10] See Chapter 7, Sections 2.2–2.4, pp. 166–171.

fictions' throughout the eighteenth century, having no real meaning yet were remarkably useful for practical calculations. Even as late as 1831, the celebrated mathematician de Morgan wrote:

> The imaginary expression $\sqrt{(-a)}$ and the negative expression $-b$ have this resemblance, that either of them occurring as the solution of a problem indicates some inconsistency or absurdity. As far as real meaning is concerned, both are equally imaginary, since $0 - a$ is as inconceivable as $\sqrt{(-a)}$.[11]

His personal conceptions, which he shared with his peers, had algebraic aspects that allowed him to operate successfully with negative and complex numbers yet had embodied aspects that continued to be problematic.

Nevertheless, changes in conception were already spreading through the mathematical community. At the turn of the nineteenth century, at least three mathematicians (Wessel[12] in Denmark, Gauss[13] in Germany and Argand[14] in France) began to embody complex numbers by imagining $x + iy$ to be the point (x, y) in the plane. The complex number i was now seen, not just as a fictitious symbol, but as a genuine point $(0, 1)$ on the vertical axis, one unit above the origin. The problem that the square of a number might be negative began to be seen in a new light. Previously the argument said that the square of a positive or negative number is positive. Now this argument could be seen to apply only to numbers on the x-axis. It need not apply to the square of i because this does not lie on the horizontal number line, but at point on the y-axis a unit distance *above* it.

Nowadays, we can think of multiplication of complex numbers as transformations of the plane. Multiplying by complex number $re^{i\theta}$ magnifies the distance from the origin by a scalar factor r and turns the plane about the origin through an angle θ. The complex number i at the point $(0,1)$ has polar coordinates $r = 1$, $\theta = \pi/2$ and so multiplying by $i = e^{i\pi/2}$ turns the plane through a right angle.

In this way the symbolic manipulation of complex numbers is blended with the embodied transformations of geometry to give a new knowledge blend with complex numbers represented as points in the plane and the arithmetic of symbols given by geometric transformations.

In the nineteenth century, many old problems were given new solutions using complex numbers. Very quickly, the philosophical difficulties

---

[11] De Morgan (1831).
[12] Wessel (1799).
[13] Gauss worked with complex numbers as early as 1797. He used the concept of the complex plane in a public lecture (Gauss, 1831).
[14] Argand (1806).

associated with these numbers ceased to be a problem. They were represented as physical points in the plane and could be 'seen' as a new way of looking at old problems.

This historical development reinforces the observation in Chapter 7 that the development of mathematical ideas need not always build from embodiment to symbolism. The proposed Brunerian sequence through enactive, iconic and symbolic does not necessarily follow this apparently self-evident sequence at all levels. The symbolism of the solution of quadratic and cubic equations developed operational meanings long before any embodiment was imagined. Sometimes enactive ideas in more advanced mathematics are recognized explicitly only *after* visual iconic ideas. For instance, in my own personal development of the calculus, to be discussed in Chapter 11, I developed a dynamic visual approach to differentiation[15] at least a decade before I realized its embodied/enactive underpinning by moving my hand along a curve to sense its changing slope and represent it visually as the slope function that leads to the derivative.[16]

7. The Birth of Modern Formal Mathematics

7.1 *The Crisis of Meaning in Geometry*

During the latter part of the nineteenth century, *Homo sapiens* was reaping the benefits of mathematical science, but, at the same time, cracks were beginning to appear in the theory. For more than two thousand years, Euclidean geometry had been the bastion of mathematical rigor and proof. Even though pictures were drawn to represent the ideal figures, the main theoretical basis lay in setting out verbal definitions and making logical deductions. Highly subtle difficulties arose in making certain that the verbal definitions and deductions were self-contained and did not depend on any implicit assumptions based on our perceptions of the pictures. For instance, one of the axioms of geometry, the 'parallel postulate', phrased in a version known as 'Playfair's axiom',[17] says: 'for each line L and point P not on L, there exists precisely *one* line through P that is parallel to L' (Figure 9.14).

In the physical world we live in, this idea is self-evident. If we tilt the line through P a little, it will meet the line L on one side and if we tilt it the

---

[15] Tall (1986a).
[16] Tall (2009).
[17] Playfair (1860), p. 291.

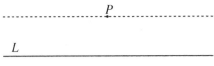

Figure 9.14. The parallel axiom.

other way it will meet *L* on the other side. The embodied world we imagine in our minds is like that. When we perform a thought experiment on the picture, the parallel postulate is clearly true. However, it had an annoying feature that – no matter how individuals tried over the centuries – it did not seem to be possible to either prove it to be true as a consequence of the other axioms, or to show that it was independent of them.

In the nineteenth century, Bolyai and Lobachevsky revealed a new way of looking at the problem.[18] The parallel postulate, as phrased, depends subtly on our embodiment of the world. We see the picture naturally on a flat plane and it did not occur to classical geometers to think of the problem in any other way. However, by considering geometry on other types of surfaces, and interpreting the terms 'point', 'line' and 'parallel' in appropriate ways (e.g., a 'line' might be the shortest distance between two points on a curved surface; two 'lines' might be considered 'parallel' if they never meet), new forms of geometry were invented in which the parallel postulate was no longer true.

For instance, we might invent a new system in which, given a 'point' *P* not on a 'line' *L*, it is possible to have no 'lines' through *P* that are 'parallel' to *L*; it might also be possible to invent other systems in which there might be more than one 'parallel line'.

Bolyai and Lobachevsky did just that. They designed new geometries called 'elliptic' geometry that had no parallel lines through a given point, and 'hyperbolic' geometry that had several. Later, the great French mathematician Henri Poincaré described a particularly simple form of hyperbolic geometry.[19] He imagined his 'points' and 'lines' to be inside a particular fixed circle *C*. He defined a 'point' to be any point inside *C* and a 'line' to be the part of any circle inside *C* that met the circle *C* at right angles. Given any two 'points' *P*, *Q* (inside *C*) he was able to show (by Euclidean geometry) that there was precisely one 'line' through *P* and *Q* (a circle meeting *C* at right angles). (Figure 9.15.)

---

[18] See http://en.wikipedia.org/wiki/Hyperbolic_geometry (Accessed August 29, 2012).

[19] Poincaré described a model originally proposed by Beltrami (1868). See http://en .wikipedia.org/wiki/Poincaré_disk_model (Accessed August 29, 2012).

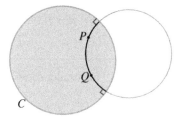

Figure 9.15. A single 'line' through two 'points' *P*, *Q*.

As only points inside circle *C* are counted as 'points', two 'lines' are considered to 'meet' in a 'point' only if that 'point' is inside the circle. This means that, given a 'line' *L* and 'point' *P* not on *L*, there may be many 'lines' through *P* that do not 'meet' *L*. (Figure 9.16.)

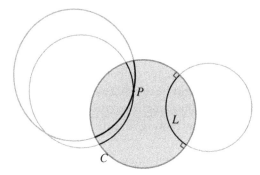

Figure 9.16. Two 'lines' through *P* that do not meet the 'line' *L*.

If we say two 'lines' that do not meet are 'parallel' then, in this geometry, there are many 'lines' through *P* that are 'parallel' to the 'line' *L*. This is an example of a hyperbolic geometry with very interesting properties. For instance, as the 'lines' are actually parts of circles, we can measure the 'angle' between two 'lines' by measuring the angles between the tangents to those circles. This measure of angle is very interesting, for if we define a 'triangle' to consist of three 'lines', then the sum of the angles inside a 'triangle' no longer add up to 180°. The sum of the 'angles' in any 'triangle' in this geometry is always *less* than 180°!

On the other hand, if we study geometry on a sphere, which is, after all, the essential shape of our Earth, then we can take straight lines to be great circles and we can measure angles between them again in terms of the angles between the tangents to the great circles at the points of intersection. As we saw in Chapter 8, the angles in any spherical triangle always add up to *more* than 180°. For instance, we can easily take two great circles through the north pole, *A*, at right angles and take the base of the spherical triangle *BC* on the equator to find a triangle where all three angles are right angles! (Figure 9.17.)

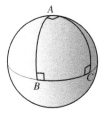

Figure 9.17. A spherical triangle with three right angles.

These new geometries revealed Euclidean geometry in a new light. For more than two thousand years, human beings envisaged points and lines as entities in a plane with planes lying in our familiar three-dimensional space. Now we needed to take account of other possibilities.

In a moment of inspiration in a beer cellar, the great German mathematician David Hilbert suddenly realized that the names we give to concepts are not what matters. It is immaterial whether the concepts are called 'points', 'lines' and 'planes'; they could just as well be called 'tables', 'chairs' and 'beer mugs'.[20] They could be any other kind of entities, such as the 'points' and 'lines' in Poincaré's geometry or on the sphere. They could be completely different entities. What matters is that the named concept satisfies appropriate properties specified in a formal definition. This shift of attention, from 'known objects' to 'concepts given only by their properties', emancipated mathematics from the confines of a single embodiment and allowed us to conceive of formal ideas specified only by their axiomatically defined properties.

From that point on, the theory of mathematics moved away from concepts based on our sensory perception to formal concepts defined in terms of set-theoretic definitions and formal proofs. However, this did not remove intuition from mathematics; it *extended* it. Mathematicians found that formally defined objects often led to theorems that could be imagined in unsuspected new ways. The strange square root of a negative number was imagined as a point in the plane, and the equally peculiar idea that through a given point there could be several lines parallel to a given line can be visualized using the Poincaré model. The difference is that these strange ideas have formal definitions in a coherent context where their properties can be deduced by formal proof.

[20] Reid (1996), p. 57.

7.2 *The Arithmetic of Infinity*

Geometry was not the only part of mathematics that was in a state of flux in the nineteenth century. In analysis, mathematicians were using infinite series to get good approximations to mathematical functions after the manner pioneered by Euler. However, such series presented subtle problems. For the infinite series

$$\tfrac{1}{2} + \tfrac{1}{4} + \tfrac{1}{8} + \cdots .$$

the sum of two terms is

$$\tfrac{1}{2} + \tfrac{1}{4} = \tfrac{3}{4},$$

which is $\tfrac{1}{4}$ less than 1.

The sum of three terms is

$$\tfrac{1}{2} + \tfrac{1}{4} + \tfrac{1}{8} = \tfrac{7}{8},$$

which is $\tfrac{1}{8}$ less than 1, and as each succeeding term is added, the difference between the sum and the number 1 is halved.

After adding n terms, the sum is

$$\tfrac{1}{2} + \tfrac{1}{4} + \cdots + (\tfrac{1}{2})^n = 1 - (\tfrac{1}{2})^n .$$

It is therefore 'reasonable' to suppose that the sum of *all* the terms is

$$\tfrac{1}{2} + \tfrac{1}{4} + \cdots + (\tfrac{1}{2})^n + \cdots = 1 .$$

Or at least, it is incredibly *close* to 1. But if we allow ourselves to add up infinite sums like this, what is the sum of the following?

$$1 - 1 + 1 - 1 + 1 - \cdots .$$

If we bracket the terms thus:

$$(1 - 1) + (1 - 1) + (1 - 1) + \cdots ,$$

we get

$$0 + 0 + 0 + \cdots ,$$

which is zero, but if we bracket it thus:

$$1 - (1-1) - (1-1) - \cdots,$$

we get

$$1 - 0 - 0 - \cdots,$$

which is 1. Does this mean that $0 = 1$? Or have we done something illegal?

7.3 *The Development of a Formal Approach*

Prior to the nineteenth century, mathematics consisted of practical and theoretical ideas, developed from natural origins. Newton's major work, the *Principia*, had the full title *Philosophiæ Naturalis Principia Mathematica* which is Latin for "The Mathematical Principles of Natural Philosophy". From natural philosophy grew 'natural science' which uses the Latin term 'scientia' (knowledge) to describe the science of nature. Theoretical aspects of mathematics were based on natural origins.

However, the crises that developed in the nineteenth century caused a rethinking of the foundations of mathematics. Instead of basing arguments on natural origins, mathematicians began to specify concepts using formal definitions based on carefully selected properties as a basis for mathematical proof. Instead of trying to prove things that are 'obvious', such as the parallel postulate in geometry, or the fact that for any two numbers a, b, then $a + b = b + a$, mathematicians selected certain properties such as these and took them as foundational *axioms* in new theories. The statement that

$$a + b = b + a \quad \text{for all } a, b$$

is conceived as a basic axiom (the 'commutative law') along with a list of other rules that define number systems. These basic axioms are selected in such a way that other properties of the defined number systems can be deduced from them. This is quite a subtle process and needs a very careful choice of generative axioms.

More generally, mathematicians developed their theories by defining all the mathematical concepts they require and using the definitions as a basis for logical deductions of the properties of these concepts. For instance, they got out of the impasse of the exact meaning of the infinite sum

$$\tfrac{1}{2} + \tfrac{1}{4} + \tfrac{1}{8} + \cdots$$

by focusing not on the process of computing the sum for more and more terms, but on the specific value that these sums get closer to. The limit is this value. In this case the limit is 1. An infinite sum that gets close to a specific limit is said to be *convergent*.

In the case of the attempted sum

$$1 - 1 + 1 - 1 + 1 - \cdots$$

the sum of 2 terms is 0, of 3 terms is 1, of 4 terms is 0, and the sum oscillates between 0 and 1. It does not get close to any single limit value and the infinite sum is not convergent. This distinction between infinite sums that have limits and those that do not allows us to focus on the theory of limits for convergent sums and exclude all cases that are not convergent. In this way a mathematician can build a theory of convergence that restricts consideration only to convergent sums to give a rich and consistent theory.

7.4 *New Views of Mathematics*

At the turn of the twentieth century, new foundations of mathematics were developed in several different directions, each of which focused on different aspects of the whole enterprise. Of these, three distinct philosophies came to the fore: *intuitionism, logicism* and *formalism*.[21]

Intuitionism is a theory formulated by Brouwer, based on the philosophy of Kant, that mathematics develops from our intuitions of space, time and number and that theorems should be deduced directly from these fundamental ideas in a finite number of steps. In particular, intuitionism accepted potential infinity (there are as many numbers as we wish) but rejected actual infinity (the concept of 'all' numbers); it also rejected proofs by contradiction.

Logicism is an approach to mathematics introduced by Gottlieb Frege and extended by Bertrand Russell and Alfred North Whitehead where the interest is focused on the use of quantified statements and the mechanism of logical deduction.

Formalism is an approach advocated by David Hilbert that is based on the use of axioms and definitions and the proof of theorems in a finite number of logical steps. Unlike the logicist approach, which was based on the pure development of logic, Hilbert saw the formal approach starting with genuine real-world problems, moving to a new level depending entirely

---

[21] See, for example, Snapper (1979) for more details.

on specified axioms and logical deduction. He spoke of this in his famous lecture of 1900 that focused on the new axiomatic framework for mathematics and specified his list of 23 major problems that were central to the development of mathematics in the twentieth century:

> Surely the first and oldest problems in every branch of mathematics spring from experience and are suggested by the world of external phenomena. Even the rules of calculation with integers must have been discovered in this fashion in a lower stage of human civilization, just as the child of today learns the application of these laws by empirical methods.... But, in the further development of a branch of mathematics, the human mind, encouraged by the success of its solutions, becomes conscious of its independence. It evolves from itself alone, often without appreciable influence from without, by means of logical combination, generalization, specialization, by separating and collecting ideas in fortunate ways, in new and fruitful problems, and appears then itself as the real questioner.[22]

In developing a formal approach, he realized that axiomatic systems often developed out of specific problems. For instance, he referred to the intuitive basis of mathematical ideas, such as the order relation $a > b > c$ being visualized as three successive points in order on a line. The subtle part of a formal axiomatic approach is not that the symbols fail to have meaning. On the contrary, they have *multiple* meanings. They apply not just to a particular example that satisfies the given definitions, but to *any* example that satisfies the definitions.

This extends mathematics from working with a particular theory in a particular context to a general theory that applies in *all* contexts satisfying the axioms. It was this pragmatic view of the formal approach that found most favour in the mathematical community.

Broadly speaking, mathematicians focused on genuine problems, developed general theories, and established the truth of propositions using formal definitions and deductive proof. En route, they might develop new ideas that may depend on the symbolism and logical deductions rather than on any embodiment, just as Jerome Cardan developed new extensions to negative and imaginary numbers that at the time had no embodiment. Such theories might eventually develop a new embodiment just as the incomprehensible notion of complex numbers arising from the algebra of the seventeenth century were embodied as familiar points in the plane. With the arrival of the formalism of Hilbert, mathematics at last had a full axiomatic basis.

---

[22] Hilbert (1900).

7.5 *The Flaw in Formalism*

The glow of the new formalism lasted for thirty years. In 1931, Kurt Gödel used these very axiomatic methods to produce a theorem that struck a body blow to formalism.[23] He used an infinite counting argument to prove that there must be theorems in arithmetic that are definitely true, but for which no finite proof exists. Essentially, the formalist approach was flawed because it sought to accomplish more than it could hope to achieve. A set (for instance the set of counting numbers) might be *infinite*, but each proof about properties of a set had to be performed in a *finite* number of steps so that it could be written down. Gödel showed that there are simply too many theorems to prove about an infinite set for them all to be achieved in a finite number of steps.

Despite the apparently mortal blow, there are still many theorems that *can* be proved in axiomatic systems. The sights simply need to be set lower. Instead of trying to prove *all* theorems in an axiomatic system (which Gödel showed is not possible), professional mathematicians continue to use a formal presentation of mathematics to specify and prove many theorems that are amenable to the formalist paradigm. This has generated a vast corpus of formal theory.

Controversies continue unresolved. Some mathematicians continue to insist on giving explicit constructions of mathematical entities, and do not allow proof by contradiction. This is a valid approach in its own right with much to recommend it. In the end, however, the choice that is likely to lead to the greater conquests is the one that offers the greater power and at the moment, it is Hilbert's formalism that continues to predominate, while steadily being extended as mathematics expands.

7.6 *Embodied Foundations for Formalism*

Formal theorems need to be conceived in the first place, and this is done by human brains working with mental images to relate ideas together to imagine what theorems might be usefully proved before they are put in a logical sequence. When the veteran mathematician Jacques Hadamard enquired of his peers what mental processes they used in doing research, he found that they used all kinds of mental imagery. Einstein explained to him:

> The words of language, as they are written or spoken, do not seem to play any role in my mechanism of thought. The psychical entities which seem to

---

[23] Gödel (1931).

serve as elements in thought are certain signs and more or less clear images which can be 'voluntarily' reproduced and combined.

There is, of course, a certain connection between those elements and relevant logical concepts. It is also clear that the desire to arrive finally at logically connected concepts is the emotional basis of this rather vague play with the above mentioned elements. But taken from a psychological viewpoint, this combinatory play seems to be the essential feature in productive thought – before there is any connection with logical construction in words or other kinds of signs which can be communicated to others.

The above mentioned elements are in my case, of visual and some of muscular type. Conventional words or other signs have to be sought for laboriously only in a secondary stage, when the mentioned associative play is sufficiently established and can be reproduced at will.... the play with the mentioned elements is aimed to be analogous to certain logical connections one is searching for – when words intervene at all, they are, in my case, purely auditive, but they interfere only in a secondary stage as already mentioned.[24]

The thinking processes of Einstein are here based initially not on words, but on 'visual' images and 'some of muscular type'. These sensori-motor perceptions 'embody' high-level ideas that can later be reflected upon and expressed in words, which Einstein then 'hears' rather than sees.

Other scientists also use personal schemes of mental representation based on mental thought experiments with physical objects. The physicist Richard Feynman, for instance, developed his own method of attempting to understand theorems put forward by mathematicians.

I had a scheme which I still use today when somebody is explaining something that I'm trying to understand: I keep on making up examples. For instance, the mathematicians would come in with a terrific theorem, and they're all excited. As they're telling me the conditions of the theorem, I construct something which fits all the conditions. You know, you have a set (one ball) – disjoint (two balls). Then the ball turns colors, grows hairs, or whatever, in my head as they put more conditions on. Finally they state the theorem. Which is some dumb thing about the ball which isn't true for my hairy green ball thing, so I say 'False!' ... I guessed right most of the time, because you can get used to this ultra-fine cutting business and guessing how it will come out.[25]

[24] Einstein, quoted in Hadamard (1945), pp. 142–3.
[25] Feynman (1985), p. 85.

Here we have two examples of mathematical scientists who built their ideas on thought experiments rooted in their bodily experience. It is for this reason that we build a simple theory of mathematical development including an 'embodied' mode of activity. This operates in a quite different manner from the manipulation of symbols and the logical proof of theorems. In the embodied mode one imagines a situation in which the required conditions hold to perform a *thought experiment* to see if the consequences given in the theorem follow.

Not all mathematical researchers admit to using such perceptual embodied thoughts in their research. They have moved on from their childhood relationships with the world, basing their mathematical thoughts not on physical perception, but on the manipulation of symbols and the logical deductions of mathematical proof. However, there are also many professional mathematicians who imagine relationships embodied through thought experiments to suggest possible theorems that can be formulated and proved axiomatically. And, more interestingly, formal proof can sometimes lead to new theorems that link back to more sophisticated forms of embodiment and symbolism so that the development can go full circle. The biological brain builds from embodiment, through symbolism and on to formalism and then on to higher formal levels of embodied and symbolic thought.

8. The Role of the Computer

The invention of the computer halfway through the twentieth century gave rise to completely new possibilities, for computers can perform in ways that complement the human mind. Where the brain is rich in associations but liable to error, the computer currently has no innate intelligence, yet can carry out complex computations almost instantaneously and totally accurately (given bug-free software). Where the individual may need to carry out mental arithmetic or algebraic manipulation to solve a problem, the computer can be programmed to carry out these calculations and manipulations at the behest of the human operator.

I remember as a teenager learning about organic chemistry and the way in which carbon is the basis of huge complex molecules that form the foundation of life. Silicon comes in a poor second in this respect. I remember speculating whether silicon could be made to provide a basis for an alternative life form. Little did I realize then that silicon would provide the foundation on which computer processors would be built.

Suddenly, *Homo sapiens* has the opportunity for a further leap in tool making. This new tool, the computer, is more than something that can be used by actions of the individual, like a club, or a spear. It is no longer passive, responding only to the actions of the user, nor is it crudely mechanical. Instead it can store data, represent it by images on a screen (coordinated with sound and other multimedia output), and can act upon the data in a manner specified in the software by the programmer.

This has profound effects, not only for the global economy, but also for the growing mental conceptions of the child learning mathematics. In geometry, objects can be drawn by the computer software and manipulated by the child using an appropriate interface, so that simple actions by the child (moving a mouse or moving a finger over a touch-sensitive screen) can cause corresponding actions to the images. Thus the child can explore geometric concepts using an embodied human interface (hand movements) to see effects that may give insight into higher-level geometric relationships.

In his book *The Psychology of Learning Mathematics*[26], first published in 1971 before the advent of computer graphics, Richard Skemp remarked that human beings had input and output for words and symbols – the spoken voice acted as a loudspeaker, putting out sounds to be heard by the human ear. However, although the human could take in visual information through the eye, there was no comparable projector for visual output other than broad gestures and physical actions. Now the computer, suitably programmed, offers the possibility of highly sophisticated visual output under the control of the individual. As hardware and software develop, the control of graphical displays can be performed by gestures, giving more intimate interaction between human embodiment and symbolically computed visualizations.

In arithmetic, algebra and calculus, the leap forward is equally profound. Symbols that were previously written on paper and actively manipulated by the mind of the individual can now be programmed into software, to be manipulated with little further intervention by the user. The notion of procept acting dually as process and concept takes on a new and even more powerful role. The human operator can specify the concept in terms of the known formulae and the computer can do the calculation and manipulation.

The balance between concept and process changes, with the human focusing more on the concept and the computer taking care of the process.

Yet another stride is taken forward by *Homo sapiens*. Routine aspects of mathematics can be devolved to a computer support, leaving the mind of

---

[26] Skemp (1971).

the individual to focus on more subtle problem-solving aspects. The combination of *Homo sapiens* and computer provides a new twist to the tale of human evolution in mathematics. It is an essential element of mathematical growth in this new technological age that underlines the fact that the mathematics of today is not the final solution, but our current step in the continuing evolution of mathematical thinking.

9. Summary

In this chapter we have looked at some of the key ideas that occurred in the evolution of mathematics such as the use of language and symbolism to develop new ways of conceptualizing geometry and performing arithmetic.

Egyptian arithmetic used procedures of doubling and halving with whole numbers and unit fractions. Later various civilizations developed their own forms of notation for numbers, each with its own advantages and disadvantages. The modern choice of decimal arithmetic based on ten digits, a decimal point and a minus sign is a highly subtle framework that represents numbers of any size, positive or negative, and enables the operations of arithmetic to be carried out in efficient and flexible ways.

Greek arithmetic and geometry both developed from embodiment. Euclidean geometry used language to formulate Platonic geometric notions in a coherent conceptual framework while Greek arithmetic pictured number concepts as arrays of pebbles that led to ideas of square numbers, triangular numbers, rectangular numbers and prime numbers (that are not rectangular). However, the study of geometry using ruler and compass constructions revealed magnitudes that were not expressible as ratios of whole numbers, leading to separate developments of embodied geometry and symbolic arithmetic.

Greek geometry evolved using ratio and proportion and the subtle notion of continued fraction where quantities are compared but not given a full arithmetic. It was only when Descartes refined Euclidean geometry to include a chosen unit length that the full arithmetic of magnitudes became available and led to his link between geometric embodiment and algebraic symbolism in the Cartesian plane.

Algebraic symbolism developed from expressions for formulating generalized statements (such as the use of 'heap' in ancient Egypt where problems were solved by direct methods of calculation) to the embodied methods of solution expressed verbally by Al-Khwarizmi. The solution of cubics involved the use of the square root of a negative number that could be operated on but had no initial embodied meaning.

The link supplied by Descartes between the pure embodiment of geometrical figures and the symbolic representations of algebra led to the creative blending of the worlds of embodiment and symbolism. This led in turn to the calculus for calculating and modeling the rate of change of quantities and their cumulative growth.

Creative use of symbolic computations with complex numbers revealed new relationships between seemingly unrelated concepts, such as the exponential e^{ix} and the trigonometric functions $\cos x + i \sin x$. The visualization of complex numbers as points in the plane finally blended the geometry of transformations of the plane and the symbolism of complex arithmetic after several generations of conflict.

Foundational problems in the use of infinitesimals in calculus and long standing concerns with Euclidean geometry were addressed by the introduction of a formal axiomatic approach in the nineteenth century. Though flawed because it cannot deliver proofs of everything, the axiomatic formal approach is still capable of building a huge body of coherently organized mathematical knowledge and has become the standard format for presenting modern mathematical proof.

This reveals the evolution of mathematics based initially on natural foundations of practical and theoretical ideas in:

> human *embodiment* to formulate meaningful mathematical ideas developing from perceived objects to imagined Platonic perfection,
>
> *operational symbolism* in arithmetic and algebra that is compressed to give increasing computational power,

to be later transformed into

> *formal definition and proof* to construct deductive mathematical theories.

IV

University Mathematics and Beyond

10   The Transition to Formal Knowledge

This chapter considers the challenges that students face as they make the transition from the embodiment and symbolism of school mathematics to formal mathematics at university based on set-theoretic definition and formal proof. The framework of three worlds of mathematics will be used to analyze supportive and problematic aspects of fundamental definitions including sets, relations, functions, equivalence relations and order relations. There follows a review of the formal construction of the real numbers and how students attempt to make sense of the concept of limit in mathematical analysis. This reveals a spectrum of different personal conceptions from 'natural' approaches based on previous meanings of embodiment and symbolism to a 'formal approach' based on making deductions from formal set-theoretic definitions. The chapter analyses how some students 'give meaning' to the definition from their embodied and symbolic experience, and some 'extract meaning' directly from the definition by learning to formulate formal proofs from formal definitions, with varying levels of confidence and disaffection, depending on the supportive and problematic aspects of their development. Various different methods of analysis of data are considered and related to the long-term framework for mathematical thinking presented in this book.

1. Major Changes from Embodiment and Symbolism to Formalism

The shift from the practical and theoretical development of embodied objects and symbolic operations to the formalism of axiomatic systems involves significant changes in meaning. A student who has studied Euclidean geometry has experience of building a knowledge structure where theorems are deduced from axioms and previous theorems. However, this involves principles such as congruence or the properties of parallel lines rather than the quantified set-theoretic deductions in formal proof. Meanwhile, proof in arithmetic and algebra, based on the 'rules' of arithmetic, is also a useful prelude to formal proof from axioms.

School mathematics is based on embodied operations in geometry or arithmetic that arise naturally in practical situations, evolving into theoretical definitions and deductions that evolve from practical experiences. The shift to an axiomatic formal approach is likely to be problematic because formal operations do not require any procedure of operation to be specified. All that is required is that for two elements x, y in a given set, there is a third element written as $x \circ y$ that satisfies properties such as $x \circ y = y \circ x$.

In a formal approach, it is essential to focus on the properties of an operation, without needing to say how to define it. In this way, all formal proofs deduced from specific axioms and set-theoretic definitions will work in *any* system satisfying those axioms and definitions, regardless of the particular procedure used to perform the operation.

The terms 'natural' and 'formal' are consistent with their use in history, where 'natural philosophy' and 'natural science' were used to describe the study of natural phenomena using geometry, arithmetic, algebra and calculus before the introduction of Hilbertian formalism.

Given the evident power of formal proof, it is the mode of operation for presenting research mathematics by experienced mathematicians. But the changes in meaning required in passing from earlier embodied and symbolic experience to formal reasoning cause the transition to axiomatic formalism to be problematic for many undergraduates. The origins of these difficulties lie in our met-befores, which may involve implicit properties that are not explicitly specified in the formal definition.

2. Sets and Relations

The challenges underlying a formal approach to mathematics may be illustrated by a study of the foundational ideas of sets and relations.

The transition to formal mathematics is built on the concept of set. This is not given a formal definition (at least not until later developments in logic are introduced). Therefore students must build on their familiar experience to make sense of it. Fundamentally, most mathematicians recognize a set S as something that has elements, or members, so that for any x whatever, it can be determined whether x is a member of S (written $x \in S$) or not ($x \notin S$).

Building on the implicit notion of set, various new constructions can be introduced, such as the set $A \times B$, which is defined to be the set of all ordered pairs (x, y) where $x \in A$ and $y \in B$. Each element in $A \times B$ relates to precisely one element in A and one element in B. That is all. No more assumptions need to be made. However, in the case of the set $\mathbb{R}$, which can be embodied by the number line, the set $\mathbb{R} \times \mathbb{R}$ can be visualized in terms of points in the plane $\mathbb{R}^2$. The mental picture may be less easily visualized for more general sets such as $\mathbb{R}^2 \times \mathbb{R}^3$ or $\mathbb{C} \times \mathbb{C}$.

A *relation* between two sets A, B is defined to be *any* specified subset R of $A \times B$. That's it. There is no restriction placed on what kind of subset it might be. However, specific types of relations – such as functions, order relations and equivalence relations – may be conceptualized in individual ways that are affected by the student's previous experience. As a consequence, students may imagine relations as having different implicit properties from those intended by the definitions, as we shall now see.

2.1 *Functions*

A *function* from a set A to a set B is a relation F that satisfies two further properties:

(F1) For each $x \in A$ there exists an element $y \in B$ such that $(x, y) \in F$.
(F2) If $(x, y_1), (x, y_2) \in F$ then $y_1 = y_2$.

Properties (F1) and (F2) together say that for each $x \in A$ there is precisely *one* element in $x \in B$ such that $(x,y) \in F$. The element y may be written as $F(x)$, enabling us to imagine the set F as the *graph* of the function consisting of all ordered pairs $(x, F(x))$ for $x \in A$. The graph is written as $F : A \to B$, where A is called the domain and B the target (or co-domain).

In the case where this is embodied as the graph of a real function $F : A \to \mathbb{R}$ (where the domain A is a subset of $\mathbb{R}$) then (F1) tells us that there is a point $F(x)$ such that $(x, F(x))$ is on the graph and (F2) tells us that this is the only one. It gives 'the vertical line test' to check if a relation is a function. (Figure 10.1, overleaf.) Draw a vertical line through any point $x \in A$ to see that it meets the graph in just one point, which will be $(x, F(x))$.

Apart from this, the formal definition makes no further restriction on functions.

The functions met in school mathematics have various familiar features that affect the meaning of the function concept. For instance, a function is usually given by a formula made up of polynomials, trigonometric

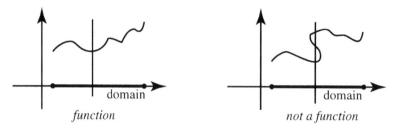

Figure 10.1. The vertical line test.

functions, exponentials and logarithms – all of which have recognizable shapes. In the transition from school to university, these met-befores may suggest implicit properties that a function must have, for instance, it is usually given by a single formula and students rarely have experience of a function having different formulae on different parts of the domain.

In a study of 36 students in the last year of secondary school and 109 first-year university mathematics students, MdNor Bakar asked which of a number of pictures represented functions.[1] (Figure 10.2.)

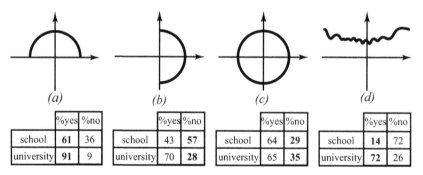

	%yes	%no			%yes	%no			%yes	%no			%yes	%no
school	61	36		school	43	57		school	64	29		school	14	72
university	91	9		university	70	28		university	65	35		university	72	26

Figure 10.2. Which of the sketches could represent functions? Give an explanation.

Graph (a) was problematic for school students, with several saying 'if it were a function, the graph would continue, not stop,' or 'functions are usually continuous, needs a condition.' The term 'continuous' here refers to the dynamic continuity of the embodied action of drawing the curve with the expectation that it will continue to flow and not stop suddenly, which is characteristic of most examples in school mathematics.

---

[1] Bakar & Tall (1992).

There is also an implicit assumption in the question that the pictures represent y as a function in x, so it was expected that students would say that picture (b) is not a function. However, two university students who declared it was a function commented in ways that suggested that x is a function of y, one writing 'look at it a different way', the other writing the equation as $f(y) = x$.

Two thirds considered (c) to be a function, which is perhaps not surprising given that it is sometimes described as an 'implicit function', even though it doesn't satisfy the vertical line test.

Graph (d) was rejected by three quarters of the students in school and a quarter at university. Their reasons included 'no regular pattern,' 'too irregular,' 'too complicated to be a function.' Experience in school refers to familiar functions given by an explicit formula, and the graph did not fit their mental image.

These problematic aspects may be addressed directly specifically by encouraging students to reflect on the precise meaning of the formal definition. For instance, it is essential to focus on what the definition says and what it doesn't say. Axiom (F1) says for each x there is a y, but it doesn't say that different xs must have different ys. Nor does it say that every y must be related to some given x. Nor does it say that the function must be given by a specific formula. By considering a range of examples illustrating different aspects of the function concept, a professor as mentor may assist students to refine their personal conceptions.[2]

2.2 *Relations between Elements in the Same Set*

When the two sets A and B are the same, we speak of *a relation on A*. This is simply a specific set R of ordered pairs (x, y) where $x, y \in A$. It may be symbolized to look like a regular relation by writing xRy to mean $(x,y) \in R$. For instance, when the relation R given by

$$R = \{(x, y) \in \mathbb{N} \times \mathbb{N} \mid x < y\}$$

is written as xRy, this corresponds precisely to the familiar idea $x < y$ where the symbol R is replaced by '<'. It can be pictured visually as a relation by plotting all the points (x, y) where x and y are whole numbers and marking the subset for which $x < y$. (Figure 10.3.)

However, this picture is rarely used. Instead the relationship of order is more usually embodied by marking two whole numbers x, y on the number line where $x < y$ is represented by drawing x to the left of y. (Figure 10.4.)

---

[2] Akkoc & Tall (2002); Bayazit (2006).

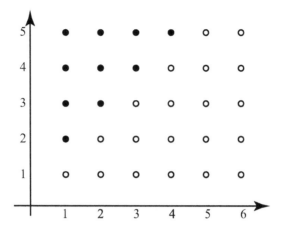

Figure 10.3. The relation $x < y$ as the subset denoted by black discs.

Figure 10.4. The relation $x < y$ where x is to the left of y.

The picture of a relation on A as a subset of $A \times A$ is intended to represent the full set of ordered pairs. The alternate representation of pairs in the original set A is seen more in terms of two generic elements that can be placed anywhere in A and may be imagined moving around to represent different pairs. Some relations, such as functions, are usually represented as subsets of the Cartesian product (as in Figure 10.3). Others, such as order or equivalence, are usually represented in terms of the relation between elements of the set itself (as in Figure 10.4). This can lead to problematic meanings, as we will see later in the case of equivalence relation.

2.3 *Order Relations*

An order relation is inspired by the idea of placing the elements of a set in a given order. The notion of order in number systems given in the previous chapter can be modified to apply to any set.

An order relation on a set A is a set R of ordered pairs (x, y), where we write $x < y$ if the ordered pair $(x, y) \in R$, which satisfies:

(O1) Given $x, y \in A$, then *precisely one* of the following holds:

$x < y$ or $y < x$ or $x = y$,

(O2) If $x < y$ and $y < z$ then $x < z$.

Axiom (O1) is called *the law of trichotomy*. Only one of the three relations can hold at once. It implies that if $x \neq y$ then either $x < y$ or $y < x$ but not both. As examples, we have the natural numbers $\mathbb{N}$ or the real numbers $\mathbb{R}$ with the usual order that allows them to be embodied by visualizing them on a line from left to right so that if $x < y$ then x is to the left of y.

Likewise we can put the twenty-six letters of the alphabet in alphabetical order, $A < B < \cdots < Z$. This can be extended to the alphabetical order of words where if the first letter of one word comes before the first letter of the second, then the first word is placed before the second, but if first letters are the same, the order is determined in the same way by looking at the second letter, then the third and so on. For example, we would have $AAB < AB < B < BC < BDA < \cdots < ZZZZ$.

However, the order need not be alphabetic. An order relation on a set of words simply requires them to be placed in a specific sequence, and there is no restriction on how this is done. For instance, we may choose to order the three words *CAT*, *SAT* and *MAT* as $MAT < CAT < SAT$.

The notion of order relation is far more general than anything a student will have met before; for instance, one can take the set of natural numbers $\mathbb{N}$ and an extra element ω that is different from them all, then define an order on the extended set consisting of the elements of $\mathbb{N}$ and the element ω by using the standard order on $\mathbb{N}$ and defining $n < \omega$ for all natural numbers n. In this sense we can embody a context in which the usual set of natural numbers potentially continues forever, though nevertheless there is an additional element that satisfies $n < \omega$ for all of them.

This is a new and destabilizing idea, blending together the familiar order of whole numbers with an extra element that is 'bigger than them all'. This conflicts with familiar met-befores that the whole numbers grow 'without limit' and will be problematic for a learner who cannot imagine that anything can be 'bigger than all the natural numbers.' The element ω is not 'bigger' than all the natural numbers. It simply satisfies the formal order $n < \omega$ in the set consisting of $\mathbb{N}$ and the additional element ω. Nevertheless, the human brain, rich with connections built up over the years, naturally uses these links, consciously or unconsciously, and it requires a great effort of will to attempt to focus only on links built up through formal proof from definitions.

2.4 *Equivalence Relations*

The concept of equivalence occurs throughout embodiment and symbolism. For instance, there is the equivalence of fractions, algebraic expressions, free vectors, and so on, in arithmetic and algebra. There are also forms of equivalence in Euclidean geometry in terms of congruence of triangles and parallel lines.

Formally, an *equivalence relation* ~ on a set S is defined to satisfy the axioms:

(E1) $x \sim x$ for all $x \in S$,
(E2) If $x \sim y$ then $y \sim x$,
(E3) If $x \sim y$ and $y \sim z$ then $x \sim z$.

Notice that (E3) is precisely the same as (O2); however, the two identical looking axioms operate in different contexts and behave differently.

For instance, consider the following axiom:

(E3)′ If $x \sim z$ and $y \sim z$ then $x \sim y$.

In the context of the axioms (E1) and (E2), the axiom (E3)′ can be used to establish (E3) as follows:

Given the left-hand side of (E3): $x \sim y$ and $y \sim z$. By (E2) this gives $x \sim y$ and $z \sim y$, and then (E3)′ implies $x \sim z$.

The converse follows by a similar argument, so in the context of an equivalence relation, (E3) and (E3)′ can be interchanged and either can be used as part of the definition.

However, in the context of order, the two axioms are not equivalent. Given the order relation $m < n$ on the set of whole numbers, axiom (E3) is satisfied but (E3)′ is not. From $2 < 5$ and $5 < 9$ we may deduce that $2 < 9$, but the inequalities $3 < 5$ and $2 < 5$ do not imply $3 < 2$.

This leads to a surprising principle, which is important to make explicit:

The contextual role of an axiom or definition: A single axiom or definition may operate in different ways in different contexts and a formal structure depends not only on the roles of individual axioms and definitions but also on the interplay between them all within the specific context.

For instance, the notion of a relation on $\mathbb{R}$ is defined to be a subset of $\mathbb{R}^2$. Yet when Abe Chin asked the following question in a highly rated mathematics department[3], most students either did not respond or said that they did not understand the question:

---

[3] Chin (2002); Chin & Tall (2001, 2002).

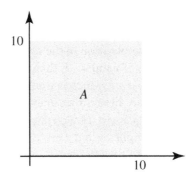

Figure 10.5. The relation A as a subset of $\mathbb{R}^2$.

$A = \{(x, y) \in \mathbb{R}^2 \mid 0 < x < 10, 0 < y < 10\}$. Is A an equivalence relation on $\mathbb{R}$?

The subset A is the interior of a square in the plane. (Figure 10.5.) It is not an equivalence relation because it fails to satisfy (E1). For instance, $11 \in \mathbb{R}$ but $(11, 11) \notin A$.

Out of 15 first-year and 15 second-year mathematics students interviewed, *no* first-year student and just one second-year student gave a correct response (using the counter-example $(11, 11) \notin A$). Of the others, those who wrote comments were all able to write down the three axioms, but often said that they did not understand the question and none mentioned the necessity that (E1) must apply to *all* elements in the set.

On closer investigation, it became apparent that the students thought of an equivalence relationship not as a subset of $A \times A$ as in Figure 10.5, but as a relationship between elements in A.

This interpretation became even more apparent in a question asked of 277 students in the same university:[4]

> Let $X = \{a, b, c\}$ and the relation $\sim$ be defined where $a \sim b$, $b \sim a$, $a \sim a$, $b \sim b$, but no other relations hold. Is this an **equivalence relation**? If not, why?

Again, this is not an equivalence relation because $c \sim c$ is not specified, even though $c \in X$, violating (E1). However, only 139 students (50%) gave a correct response with a correct supporting reason. Sixty-eight others (25%) gave the correct answer but offered an incorrect reason, claiming that the relation is *not transitive*.

---

[4] Chin & Tall (2002).

The relation is certainly transitive, because whenever $x \sim y$ and $y \sim z$ are satisfied then so is $x \sim z$. Because the relationship is specified only between the two elements a and b, any application of the transitive law must be trivially true. For instance, given $a \sim a$ and $a \sim b$, then putting $x = a, y = a, z = b$ gives $x \sim z$, which translates to $a \sim b$, which is true.

The problematic met-before here is that in many situations the transitive law implicitly assumes that x, y, z are *different*. For instance, the order relation $x < y$ automatically implies x and y are different and is embodied by points on a line where x is to the left of y.

In examples that the students have met before, the relation concerned may require the elements involved to be different. For instance, if the notion of two lines in a plane being parallel is defined by the fact that they do not meet, then a line cannot be parallel to itself because it meets itself all along its whole length. In this case, (E1) fails but (E2) is true. Meanwhile (E3) is true in the case that a, b, c are all different, but it fails if a and c are the same and a is parallel to b (because then a is parallel to b and b is parallel to a but a is not parallel to a).

The Greeks treated the notion of congruence as a relation between two *different* triangles, so they did not allow a triangle to be congruent to itself, even though today we would be happy to allow this as part of a modern theory to allow congruence to be an equivalence relation.[5]

The same occurs with relations in everyday life. I have a brother Graham. He is my brother and I am his brother, but only a mathematician might say that I am my own brother.

When we make statements in everyday arithmetic, we use the information to say precisely what we know, for instance, we say that '3 + 2 is equal to 5' and '3 + 2 is less than 6', but rarely that '3 + 2 is *less than or equal* to 6' as we already *know* that it is not equal. With such a background of experience, our interpretation of the notion of an equivalence relation can involve subtle met-befores that are not explicitly given in the set-theoretic definition. In particular, the symmetric law $a \sim a$ on the set S must apply to *all* $a \in S$ and the other two laws must include the possibility that the elements involved need not be different.

These examples reveal the rich connections built up through previous experience that may cause problematic met-befores in new situations that students face in their transition to formal mathematical thinking.

---

[5] Amazingly, the notion of 'congruence' is not given a name in the theory of Euclid. It is a process to go through to show that two (different) triangles that have certain corresponding properties, such as having all three corresponding sides equal, would then have all other attributes equal.

3. Real Numbers and Limits

The shift from rational numbers to real numbers proves to be a major watershed for many students. In school, students meet irrational numbers such as $\sqrt{2}$, π and e, and begin to realize that the number line has numbers on it that are not rational, though it is not clear precisely what these irrational numbers are.

Historically the problematic nature of these new numbers is reflected in the name *irrational*, meaning they are not rational numbers calculated by dividing one whole number by another. John Monaghan found that some students aged sixteen to eighteen sensed that these additional numbers were somehow 'improper'.[6] They could not be produced by a simple calculation with whole numbers. They had infinite decimal expansions, such as $\sqrt{2} = 1.414\ldots$ and these were often considered as 'infinite' numbers, not because they were infinite in size, but because they were infinite *in extent*. They could never be calculated accurately because the decimals go on forever.

A particular case is the repeating decimal $0.999\ldots$. This can be approximated by working it out to, say, n decimal places, which equals $1 - (1/10^n)$. This approximation can get as close as one likes to 1, *but it is never equal to 1*. The result is that the vast majority of students, and many teachers, believe that $0.999\ldots$ is not equal to 1; it is *just less*.[7]

Given the widespread occurrence of this interpretation, there must be an underlying reason for it. The biological brain must deal with a term $s_n = 1 - (1/10^n)$, and consider what happens 'as n increases'. It may be hypothesized that the brain makes sense of each term in the same way, so it imagines a single variable term that changes and increases as n increases. This is a compression of knowledge from a sequence of different terms to a single varying term. This variable term can get as close as we like to 1 but is never equal to it, so it is natural to conceive the limiting case as a quantity that is arbitrarily close to, but never equal to 1.

The idea that quantities can be 'arbitrarily close' or 'arbitrarily small' is a phenomenon that leads naturally to a mental concept that is arbitrarily small, but not zero. Such a notion arises both in embodiment and in symbolism.

This idea of being arbitrarily small, but not zero, is consistent with our experience of points marked with a pencil or lines drawn on paper.

[6] Monaghan (1986).
[7] Cornu (1991).

A point drawn in this way is small, but not so small that it cannot be seen, so it may be imagined as being 'as small as possible'. A line, though thin, has a physical width and, in the quest for precision, it is drawn practically as thin as possible. But it is not drawn without any thickness at all. As a result, our imagination of points and lines based on perception is as small as possible and as thin as possible. Even though we may propose the Platonic idea of a point having position and no size and a line having length but no breadth, this must operate in the same biological brain with the practical met-befores of points and lines that *do* have a size, which are as small as possible.

This is evident in the history of calculus, where Leibniz formulated his 'principle of continuity' that said:

> In any supposed transition, ending in any terminus, it is permissible to institute a general reasoning, in which the final terminus may also be included.[8]

In a supposed transition with a sequence of terms such as $\frac{1}{2}, \frac{1}{4}, \ldots,$ $(\frac{1}{2})^n, \ldots$ which get smaller and smaller but are always positive, Leibniz's principle suggests that the 'final terminus' is a quantity that is arbitrarily small but positive. An infinitesimal is a natural product of the functioning of the human brain.

In the same way, an infinite decimal expansion such as $1/3 = 0.333 \ldots$ or $\sqrt{2} = 1.4142 \ldots$ is often imagined initially as *approaching* the limit, rather than *being* the limit.

In 1986[9], I used the principle of continuity of Leibniz to describe the notion of *generic limit*, which need not be a limit in the mathematical sense but 'is the concept of limit that the individual holds in his or her mind as a result of extrapolating the common properties of the terms of the sequence.' This idea was also extended to various other related concepts such as a *generic tangent*[10], which may not be a true tangent, but is drawn as a line that 'touches the curve at a single point and does not cross it.' Generic ideas arise from considering specific examples as typifying a more general concept.

A telling example of this phenomenon occurred in the work of one of my research students, Lan Li, who asked undergraduate students studying for a degree in teaching mathematics:

---

[8] Leibniz, translated in Child (1920), p. 147.
[9] Tall (1986a, b).
[10] Tall (1986b), p. 74.

(A) Can you add $0·1 + 0·01 + 0·001 + \ldots$. and go on forever and get an exact answer? (Y/N)

(B) $1/9 = 0 \cdot \dot{1}$. Is 1/9 equal to $0 \cdot 1 + 0 \cdot 01 + 0 \cdot 001 + \ldots$? (Y/N)

The favoured response was *No* to (A) and *Yes* to (B).[11] Interviewing the students at the time, it became evident that the symbolism was being read from the left to the right so that $0 \cdot 1 + 0 \cdot 01 + \ldots$ represents a potentially infinite process that can never be completed but the second shows how $1/9 = 0 \cdot 1 + 0 \cdot 01 + \ldots$ can be divided to get as many terms as desired.

During this course, I did my very best to give the students experience of programming convergent sequences, to see that some converged faster than others, and I carefully explained that an infinite decimal is a notation for the *fixed quantity* to which the sequence of finite approximations can get as close as is practically required. I gave examples to illustrate the principle. In particular, I showed that $0.999\ldots9$ to n decimal places is equal to $1- (1/10^n)$ and that, for any given positive value of ε, we can find an N such that if $n > N$, then $0.999\ldots9$ to n decimal places differs from 1 by less than ε. I explained that N can be found by writing $1/\varepsilon$ as a decimal and choosing N such that $10^N > 1/\varepsilon$; then, whenever $n > N$, we have $1/10^n < \varepsilon$ and so the difference between 1 and $0.999 \ldots 9$ to n decimal places is less than ε as required. I focused on the fact that the limit was the *fixed number* that the sequence tended to, according to the definition.

Before the class, most of the students (21 out of 25) believed that 0.999… is less than 1, and I felt confident that I could change their views by giving a coherent explanation. Two weeks later I repeated the question and 21 out of the 23 present at the time still replied that 0.999… is less than 1. In the discussion that followed, the main argument put forward by the students was that they were sure that '0.999 repeating' never quite reached 1, so it was not proper to attempt to *define* it to be otherwise.

When Lan Li, the research student working with me, wrote up the experiment for her master's degree, she said that it was not proper for her to write that her supervisor failed to explain the idea satisfactorily. My response was that if this had happened when I was trying my best to give a good explanation, then there must be a serious underlying reason.

As I reflected on this and other evidence, I recalled another study that amazed me at the time, but made more sense upon reflection. Nicholas

---

[11] See Li and Tall (1993). The response *Yes* to (a) and *No* to (b) was given by 18 out of 25 students (72%) before the course and 14 out of 23 (61%) after.

Wood questioned pure mathematics students who had received more than a year's training in analysis techniques. When he asked 'Is there a *least* positive real number?' and 'Is there a *first* positive real number?' a sizeable minority said there was a first, but not a least.[12]

There are underlying experiences that can give rise to these conflicting responses. Geometrically and algebraically there cannot be a least positive real number x, because $\frac{1}{2}x$ is still positive and smaller. However, in the symbolism of arithmetic, writing a number to, say, four decimal places, there *is* a first nonzero number, namely 0.0001 so, perhaps this is extrapolated to the case of an infinite number of places in the form 'zero point zero, zero, zero, repeating, with a one at the end.' This seems to relate to the difference $1 - 0.999\ldots$, which may be imagined as a string of zeros with a one in the 'last' decimal place.

Lakoff and Núñez expressed the general idea in terms of what they termed as the 'basic metaphor of infinity':

> We hypothesize that all cases of infinity – infinite sets, points at infinity, limits of infinite series, infinite intersections, least upper bounds – are special cases of a single conceptual metaphor in which processes that go on indefinitely are conceptualized as having an end and an ultimate result.[13]

Formulated in these terms, this is essentially a restatement of the principle of continuity of Leibniz, although the authors formulate it in a new way. For instance, they explain the notion of infinite decimal in terms of a succession of finite decimal representations $R_1, R_2, \ldots$ where R_n is the set of real numbers that have decimal representations with n decimal places. The Basic Metaphor of Infinity is invoked to declare that the system has an end and an ultimate result that is the set R_∞ of infinite decimals. Lakoff and Núñez explain that the elements of R_∞ are not the real numbers but the numerals that are *names* for the real numbers and their precise meaning requires further applications of the Basic Metaphor.

At this point, what they do not say is that – for the student and for the vast majority of ordinary mortals – infinite decimals are slightly strange (improper) numbers that are infinite in extent but implicitly share the properties experienced with finite decimals.

In the finite case the different numerals in R_n are all different decimals. To the biological brain using the same neural circuits to interpret these

---

[12] Wood (1992).
[13] Lakoff & Núñez (2000), p. 158.

improper numbers, different infinite decimals also have *different* values. The finite sequence 0.999…9 (to n decimal places) is less than 1.000 … 0, *so the improper number 0.999… is less than 1!*

The evidence lies not only in the many responses from students that support this view, but also in the amazing result of Wood that a substantial number of undergraduates believe that there is not a least positive number, but there is a *first* positive number, which in R_n is 0.000 … 01 and leads to the belief that the first positive real number in R_∞ is 'zero point infinite zeros, one' that can be written as $1 - (0.999 …)$.

This illustrates the need to complement a top-down cognitive science 'idea analysis' with a bottom-up cognitive development analysis of how students make sense of new ideas based on their previous experience. In *Where Mathematics Comes From* by Lakoff and Núñez, and *The Way We Think* by Fauconnier and Turner, the analyses of conceptual blends are performed using high-level concepts that are available in various ways to modern philosophers, mathematicians and cognitive scientists. Such concepts are not usually available to individuals attempting to make sense of new ideas for the first time. For instance, Gilles Fauconnier and Mark Turner interpret the complex numbers as an emergent blend using the modern axiomatic notion of field, which was certainly not available to the individuals earlier in history. What is more important, both in history and in the development of students, is to try to understand how individuals may make sense of a system not just in terms of the viewpoint of an expert, but *from the viewpoint of the learner*, or more precisely, in terms of the learner's personal met-befores.

In attempting to describe how students understand real numbers and limits, it is essential to see where the students are coming from. They come from experiences with what I shall call 'good-enough' arithmetic, using calculations to an appropriate accuracy to get an answer that is good enough for the purpose in hand. Good-enough arithmetic concerns the practical mathematics of the world that we live in, where straight lines are drawn with physical implements and quantities are given to an appropriate accuracy. Sometimes it is good enough for π to be 3.142 or $\frac{22}{7}$ and, in a given situation, either of these may be satisfactory whereas in other situations a more accurate value may be required. For a carpenter or an engineer, the practical mathematics of good-enough arithmetic is good enough.

As learners grow in sophistication, they learn the strengths and weaknesses of good-enough ways of operating with numbers. They know that if they cut a quantity in half, then in half again and so on, theoretically this can go on forever, though in a very practical sense the quantity is soon so small that it cannot be further divided.

Good-enough arithmetic works in everyday calculations, but it is not perfect. Floating point arithmetic on computers gives sufficiently accurate answers for most practical purposes, but it does not satisfy all the rules of arithmetic. For instance, $(a + b) - a$ may not equal b in a practical calculation when $a = 1$ and $b = 10^{-1000}$ because $a + b$ is rounded to 1 as a floating-point number with a limited number of places and the result is $(a + b) - a = 1 - 1 = 0$, even though $b \neq 0$. More seriously, calculating ratios of small numbers can give huge errors, and good-enough arithmetic becomes problematic for calculating numerical derivatives in the calculus.

Expert mathematicians, seeking perfection, move from good-enough arithmetic to the theoretical mathematics of real numbers to obtain perfect arithmetic. At a higher level, this leads to the formal limit concept. However, many practical professionals in engineering and other occupations essential for our society do not require the formal notion of limit, only a firm grasp of good-enough arithmetic and the ability to model problems and calculate solutions to the required accuracy.

This illustrates the difference between a *theoretical* limit related to the need to think coherently with good-enough arithmetic in applications and the *formal* limit as given by the formal definition in mathematical analysis.

Pure mathematicians see the formal limit concept as a watershed. Students who can operate with it in a formal way are believed to have the potential to become genuine mathematical thinkers to formulate proofs in axiomatic formal mathematics. The reality is somewhat different. Students meeting the concept in their first course of real analysis must build on their current knowledge structures. They may do this in qualitatively different ways from the formal mode of thinking seen as the ultimate form of expression by expert pure mathematicians.

Applied mathematicians are content with a theoretical approach that uses pure mathematics to formulate mathematical models in applications to solve and predict the possible outcomes of a given situation.

3.1 *Mathematical Constructions of the Real Numbers*

In the latter part of the nineteenth century, the concept of real number was given a formal construction in different ways by Georg Cantor[14] and Richard Dedekind[15].

[14] Cantor (1872).
[15] Dedekind (1872).

Cantor's method began with a particular type of sequence, $s_1, s_2, \ldots, s_n, \ldots$, of rational numbers introduced by Cauchy, where the terms of a sequence 'get close to each other' in the following sense:

> **Definition:** A Cauchy sequence is a sequence $s_1, s_2, \ldots, s_n, \ldots$ of numbers so that, given any rational $\varepsilon > 0$, a value of N can be found so that when $m, n > N$, the difference between s_m and s_n is less than ε.

Given two Cauchy sequences $a_1, a_2, \ldots$ and $b_1, b_2, \ldots$ then we can consider whether the sequence $a_1 - b_1, a_2 - b_3, \ldots$ tends to zero. If this happens then we can say that two such Cauchy sequences are 'equivalent'.

This idea essentially allows us to say that equivalent Cauchy sequences have the same limit without actually needing to calculate the limit itself. Cantor's idea was to *define* a real number to be given by a Cauchy sequence of rational numbers, where two equivalent sequences defined the same real number. A rational number r gives rise to a constant Cauchy sequence where every term is equal to r. The rational numbers can then be regarded as special cases of real numbers[16] and are now a subset of the extended system of real numbers.

Dedekind's method, inspired by Cantor, envisaged the rational numbers on the line being cut into two disjoint sets, L and U, in such a way that every rational in L is smaller than every rational in U. This separates all the rationals into a lower set L and an upper set U, something like Figure 10.6.

$$L \qquad\qquad U$$

Figure 10.6. A cut on the rational number line into sets L (grey) and U (black).

This picture represents only *rational* numbers and leads to essentially two distinct forms of cut. One occurs at a rational number r, where L is the set of rational numbers less than r; U is the set of rationals greater than r; and r itself is included either in L or in R, which will be here chosen in L for definiteness. The other does *not* occur at a rational number, such as happens when U is the set of all positive rationals with square greater than 2, and L contains the rest. Essentially this cut corresponds to a new type of number that is *not* rational, namely $\sqrt{2}$.

Dedekind defined an addition for cuts by adding the elements in the two lower sets together and those in the two upper sets together to give

---

[16] A subtle use of the idea that the rational numbers and their arithmetic are the same crystalline concept as the equivalence classes of constant sequences.

the sum as a new cut. He defined subtraction, multiplication and division of cuts, which needed a little more ingenuity to cope with negative values. These 'cuts' were now considered as 'numbers', some corresponding to the rational numbers where the cut occurs and some new cuts that are the *irrational* numbers. Dedekind's methods effectively expanded the number line to include both rationals and irrationals. In a very 'real' sense, both Cantor and Dedekind 'completed' the number line by introducing the irrationals.

Once the number line is seen to be 'complete', with both rationals and irrationals, the scene is set for a rigorous approach to the calculus in terms of the theory of mathematical analysis.

The completion was later christened 'the Cantor-Dedekind Axiom', stating that

The real numbers are order-isomorphic to the geometric line.[17]

This essentially fulfils the vision of Descartes, who saw points in the plane expressed as pairs (x, y) of numbers and, in particular, points on the x-axis in a direct ordered correspondence with the number line. The real number line is now seen as a blend of geometric points and symbolic decimals.

The real number system $\mathbb{R}$ satisfies the axioms for an ordered field, together with the completeness axiom, which states

(C) Any Cauchy sequence in $\mathbb{R}$ tends to a specific limit in $\mathbb{R}$.

For instance, the sequence of approximations, $a_1 = 1.4$, $a_2 = 1.41$, $a_3 = 1.414$, ..., where a_n is the value of $\sqrt{2}$ to n decimal places, is a Cauchy sequence (because for $m, n > N$, the terms a_m and a_n agree at least for N decimal places, so they differ by at most $1/10^N$).

The completeness axiom (C) essentially guarantees that any infinite decimal has a numerical value. Later we will show that any ordered field satisfying the axiom of completeness has the same arithmetic structure as the arithmetic of infinite decimals and that it has a unique crystalline structure that fits together in such exquisite ways that mathematicians imagine it as a unique Platonic object.

To be able to build this new level of mathematical sophistication, we must now introduce the formal notion of limit.

---

[17] See, for instance, The Cauchy-Dedekind Axiom in Wikipedia, retrieved from http://en .wikipedia.org/wiki/Cantor-Dedekind_axiom (Accessed July 28, 2012).

3.2 *Introducing the Limit Concept*

The formal definition of the limit concept states that a sequence $a_1, a_2, \ldots,$ $a_n, \ldots$ tends to a limit a (which is fixed) if the following condition is satisfied:

Given any $\varepsilon > 0$, there exists a whole number N such that
$n > N$ implies $|a_n - a| < \varepsilon$.

Making sense of this definition is problematic, not least because it has several quantifiers. Written in symbolic language using the quantifiers $\forall$ (for all) and $\exists$ (there exists), it becomes

$$\forall \varepsilon > 0, \ \exists N \in \mathbb{N} \quad \text{such that} \ \forall n > N, \ |a_n - a| < \varepsilon.$$

This involves three quantifiers nested within each other, alternating 'for all' and 'there exists' in a manner that can be complicated to handle. Furthermore, the constructions of the real numbers formulated by Cantor and Dedekind are based on visual imagery and experience of operating with numbers. The formalism of Hilbert is intended to be based purely on set-theoretic deductions in terms of a system satisfying the axioms of a complete ordered field.

We begin our exploration of student conceptions of the limit concept based on a longitudinal study in which Marcia Pinto interviewed eleven students on seven occasions at intervals throughout a twenty-week analysis course[18], seeking underlying themes using grounded theory.[19] The grounded theory data led to categories that distinguished whether the student constructed the concept of limit by *giving meaning* to the definition based on the student's concept image or *extracting meaning* from the definition by operating with the quantified definitions to build formal proof. These two approaches are related to *a natural approach* building on the concept image and *a formal approach* building formal theorems based on the formal definition.

The concept image as defined in Tall & Vinner 'includes all the mental pictures and associated properties and processes.'[20] This underlines the need to include not only pictures, but also symbolism, as encountered in practical and theoretical mathematics. This is consistent with the historical

[18] Pinto (1998); Pinto & Tall (1999, 2001, 2002).
[19] Strauss & Corbin (1990).
[20] Tall & Vinner (1981), p. 152.

use of the term 'natural' in 'natural philosophy' including geometry, arithmetic, algebra, and calculus to describe natural phenomena prior to the introduction of formal mathematics at the end of the nineteenth century. This leads to a categorization of the development of proof into:

- A natural approach based on theoretical mathematics involving embodiment, or symbolism, or a blending of the two;
- A formal approach using the formal mathematics of set-theoretic definition and deduction.

We begin by considering the data from four selected students.[21]

4.1 *A Natural Approach Blending Embodiment and Symbolism*

Student Chris typified an approach building from embodiment and symbolism to construct the formal definition. To write down the definition of convergence, he drew a picture and imagined the dynamic process as the

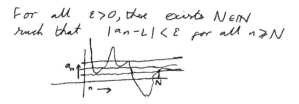

Figure 10.7. Chris's conception of the limit concept.

sequence (a_n) of terms tended to the limit L. (Figure 10.7.)

As he drew the diagram, he motioned with his hands to suggest the ideas underlying the definition, saying:

> I don't memorize that [the definition of limit]. I think of this [the picture] every time I work it out, and then you just get used to it. I can nearly write that straight down.
>
> I think of it graphically ... you got a graph there and the function there, and I think that it's got the limit there ... and then ε once like that, and you can draw along and then all the ... points after N are inside of those bounds.... When I first thought of this, it was hard to understand, so I thought of it like that's the n going across there and that's a_n.... Err, this shouldn't really be a graph, it should be points.

---

[21] The material in the following section is based on the doctoral research of Marcia Pinto (1988).

In his final remark, he recognized that he had drawn a continuous graph with a motion of his pencil, instead of a sequence of points. However, the thrust of his dynamic argument remained valid and allowed him to build up the formal definition from his embodied imagery.

Throughout the whole course he seemed to be negotiating with the ideas. For instance, he believed that a formal proof must include *all* the logical steps to build from the given assumptions. He did not allow the quotation of results previously established because he was adamant that each 'proof' must be complete in itself. It was not until the eighth week of the twenty-week course that he gave up this ideal when his proofs became interminably long.

He also played with various possible alternatives for definitions. For instance, instead of starting with ε and looking for a value of N, he considered starting with N to find ε, before deciding that the standard definition is more appropriate.

He enjoyed the tension of the challenge. He had clearly faced mathematical challenges before and felt the thrill of success. Now he was maintained on an emotional high level that seemed to give him pleasure even when under stress. He always looked for clarity and precision in his ideas, and surmounted errors by refocusing his attack.

Chris's approach developed a rich blend of embodiment, symbolism and formalism where formal ideas were supported by embodied imagery and fluent symbolic operations. His approach is 'natural'. It 'gives meaning' to the definition focusing on dynamic visual imagery and blending this with meaningful manipulation of quantified symbolic definitions.

4.2 *A Formal Approach Based on Definition and Proof*

Student Ross coped with the definition by repetition:

> Just memorizing it, well it's mostly that we have written it down quite a few times in lectures and then whenever I do a question I try to write down the definition and just by writing it down over and over again it gets imprinted and then I remember it.

When he investigated the limit of a sequence, he used the definition. He declared that the constant sequence 1, 1, 1, ... tends to 1, because, given any $\varepsilon > 0$, take $N = 1$ and for $n > 1$ we have $|a_n - 1| = 0$, so clearly $|a_n - 1| < \varepsilon$ as desired.

Many other students, however, have the linguistic met-before that the phrase 'tends to' means 'gets close to, but is not equal to the limit.' This is emphasized by many examples such as $1/n$, which *tends* to 0, but the term $1/n$ is never actually zero itself.

Many students consider a constant sequence as a special case that feels different from a sequence that tends to a limit, getting ever closer to the limit, which it never reaches. Ross had a much more subtle insight. He thought very carefully about the idea of convergence and realized that for a certain value of ε, some sequences would require much larger values of N than others, and so one could talk about some sequences converging more slowly than others. In a later tutorial, he brought this topic up and declared that the constant sequence is 'the fastest converger of all'. This is the mark of a true mathematician. While other students might include the constant sequence as a separate case, Ross considered it as a central example.

Ross drew a picture in interview (Figure 10.8), but insisted that he built his ideas by thinking about what was happening dynamically. In an interview, he explained:

> Well, before … I saw anyone draw that, it was just umm … thinking basically as n gets larger than N, a_n is going to get closer to L, so that the difference between them is going to come very small and basically, whatever value you try to make it smaller than, if you go far enough out then the gap between them is going to be smaller. That's what I thought before seeing the diagrams … something like that.

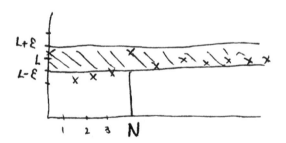

Figure 10.8. Ross's sketch of convergence.

In his responses he used dynamic metaphorical language in which 'n gets larger than N,' 'a_n is going to get closer to L,' 'the difference between them is going to come small,' 'the gap between them is going to be smaller.' Thus, although he did not build his ideas from a conceptual embodiment in a picture viewed dynamically, he used functional embodiment of the dynamic changes in the process of tending to a limit. In doing so, he built on the formal definition and suppressed his concerns over the problematic nature of his visual interpretation of the limit concept.

Over time he became highly proficient in manipulating the logical symbols, such as using the quantifiers $\forall$ (for all) and $\exists$ (there exists). He realized that to show a 'for all' statement is false needs just one counter-example and using the symbol $\neg$ for 'not' leads to the simple rule that one can replace $\neg\forall$ by $\exists\neg$. In the same way, to show that a 'there exists' statement is false requires the proof that the statement is false in all cases, so $\neg\exists$ can be replaced by $\forall\neg$. He used these principles to deduce what is meant for a sequence not to be convergent by writing

$$\neg\left(\forall\varepsilon > 0 \, \exists N \, \forall n > N : |a_n - L| < \varepsilon\right)$$

and moving the negation sign successively over the quantifiers, swapping them around to get

$$\exists\varepsilon > 0 \, \forall N \, \exists n > N : \neg|a_n - L| < \varepsilon$$

so

$$\exists\varepsilon > 0 \, \forall N \, \exists n > N : |a_n - L| \geq \varepsilon$$

Ross is a 'formal' learner, building a rich knowledge structure for the thinkable concept of limit by following through the proofs and getting a sense of the meaning of the logical structure. He uses logical symbolism to represent the definition in a compact form and manipulates it easily and logically while also thinking about the limit process as a functional embodiment as the terms get as close as desired to the limiting value.

4.3 *A Problematic Embodied Route*

Colin based his idea of convergence on the embodied movement along a descending curve that he drew and described in dynamic terms (Figure 10.9), saying:

> ... um, [I] sort of imagine the curve just coming down like this and dipping below this point which is ε ... and this would be N. So as soon as they dip below this point then ... the terms bigger than this [pointing from N to the right] tend to a certain limit, if you make this small enough [pointing to the value of ε].

He was not able to formulate this idea in a way that enabled him to produce a formal proof. For example, when asked to prove the following

If $a_n \to 1$, prove that there exists $n \in \mathbb{N}$ such that $a_n > \frac{3}{4}$ for all $n > N$,

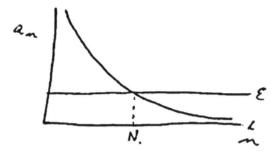

Figure 10.9. Colin's mental image of convergence.

he said:

> It seemed to be a silly question that … if a_n tends to 1 then if you question when a_n is greater than $\frac{3}{4}$ … this is a bound, it seems … I don't know why.

It seemed self-evident to him that if the terms get closer to 1, eventually they must be bigger than $\frac{3}{4}$. However, there is not a specific formula given for a_n or a numerical value for ε, so it is not possible to calculate a numeric value for N.

As the course progressed, he sensed the conflict between his embodied imagery and the formalism. For instance, his dynamic imagery suggested that 0.999… (zero point nine repeating) gets 'closer and closer' to 1 without reaching it, but the formal definition tells him that the limit *is* 1. Towards the end of the course, the problematic aspects of his conception of limit remained, as he commented:

> It's sort of … I understand it should be 1 … and that the limit of the sequence is actually 1 just … It's down to notation. It just it's a bit hard to let go of 0.9999 recurring …

4.4 *A Problematic Symbolic Route That Is Essentially Procedural*

Student Rolf built on his symbolic experience with algebra and arithmetic to interpret the definition of convergence as a calculation. For him the definition said:

> specify the formula for the nth term of the sequence and how small you require ε and I will be able to compute the value of N so that when $n > N$, then the nth term differs from the limit by less than ε.

He was able to use this computational procedural approach to deal with specific cases where he was given an explicit formula for the term and a numerical value of ε to work with. For him the procedure was operational in specific cases, but it was not meaningful if he did not have an explicit formula and a numerical epsilon to use in a computation. Over time, he explained that he was beginning to become accustomed to the definition without really understanding what is going on.

> Err ... I (once?) thought the definition was stupid. I once thought there was no point in having ... complicated definitions. But now I think it's okay. I mean, *I am getting used to it*, but I thought the definition was, err, I didn't really fully understand the definition.

However, he could not understand what it meant to say that a sequence does *not* tend to a limit L:

> ... it's a pretty useless definition, isn't it? Do you see what I'm saying? Because if it doesn't tend to a limit, then you then ... what you are going to imply for L? I think that's the definition, but it's pretty useless.

Rolf was not comfortable studying analysis. He sensed how limits worked dynamically and could verify the limit definition by a calculation if he had the necessary information, but he did not grasp how to reason with the formal definition in formal proofs. After a term he changed his course to read applied mathematics.

4.5 *Classifying Routes to Formal Mathematical Thinking*

The four examples in the preceding section are carefully selected from eleven student responses to represent a spectrum of individual conceptions of the limit. Broadly speaking, they can be seen as conceptions that have a range of differing supportive and problematic aspects.

Chris built by extracting meaning from visual thought experiments and blended his embodiment with quantified symbolism to succeed in developing formal proof. In general, for a natural learner building from embodiment, it is essential to translate embodied reasoning into quantified symbolism.

Ross took a fundamentally formal approach, extracting meaning from the definition by repeating it and working through the proofs until he had sufficient familiarity to reflect on them and make sense of the axiomatic formalism. He had a supportive logical knowledge structure, but he suppressed his imagery, which he found to be limited, even problematic.

His focus on verbal logic enabled him to make sense of aspects that many students found to be problematic (such as the convergence of constant sequences) as coherent parts of a supportive formal knowledge structure.

Colin attempted to build his idea of a limit by extracting meaning from embodied imagery but was unable to make sense of the multiple quantifiers. He had an intuitive sense of the limit concept but various aspects of his imagery, such as a sequence 'approaching a limit', proved to be problematic in making sense of the formal definition.

Rolf was classified as 'extracting meaning' from the definition but was unable to cope with the quantifiers. He based his arguments on symbol manipulation and did not draw pictures. If the formula for the nth term was given, for a given numerical value of epsilon, he could calculate a numerical value of N, so he was building on his natural symbolic experience but did not develop into a full formal approach.

Figure 10.10 shows the full cognitive development of proof, from specific and generic examples in practical mathematics, natural embodied and symbolic proof in theoretical mathematics that may develop into formal proof based on quantified set-theoretic axioms and definitions.

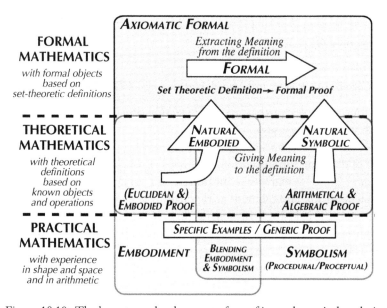

Figure 10.10. The long-term development of proof in mathematical analysis.

5. Comparison of Theoretical Frameworks

The broad picture of the long-term development of proof has been categorized in a number of ways. Janet Duffin and Adrian Simpson used the term 'natural' to denote an approach building naturally on previous experience as opposed to an 'alien' approach in which the learner is willing to accept the definitions and work with them without needing to give them a specific meaning.[22] They also spoke of a 'conflicting' approach where the student was impeded by conflict between previous experience and new formal ideas. Pinto and Tall adopted the terminology for a 'natural' approach, but used the term 'formal' to describe the derivation of formal proof while noting that conflict could arise from both these approaches.[23]

Working at about the same time, Keith Weber saw three categories, naming them 'natural', 'formal' and 'procedural' as follows:

- a *natural* approach, giving an intuitive description and using it to lead to formal proof,
- a *formal* approach, where students had little initial intuition but could logically justify their proofs,
- a *procedural* approach, in which students learnt the proofs given them by the professor by rote without being able to provide any formal justification.[24]

In addition, he analyzed the teaching style, where the professor concerned began with an initial *logico-structural* style in which he guided the students into constructing a sequence of deductions to prove a theorem. He divided his working space on the board into two columns, with the left column to be filled in with the text of the proof and the right column as 'scratch work'. He wrote the definitions at the top of the left column and the final statement at the bottom, and then used the scratch work area to translate information across and to think about the possible deductions that would lead from the assumptions to the final result.

Interpreted in problem-solving terms, he wrote 'what is known' (the hypotheses), 'what is wanted' (the conclusion) and sought to find 'what to introduce' to build a formal argument from hypothesis to conclusion.

---

[22] Duffin & Simpson (1993).
[23] Pinto & Tall (1999).
[24] Weber (2004).

Later in the course, he wrote his proofs in a more sequential *procedural* style, writing the proof down in the left column and using the right column to work out detail, such as routine manipulation of symbols. When the topic shifted emphasis to a geometric approach, he used what Weber termed a *semantic* style, by drawing pictures and introducing ideas visually, essentially building from embodiment to formal proof.

The students' responses in examinations related to the teaching style. In topics presented in a logico-structural or procedural manner, of six students interviewed, four responses were classified as formal, one as procedural and one natural. In topics taught in a semantic style, there were no formal responses, one was procedural and five were natural. Logical and structural teaching resulted in more formal responses while visual embodiments resulted in more natural responses.

Lara Alcock and Adrian Simpson used grounded theory to study two parallel analysis courses with the same syllabus, 'covering formal, definition-based approaches to convergence of sequences and series and the completeness of the real numbers'.[25] One gave standard lectures and the other used cooperative learning based on the book, *Numbers and Functions: Steps into Analysis*, by Robert Burn.[26] In the latter the students learned about analysis concepts as a natural extension of school arithmetic and algebra, working together to make calculations with sequences that tend to zero, to build formal ideas by giving meaning to quantified symbolic definitions.

Interviewing eighteen students in pairs, they found the data led to an analysis into 'visual' and 'non-visual' approaches. The visual students introduced diagrams, made gestures while explaining and preferred pictures to algebraic explanations. The non-visual students used algebraic notations, did not introduce diagrams, and were not inclined to use pictures in reasoning. Nine students were classified as visual, seven as non-visual, and two were not classified because their partner dominated the interview. In particular, when a pair included a visualizer and a non-visualizer, when the visualizer explained reasoning based on visual images, the non-visualizer usually remained silent.

The students were subdivided into three bands. In the lower band visualizers referred to limited visual information, but neither they nor non-visualizers coped with definitions or arguments.

In the middle band, the visualizers base their ideas on embodiment with some links to the definition, while they shared with non-visualizers an

---

[25] Alcock & Simpson (2004, 2005).
[26] Burn (1992).

incomplete understanding of the formal concepts and relied on the book or the lecturer as the source of authority.

The higher visual band blended together embodiment and symbolism to develop a quantified formal approach. The higher non-visual band built from algebraic experience to a quantified formal approach.

In a later paper, Lara Alcock and Keith Weber collaborated to produce a two-part analysis of the development of proof categorized as 'semantic' and 'syntactic'.[27] They describe a semantic approach 'in which the prover also makes use of his or her intuitive understanding of the concepts' and a syntactic approach in which 'the prover works from a literal reading of the involved definitions'.

In the three-world framework, the visual-symbolic analysis may be considered in terms of the relationship between conceptual embodiment and operational symbolism, while the semantic/syntactic analysis relates more to the transition from embodiment and symbolism to axiomatic formalism. There may be differences in detail, but the broad development may be represented by Figure 10.11.

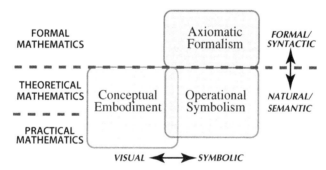

Figure 10.11. A two-by-two analysis of the growth of mathematical thinking and proof.

This framework is directly related to Bruner's enactive-iconic-symbolic modes of operation in general cognitive development. The three-world framework combines enactive and iconic as conceptual embodiment and sub-divides symbolism into the operational symbolism of arithmetic and algebra and the increasing verbal reasoning leading to the logic of axiomatic formalism. This provides a two-way analysis between the visual and symbolic in school mathematics where the visual is verbalized and the symbolism is generalized to translate into the quantified set-theoretic logic of

[27] Alcock & Weber (2004).

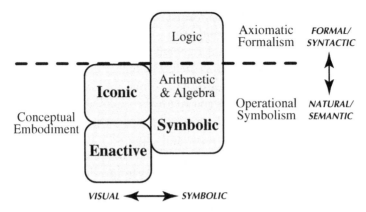

Figure 10.12. Bruner's three modes and the three worlds of mathematics.

axiomatic formalism (Figure 10.12). Even though logic is here represented as a higher level of symbolism, it should be remembered that Hilbert's reformulation of Euclidean geometry is a verbal and logical extension of the enactive and iconic development of geometry.

5.1 *Reviewing the Data in Terms of Natural and Formal*

An alternative two-part analysis focuses on the development from natural mathematics based on embodiment and symbolism to formal mathematics based on set-theoretic definition and formal proof.

Our concept images are based on our previous experience, including both mental pictures and symbolic processes. Natural thinking builds from natural experiences using thought experiments and symbolic operations. Formal thinking arises from choosing quantified axioms and definitions selected to specify a particular formal situation, constructing a sequence of theorems by formal deduction from the axioms, definitions and previously proven theorems. (Figure 10.13.)

Emotional aspects enter into the mix, as individuals with confidence in their ability to face new ideas may build either naturally from their previous experience or formally in the new axiomatic formal framework. Meanwhile, students who find mathematics problematic and lack confidence may find the subject a source of anxiety and either lose heart or seek to avoid the anti-goal of failure by focusing on the alternate goal of learning procedurally to be able to reproduce proofs in an examination.

There is a huge difference between the embodiment and symbolism of school mathematics and axiomatic formal thinking at university. As a

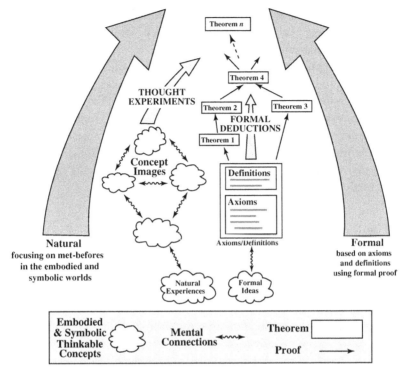

Figure 10.13. Natural and formal routes to build proofs.

university teacher and examiner over many years, I have observed in many situations how students prefer problems that are solvable by well-rehearsed algorithms rather than the subtleties of formal proof.

As an awarder prescribing the grades on a higher mathematics paper taken only by exceptional eighteen-year-olds, the candidates almost unanimously selected long and technical algorithms in the calculus rather than elementary formal proofs in group theory that could be answered in a few lines. In a first-year mathematical analysis course, students preferred to use tests of convergence involving calculations rather than problems requiring proofs. In linear algebra, students are more likely to answer questions solving linear equations. In group theory they preferred to tackle problems involving symbolic manipulations such as operating with permutations. In complex analysis, the first choice usually combines visual and symbolic methods in contour integration. In every case, the students preferred 'safe' questions using routines that they had practiced as an extension of the symbolic world of calculation and manipulation rather than the transition into axiomatic proof. Questions requiring even minimal problem solving in formal theory are less likely to be attempted if they involve more than simply reproducing a theorem learnt by rote.

This emphasizes the enormous gulf between the parallel worlds of embodiment and symbolism and the subsequent axiomatic formal world. It is for this reason that I retain the three-part structure of the three worlds of mathematics rather than reduce it to fewer categories. It reflects the major change in mathematical thinking that distinguishes the more fundamental natural worlds of embodiment and symbolism from the distinct axiomatic formal world used for communication of research results by research mathematicians.

6. The Bigger Picture

The data used for the building of the framework has been based mainly on the development of mathematical analysis. However, in Chapter 8 and in the earlier part of this chapter, other aspects of the development of mathematical thinking have been considered that offer a variety of different contexts that combine embodiment, symbolism and formalism in various ways.

Hilbert's formalism takes the formal embodiment of Euclidean geometry to set-theoretic formalism that refers only to the relationship between formal entities consisting of 'points', 'lines' and 'planes' that he observed could just as easily be called 'tables', 'chairs' and 'beermats'. This builds from embodiment to formalism without any reference to the operational symbolism of measurement.

The proof of the area of a spherical triangle in Chapter 8 is an essential blend of embodiment of the sphere and the operational symbolism of the computation of surface area. This is a theoretical argument that does not need to be translated into an axiomatic formal proof.

A variety of possible developments of mathematical proof is outlined in Figure 10.14.

Natural proof builds on concept imagery involving embodiment and symbolism, which may build on embodiment, symbolism, or a blend of the two. A default form of proof occurs through a procedural development that essentially builds on rote-learning proofs for reproduction in examinations. This should not be confused with individuals who commit proofs to memory so that they can reproduce them and reflect upon their content to make sense of them. Formal proof involves making coherent deductions based on set-theoretic definitions.

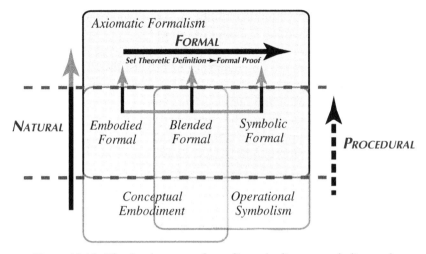

Figure 10.14. The development of proof in embodiment, symbolism and formalism.

The vertical arrows representing the development from natural to formal are shaded black in the lower portion and grey at the top. This represents the observation that proofs often remain in the theoretical world of natural embodiment and symbolism without shifting to the formal world of set-theoretic definition and proof.

Most of us work with natural embodiment and symbolism. Many professional mathematicians are happy to accept such proofs on the understanding that they *could* be expressed in a more formal manner, should that be desired.

Formal proof becomes essential to ensure (as best we can) that the proofs that we present are not dependent on hidden assumptions that may later become problematic. Although natural proof depends on the specific context and may be generalized theoretically, formal proof represents a distinct shift to basing mathematical thinking on quantified reasoning that applies to *any* context that satisfies the set-theoretic axioms and definitions.

7. Reflections

The three-world framework reveals the development from the theoretical mathematics of perception and operation to the formal mathematics of definition and deduction to be a huge challenge for students. Formal knowledge structures can be developed in a spectrum of different ways, from natural approaches using embodied and symbolic experience that give meaning to definitions and relationships, to formal approaches extracting meaning from the definition using formal proof.

Students have varying preferences that involve both cognitive and emotional aspects. They may gain confidence or become disaffected through making, or failing to make, sense of a natural or formal approach.

In Chapter 11, we will use the framework from embodiment and symbolism to formalism to explore the cognitive development of the calculus and mathematical analysis. We will then continue the journey building formal knowledge structures in more advanced mathematical thinking.

11   Blending Ideas in the Calculus

The calculus is the crowning glory of classical mathematics, giving us the power to calculate how things change (differentiation), how they build up (integration) and the relationship between the two (the fundamental theorem of calculus). These ideas can be embodied visually and dynamically as the changing slope of a curve and the area underneath the curve, which extend to a vast range of applications to calculate the rate of change of quantities and how they accumulate. Yet, over the centuries, the calculus has been the subject of ongoing critical debate.

Controversy persists precisely because the calculus deals with arbitrarily small quantities and potentially infinite processes. This problem was formally resolved in the nineteenth century by defining the limit concept in terms of a challenge, specifying the accuracy desired and seeking a way of calculating to within this desired accuracy. It involves the famous epsilon-delta approach: 'tell me how close you would like to be (a positive value epsilon) and then I will tell you a value (delta) so that when the input is within delta, then the output is within epsilon.'

The introduction of the epsilon-delta challenge made it possible for expert mathematicians to build the modern theory of mathematical analysis, but, as we saw in Chapter 10, it is often problematic for students meeting the calculus for the first time. Their mathematical knowledge structures are based on the embodied world of geometry and graphs, and the symbolic world of arithmetic and algebra. These are related to a physical world in which objects move around in a continuous fashion and graphs are drawn continuously with a dynamic movement of the hand, where the word 'continuous' is used in an embodied dynamic sense, perceived through our senses. This form of continuity will be described as *dynamic continuity*, to distinguish it from the formal epsilon-delta definition of continuity given by the limit concept.

The dynamic and formal meanings of continuity are often seen as fundamentally different.[1] Dynamic continuity relates to physical perception and action, moving objects in the world and drawing graphs dynamically by hand, or visually on a computer screen. These experiences give a dynamic meaning to the notion of 'continuity' that we all share.

What we perceive with our eyes and what we can conceive in our minds are subtly different. Concepts arise in the human brain as neurons fire in consort. The framework of three levels of consciousness by Merlin Donald[2] – which informed the construction of thinkable concepts in Chapter 2 – is particularly relevant here.

The first level of consciousness takes place in a fraction of a second as the brain forms a selective binding of the firing of various neuronal structures to form an interpretation of human perception as a thinkable concept. The second level of consciousness is the short-term awareness that occurs over periods of seconds as these selective bindings change over time. It is this level of operation that gives the perception of dynamic continuity that informs our senses. The third level of consciousness is our extended awareness that reflects on events and conceptions encountered at different times to build into more extended knowledge structures.

This framework is particularly insightful in the calculus. Given that selective binding is performed over a short period of time (around a fortieth of a second or so), the human mind is unable to perceive much shorter events. However, through short-term awareness it can trace the dynamic changes that occur over time as a continuous flow.

For instance, if we attend a game of football, we may see a football player kick the ball and watch it glide continuously between the posts. Watching the same game on a film, we see a succession of still pictures played one after another at around twenty-five to thirty frames a second, yet the brain still sees it as a dynamically continuous movement.

We can gesture in the air and draw a graph on a piece of paper to sense the dynamic continuous change in a quantity. We may look at a static graph on a computer screen that is made of discrete pixels almost too small to distinguish and cast our eye along it to see it representing dynamic change. We can see a static area under a graph between two vertical lines and imagine the area changing continuously as a vertical side is moved, enabling us to conceptualize an area as a dynamically varying quantity. In this way we have a dynamically continuous perception of the changing world around us.

---

[1] See, for example, Núñez et al. (1999).
[2] Donald (2001).

1. The Origins of the Concepts of the Calculus

The Greeks imagined various processes that could be repeated again and again to conceive of potential infinity and to argue about the existence of an actual infinity. They debated whether the operation of subdividing a quantity would eventually produce a tiny indivisible element or an infinitesimal quantity that could be continually subdivided further.

Archimedes privately used infinitesimal methods to calculate areas that he regarded as being made of a large number of lines or very thin strips. Yet the proofs that he published replaced these methods by logical arguments using false position.

The early seventeenth century saw a resurgence of methods using either infinitesimals or indivisibles to calculate areas and slopes of tangents that flowered in the calculus of Newton and Leibniz.

At this time, Newton's professor at Cambridge, Isaac Barrow, was using the concept of infinitesimal with a clear cognitive meaning, writing in his *Lectiones Geometriae*:

> To every instant of time, or indefinitely small particle of time, (I say instant or indefinite particle, for it makes no difference whether we suppose time to be made up of instants or indefinitely minute timelets); to every instant of time, I say, there corresponds some degree of velocity, which the moving body is considered to possess at the instant.[3]

To calculate an area, he viewed it being made up of lines, though he agreed that it might be preferable to replace them by very narrow rectangles, maintaining that 'it comes to the same thing whichever way you take it.'

Using geometrical methods, he was able to calculate the slope of tangents and areas under curves, revealing a relationship between them that was the precursor of the fundamental theorem of calculus.

Both Newton and Leibniz read Barrow's work. Newton made three distinct attempts to explain how to imagine and calculate changing quantities. He started from Barrow's ideas and considered a quantity x varying continuously with time that he called a *fluent*, having a velocity that he called a *fluxion*, denoted by $\dot{x}$. Calculating fluents led to the notion of differentiation, the process of finding a fluent given a fluxion led to integration, and the amazing inverse relationship between the two is the Fundamental Theorem of Calculus.

---

[3] Isaac Barrow (1670), as translated by Child, p. 38.

His methods of calculation can be seen in his second approach to the calculus where he considered a small change o in x and calculated the ratio of the change in x^n to that in x as $((x + o)^n - x^n)/o$, using the binomial expansion (which he had himself formulated) to reduce the expression to

$$nx^{n-1} + o(\tfrac{1}{2} n(n-1)x^{n-2} + \cdots)$$

He then declared that when o becomes small, it could be neglected to give the slope as nx^{n-1}.

In his third method he considered the calculation in the Greek style by comparing ratios, where the *prime ratio*

$$(x + o)^n - x^n \text{ to } o$$

eventually becomes the *ultimate ratio*,

$$nx^{n-1} \text{ to } 1.$$

Even in this version, there is a subtle step from prime to ultimate ratio that is not fully explained.

Meanwhile, Leibniz imagined dx and dy to be the components of the tangent vector and saw dy/dx simply as the ratio of two finite quantities, dy divided by dx. (Figure 11.1.)

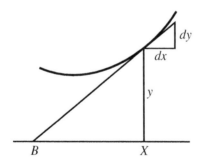

Figure 11.1. The Leibniz definition of dx and dy.

From the figure he noted that

$$\frac{dy}{dx} = \frac{y}{BX}$$

and so he could compute dy/dx if he knew the ordinate y and the subtangent BX.

However, to find the subtangent required him to know the slope of the tangent first, and this was what he was trying to find. His solution was to imagine the curve as a polygon with an infinite number of infinitely small sides so that he was able to visualize the tangent as extending a side of the polygon:

> We have only to keep in mind that to find a tangent means to draw a line that connects two points of the curve at an infinitely small distance, or the continued side of a polygon with an infinite number of angles, which for us takes the place of the curve.[4]

In the case of $y = x^2$, he calculated $dy = (x + dx)^2 - x^2$ and found

$$\frac{dy}{dx} = 2x + dx.$$

He then affirmed that, if dx was infinitesimal, it did not change the finite value $2x$ when added on. So

$$\frac{dy}{dx} = 2x.$$

He justified this argument by the imaginative use of quantities of very different sizes, saying:

> There are different degrees of infinity or of infinitely small, just as the globe of the Earth is estimated as a point in proportion to the distance of the fixed stars, and a play ball is still a point as compared to the radius of the terrestrial sphere, so that the distance of the fixed stars is an infinitely infinite with respect to the diameter of the ball.[5]

Bishop Berkeley, playing the role of the 'plain man', attacked both the fluxions of Newton and the infinitesimals of Leibniz, claiming that human sense is 'strained and puzzled with the perception of objects extremely minute', which seem to be 'ghosts of departed quantities' that 'exceed all human understanding'. For example, he asserted that

> ... to conceive a Quantity infinitely small, that is, infinitely less than any sensible or imaginable Quantity, or any the least finite Magnitude, is, I confess, above my Capacity. But to conceive a Part of such infinitely small Quantity, that shall be still infinitely less than it, and consequently though

---

[4] Quoted from the translation in Struik (1969), p. 276.
[5] Quoted from Struik (1969), p. 280.

multiply'd infinitely shall never equal the minutest finite Quantity, is, I suspect, an infinite Difficulty to any Man whatsoever ...[6]

He who can conceive the beginning of a beginning, or the end of an end, somewhat before the first or after the last, may be perhaps sharpsighted enough to conceive these things. But most Men will, I believe, find it impossible to understand them in any sense whatever.[7]

Berkeley's criticism is well formulated in the everyday 'common sense' of practical mathematics, even in the theoretical mathematics encountered in school, and his arguments remain strong to this day. Yet, we will later see in Chapter 13 that an alternative possibility arises in the world of formal definition and deduction where it is possible to define the real numbers to be a subfield of a larger system that can satisfy the order axioms. This will allow us to contemplate elements in a larger system that are greater than zero but smaller than any positive real number.

Such a view was not available to Berkeley or to his contemporaries, and he made other criticisms of the calculus such as disputing the technique that claims that dx is non-zero to calculate the ratio dy/dx and then setting dx equal to zero to calculate the limit.

The dispute continued in succeeding centuries. In the nineteenth century, Cauchy spoke of variable quantities that could 'become' infinite or infinitesimal:

One says that a variable quantity becomes infinitely small when its numerical value decreases indefinitely in such a way as to converge to the limit zero.[8]

Meanwhile, in England in 1803 the pragmatic Cambridge mathematician Robert Woodhouse criticized the cumbersome notation of Newton because the first derivative of x was represented as $\dot{x}$, and the tenth derivative would require ten dots over the symbol. He suggested a modification of the Leibniz notation that continues in use today. He defined δx and δy to be corresponding finite increments in x and y, Δx and Δy to denote corresponding infinitesimal increments, and dx, dy to denote the differentials. Thus if $y = x^2$, one would have

---

[6] Quoted from *The Analyst*, edited by Wilkins (2002), p. 3.
[7] Wilkins (2002), p. 21.
[8] Cauchy, quoted from Boyer (1923/1939), p. 273. Cauchy's ideas have been debated over the years. My own cognitive view is that he based his ideas of sequences that tended to zero, but then used the sequences as mental objects that he could manipulate, thus encapsulating a process as a mental object.

$$\delta y = (x + \delta x)^2 - x^2 = 2x\,\delta x + \delta x^2 \quad \text{(for finite } \delta x)$$

$$\Delta y = 2x\,\Delta x + \Delta x^2 \quad \text{(for infinitesimal } \Delta x)$$

and

$$dy = 2x\,dx \quad \text{(for infinitesimal } dx).$$

This notation works in practice and corresponds to the perceptual imagery of quantities being so very small that they make no difference in a finite calculation. However, it does not satisfy the logical need to make sense of infinitesimal concepts. The problem was eventually resolved by eliminating the need for infinitesimals. The breakthrough came by using the epsilon-delta definition of limit in a purely arithmetical approach advocated by Karl Weierstrass. This effectively avoided actual infinitesimals and returned to the potentially infinite idea of specifying a required error of at most epsilon to seek an input within an error delta to produce the required accuracy. This gave mathematical analysis a new and rigorous foundation. At the same time it led to a formal break with the past and the rejection of the infinitesimals of Leibniz.

2. Problematic Aspects in Teaching

The introduction of the limit concept enabled mathematical experts to build formal knowledge structures with new formal concepts that offer powerful new ways of proving theorems. However, the limit concept proved to be problematic for beginning students and their difficulties were not helped by the convoluted disputes over the meaning of the concepts in the calculus.

In the United Kingdom, the mid-twentieth century version of calculus still depended on the ideas introduced by Woodhouse a century and a half before. The received wisdom was that if y is a function of x and, as x increases to $x + \delta x$ so y increases to $y + \delta y$, then, as δx gets small, if the slope $\delta y/\delta x$ tends to a fixed limit, the symbol dy/dx is *defined* to be that limiting value:

$$\frac{dy}{dx} = \lim_{\delta x \to 0} \frac{\delta y}{\delta x}.$$

The symbol dy/dx no longer has the sense given to it originally by Leibniz or subsequently by Woodhouse. As Geoffrey Matthews wrote at the time:

> dy/dx is simply a notation, signifying the gradient of the curve in question. It is not to be considered here as a ratio, as $\delta y/\delta x$ is, but just a handy way of expressing 'the limit as $\delta x \to 0$ of $\delta y/\delta x$'.[9]

[9] Matthews (1964).

His view was firmly supported by Hilary Shuard and Hugh Neill in their book, *Teaching the Calculus*:

> The student … has to learn that, in spite of all the evidence to the contrary, which seems to him to build up from statements such as
>
> $$\frac{dy}{dx} \times \frac{dx}{dt} = \frac{dy}{dt}$$
>
> *dy/dx* is not a symbol for a fraction, but for the limit of the gradient of a chord.[10]

It was expressed even more forcefully in one of the earlier versions of the *School Mathematics Project Advanced Mathematics*:

> '*dy/dx*' must, at least for some considerable time, be regarded as an insepar-able whole, just as 'δx' is. It does not in any simple or straight-forward way mean anything like '*dy* divided by *dx*', and a statement such as
>
> $$\frac{dy}{dx} \times \frac{dx}{dt} = \frac{dy}{dt} \quad \text{by cancelling } dx$$
>
> is just so much gibberish.[11]

With this damning opinion of a symbolism that looks like a quotient and acts like a quotient, what are students to think? Essentially they are not only being presented with the goal of understanding the limit concept, but the anti-goal of avoiding thinking of the derivative as a quotient.

They are told that the symbol *dy/dx* means 'the derivative of y *with respect to* x' and are then told that the symbol *dx* in $\int f(x)\, dx$ now means 'the integral of *f(x)* with respect to *x*'.

Having been told that *dy/dx* is not a quotient, when students meet dif-ferential equations such as

$$y\frac{dy}{dx} = x$$

they may then be told that the solution is found by 'multiplying through by *dx* and integrating the result' to get

[10]   Neill & Shuard (1982).
[11]   Schools Mathematics Project (1982), p. 221.

$$\int y \, dy = \int x \, dx$$

giving

$$\tfrac{1}{2} y^2 = \tfrac{1}{2} x^2 + c.$$

These techniques are taught instrumentally around the world, so that students can carry out procedures to use in applications and to give answers on tests. They are told that they must avoid thinking about ideas in certain ways that seem natural to them, in an emotionally charged manner that counsels them to avoid thinking about the derivative as a quotient of lengths. Skemp's theory of goals and anti-goals discussed in Chapter 5 reveals that this can be explained not only in terms of high-level intellectual dispute, but also in terms of fundamental human reactions to problematic aspects of knowledge.

As social creatures we repeat the ideas passed down to us and, in turn, we pass them on to our students. Our met-befores, born out of cognitive conflict, are passed on to successive generations to be learnt and feared as problematic met-befores that must be avoided. The consequence is a change, from the goal of relational understanding blighted by conflict, to the goal of learning procedures to achieve pleasure in acquiring techniques that are useful in applications and in passing examinations.

2.1 *Using Computer Software to Represent Calculus Concepts*

The arrival of personal computers in the 1970s provided new ways of conceptualizing the calculus. However, computers used in the 1980s for numerical calculations could produce catastrophic errors when dividing one small number by another. For instance, one might hope to show that the numerical value of the slope for $\sin x$ at $x = \pi / 3$ tends to the derivative $\cos(\pi / 3) = \tfrac{1}{2}$. A BBC computer with floating point arithmetic calculated the values of $(\sin (\pi/3 + h) - \sin (\pi/3)/h$ for $h = 1/10^n$ as n increases from 1 to 10 as follows:

0.455901884, 0.495661539, 0.499954913, 0.499980524, 0.499654561,
0.500585884, 0.465661287, 0.232830644, 0,   0.

The first four values increase towards the expected limit 0.5, but then the values go haywire as numerical errors come into play. The last two results are zero because floating point arithmetic returns the value zero for the numerator while the denominator is non-zero.

More modern software calculates to a far greater accuracy so that these errors are less likely to be revealed, although they still remain in floating point arithmetic when the differences are very small.

The early pioneers who developed software to represent ideas in calculus were often as much concerned to 'tame the beast' of numeric computation to present satisfactory outputs as they were to think of ways of using technology to give conceptual insight.

Symbol manipulation software introduced a new element of perfection, but even this needed to be interpreted in an appropriate way to make sense of the symbolic solution of a problem.

3. A Locally Straight Approach to the Calculus

Given the human capacity to put together short events of around a fortieth of a second and to link them together smoothly as a continuous perception, dynamic computer graphics are ideal for representing human perceptions of change and growth. What is essential is a curriculum that builds on the strengths of the knowledge structures of the learner.

The framework of three worlds of mathematics deals precisely with this situation. It enables the learner to embody the human perception of continuous change, use good-enough arithmetic to obtain a numerical approximation, and then to seek the perfect symbolic expression for the derivative. At the same time, there is already ample evidence that the focus on the formal limit without the students having any experience of the formal axiomatic world is problematic.

While a combination of geometric, arithmetic and symbolic aspects are found in reform calculus in the United States[12], the presentation is in the form of an interplay between graphic, symbolic and analytic representations rather than a focus on the particular strengths of various aspects of the blend.

An approach that takes the student's cognitive development into account may begin with the embodied experience of dynamic change and seek to calculate the rate of change using good-enough arithmetic and algebraic manipulation.

The strategy is to use dynamic graph-plotting software to zoom in on any part of a graph. The graphs in the student's experience are usually

---

[12] Gleason & Hughes Hallett (1994).

combinations of standard functions (including polynomials, rational functions, trigonometric functions, exponentials and logarithms). All of these share a common property.

As one zooms in on the graph and looks at a smaller and smaller piece under higher magnification, the graph gets less and less curved until a small portion highly magnified looks like a straight line. A graph with this property is said to be *locally straight*.

The idea of local straightness is a variant on the insights of Leibniz. If he had access to the tools that we have today to look at curves under high magnification, he would be able to *see* a vision that is more perfect than his own conception of a smooth curve as a polygonal graph with an infinite number of infinitesimally straight sides. A polygon has *corners*, which involves tiny turns. They may be tiny, but they are there. A locally straight approach zooms in on the curve and, if the function is differentiable, then the graph looks locally straight. For a differentiable function, there are no corners visible anywhere. The vision is perfect.

This gives a distinction between those graphs that are dynamically continuous (meaning they can be drawn in a movement of the hand using a pencil that does not leave the paper) and those that are locally straight, which are precisely those graphs that have a slope function. A graph may have extremely tiny wrinkles on it that are not picked up at a given scale when drawing with a physical pencil. So it may be dynamically continuous without being locally straight. The wrinkles become visible only when the graph is visualized under appropriately high magnification.

This offers students a new way of visualizing the difference between continuity and differentiability that is not part of the traditional approach focusing only on graphs that are differentiable. It also has a further bonus. The components of the tangent vector may be denoted by dx and dy, so that the derivative dy/dx may be conceived as a quotient of finite lengths. This removes the need to give students an anti-goal to avoid thinking of the derivative as a ratio. It offers in its place the positive goal of relational understanding of differentiability in terms of local straightness under appropriate magnification, linking this to the computable symbolism of differentiation and integration.

3.1 *The Slope Function of a Locally Straight Graph*

A locally straight approach to the calculus begins with human perception of the graph of the function itself, which we can trace with our finger and see as an object drawn practically on paper or mentally in our mind's eye

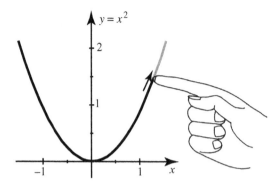

Figure 11.2. Tracing a graph to see and feel the graph as an object.

(Figure 11.2). This enables us to *feel* the continuity of the graph as dynamic continuity. But it does not yet tell us much about the changing slope.

Now imagine sliding the hand along the curve to let the slope of the hand follow the changing slope (Figure 11.3). This is an operation on a visible object (the graph) and it builds the embodied sense of the changing slope of the curve.

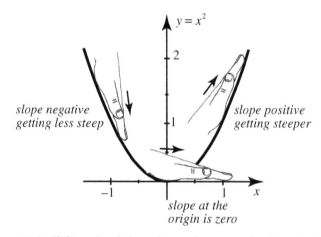

Figure 11.3. Sliding a hand along the graph to sense the changing slope.

To see the changing slope, imagine moving a magnifying glass along the curve to *see* the slope change as the magnifying glass moves along (Figure 11.4). For the graph of $y = x^2$ the slope will be seen to be downwards (negative) to the left of the origin, zero at the origin, with the slope continuing to increase in value. One or two key points may give a sense of

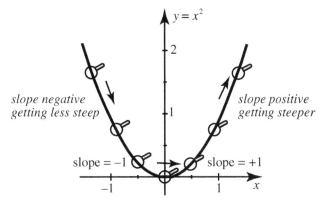

Figure 11.4. Moving a magnifying graph along the curve to see the changing slope.

size, for instance, the slope is about –1 when $x = -\frac{1}{2}$, zero at the origin, and about 1 at $x = \frac{1}{2}$.

Now let the graph be drawn using software to plot the line through close points (x, x^2), $(x + h, (x + h)^2)$, for fixed h. This line is called a *practical tangent* at the point x. Figure 11.5 shows the practical tangent being drawn

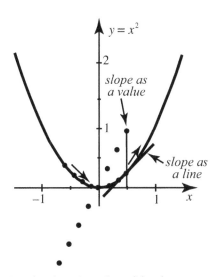

Figure 11.5. Plotting the changing value of the slope on a computer as a new graph.

for $h = 0.01$ at a sequence of points on the graph $y = x^2$ and the value of the slope being plotted. For each value of x the practical tangent is drawn at the same time as the value of the slope is drawn as a dot. The dots remain as the successive practical tangents are drawn and removed, to leave a sequence of points representing the changing value of the slope.

In practice, the picture does not require h to be arbitrarily small; in many familiar cases, a value such as $h = 0.1$ or 0.001 will do.

There is also another aspect to this simple idea. We can draw a practical tangent from $(x, f(x))$ to $(x + h, f(x + h))$ for *any* function f for which the values $f(x)$ and $f(x + h)$ are defined. In particular, if the graph is locally straight, then, for small h, the practical tangent looks indistinguishable from the theoretical tangent. This relates to the way that Leibniz imagined a tangent through two points on the curve that are an infinitesimal distance apart.

It also relates to the cognitive development of the learner, shifting from the *practical mathematics* of childhood to the *theoretical mathematics* of conceptual embodiment of graphs and operational symbolism of algebra blended together to give the calculus. To grasp the practical and theoretical significance of the changing slope based on human perception and action can be achieved *before* looking at the formal definition of the limit.

In the case of the function $y = x^2$, the changing values of the slope look as if they are in a straight line. But what is its equation? All this requires is to switch from insightful embodiment to precise symbolism.

The slope from (x, x^2) to $(x + h, (x + h)^2)$ is

$$\text{slope} = \frac{(x + h)^2 - x^2}{h} = \frac{2xh + h^2}{h} = 2x + h$$

This is a straight line, and for small values of h, it looks like the graph of $2x$. The graph of $2x$ represents the changing slope of the original graph, allowing us to see the slope function *as a whole*.

This focuses on the *structure* of the graph of the function, how it rises and falls, and how its slope changes. It involves *embodied compression* through the operation of looking along the visible graph of the function (as a base object) and traces its changing slope and draws the *effect* of the operation as a new graph: the graph of a slope function. Instead of the *symbolic compression* encapsulating a limiting *process* into a limit *object* (the derivative), it is an *embodied compression* that operates on an *object* (the graph) to give a new *object* (the graph of the slope function). The student can now *see* the derivative as the changing slope function. The new task is to symbolize this vision of the slope function by calculating a good-enough arithmetic approximation, or better still, a perfect symbolic representation.

This vision of the slope function, made possible by the computer, is quite different from the traditional pre-computer approach. The latter 'simplifies' the symbolic calculation by starting with x as a *fixed* point, and calculating the slope through two nearby points on the curve over x-values x and $x + h$, and taking the limit as h tends to zero. It then allows x to vary again to give the overall derivative. This involves the mystery of working out the quotient $(f(x + h) - f(x))/h$ assuming that h is non-zero and then concluding the argument by putting $h = 0$. It is based on a potentially infinite limit process that leads to an object whose existence needs to be established.

A locally straight approach works with the *whole graph* and operates on it to visualize the changing slope. This is a far more natural approach as it builds on the student's natural perception and action to produce a visible graph of the slope function. The task is then to *calculate* the slope function that is visible for all to see.

In the case of the function x^2, the slope function visibly stabilizes on $2x$. It gives the best of both worlds – embodied and symbolic – to see, feel, and sense the changing slope of the original function and to see the *effect* of tracing the changing slope as a new embodied object. This slope function can then be linked to the corresponding symbolism and the formal idea of limit can be introduced later when the need for it becomes apparent in developing the standard rules for calculating the symbolic derivative for combinations of functions.[13]

More generally, one starts with the graph of a function f and looks along it to perform the operation D that gives the graph of the stabilized slope function Df. After one has visualized the graph of Df in one's imagination, the value of $Df(x)$ at a particular point x equals the quotient dy/dx of the components of the tangent.

---

[13] There are many individuals in the mathematics community who were *horrified* by this approach as their experience taught them that they had to find the derivative at a point first and then to vary it to get the derivative function. They know that there are issues about fixing h first, related to the subtle distinction between a *uniform* change in h over the whole domain and a *pointwise* change in h at a specific point. This issue can be addressed much later by looking at $f(x) = 1/x$, which jumps at the origin and requires x and $x + h$ to be on the same side of the origin. This example shows why, at a later formal stage in mathematical analysis, it is necessary to distinguish between continuity at a single point and uniform continuity.

3.2 *The Slope Functions of Standard Functions*

The combination of embodiment and symbolism allows a fruitful exploration of all the standard functions x^2, x^3, x^n, sin x, cos x, e^x and ln x to seek an embodiment of their slope functions. For instance, looking along the graph of sin x (with angles in radians) reveals the slope function shaped like cos x while the graph of cos x has a slope function that looks like sin x upside down, so it is *minus* sin x (Figure 11.6).

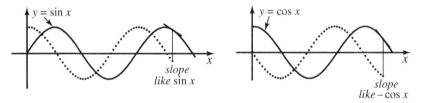

Figure 11.6. The slope of sin x is cos x and the slope of cos x is sin x upside down.

When I first programmed this in the *Graphic Calculus* software[14], I included the possibility of drawing successive tangents at various speeds and included an option to stop it so that the teacher as mentor could discuss the relationship between the slope of the practical tangent and the corresponding value plotted simultaneously to build the slope graph.

I longed for the time when computer technology would advance far enough to plot so many points that it would look like a dynamically continuous graph building up on the screen.

The opportunity came quicker than I expected when the British BBC computer switched from an 8-bit processor to a 32-bit RISC chip in the mid-1980s and the program suddenly ran a hundred times faster. I set the program to plot so many points on the slope function that they appeared as a growing connected graph. My human eye proved to be incapable of correlating the smoothly moving tangent and the smoothly growing slope graph. It all happened too fast for coherent selective binding. The conceptualization needs a steady click-click-click moving the practical tangent along in steps to enable my mind to correlate its changing slope with a succession of explicit points on the slope graph. Again, we are reminded of the need to create representations that can be interpreted sensibly by our human perception.

[14] Blokland & Giessen (2000).

3.3 *The Exponential Function*

Moving on to the case of graphs of the form k^x where k is a constant, an investigation of the slopes of 2^x and 3^x reveals both have steadily increasing graphs, and each has steadily increasing slope functions. However, the graph of 2^x has a slope graph that is lower than the original, while 3^x has a slope graph that is higher (Figure 11.7).

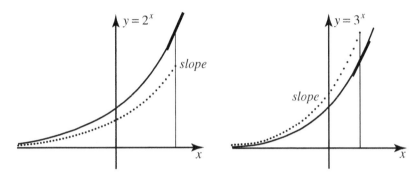

Figure 11.7. The slopes of $2x$ and $3x$.

Our dynamically continuous perception can imagine k changing continuously from 2 to 3, suggesting that somewhere between 2 and 3 there should be a value e such that the graph of e^x and its slope function are the same.

Suppose that this function can be approximated by a (possibly lengthy) polynomial,

$$e^x = A + Bx + Cx^2 + \cdots$$

then this must equal its derivative,

$$B + 2Cx + 3Dx^2 + \cdots .$$

Putting $x = 0$, using $e^0 = 1$ gives $A = 1$, and comparing term by term gives $B = A, 2C = B, 3D = B, \ldots$, so $B = 1$, $C = \frac{1}{2}$, $D = \frac{1}{(2 \times 3)}, \ldots$ and

$$e^x = 1 + x + x^2 / 2! + \cdots x^n / n! \cdots \quad \text{where } n! = 1 \times 2 \times \cdots \times n.$$

Putting $x = 1$ gives

$$e = 1 + \frac{1}{1!} + \frac{1}{2!} + \cdots + \frac{1}{n!} + \cdots$$

which is easily calculated by writing down 1, dividing it by 1, then by 2, then 3, and so on, adding the results to find *e* to, say, 10 decimal places:

1	1.0000000000
divide by 1 gives	1.0000000000
divide by 2 gives	0.5000000000
divide by 3 gives	0.1666666667
divide by 4 gives	0.0416666667
divide by 5 gives	0.0083333333
divide by 6 gives	0.0013888889
divide by 7 gives	0.0001984127
divide by 8 gives	0.0000248016
divide by 9 gives	0.0000027557
divide by 10 gives	0.0000002756
divide by 11 gives	0.0000000251
divide by 12 gives	0.0000000021
divide by 13 gives	0.0000000002
divide by 14 gives	0.0000000000
divide by 15 gives	0.0000000000
Total =	2.7182818285

The constant e is 2.7182818285 to ten decimal places (as the subsequent terms are each less than a tenth of the previous one and so their total will not change the tenth decimal place).

For an expert, this approach involves hidden problems, such as the idea that e^x is given by a polynomial of unspecified length. However, for a student coordinating good-enough arithmetic with dynamically changing graphs, it offers a natural extension of previous experience. In particular, by personally calculating *e*, the student experiences *why* the later terms become so small that they become irrelevant.

4. Leibniz Revisited

We saw that Leibniz expressed the derivative of a relationship between variables *x* and *y* as the ratio dy/dx where dy and dx are the components of the tangent vector. These components may be called *differentials*. They are the same differentials that appear in differential equations.

It was only the need to calculate the slope of the tangent vector that caused Leibniz to introduce infinitesimal arguments. Now that we can use dynamic computer imagery to represent his embodied ideas, we can take his lead to define dx and dy as *the components of the tangent vector* and to define the derivative as the quantity dy/dx. As we zoom in on the curve, and the graph looks locally straight, we can *see* the derivative to be the slope of the graph at the point x.

The horizontal component of the tangent can be any real number dx and, using the modern function notation $y = f(x)$, if the derivative $f'(x)$ is known, then the vertical component dy is

$$dy = f'(x)dx.$$

This meaning of dx and dy as components of the tangent vector begs one question, which Leibniz could solve only by introducing infinitesimals, that is to say clearly what is meant by the concept of 'tangent'.

4.1 *What Is a Tangent?*

The concept of tangent arises from embodiment in geometry, from the Latin verb *tangere*, meaning to 'touch'. A tangent to a circle is a straight line that is imagined to touch a circle at precisely one point (or, as is sometimes said, at 'two coincident points'). If this is generalized to speak of a tangent to a more general curve, it may continue to evoke the met-before that a tangent 'touches the graph at one point, and does not cross it.' This introduces a problematic aspect. It evokes a conception of the tangent that I term a 'generic tangent'.[15] This need not be a mathematical tangent; it is a straight line that 'touches but does not cross the graph.' For instance, the function given by

$$f(x) = \begin{cases} x & (x \le 0) \\ x^2 + x & (x > 0) \end{cases}$$

has a tangent $y = x$ at the origin; however, this is often rejected by students because it coincides with the graph to the left. In such circumstances, students often move the tangent line around a little to draw a generic tangent that touches the graph at only one point. (Figure 11.8.) In a study comparing students who had been taught by a locally straight approach compared with others following a traditional approach, 46% (30 out of 65) traditional students drew a generic tangent while only 20% (8 out of 40) following a locally straight approach did so.[16]

The problematic nature of a generic tangent may arise in part from the belief that the limiting secant never reaches the exact position of the

---

[15] Tall (1986a, b).
[16] Tall (1986a, b).

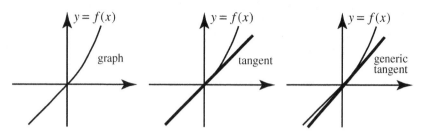

Figure 11.8. A generic tangent to a graph (at the origin).

tangent. However, a more likely source is the met-before of a tangent to a circle that touches the circle at one point only and does not cross it.

To resolve the problem requires a wider consideration of the notion of the tangent and what it means to say that a graph has a tangent at a point. Again local straightness gives a precise solution. The graph has a tangent at a point if and only if it is locally straight there. Zooming in on a graph focusing on a particular point where the graph is locally straight reveals that the graph and its tangent soon look indistinguishable. The tangent is 'the best linear approximation' to the curve at the given point. Far from touching the curve at just one point, when it is drawn with a pencil of finite thickness, in the magnified picture the tangent and the graph look exactly the same, to within the physical accuracy of drawing.

This includes the conception of a tangent to a straight line (where the tangent is identical with the line), or at a point of inflection, passing from one side of the curve to the other. Both of these occur in the calculus and are problematic for a student who thinks a tangent 'touches the curve at just one point and does not cross it.'

5. Parametric Functions

The idea of the derivative as the ratio of the components of the tangent also works in the case of parametric and composite functions.

A parametric function $x = x(t)$, $y = y(t)$, which is usually drawn as a curve in two-dimensional (x, y)-space, can also be imagined as the curve $(t, x(t), y(t))$ in three-dimensional t-x-y space to see the value of x and y vary with t. For instance, Figure 11.9 shows the parametric curve $x = \cos(t)$, $y = \sin(t)$ plotted on a computer screen with the three-dimensional view in the top left and the projections onto the three coordinate planes in the other three windows.

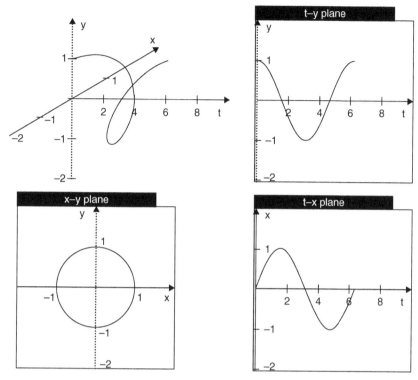

Figure 11.9. The parametric curve $x = \cos t$, $y = \sin t$ in three-space with projections onto the three coordinate planes.

The software[17] allowed the three-dimensional picture to be rotated in space to look at it from different angles to reveal the three projections. It also allowed a practical tangent to be drawn to the curve at any chosen point with parameter t that is good enough to represent the theoretical tangent with components dt, dx, dy. The value dt can then be any length with dx and dy calculated as

$$dx = x'(t)dt, \quad dy = y'(t)dt.$$

Figure 11.10 shows the tangent vector and its components dt, dx, dy in three dimensions (top left) with the projections on the coordinate planes.

---

[17] This software was written for the *Real Functions and Graphs* (Tall 1991b) and is no longer available for modern computers.

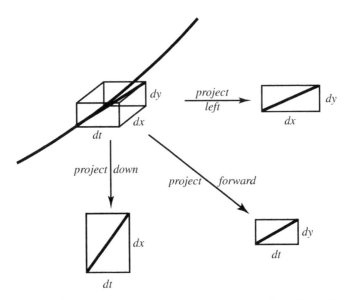

Figure 11.10. The components of the tangent vector in three dimensions as
dt, dx, dy.

In the x-y plane, the tangent has components dx, dy and its slope is

$$\frac{dy}{dx} = \frac{y'(t)dt}{x'(t)dt} = \frac{y'(t)}{x'(t)}$$

or, using the Leibniz notation $x'(t) = dx/dt$, $y'(t) = dy/dt$,

$$\frac{dy}{dx} = \frac{dy}{dt} \bigg/ \frac{dt}{dx}.$$

Because dt, dx, dy are all *lengths* in this interpretation, the equation is valid as quotients. Because dt can always be taken to be non-zero, the only technicality occurs when $dx = 0$ and here, as a point on the graph is traced in time, it can be seen that the tangent is perpendicular to the x-axis. (Figure 11.11).

6. Composite Functions and the Chain Rule

When I programmed the original software[18] in Figure 11.9, I had the idea of using the same software to draw a composite function $x = f(t)$ and $y = g(x)$

---

[18] Tall (1991b).

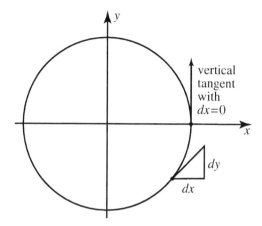

Figure 11.11. A vertical tangent for a parametric function with x and y as functions of t.

by allowing y to be input as a function of x which then gave a parametric function in the form $x = f(t)$, $y = g(f(t))$. When submitted for a volume published by the Mathematical Association of America, this idea affronted a reviewer, who declared that it was essential to see the graph of a composite function as a function of a function, not as a special case of a parametric function. The article was published[19] on condition that I remove the offending section. The reviewer's problem related to his inability to see a general composite function $f : A \rightarrow B$, $g : B \rightarrow C$ as a subset of $A \times B \times C$ in the form $(t, f(t), g(f(t)))$. I suggest that the problem is not mine, but that it arises from a view of the mathematics that insists on a particular viewpoint and lacks conceptual flexibility. The section removed was quickly accepted as a separate paper in another journal.[20]

The insight of this view reveals a composite function in t-x-y space where the components of the tangent vector are again dt, dx, dy. The value of dt can be any real number and $dx = f'(t)\, dt$, $dy = g'(x)\, dx$.

If dt is non-zero, we can then operate with dt, dx, dy as lengths, to get the 'chain rule' in the form

$$\frac{dy}{dt} = \frac{dy}{dx} \times \frac{dx}{dt}$$

or, in function notation,

$$h'(t) = g'(x)f'(t) = g'(f(t))f'(t).$$

Here the differentials dt, dx, dy are the sides of a box in three-space, so the value dx can certainly be cancelled to interpret the equation in the usual way. There is, however, a singular case, which happens when $f'(t) = 0$ and so $dx = f'(t) \, dt$ is also zero and cannot be substituted into the equation. The problem is no big deal. If $dx = 0$ then $dy = g'(x) \, dx$ is also zero and so $h'(t) = dy/dt = 0$ (where $dt \neq 0$) and the chain rule in the form $h'(t) = g'(x)f'(t)$ remains true because both sides are zero.

This singular case caused mathematicians to see the need for a full formal proof of the chain rule using epsilon-delta analysis. This is part of the vast edifice of modern mathematical analysis that is a tribute to the ingenuity of *Homo sapiens*, thinking in ways that are far beyond that of any other species. But it is a difficult transition for students meeting the calculus for the first time. What is far more appropriate is an approach building from the experience of dynamic embodiment, good-enough arithmetic and the familiar manipulation of symbols where dy/dx is the quotient of the components of the tangent vector. This enables the learner to build on practical and theoretical mathematics in their first calculus course, to choose later whether to remain with a theoretical approach where practical problems are modelled and solved symbolically, or to move to a formal approach in mathematical analysis.

7. Inverse Functions

Inverse functions also work naturally in the Leibniz notation, for if $y = f(x)$ is one-one and has an inverse function $x = g(y)$, then the inverse has a graph found by interchanging the axes, (reflecting in the line $y = x$). (Figure 11.12.)

This simply interchanges the component of the tangent vectors so that the derivative of the inverse is the reciprocal of the derivative of the original:

$$\frac{dx}{dy} = \frac{1}{dy/dx}.$$

In the case of $y = \ln(x)$, the inverse is $x = e^y$, with derivative

$$\frac{dx}{dy} = e^y$$

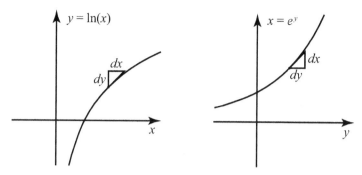

Figure 11.12. The inverse function is found by interchanging the axes.

or

$$\frac{dx}{dy} = x$$

so the derivative of the original function $y = \ln(x)$ satisfies

$$\frac{dy}{dx} = \frac{1}{x}.$$

This completes the list of standard derivatives that are the basis of a first course in calculus.

8. Introducing the Limit Concept

A student who has grasped the embodied meaning of the changing slope of a (locally straight) function as a new function that can be visualized is ready to tackle the notion of limit. He or she can 'see' that the slope function of a locally straight function is again a function. The challenge is to *calculate* it.

Calculus is more than *looking* at graphs and *guessing* the formula for the derivative. As soon as we have slightly more complicated functions, such as $x \sin x$ or $e^{1/x}$, then 'looking and guessing' is no longer feasible. Now that the slope function has a perceptual image to embody its ultimate form, it is time to introduce the limit concept to use it to derive the rules of calculus to differentiate more complicated functions.

8.1 *The Rules for Differentiation*

Having visualized the picture of the slope function and introduced the concept of limit, the next step is to work with functions $f(x)$, $g(x)$ whose derivatives are known and to calculate the derivatives of combinations such as $f(x) + g(x)$, $f(x) - g(x)$, $f(x)\, g(x)$, $f(x)/g(x)$ and $f(g(x))$.

Addition and subtraction are fairly self-evident and the derivative of the composite $f(g(x))$ has already been performed in a previous section.

This leaves the laws for a product and quotient. Leibniz had the bright idea to see the product uv as the area of a rectangle and, when u increased to $u + du$ and v to $v + dv$, the rectangle increased in size to

$$(u + du)(v + dv) = uv + u\,dv + v\,du + du\,dv$$

so the actual increase is

$$u\,dv + v\,du + du\,dv.$$

Dividing by dx gives the change in slope as

$$u\frac{dv}{dx} + v\frac{du}{dx} + du\frac{dv}{dx}.$$

As dx tends to zero, if we know that u and v are locally straight giving finite derivatives du/dx and dv/dx, then as dx tends to zero, so does du, giving the derivative uv as

$$u\frac{dv}{dx} + v\frac{du}{dx}.$$

A similar argument gives a formula for the derivative of a quotient u/v.

8.2 *Non-differentiable functions*

A first course in calculus usually focuses on the regular functions given by a combination of the standard functions. This necessarily gives the impression that functions are usually differentiable, setting up the met-before that later ideas in mathematical analysis can be monstrous. An embodied approach, however, can offer insights as to what it means to be *non*-differentiable. This may be a function whose graph has a corner, such as $|\sin x|$ with corners at every multiple of π. (Figure 11.13.)

It may also be a function that is so wrinkled that it *never* looks straight under high magnification. Such a function is the *blancmange function*, built up by starting with the sawtooth function

$$s(x) = \begin{cases} x & (0 \le x \le \tfrac{1}{2}). \\ 1 - x & (\tfrac{1}{2} \le x \le 1) \end{cases}$$

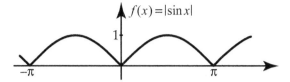

Figure 11.13. A function with corners.

and repeating the values in every unit interval, $s(x + n) = s(x)$ for every whole number n.

The blancmange function is built by constructing successively half-size sawteeth $s_n(x) = \frac{1}{2^{n-1}} s(2^{n-1} x)$ and adding them together to get

$$b_n(x) = s_1(x) + s_2(x) + \cdots + s_n(x)$$

The blancmange function itself, $bl(x)$, is the limit of this sequence of sums (Figure 11.14).

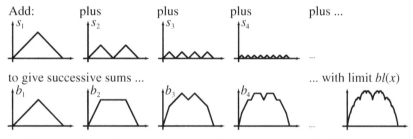

Figure 11.14. Adding successively smaller sawteeth to get the blancmange function.

In the practical world of drawing pictures, it is only necessary to add on as many sawteeth as are necessary to stabilize the picture drawn with a pencil or with pixels on a computer screen. A high-resolution display may be a thousand pixels or so high. In this case it only needs ten iterations to give a 'good-enough' picture. Any additional sawteeth become so small that what they add lies within the size of a single pixel. More sawteeth may be required if the graph is magnified to reveal higher detail.

The graph is visibly dynamically continuous in the sense that it can be drawn by a continuous stroke of a pencil. Higher detail arises as one imagines the graph drawn at higher magnification using the same pencil. If required, it is a routine calculation to show that the function is formally continuous, but that is not required in a first calculus course.

To see why the blancmange function is nowhere differentiable can be shown by an embodied argument that can later be transformed into a formal proof if that is required. The strategy is to superimpose the successive approximations to the blancmange function. (Figure 11.15.) This reveals the curve as a fractal with small blancmanges everywhere, some clearly recognizable, others disguised by being sheared vertically as they stand on straight-line segments that are at an angle.

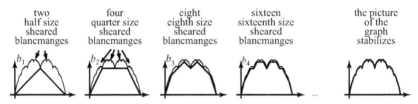

Figure 11.15. Blancmanges everywhere!

This is because the sum giving the blancmange can be broken up into the sum of the first n saw-teeth plus the rest. The blancmange is

$$b_1(x) + (s_2(x)) + s_3(x)) + \cdots)$$

which is $b_1(x)$ plus a *half-size blancmange*. It is also

$$b_2(x) + (s_3(x)) + s_4(x)) + \cdots)$$

which is $b_2(x)$ plus a quarter-size blancmange, and, in general, the blancmange function is $b_n(x)$ plus a $(\frac{1}{2})^n$ size blancmange. However much the graph is magnified, it is possible to choose a value of n to see it as a straight-line segment arising from $b_n(x)$ with a tiny blancmange growing on it. You will need to do this in your mind's eye, for where the graph is very steep, the added blancmange will be swamped within the steep line of pixels, as you can see by squashing a picture horizontally to see what happens as the line becomes steeper. (Figure 11.16.)

Figure 11.16. What happens to a part of the blancmange as the slope gets steeper.

In general, there are two kinds of points on the graph, those at values of x precisely of the form $k/2^n$ for any integers k, and n ($n \geq 0$), where the graph comes down vertically from the left and goes up vertically to the right. Here, under high magnification the graph looks like a half-line pointing upwards. Everywhere else, the graph is locally a tiny blancmange sheared on a small line segment that may be easily seen if the segment is not too steep, but if it is nearly vertical, the up-and-down oscillations may be submerged in a vertical line of pixels.

This shows that what we can see in our mind's eye is subtler that what can be represented on a computer screen. We can imagine a blancmange on a line segment, but a computer picture with a nearly vertical line may not distinguish the two.

This relates to the levels of consciousness formulated by Merlin Donald where our real-world perceptions are limited by our capacity to distinguish small details in vision and in time but our extended thinking skills enable us to imagine ideas that we cannot represent in practice.

The development of the calculus in history and in the individual have led to the idea that most functions are differentiable almost everywhere, except at a few singular points. We can now use software to 'see' graphs that are everywhere continuous, but nowhere differentiable.

In a given picture we may not even be able to see the difference between a function that is everywhere differentiable and one that is nowhere differentiable. For instance, the tiny blancmange function $n(x) = bl(1000x)/1000$ is only a thousandth the size of the original. I call this 'the nasty function'. If we take *any* differentiable function $f(x)$ and add the nasty function, then $f(x)$ is differentiable everywhere and $f(x) + n(x)$ is differentiable nowhere. Yet the two graphs look exactly the same when drawn at a scale that loses the additional information given by the added function $n(x)$.

The reason for this is that the physical drawing is performed using a pencil that draws a fine line that has a thickness that covers both graphs. When drawn on a computer screen at a certain scale, the nasty wrinkles are subsumed within the pixels. It is only when these graphs are magnified a thousand times that one looks locally straight while the other has visible blancmanges growing on it. (Figure 11.17 overleaf.)

An embodied approach to the calculus is so much more than a naïve approach suitable to teach novice learners, it reveals genuine insights into why we must refine our embodiment in our imagination and make it more precise by introducing exact symbolism and, at a suitable stage, formal definitions. This offers more sophisticated ways to imagine new embodiments that give a natural meaning to concepts that had seemed monstrous.

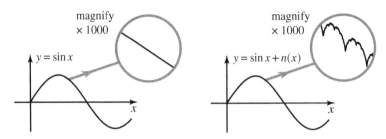

Figure 11.17. Two graphs that look the same at one level but are very different magnified.

9. From Dynamic Embodied Continuity to the Formal Definition

In an embodied sense, a dynamically continuous function is one whose graph can be drawn without taking the pencil off the paper. Imagine this in the mind's eye, and then imagine focusing on a tiny section of it and stretching it horizontally. As the horizontal scale is increased and the vertical scale stays the same, it becomes flatter. On a computer screen we can embody this process by drawing any graph in a window and allow the individual to select a tall thin rectangle that will then be expanded to fill a whole window. This happens even with the blancmange function at $x = \frac{1}{2}$, where under equal magnification it would look like a vertical half-line but, stretched horizontally in a fixed window, the graph pulls flat to look like a horizontal line. (Figure 11.18.)

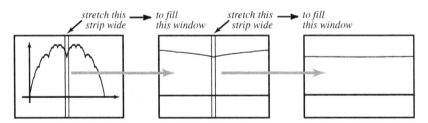

Figure 11.18. Stretching a continuous curve horizontally reveals a straight horizontal line.

The picture on a computer screen is built up of pixels of a tiny but non-zero size, so what we see onscreen with our human visual apparatus is a horizontal line of pixels. To be able to 'pull the graph flat' around a point $(x_0, f(x_0))$, suppose the pixel is height 2ε and $(x_0, f(x_0))$ is in the centre of a pixel, then we must find a width δ such that when x is in the interval $x_0 - \delta < x < x_0 + \delta$ then $f(x_0) - \varepsilon < f(x) < f(x_0) + \varepsilon$ (Figure 11.19).

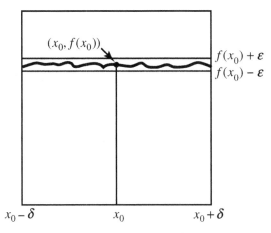

Figure 11.19. The property of continuity.

This embodied approach to continuity leads to the formal definition:

The function f is formally continuous at x_0 if:

Given $\varepsilon > 0$ then $\delta > 0$ can be found so that
$x_0 - \delta < x < x_0 + \delta$ implies $f(x_0) - \varepsilon < f(x) < f(x_0) + \varepsilon$.

Various authors have suggested that the formal definition of continuity gives bizarre results. In *Where Mathematics Comes From*, Lakoff and Núñez declare that the formal definition of continuity is fundamentally different from the natural dynamic form of continuity. Their argument is formulated by listing properties of embodied continuous perception and formally discrete mathematical definitions and revealing a huge disparity between the two. For example, 'natural' continuity implicitly involves a certain smoothness – that 'natural graphs' have tangents at every point, except possibly at a few exceptions where they may have corners.[21]

This idea of a 'natural graph' is much better conceptualized by using the embodied theory of dynamic continuity and local straightness. Here there is a clear 'natural' distinction between graphs that are smooth with tangents at most points and graphs that are merely continuous in a dynamic

---

[21] Lakoff & Núñez (2000), p. 307.

sense. If students were to follow a 'locally straight' approach to calculus in the sense described in this chapter, then they have the potential to be able to imagine functions being continuous but not differentiable – a conception that is virtually unthinkable in the classical approach.

I am quietly amused to note that the more general functions met in American college calculus courses are usually given by separate formulae on different intervals and so they are differentiable at all but a finite number of points. This leads to a technique of testing differentiability, first over intervals where a formula is given, then a separate consideration at points where there are corners. If the idea of 'local straightness' were adopted, not only would that mean that the functions in college calculus would be locally straight except at corners with different left and right derivatives, but that there would also be an embodied visual meaning to underpin the full range of ideas relating both to differentiability and to 'natural' dynamic continuity. It can even give insight into the apparently 'monstrous' properties of formal continuity.

In Chapter 10, I noted the principle that 'the meaning of an axiom or definition depends on its context.' For example, the transitive law has a very different meaning as part of the definition of an equivalence relation from its role in the definition of an order relation. Likewise, the definition of continuity operates very differently in different contexts. In formal mathematics, when the definition is applied to operate only on the rational numbers, for example, it can have quite different properties.

The function $f : \mathbb{Q} \to \mathbb{Q}$ defined by

$$f(x) = \begin{cases} 1 & \text{if } x^2 > 2 \\ 2 & \text{if } x^2 < 2 \end{cases}$$

is continuous everywhere in its domain but has a jump either side of $-\sqrt{2}$ and $+\sqrt{2}$. However, these jumps occur *outside* the domain of the function at irrational points. The function satisfies the formal definition, and, if one takes a point $x_0 \neq \pm\sqrt{2}$, the analysis of Figure 11.19 still holds good. One simply chooses δ so that the interval from $x_0 - \delta$ and $x_0 + \delta$ to exclude the two points where the jump occurs to get a picture where the graph pulls flat.

To make a natural transition from embodiment to formalism requires working in an appropriate context where the ideas of embodiment translate naturally to formalism. The notion of dynamic continuity pictured in Figure 11.9 starts at some point $(a, f(a))$, continuing (in a dynamic sense) through *all* the points in between to the end of the stroke at $((b, f(b))$. This suggests that the continuous graph is drawn on a closed interval $[a, b]$. It is known that a continuous function on a closed real interval is uniformly continuous. This means that for a given positive ε one can find a single value of δ to satisfy the continuity condition throughout the whole interval.

In this context we can now show that formal continuity implies embodied continuity. To draw a formally continuous function over a closed interval $[a, b]$ with a given pencil, we note that a mark made with the pencil has a finite size and so the graph is drawn by dragging the pencil to *cover* the formally defined curve.

The proof involves choosing a value of $\varepsilon > 0$ sufficiently small so that a square of side length ε can easily be covered by the pencil mark. Use this value of ε to find a value δ, such that, for every value of t in the interval centre x, width δ, the value of $f(t)$ lies in a vertical range with centre $f(x)$ and total height ε.

(Technically δ must satisfy $|x - t| < \tfrac{1}{2}\delta$ implies $|f(x) - f(t)| < \tfrac{1}{2}\varepsilon$).

If it happens that $\delta > \varepsilon$, replace δ by the smaller value ε to enable the rectangle width δ, height ε to be covered by the mark made by a pencil point. Draw successive rectangles at steps δ apart, each of which has its middle point centred on the graph, then the graph in the interval within the rectangle will lie completely within the rectangle. Then place the pencil point over successive rectangles and drag it along the curve to get a dynamically continuous graph. (Figure 11.20.)

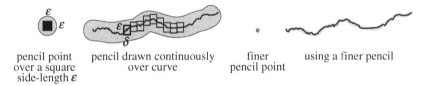

pencil point over a square side-length ε pencil drawn continuously over curve   finer pencil point   using a finer pencil

Figure 11.20. A physical drawing of a continuous function over an interval.

By using a finer pencil (and many more tiny squares), the curve drawn will begin to look like the desired picture of the graph. It is this embodied picture we see on a piece of paper or on a computer screen. If the pencil is thick, or the pixels on a screen are large, then what we see may look crude, but what is important, is not the picture on the screen, but the picture we have in our mind's eye.

Now we can see why a dynamically continuous function (such as the graph of $\sin x + n(x)$ in Figure 11.17) may look smooth at a regular scale when it is fact nowhere differentiable. The tiny wrinkles are covered by the thickness of the drawing of the graph.

This tells us that we cannot tell from a single picture alone whether a given real function is differentiable. We need to know that it is guaranteed to be locally straight, or how to calculate it so that we can compute its derivative.

10. The Area under a Continuous Graph

The area drawn under a continuous graph between two vertical lines can be perceived as having a specific numerical value. Leibniz and Newton both saw the area calculated under the graph of y from a fixed point a on the x-axis to a variable point x as a variable quantity A depending on x. (Figure 11.21). A formal mathematician requires the area to be proved to exist and to be calculated using a limiting argument. The common sense of our perception of the area under a continuous curve allows us to *see* the area. The problem is to *calculate* it, not just as a number for a specific area, but also as a function $A(x)$ that varies as x varies.

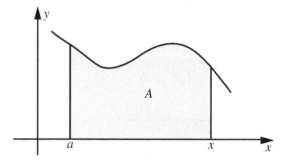

Figure 11.21. The area $A(x)$ under the curve from a to x.

To calculate A, Leibniz imagined it as being made of up thin strips with height y and width dx (Figure 11.22).

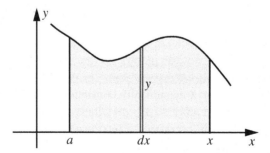

Figure 11.22. The area is made up of strips width dx, height y.

He saw the area as the sum of all the strips size $y\,dx$ and wrote it in Latin as 'summa $y\,dx$' using an elongated S for the word 'summa' to give

$$A = \int y\,dx.$$

If the area is calculated from a different starting point b, the value of A is changed by the area under the curve between a and b, so the area function in general is

$$A = \int y\,dx + c$$

where c is called the constant of integration.

10.1 *The Fundamental Theorem of Calculus*

Leibniz didn't calculate the area by adding up the strips directly. Instead he envisaged that, when x is increased by a quantity dx, the area A is increased by a quantity dA which is the area of a very thin strip width dx, height y. (Figure 11.23.)

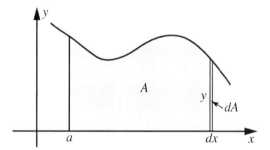

Figure 11.23. The increase dA in area equals $y\,dx$.

The thin strip of area dA is not an exact rectangle as the top is part of the curved graph. For a continuous function, however, the final strip width dx can be taken so small that when the strip is stretched horizontally, then the graph will pull flat and the increase in area looks like a rectangle width dx, height y (Figure 11.24).

Using good-enough arithmetic, the area is

$$dA = y\,dx.$$

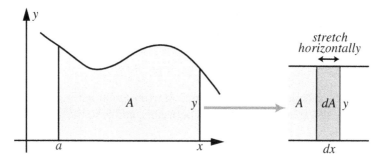

Figure 11.24. Stretching a thin strip that pulls flat.

Any error that occurs because the curve is not precisely horizontal is contained within the thickness of the pencil line used to draw the graph.

Dividing the equation through by dx, Leibniz obtained the relation:

$$\frac{dA}{dx} = y.$$

The two equations

$$A = \int y\, dx + c \quad \text{and} \quad \frac{dA}{dx} = y$$

express in the simplest terms that the operations of integration and differentiation are essentially inverses of each other, giving the *Fundamental Theorem of Calculus*. This is an amazing compression of knowledge, expressing the essential connection between change and growth in two brief equations!

When calculating the area using a large number of thin strips, one may wonder whether the sum of many tiny errors may add up to something non-zero. I can still remember that when I met this idea as I learned the calculus at the age of sixteen, I was concerned that a large number of small errors might build up to give a significant error. But the theory worked in the mathematics I was studying and gave the right answers, so I suppressed my reservations and got on with using the ideas that were successful in solving the problems I was given. I now know that, while a discussion of this problem may not be appropriate in a first calculus course, it can be resolved using a variant of the notation of Newton and Leibniz.

The interval from a to b can be subdivided into strips $a = x_0 < x_1 < \cdots < x_n = b$ where $x_r - x_{r-1}$ is written as dx_r. The sum of the rectangular strips width dx_r, height $y_r = f(x_r)$ can be written as

$$\sum_{a}^{b} f(x)dx_r.$$

For a continuous function $f(x)$, given any $\varepsilon > 0$, it is possible to find $\delta > 0$ so that if each strip has width less than δ, then the variation in the strip can be made less than $dx \times \varepsilon/(b - a)$. This particular value is chosen so that the total variation in all the strips is less than

$$(dx_1 + \cdots + dx_n) \times \varepsilon / (b - a)$$

which, because $dx_1 + \cdots + dx_n = (b - a)$, gives a total variation less than ε.

In this way, this sum of the strips $\sum_{r=1}^{n} y_r \, dx_r$ where $y_r = f(x_r)$ for any selected value of y in the rth strip, will be a 'good-enough' approximation to the area. Simplifying the notation further, the area from a to b calculated using finite strips can be written as

$$\sum_{a}^{b} y \, dx.$$

For a continuous function $y = f(x)$ the strip-widths can be taken small enough to give a good-enough numerical approximation to the actual value for the area, where the precise value (given by the formal limit concept) may be written in the compact Leibniz notation as

$$\int_{a}^{b} y \, dx.$$

10.2 *The Area-So-Far Function*

The area function from a fixed point a to a variable point x can be calculated numerically and the cumulative 'area-so-far' function can be simultaneously plotted as a sequence of points. (Figure 11.25.)

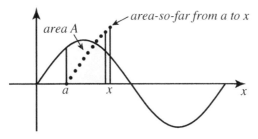

Figure 11.25. Area-so-far from fixed point a to x.

This 'area-so-far' function plots the cumulative sum adding the areas of successive strips. As the widths of the strips get smaller, the graph of the area-so-far function stabilizes upon the actual area function, which is locally straight, because the original graph is continuous. If we were to draw the graph of the precise area function A and look at the actual tangent at a point, then its components may be denoted by dx and dA. (Figure 11.26.)

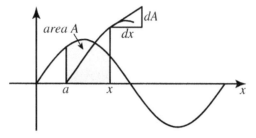

Figure 11.26. The tangent to the area function with components dx and dA.

Taking a thin strip, magnification of the area function looks locally straight, as in Figure 11.27.

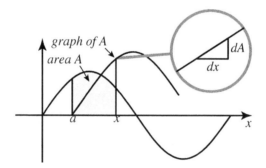

Figure 11.27. Magnifying the area function.

We are now at the root of the Leibniz problem. Leibniz proposed obtaining the areas under the graph of y by summing the strips $dA = y\,dx$ which effectively calculates not the area under the graph, but the area of the staircase of rectangles whose tops are shaded in Figure 11.28.

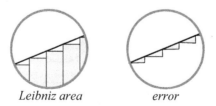

Leibniz area   *error*

Figure 11.28. The Leibniz area and its error.

Here we see that, taking finite widths of strips, there *is* an error. However, if the function is *continuous*, by the argument presented earlier, all these errors added up together can be made as small as is required so that the calculation is good enough for any practical purpose. Indeed, by making the error suitably small, it will lie within the line of pixels or inside a pencil line drawing the graph, reminiscent of Leibniz's visionary idea that adding a line to an area does not change the area by any significant quantity. (Figure 11.29.) Indeed, because the graph is *continuous* in the embodied sense, given any error $\varepsilon > 0$, we can choose a fine pencil drawing a line of thickness $\pm \frac{1}{2} \varepsilon (b - a)$ high and then choose a value of δ so that the variation in y in a strip width δ is less than $\pm \frac{1}{2} \varepsilon (b - a)$, then the total error in area between a and b is less than ε.

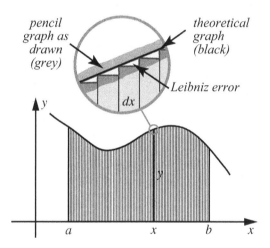

Figure 11.29. Making the error as small as desired so that it lies within a pencil line.

10.3 *Positive and Negative Area Calculations*

In Chapter 7, we saw that the introduction of signed numbers in algebra causes greater complexity in visual representations. This is usually solved as I have done above, by drawing pictures where the graph is above the *x*-axis. However, when calculating the area of a strip by multiplying the height y of the strip by the width dx, either or both of the quantities y and dx can be positive or negative. The value of y is negative when the graph is below the axis and the step dx can be negative if the sum is performed from right to left. All combinations are possible. (Figure 11.30.)

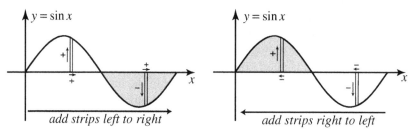

Figure 11.30. Adding strips in different directions.

The areas shaded give a negative result (multiplying a positive by a negative); those unshaded are positive (either positive times positive or negative times negative). This reveals the idea of orientation, with an area changing sign if it is turned over to face the other way. Again, an embodiment, in terms of dynamic movement, offers a new insight.

In practice, mathematicians usually avoid this by defining the integral from b to a for $a < b$ to be

$$\int_b^a f(x)dx = -\int_a^b f(x)dx.$$

However, as discussed in Chapter 7, although the introduction of negative quantities usually makes embodiment more complicated, as here, a picture of the main idea can give significant insight.

10.4 *Functions That Are Differentiable a Finite Number of Times*

Embodiment can give insight to highly sophisticated mathematical ideas. For example, the blancmange function is continuous, so, by the fundamental theorem, $B(x) = \int_a^x bl(x)dx$ is differentiable with derivative $bl(x)$. This means that $B(x)$ is differentiable everywhere once, but nowhere twice. If we integrate $bl(x)$ 27 times to get a function $C(x)$, then this will be differentiable precisely 27 times and not 28.

By embodying the ideas of the calculus, we can mentally imagine situations that are way beyond the understanding of the unprepared use of 'common sense'. This is the amazing genius of the human brain. It may not make sense to the unprepared mind without the requisite experience, but it reveals the human capacity of our mathematical thinking that takes us far beyond naïve intuition.

11. Differential Equations

Differential equations tell us something about the rate at which a quantity is changing and our challenge is to find the quantity itself. A differential equation might be something like

$$\frac{dy}{dx} = 2x$$

which is usually read as 'the derivative of y with respect to x is $2x$' and has the solution $y = x^2 + c$. However, the differential equation

$$\frac{dy}{dx} = \frac{x}{y}$$

is more interesting because its solution does *not* give y as a function of x. It can be written more insightfully as a *differential* equation

$$y\,dy = x\,dx$$

that specifies dx and dy as the components of the tangent vector to the solution curve. This can be embodied in a computer program by allowing the user to point anywhere in the graph window as the software plots a short line segment whose slope is given by the differential equation.[22] (Figure 11.31. See overleaf.[23])

Clicking the mouse can deposit the segment and drawing segments end to end can give the learner the sense of controlling the solution by following a curve whose direction is given by the differential equation.

Notice that substituting $y = 0$ with $x \neq 0$ in the equation $y\,dy = x\,dx$ gives $dx = 0$ showing that the solution curve has a vertical tangent when it crosses the x-axis. This would cause a problem if we seek a solution in which y is a function of x. However, if x and y vary, say as a function of time t, then the differential equation can have a more general solution curve following the direction given by the changing tangent.

Adding together successive steps for the differential equation $y\,dy = x\,dx$ to get a good-enough approximation starting at (a, b) and ending at (x, y) gives

---

[22] Blokland & Giessen (2000).
[23] In the picture, the line segment is drawn calculating the direction at the midpoint. This gives a better approximation to the tangent direction, which in turn gives a better approximation to the required solution.

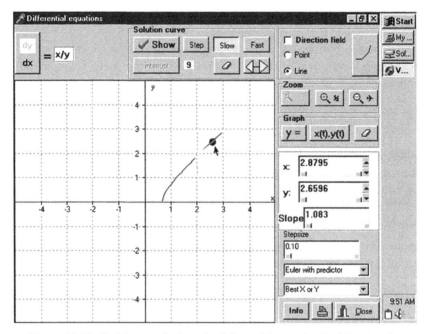

Figure 11.31. Building a solution of a differential equation by following the direction it specifies.

$$\sum_{b}^{y} y\, dy = \sum_{a}^{x} x\, dx$$

leading to the symbolic integral

$$\int_{b}^{y} y\, dy = \int_{a}^{x} x\, dx.$$

There is subtle point here that need not be overemphasized in a first calculus course, but is a phenomenon ignored by many who solve differential equations. In the original definition of the sum of strips, the stripwidths dx and dy are positive. In the differential equation $y\, dy = x\, dx$, the signs of dx and dy may change depending on the values of x and y. For instance, if x is positive and y is negative, then dx and dy must have opposite signs. Following along a solution curve can easily change direction, as in the solutions of the current differential equations in the form $\frac{1}{2}y^2 = \frac{1}{2}x^2 + c$, which are hyperbolas of the form

$$x^2 - y^2 = k$$

for some constant k. In real-world examples, a dynamic solution involves the point (x,y) moving along part of one arm of a hyperbola in Figure 11.31, where x and y vary in time.

This can be perceived by the human senses by software that enables the user to point and click to lay a short line segment down in the direction constrained by a differential equation. By fitting each successive line segment one after another, it is possible to *see* and *feel* the solution curve as a locally straight curve whose direction is always given by the differential equation.[24]

This is not a simple-minded solution that applies only to first-order differential equations. It is a highly sophisticated idea that applies equally well to a whole system of differential equations in one independent variable t. For instance, simultaneous first-order differential equations of two variables x and y that are functions of time t are of the form

$$\frac{dx}{dt} = f(t, x, y), \quad \frac{dy}{dt} = g(t, x, y).$$

These can be visualized in three-dimensional t-x-y space, with the tangent vector (dt, dx, dy) specified by

$$dx = f(t,x,y)dt, \quad dy = g(t,x,y)dt$$

in the direction $(1, f(t, x, y), g(t, x, y))$. The solution through a specific starting point is just a curve that follows the changing direction of the tangent.

A second-order differential equation

$$\frac{d^2 x}{dt^2} = f\left(t, x, \frac{dy}{dx}\right)$$

can be turned into two simultaneous differential equations by introducing a new variable $v = dx/dt$ to give

$$\frac{dx}{dt} = v, \quad \frac{dy}{dt} = f(t,x,v)$$

and visualized in the same way.

---

[24] To enable the solution to follow an implicit curve, the algorithm for a given step s can set the sign of s at the beginning to choose one direction or the other, and then successively calculate the value of dy/dx from the equation, changing the sign of s whenever dy/dx changes sign and assigning the value of s to whichever of dx or dy has the larger absolute value. The actual length of each step will then always be less than $\sqrt{2}|s|$.

More generally, any system of differential equations of any order can be reduced to a system of first-order differential equations. This reveals the simple case of the first-order differential equation as a generic concept that generalizes to the general case with n variables $x_1, \ldots, x_n$ depending on the independent variable t. Solving a system of differential equations in an embodied sense means following the direction given by the system to build a solution curve in a higher-dimensional space.

The space involved has components $(t, x_1, \ldots, x_n)$ and has dimension $n + 1$, which will stretch our human imagination. However, we can still see it in two dimensions by imagining the projections on the n coordinate planes t-x_1, t-x_2, $\ldots$, t-x_n and, as the point $(t, x_1, \ldots, x_n)$ moves through $n + 1$-dimensional space, we can see its progress as a combination of the simultaneous movement in each of the n coordinate planes.

12. Partial Derivatives

The shift from functions of a single variable to functions of several variables introduces apparently more complicated ideas that traditionally are seen as not being amenable to thinking of a partial derivative $\partial z / \partial x$ as a ratio of two quantities. In this case, a function of two variables $z = f(x, y)$ is defined to have partial derivatives given by

$$\frac{\partial z}{\partial x} = \lim_{h \to 0} \frac{f(x+h, y)}{h}, \quad \frac{\partial z}{\partial y} = \lim_{h \to 0} \frac{f(x, y+h)}{h}.$$

These satisfy the identity

$$dz = \frac{\partial z}{\partial x} dx + \frac{\partial z}{\partial y} dy.$$

The different symbols dx, ∂x and dy, ∂y emphasize that they cannot be cancelled, for then the equation would become $dz = \partial z + \partial z$, whatever that means. This suggests that perhaps the partial derivatives should not be considered as quotients. However, this is not so. The problem lies not in the mathematics, but in the *notation*.

The function $z = f(x, y)$ gives a surface in three dimensions in which a point (x, y) in the horizontal plane gives a point on the surface a distance z vertically above. The tangent plane through the point (x, y, z) on the surface cuts the vertical plane where y is constant in a curve that has a tangent with components dx and dz_x. It cuts the vertical plane where x is constant in a curve with tangential components dy and dz_y. The partial derivatives are

$$\frac{\partial z}{\partial x} = \frac{dz_x}{dx}, \quad \frac{\partial z}{\partial y} = \frac{dz_y}{dy}.$$

The total vertical change in dz to the tangent plane is simply the sum of the two vertical components $dz = dz_x + dz_y$. (Figure 11.32.)

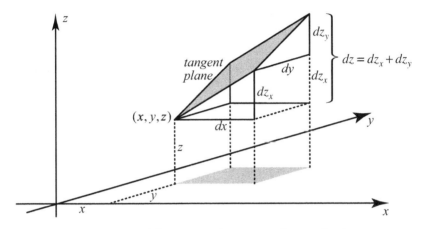

Figure 11.32. The tangent plane to a surface $z = f(x, y)$.

The new notations for the partial derivatives dz_x/dx and dz_y/dy are once again ratios of lengths where dx and dy can take any values and the corresponding increment to the tangent plane dz satisfies

$$dz = \frac{dz_x}{dx}\,dx + \frac{dz_y}{dy}\,dy.$$

where both dx and dy can be cancelled to give $dz = dz_x + dz_y$.

This shows that a locally straight approach to the calculus offers a natural interpretation of the Leibniz notation, not only in differentiation, but also in integration, differential equations and partial derivatives.

This suggests it is time for a respectful re-evaluation of the Leibniz notation. It not only gives a powerful intuitive way of making sense of the calculus, which is not found in current college calculus, but it also leads from fundamental human perception through the notion of local straightness to the formal definitions of mathematical analysis and, as we shall see later, not only to the use of infinitesimals in applied mathematics, but also to the alternative nonstandard approach to the calculus using infinitesimals.

13. The Relationship between Embodiment and Symbolism

We are now in a position to reflect on the overall framework of a locally straight approach to the calculus, which is designed to give meaning to the relationship between human embodiment in terms of perception and action and the powerful techniques of calculation enshrined in symbolic calculus. It is based first on the embodied action of tracing along a (locally straight) graph f and seeing its changing slope as the graph of a new function Df. For a locally straight graph, the slope Df at a particular point x is then seen to be the slope of the tangent in the form dy/dx where dx and dy are the components of the tangent vector.

It does not need to begin from the symbolic abstraction of finding the limit of the slope function, which involves problematic aspects of potential infinity. The case can be made for better understanding of the limit concept being introduced *after* the learner has a mental picture of the limit itself. The vision of the limiting slope function arises through the embodied picture of the changing slope of the original graph. The notion of limit can now be introduced, when the student has a mental conception of the slope function and seeks to compute it numerically using good-enough arithmetic or precisely using symbolic manipulation.

The approach offers a harmonic blending of embodiment and symbolism and leads to a meaningful use of symbolism that can be translated into the formal definitions of mathematical analysis.

The very first time this graphical approach was used to make sense of the calculus, the students involved responded in highly innovative ways.[25] For instance, when the teacher drew a curve on the blackboard with a maximum and asked how one might test for a maximum, a student, Malcolm,[26] gestured with his hand in the air following the graph going up and down, saying that the derivative would be positive, then zero at the maximum, then negative.

At the time, I believed that the software would be used regularly throughout the course. However, this proved not to be so. Once the students had developed the power of symbolism, the computer was no longer required and the students focused on meaningful use of the symbolism, now in a more flexible manner. For instance, the derivative dy/dx could be seen as a process of division of the components of the tangent – appropriate for

---

[25] Tall (1986a).
[26] Malcolm is the pseudonym for a student in the first experimental class where a graphic approach was introduced in 1985 by my colleague Norman Blackett.

differential equations – or as the concept of derivative – used symbolically to solve problems.

In the same way, the symbol $\int y\,dx$ was used to represent Leibniz's original idea of adding up strips with height y and width dx which stabilizes to a limit when the widths get smaller and smaller. This can be calculated using good-enough arithmetic with a finite number of thin strips where the symbol $\sum y\,dx$ indicates the sum of strips with height y, of finite width dx. A visual argument was used to introduce the fundamental theorem of the calculus to reveal that the derivative of the area function takes us back to the original function, so giving a meaningful embodiment of the relationship between differentiation and integration.

Fundamental to this approach is the idea of local straightness. As I wrote this final version of the chapter, I reflected back to the ideas of Newton and Leibniz and their common source of inspiration, Isaac Barrow, who revealed the first geometric form of the fundamental theorem of the calculus. These insightful ideas led to the conflict between the idea of a curve as a polygon with an infinite number of infinitesimal sides and the criticism of Berkeley, followed by three and a half centuries of dispute about the foundations of the calculus.

Then I received an e-mail from my colleague and doctoral student Anna Poynter, to say that one of her students had traced her academic lineage back to Sir Isaac Newton through the Mathematics Genealogy Project on the Internet.[27] This, of course, meant that I too (along with many hundreds of other current mathematicians) could trace my own lineage back through fourteen generations to Isaac Newton and a further generation back to Isaac Barrow. (There are even further links back to a direct line of mentors that include Galileo and Tartaglia.)

This traces a tenuous link from those early pioneers through the generations. Three and a half centuries later, the conflict concerning infinitesimals and potentially infinite limit processes has reached a new resolution in local straightness. A curve under high magnification looks like a straight line, so what we see is not a polygon with corners, however tiny the turn may be, but a curve that looks straight *everywhere*.

The modern debate on the mathematical meanings of the calculus and mathematical analysis will be considered in Chapter 13. The evolution of mathematical ideas continues in our own lifetime and is subject to

---

[27] http://www.genealogy.math.ndsu.nodak.edu/id.php?id=44620. Accessed February 14, 2013.

problematic and supportive aspects that arise in the conceptions of every one of us.

14. Reflections

This chapter reveals how the three-world model of the development of mathematical thinking offers a natural approach to the calculus, blending together embodiment and symbolism where the limit concept arises as a consequence of the need to compute symbolic derivatives of functions composed from standard functions whose derivatives are known.

It begins by magnifying graphs on a computer to see that many graphs look 'locally straight'. This offers a fundamental distinction between a graph that is dynamically continuous (because it can be drawn in a continuous movement without lifting the pencil off the paper) and a locally straight graph that has a smoothly changing slope that can be drawn as a new graph that stabilizes to become the derivative.

The approach develops into good-enough numerical methods and precise symbolism appropriate for a better understanding of the limit process and can be later developed either into the theoretical relationships of applied mathematics or the formal theory of mathematical analysis.

Skemp's theory of goals to be achieved and anti-goals to be avoided feature in this tale as mathematicians, concerned about problematic aspects of infinitesimals, turned to the alternative goal of developing mathematics through the potentially infinite limit concept. This new goal gave untold rewards in the powerful theory of mathematical analysis. But in attempting to pass the mantle on to new generations, the anti-goal of avoiding problematic ideas has unforeseen consequences.

Students are often given emotionally charged instructions to avoid thinking of dy/dx as a quotient and to conceptualize it as a limit, even though the formulae of the calculus visibly seem to operate as if it is a quotient involving symbols that can be shifted around to change differential equations into integrals.

The modern epsilon-delta approach to the calculus is intrinsically problematic for the vast majority of beginning calculus students. The result is a traditional world of calculus where students cannot achieve relational understanding, even if they desire it, and instead they are often taught to focus on the instrumental goal of learning only the procedures to use in applications and to pass exams.

The framework of three worlds of mathematics offers a basis for a flexible approach to the calculus based on a blend of embodied local straightness and symbolic operations that can operate as a foundation for a formal approach using the limit concept.

In later chapters this story will be continued to give a foundation both to the standard theory of mathematical analysis and also to unlock the meaning of an infinitesimal as a coherent formal concept that blends together formal, operational and embodied mathematical thinking.

12   Expert Thinking and Structure Theorems

In this chapter we return to the journey through the axiomatic formal world. In Chapter 8 we saw the complication involved in the initial stages of formal deduction of a relationship such as $(-a)(-b) = ab$ in an appropriate axiomatic system. In Chapter 10 we saw that first stage of dealing with definitions and deductions is highly complicated as learners attempt to make sense of the formal ideas when their minds are already full of embodied and symbolic ideas that must now be reorganized into formal definitions and proof.

Learners may develop in a variety of ways – as natural learners building structurally on embodied mental images of situations, or operationally on experiences manipulating symbols, or in a more formal way based on making deductions from formal definitions. Some may learn proofs procedurally to reproduce them in examinations.

When a learner is presented with a list of axioms, the first stage is to prove some initial theorems that enable the axioms and definitions to be used in more flexible ways. This develops from a multistructural list to a growing relational structure of formal knowledge. In the longer term it can become enriched as a crystalline concept.

For instance, a complete ordered field is formulated with a list of axioms including the axiom of completeness in the context of an ordered field. In Chapter 10 the completeness axiom was given in the form 'a Cauchy sequence always tends to a limit.' There are other ways of formulating this same axiom for an ordered field, for example, 'an increasing sequence bounded above converges to a limit,' 'a decreasing sequence bounded below converges,' 'a non-empty set bounded above has a least upper bound,' or 'a non-empty set bounded below has a greatest lower bound.' All of these different versions can be proved to be equivalent in the context of the axioms for an ordered field.

The human mind can compress the ideas further, not only into a concept in which different versions are 'equivalent', but also into a single crystalline structure: the one and only complete ordered field $\mathbb{R}$ that has formal, embodied and symbolic aspects all blended into one.

In the case of other formally defined mathematical concepts, such as a group, the concept may exist in many different forms. Examples include the group of rational numbers under addition, the non-zero rationals under multiplication, a group of transformations, or in a multitude of other examples. In group theory we have the notion of isomorphism to describe groups with a bijection (one-one onto map) between the sets that respects the group operation. Isomorphic groups are fundamentally the same and the human brain can conceive such a concept as a single crystalline structure.

Even the general concept of group has its own crystalline structure that students begin to grasp. This is illustrated by a conversation that I had with a group of thirty mathematics students beginning a course on 'the development of mathematical concepts' after a year of formal university mathematics.

Few of the students claimed to have fully understood the first-year group theory course. Some claimed that they had learnt virtually nothing. I took a positive attitude by inviting the sceptics to respond to a challenge. I told them that I had a group G in my mind. I wouldn't tell them any more than that, but I wanted them to tell me about it.

The first suggestion was that it must have an identity element that we agreed to call e. When asked about other elements, after a suggestion that perhaps e was the only element, I asked what could be said about any other element, say x. The response came that we could multiply x by x and get x^2. I then enquired about multiplying x^2 by x^2 and was given the immediate answer x^4. The explanation was given that this used the associative law so that, either way, the result is x times x times x times x.

The point had now been made. While the students did not know the group I had in mind, they had a sense of its properties and could talk to me about it, and this information followed from the growing knowledge structure each of them had constructed for the group concept.

In this chapter we will consider the longer-term development in which multistructural lists of axioms lead to theorems that relate properties and compress knowledge into crystalline formal concepts.

The journey includes the proof of a special kind of theorem, called a *structure theorem*, which proves consequences that reveal new embodied forms with precise formal meanings and symbolic methods of operation that are an inevitable consequence of the axioms. This transforms the whole nature of formal mathematical thinking. Instead of an initial multistructural system of axioms from which theorems must be proved carefully step-by-step, the developing expertise leads to crystalline concepts that have new forms of embodiment and symbolism now underpinned by the power of formal proof.

1. Comparing Novice and Expert

Keith Weber compared the ways in which four undergraduates and four doctoral students solved formal mathematical problems in group theory.[1] He found that the undergraduates were able to reproduce simple theorems but were unsuccessful when the problems became more complex. Meanwhile, he reported that 'the doctoral students appeared to know the powerful proof techniques in abstract algebra, which theorems are more important, where particular facts and theorems are likely to be useful, and when one should or should not try and prove theorems using symbolic manipulation.'[2]

A typical question was to prove whether or not the group of integers $\mathbb{Z}$ under addition was isomorphic to the group $\mathbb{Q}$ of rational numbers addition. In terms of a definition, this would mean finding a bijection between $\mathbb{Z}$ and $\mathbb{Q}$ that preserved addition, or showing that no such bijection existed. None of the four undergraduates could provide a formal response but all four graduates were able to do so.

The undergraduates focused on their memory that $\mathbb{Z}$ and $\mathbb{Q}$ have the same cardinal number and so already had a bijective correspondence between them. They had part of the idea – a bijection – but not a bijection that respected the operation of addition. The powerful met-before of the equal cardinality of $\mathbb{Z}$ and $\mathbb{Q}$ was so strong that they were unable to make any further progress.

The graduates had richer knowledge structures supporting their thinking. For instance, one immediately declared that $\mathbb{Q}$ and $\mathbb{Z}$ could not be isomorphic, first by speculating that $\mathbb{Q}$ is dense but $\mathbb{Z}$ is not, then that '$\mathbb{Z}$ is cyclic, but $\mathbb{Q}$ is not' (meaning that the element 1 generates the whole of $\mathbb{Z}$ under addition but no element in $\mathbb{Q}$ does so). This second insight shows that the additive groups of $\mathbb{Z}$ and $\mathbb{Q}$ cannot be isomorphic.

The undergraduates still saw proof as a process and sought a process to establish a bijection or not. The graduates had developed a richly connected

---

[1] Weber (2001).
[2] Weber (2001).

formal knowledge structure and knew that isomorphic groups would have the same properties and used this to solve the problem.

2. The Process of Proving and Warrants for Truth

In the process of shifting from the initial workings with definitions to the building of a succession of theorems to give a rich knowledge structure, the prover must have some idea as to what theorems might be worth proving and to conjecture what might be true. This involves producing some kind of argument to support the proposed theorem, which may not initially be a formal proof but, nevertheless, gives the prover increasing conviction that the theorem is true.

In the 1950s, the philosopher Toulmin[3] considered how general arguments were composed. In general, a proof might consist of some given **Data** that was assumed true and a form of **Proof** to establish the **Conclusion**. (Figure 12.1.)

Figure 12.1. Proving a conclusion from given data.

Toulmin, however, saw that arguments were more general than this. He suggested that a general argument began with **Data**, then had a **Warrant** for truth in the forms of arguments that support the likelihood of truth, without necessarily giving a 100% certainty, and as a consequence there would be a **Qualifier** expressing the degree of confidence in the argument supporting the **Conclusion**. The Warrant was supported by **Backing**, in the form of additional evidence, but the argument may have a **Rebuttal** that potentially refutes the conclusion, for instance, by stating conditions in which the argument would fail. (Figure 12.2, see overleaf.)[4]

This framework gives a wider context for describing how new proofs are suggested by individuals using their current knowledge structures.

Matthew Inglis and his colleagues[5] gave high-quality mathematics research students unfamiliar problems in clinical interviews to study how

---

[3] Toulmin (1958).

[4] Toulmin's framework is often presented with the box for the Warrant *below* the line between Data and Qualifier, above the Backing. However, I present it with the Warrant in the main line as I see it as part of the main argument leading to a qualified support for the Conclusion.

[5] Inglis, Mejia-Ramos & Simpson (2007).

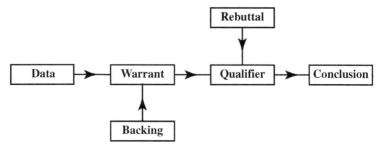

Figure 12.2. Toulmin's model of general argument.

they developed their arguments. These concerned variations of the definition of a perfect number, given as follows for a positive integer n:

> a *perfect number* n has divisors (including 1 and n) that add up to $2n$;
> an *abundant number* n has divisors that add up to more than $2n$;
> a *deficient number* n has divisors that add up to less than $2n$.

For instance, 6 is perfect (because $1 + 2 + 3 + 6 = 12$), 7 is deficient (because $1 + 7 = 8 < 14$) and 12 is abundant (because $1 + 2 + 3 + 4 + 6 + 12 = 28 > 24$).

Amongst the conjectures that were presented to the students to test if they were true or false were the following:

(A) The sum $m + n$ of two abundant numbers m, n is abundant.
(B) The product mn of two abundant numbers m, n is abundant.

Graduate student Chris responded immediately to (A) saying

> That doesn't look true.... Because the factors of $m + n$ don't really have anything to do with the factors of m or n. So it should be fairly easy to construct a counterexample.

He went on to find two abundant numbers whose sum was not abundant. Looking at (B), however, he said:

> Right, so if m and n are abundant then mn is abundant. That looks more plausible, because they are going to share factors.

This led to a sequence of arguments that ended up with a proof. Readers might like to solve both problems to see if they are, in fact, true or false. This will involve the kind of thinking that is being discussed in this section and is likely to give deeper insight than just passively reading about the ideas.[6]

---

[6] For a detailed explanation, see Inglis, Mejia-Ramos and Simpson (2007), pp.19–20.

The important observation to make is that initially the responses give warrants that are qualified, in the first case a sense that it should be 'fairly easy' to prove false, whereas the second looks 'more plausible' with the backing that the numbers are going to share factors.

A study of the responses of the six students suggested three different types of warrant:

> an *inductive* warrant-type based on evaluating one or more specific cases;
>
> a *structural-intuitive* warrant-type based on observations about or experiments with some kind of mental structure, be it visual or otherwise, that persuades them of a conclusion;
>
> a *deductive* warrant-type using formal mathematical justifications to warrant the conclusion, including deductions from axioms, algebraic manipulations, or the use of counterexamples.

These three types correspond to:

> the use of examples, typical in the first stage of problem solving (and also in the earlier practical and theoretical aspects of proof development);
>
> The use of an imagined mental structure that may be 'visual or otherwise';
>
> an argument that is essentially formal deductive from axioms or algebraic manipulation using quantified statements in generalized arithmetic.

In the three-world framework, the first of these represent specific and generic examples that arise in the practical and theoretical aspects of embodiment and symbolism. The second refers to thought experiments based on embodied images or calculations, while the third sees a switch to formal proof that we have classified either as a natural symbolic argument introducing quantifiers, or an axiomatic formal proof. The given problem is based on arithmetic operations with numbers that could be tackled without a formal knowledge framework. Here it is tackled by talented graduate students, experienced in formal proof, using their sophisticated knowledge structures to provide initial warrants for truth before moving on to seek a formal proof.

Pablo Meija-Ramos investigated a range of other problems that carried different levels of conviction from specific examples, embodied pictures, symbolic manipulations and formal proofs.[7]

---

[7] Mejia-Ramos (2008).

Two conjectures given to students were the following:

(C) The derivative of an even function is an odd function.
(D) The product of two diagonal matrices is diagonal.

The first can be imagined as an embodied picture, a symbolic relationship between functions, or something related to the formal limit definition of the derivative. The second focuses more on the symbolism of matrix multiplication. In practice, the first produced a range of responses, for example, using the symmetry of the even function f satisfying $f(x) = f(-x)$ to embody the slopes as mirror images, with the slope $f'(x)$ equaling minus $f'(-x)$. This insight was usually considered to be meaningful but did not carry the full conviction of formal proof. (Figure 12.3.)

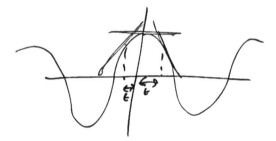

Figure 12.3. Dynamic visual picture of slope of an even function at $x = -t$ and $x = t$.

The argument produced by one such student was analyzed using the Toulmin diagram as in Figure 12.4.

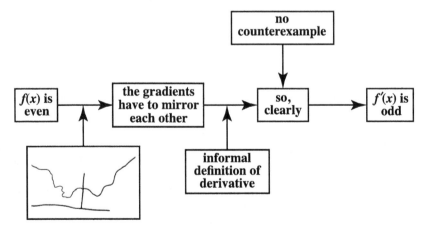

Figure 12.4. The Toulmin analysis of a visual proof by one of the students.

Here the student uses the picture as a backing to produce the warrant that the gradients have to mirror each other, with an implicit use of an informal definition and no counterexample as a rebuttal to suggest that the conclusion 'clearly' follows. When questioned, the student confirmed that although the argument was 'clear', it was not a formal proof.

Overall, the students gave a variety of arguments that were classified as 'inductive arguments' (for instance, looking at special cases such as specific polynomials with even powers), 'informal deductive arguments' (such as that in Figure 12.3) or 'formal deductive arguments'. These arguments are respectively operational symbolic, structural embodied thought experiment, and formal proof.

The case of the diagonal matrix is different as it is expressed symbolically without an obvious embodied representation. Yet even here, there are some solutions that recall the definition of matrix multiplication as a *functional* embodiment, where the rule of multiplication combines a row in the first matrix and a column in the second by multiplying the successive entries (along the row and down the column), adding them together and placing the result in the position where the row and column cross each other. This calculation was accompanied by a drawing (Figure 12.5) in which enactive gestures along row and column offer an iconic representation of the rule for multiplication to support the deductive argument.

Figure 12.5. Matrix multiplication in outline.

Mejia-Ramos summarized his data in the following terms:

Students may use any type of argument available to them when approaching a given task, and that while this may result in certain students using the same combination of arguments in two different tasks (empirical to estimate the truth of the conjecture, informal deductive to explain it and formal deductive to prove it), others may use only a formal deductive approach when such an argument is available to them, but resort to other types of arguments when faced with tasks for which the basis of a symbolic argument is not as 'fresh in their minds.'[8]

---

[8] Mejia-Ramos (2008), p. 195.

Both of these studies are designed to use the Toulmin framework to reveal the need for a qualifier that expresses a certain level of confidence rather than an all-or-nothing proof. As such they focus on the development of a formal argument, rather than the specific nature of embodiment or symbolism involved. However, the roles of embodiment and symbolism are clear in the examples given, where each example has its own specific characteristics. (A) and (B) are general properties of whole number arithmetic that benefit from theoretical symbolic arguments. (C) is a calculus problem that can be embodied as a visual picture, symbolized as a rule in calculus, or formalized in mathematical analysis. (D) is a problem in matrix algebra that is essentially symbolic but is supported by a functional embodiment to remember the formula for matrix multiplication. Each benefits from different forms of support in embodiment, symbolism and formalism to construct a proof.

3. Structure Theorems and New Forms of Embodiment and Symbolism

The axioms and definitions proposed for formal concepts are chosen by the mathematician to express generative properties that can be used as a foundation for formal development. Such axiomatic structures rarely reflect *all* the properties that are in the original examples that inspired the theory. For instance, a vector in elementary mathematics arises from generalizing the notion of vector in two and three dimensions as a quantity with magnitude and direction. But a vector space is not axiomatized to suggest this structure at all. Instead the axioms of a vector space focus only on the symbolic properties of addition of vectors and operations on vectors by elements from the associated field.

In the following discussion, the formal definition of various mathematical systems will be analyzed to show that, under specified circumstances, a formally defined concept will have structural properties that endow it with a specific embodiment and corresponding symbolism.

The ideas will be outlined in a general fashion. What is important for the general reader is to grasp that the formal definitions leads to embodied and symbolic properties. The mathematician may choose the axioms to suit specific purposes, but those axioms then have inevitable properties that result in a specific crystalline structure.

3.1 *The Concept of Vector*

A vector space V over a field F is defined formally as a commutative group V with the operation combining $\mathbf{u}, \mathbf{v} \in V$ written as $\mathbf{u} + \mathbf{v} \in V$

and multiplication of a vector $\mathbf{v} \in V$ by $a \in F$ denoted as $a\mathbf{v} \in V$ that satisfies the axioms: $(a + b)\mathbf{v} = a\mathbf{v} + b\mathbf{v}$, $a(\mathbf{u} + \mathbf{v}) = a\mathbf{u} + a\mathbf{v}$, $(ab)\mathbf{v} = a(b\mathbf{v})$ and $1\mathbf{v} = \mathbf{v}$.

An example of a vector space is the n-dimensional space F^n of coordinate vectors $(a, \ldots, a_n)$ where the coordinates $a_1, \ldots, a_n$ are all elements in the field F. This is a generalization of two-dimensional real space $\mathbb{R}^2$ or three-dimensional real space $\mathbb{R}^3$ that can be embodied as vectors in the real plane or in three-dimensional real space. Addition of vectors simply adds coordinates and multiplying by an element of F multiplies each of the coordinates by that element.

To link the formal embodiment more closely to this example, further definitions are introduced.

A vector space is said to be *finite dimensional* if it has a finite set of vectors $\mathbf{v}_1, \ldots, \mathbf{v}_n$ (called a 'spanning set') so that every vector $\mathbf{v}$ can be written as a combination $\mathbf{v} = a_1\mathbf{v}_1 + \cdots + a_n\mathbf{v}_n$ (for $a_1, \ldots, a_n \in F$). A set of vectors $\mathbf{v}_1, \ldots, \mathbf{v}_n$ is said to be *linearly independent*, if the sum $\mathbf{v} = a_1\mathbf{v}_1 + \cdots + a_n\mathbf{v}_n$ can equal zero only when $a_1 = \cdots = a_n = 0$.

If a spanning set is also linearly independent, then the representation $\mathbf{v} = a_1\mathbf{v}_1 + \cdots + a_n\mathbf{v}_n$ is *unique* in the sense that if there were two different expressions, $\mathbf{v} = a_1\mathbf{v}_1 + \cdots + a_n\mathbf{v}_n = b_1\mathbf{v}_1 + \cdots + b_n\mathbf{v}_n$, then

$$(a_1 - b_1)\mathbf{v}_1 + \cdots + (a_n - b_n)\mathbf{v}_n = 0.$$

So

$$a_1 = b_1, \cdots, a_n = b_n.$$

A set of vectors that spans a vector space and is also linearly independent is called a *basis*. In this case it can be proved that any two bases of a given vector space V have the same number of elements, and this is defined to be the *dimension* of the vector space.

In a vector space of dimension n, choose a basis $\mathbf{v}_1, \ldots, \mathbf{v}_n$, then any vector $\mathbf{v}$ can be written uniquely as $\mathbf{v} = a_1\mathbf{v}_1 + \cdots + a_n\mathbf{v}_n$, which corresponds to the vector $(a_1, \ldots, a_n)$ in the vector space F^n.

This leads to the structure theorem that any finite-dimensional vector space over a field F is isomorphic to F^n, or, to put more simply, that an n-dimensional vector space can have its elements represented as n-tuples $(a_1, \ldots, a_n)$ where the coordinates $a_1, \ldots, a_n$ are all elements in the field F. In particular, if F is the field $\mathbb{R}$ of real numbers, then a two- or three-dimensional vector space over $\mathbb{R}$ is isomorphic to two- or three-dimensional Cartesian space.

This structure theorem not only asserts that any finite-dimensional vector space over a field F is isomorphic to F^n, but it also opens the doors to link the formal structure to the worlds of embodiment and symbolism. Vectors in finite-dimensional spaces can be written using coordinates (usually as column vectors); linear maps can be written as matrices and multiplied using the symbolism of matrix multiplication. It reveals the underlying crystalline structure for a finite-dimensional vector space that is already familiar from matrix algebra.

If the field F is the field of real numbers $\mathbb{R}$, then a three-dimensional vector space V has the structure of vectors in $\mathbb{R}^3$, except that there is as yet no definition of angle between vectors (which requires additional axioms). Even so, it enables vector subspaces to be seen as lines or planes through the origin. The structure theorem now blends the formal axiomatic structure of a finite-dimensional vector space with an embodiment in space and a symbolic representation of its linear functions as matrices into a single crystalline concept.

More generally, the development from natural thinking based on embodiment and symbolism to formal thinking (in Figure 10.3) can now use structure theorems to relate formal ideas back to new forms of embodied and symbolic representations. This allows formalism, embodiment and symbolism to work together to inspire new formal theorems (Figure 12.6).

3.2 *Supportive and Problematic Aspects of Structure Theorems*

Structure theorems enable mathematicians to use new forms of embodiment and symbolism, now based firmly on formal proof, to reflect on new problems and to extend the boundaries of mathematics.

However, the new forms of embodiment and symbolism may themselves have aspects that may be supportive or problematic in possible new generalizations.

For instance, the structure theorem for a three-dimensional vector space over the real numbers may be imagined mentally as $\mathbb{R}^3$ but the selected axioms concern only the addition of vectors and multiplication of a vector by a real number. There is no mention of *angles*. The axes one may imagine are not therefore specified as being at right angles.

To be able to define angles and lengths requires more axioms, to define what is called an 'inner product' or 'dot product', which in two and three dimensions is given by $\mathbf{u} \cdot \mathbf{v} = uv \cos \theta$ where u and v are the lengths of the vectors and θ is the angle between them.

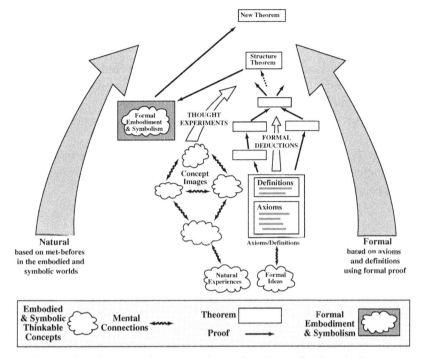

Figure 12.6. Structure theorems enhance formal proof with embodiment and symbolism.

This tells us that an embodiment of a structure given by a structure theorem certainly has the properties implied by the formal structure, but it may have additional properties that are not formally defined that can later be problematic. This happened in Euclidean geometry, which survived for more than two thousand years until it was realized that certain almost self-evident properties had not been formally included, such as the idea of a point being 'inside' a triangle, which Hilbert resolved by adding extra axioms for the idea of a point on a line being 'between' two other points on the same line.

As I will show in Chapter 13, this is happening in mathematical analysis where seeing the number line as the embodiment of a complete ordered field can act as an impediment to an extensional blend that places the real numbers in an even larger field that contains the real numbers as an ordered subfield.

This does not alter the fact that structure theorems provide ways of thinking about problems in new areas using embodied and symbolic ideas that have various warrants for truth that make them amenable to be formulated in terms of axioms and definitions to seek formal proof of relationships.

Applied mathematicians use the embodiment and symbolism to formulate problems by imagining the embodiment and formulating a symbolic model to solve, knowing that the ideas are supported by formal structures that they can use theoretically without seeking formal proofs.

The following sections outline more structure theorems in other areas of mathematics that are seminal in giving a formal underpinning to the human blending of embodiment, symbolism and formalism.

3.3 *A Finite Group Is Isomorphic to a Group of Permutations*

Practical examples of groups include groups of permutations, where the elements permute (or re-order) the elements in a given finite set. The group of permutations of n elements is called the *symmetric group of order n* and denoted by S_n. It consists of all the functions permuting the numbers $1, 2, \ldots, n$. This can be used for computational purposes. For example, the permutation of the elements $\{1, 2, 3, 4, 5\}$ that takes the order 12345 into 21453 takes 1 to 2, 2 to 1, 3 to 4, 4 to 5 and 5 to 3. This permutes the elements in two cycles, one taking 1 to 2 and 2 to 1, the other cycling 3 to 4 to 5 and taking 5 back to 3. (Figure 12.7.)

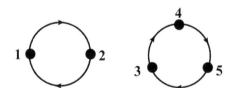

Figure 12.7. A permutation represented as cycles.

These cycles are written sequentially in brackets as (12), (345) where the elements in a bracket are permuted, with each one going to the next except the last which goes to the first. Permutations are combined by performing one followed by the other, reading from left to right. Thus the product (123) (123) takes 1 to 2 in the first bracket, then 2 to 3 in the second, taking 1 to 3 overall, while 2 goes to 3 goes to 1 overall, and 3 goes to 1 goes to 2, giving the cycle (132). This permutation turns the cycle on the right of the figure two turns clockwise, and has the same effect as one turn anticlockwise. The product (123) (123) (123) turns through three turns clockwise, turning full circle to give the identity of the permutation group. This enables the operations in the symmetric group to be embodied and calculated using cyclic permutations.

Given any finite group G with n elements, then each element $g \in G$ gives a function $f_g : G \rightarrow G$ by multiplying every element on the left by g, to get $f_g(x) = g \circ x$. By the group axioms it can be shown that f is a bijection that permutes the elements of G. Numbering the elements $g_1, \ldots, g_n$ gives a permutation of the n elements $1, 2, \ldots, n$, which is an element of the group S_n of permutations. This assignment maps elements of G to elements of S_n and preserves the group operation because $f_h(f_g(x)) = h \circ g \circ x = f_{h \circ g}(x)$. This shows that any finite group G can be represented as a subgroup of a group of permutations. Once this structure theorem is established, it allows the formal theory of finite groups to be linked to symbolic calculations.

However, mathematicians shift to a new level where equivalent structures are reconceptualized as a single crystalline structure that can be expressed in different ways. Using this way of thinking, we see a finite group not just as being *isomorphic* to a subgroup of a permutation group, but think of it *as* a subgroup of a permutation group.

Now expert mathematicians are in a completely new ball game. Finite groups are not just systems given by the axioms of a group, they can now be seen structurally as subgroups of a permutation group. If we wish to classify all finite groups, then they are subgroups of permutation groups and the abstract problem of classification becomes a more concrete exploration of finding the subgroups of permutation groups.

In practice, the permutation group S_n becomes very large as n increases and can be very complicated, so various new techniques are developed. However, they are now based on *knowing* that a finite group is a meaningful concrete structure as a subgroup of a permutation group rather than just some kind of abstract idea.

Analysing the possible structures that may occur has led to new techniques in the quest to classify all finite groups (up to isomorphism). The problem is still open, but several giant steps have been made. One involves the notion of a 'simple' group, which acts as a kind of foundational group from which all other finite groups are formed. The finite simple groups have now been fully identified, taking us a step further in the overall development of group theory.[9]

---

[9] See http://en.wikipedia.org/wiki/Classification_of_finite_simple_groups (Accessed June 1, 2012).

3.4 *An Equivalence Relation on a Set Partitions It into Equivalence Classes*

The notion of equivalence relation on a set S is formulated entirely by three axioms specifying that the relation is reflexive, symmetric and transitive. This does not have any operations defined on the set S so it does not have any obvious symbolic interpretations, though it can exist in many contexts that have additional symbolic aspects.

However, an equivalence relation consisting precisely of the reflexive, symmetric and transitive laws can be given an embodied meaning by considering elements that are equivalent to each other. Take any element $x \in S$ and consider the subset S_x of all the elements equivalent to x. This is called the *equivalence class* containing x.

Every element of S lies in an equivalence class (for instance, $x \in S$ belongs to the equivalence class S_x. If two equivalence classes have an element in common, say $z \in S_x$ and $z \in S_x$ then $z \sim x$ and $z \sim y$ and, using the reflexive and transitive axioms, we find $x \sim y$ and deduce that S_x and S_y are the same. This shows that the equivalence classes are either identical or nonintersecting, with each equivalence class being written in many ways as S_x where x is any element of the class. The equivalence classes can then be embodied as a partition of the set into distinct subsets. (Figure 12.8.)

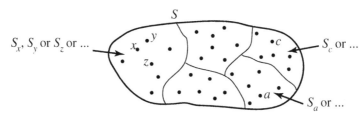

Figure 12.8. Partitioning a set S using an equivalence relation.

Conversely, it is straightforward to show that any partition gives an equivalence relation. This gives a structure theorem in which an equivalence relation on a set, given in terms of the three axioms, reflexive, symmetric and transitive, can be embodied as partitioning the set into non-overlapping subsets.

This theorem reveals the wide generality of the notion of equivalence relation. Most of the equivalence relations met in algebra – equivalent fractions, equivalent algebraic expressions, equivalent vectors, equivalence in group theory, and so on – have the relation specified by a simple rule. But it need not be so. *Any* partition of a set gives an equivalence relation.

One equivalence relation that causes some problems to students is the idea of two infinite decimals being equivalent if they represent the same real number. Here the equivalence classes have one element in every case except where a finite decimal (such as 0.65) is equivalent to an infinite decimal ending in repeating nines (such as 0.64999 ...) where the equivalence class contains precisely two elements.

3.5 *An Ordered Field Contains a Subfield Isomorphic to the Rational Numbers*

If a field F is ordered, the order relation places a limitation on the arithmetic generated by the unit element 1_F. Define the element $2_F = 1_F + 1_F$ and, proceeding by induction, for any $n \in \mathbb{Z}$, define $(n+1)_F = n_F + 1_F$ to give the sequence $1_F, 2_F, ..., n_F, ...$ in F. In a general field, the sequence might repeat, as happens in the field $\mathbb{Z}_3$ of integers modulo 3 where the sequence is $1_F, 2_F, 3_F$, where $3_F = 0_F$ and $4_F = 1_F$, and more generally in the field of integers $\mathbb{Z}_p$ for a prime number p. However, in an ordered field F, the terms $1_F, 2_F, ..., n_F, ...$ are successive sums of positive elements and so every one is positive. They must also be different, for if $m_F = n_F$ where $m_F > n_F$, then k_F is zero where $k_F = m_F - n_F$, contradicting the fact that k_F is positive and not zero.

Once we have found an infinite sequence of different terms $1_F, 2_F, ..., n_F, ...$ in our ordered field F, we include their additive inverses $-1_F, -2_F, ..., -n_F, ...$ the zero element, and the fractions m_F/n_F (for $n_F \neq 0_F$ to get a subfield isomorphic to $\mathbb{Q}$.

Again we can shift a level and regard this subfield as *being* the rational numbers $\mathbb{Q}$ and then it can be said that every ordered field *contains* the rational numbers $\mathbb{Q}$. In particular, we can use the familiar number symbols to represent rational numbers in any ordered field F, so that it has a specific crystalline substructure in the form of the rational numbers.

3.6 *Up to Isomorphism, There Is Only One Complete Ordered Field*

A complete ordered field is an ordered field with the additional axiom of completeness which we will formulate here as:

(C) An increasing sequence (a_n) bounded above by $L \in F$ tends to a limit $a \in F$ where $a \leq L$.

As we know that an ordered field F contains the rationals $\mathbb{Q}$, it already contains all finite decimals that are integers over a power of ten. We can write any finite decimal with n decimal places in the form $a_0 \cdot a_1...a_n$, where a_0 is an integer and $a_1, a_2, ..., a_n, ...$ are digits between 0 and 9. The decimal $a_0 \cdot a_1 ... a_n$ represents the rational number

$$a_0 \cdot a_1...a_n = a_0 + \frac{a_1}{10} + ... + \frac{a_n}{10^n}$$

A sequence of finite decimals in the form $a_0 \cdot a_1$, $a_0 \cdot a_1 a_2$, ..., $a_0 \cdot a_1...a_n$, ... is an increasing sequence in F, bounded above by $a_0 + 1$. By completeness, this has a unique limit $a \le a_0 + 1$. This limit a is written as the infinite decimal

$$a = a_0 \cdot a_1...a_n$$

There is some work to do to check that the arithmetic operations satisfy the axioms for a field to show that F contains a subfield isomorphic to the real numbers as infinite decimals. Then we must show that every element $x \in F$ can be written as a decimal expansion.

To find the decimal expansion for x, we begin by finding an integer m such that $m \le x < m + 1$. It is not possible to have x larger than all integers for if this happened, by completeness, the sequence 1, 2, 3, ... would be bounded above by x and then it would have a limit $k \in F$ where $k \le x$. But because k is the *limit* of the sequence then, by the definition, for any $\varepsilon > 0$, say $\varepsilon = \frac{1}{2}$, all the terms after some N lie between $k - \varepsilon$ and $k + \varepsilon$ for all $n > N$. But then, the next term $N + 1$ will lie between them, so $k - \frac{1}{2} < N + 1 < k + \frac{1}{2}$, and, in particular, $k - \frac{1}{2} < N + 1$, so the next term $N + 2$ is now *bigger* than k, which is a contradiction. So there must be some integer q bigger than x. By a similar argument, there must be some integer p smaller than x. We are now working with the familiar integers and, as we count up from p to q, we find an integer m where $m \le x < m + 1$. By an induction argument on n, we can show that x lies in the interval:

$$a_0 + \frac{a_1}{10} + \cdots + \frac{a_n}{10^n} \le x < a_0 + \frac{a_1}{10} + \cdots + \frac{a_n + 1}{10^n}$$

and then prove that x is the real number $a_0 \cdot a_1 ... a_n ...$ as the limit

$$a_0 + \frac{a_1}{10} + \cdots + \frac{a_n}{10^n} + \cdots$$

For university students in the early part of their course this is a technically difficult proof to write out in full, and even mathematicians find it tedious to write out the detail. But once established and part of the knowledge structure of the research mathematician, it can then be used as a formal algebraic structure – a complete ordered field – linked to the embodiment of the real number line and the arithmetic of decimals. The field of real numbers $\mathbb{R}$ is the unique complete ordered field that includes the rationals $\mathbb{Q}$ as an ordered subfield, the integers $\mathbb{Z}$ and the natural numbers $\mathbb{N}$.

One thing that the real numbers do *not* contain is an infinitesimal, which is 'arbitrarily small' but not zero. For instance, we might seek a positive infinitesimal $o \in \mathbb{R}$ that is smaller than all positive real numbers, but we cannot have one because $o/2 \in \mathbb{R}$ is positive and smaller.

Various experiences – such as the construction of $\mathbb{R}$ from $\mathbb{Q}$ using Dedekind cuts explained in Chapter 9 – are often described as 'completing the real number line' by 'filling in the gaps between the rationals'. This introduces a subtle met-before that is widely shared in the community: that there is 'no room' on the number line to fit in any more numbers, and certainly no room for infinitesimals.

The Cantor-Dedekind Axiom stating that the real numbers are order isomorphic to the points on a geometric line also categorically insists that once the rationals have been 'completed' then this fills up the whole geometric line.

This illustrates how the choice of a particular set of axioms gives a framework with particular properties and may be interpreted by the community to say that 'infinitesimals cannot exist.' However, it only shows that they cannot exist *as real numbers*. It does not mean that they cannot occur in another formal system, as we will see in Chapter 13.

4. Choices and Consequences

Mathematicians have control over the axioms that they choose. But then the theorems that are proved are a consequence of that choice. Choose to study a complete ordered field, and the consequence is that there can be no infinitesimals in it. Choose the epsilon-delta definition of continuity of a function, and again certain consequences follow. For instance, this might introduce monsters that are continuous almost everywhere but peculiarly discontinuous elsewhere.

A typical crazy function is given by

$$r(x) = \begin{cases} 1/n & \text{if } x \text{ is the rational number } m/n \text{ in lowest terms} \\ 0 & \text{otherwise} \end{cases}$$

The graph is then discontinuous at every rational point and continuous at every rational. This is a strange monster. The reason is that, in any interval there are both rationals and irrationals, but in any interval $a \leq x \leq b$ there are only a finite number of rationals $x = m/n$ whose values exceed a given value of $\varepsilon > 0$. Around any irrational therefore, it is possible to find an interval where all nearby points on the graph are within ε, and round any rational $x = m/n$, for $\varepsilon = 1/(2n)$, there are irrationals where points on the graph are more than ε away.

The graph is caricatured in Figure 12.9, plotted with 'large' points. If smaller points were used to approximate the graph better, then it would be seen that most points cluster around the x-axis.

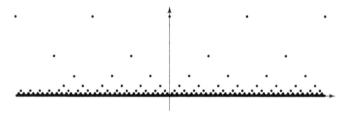

Figure 12.9. A function continuous at all irrationals and discontinuous at every rational.

The reader may think that such a bizarre function has no place in the dynamically continuous world we live in. It doesn't. Put simply, this function is not formally continuous in any interval $a \leq x \leq b$ of *real numbers*, so it would not be expected to be dynamically continuous over any interval. However, it *does* satisfy the formal definition of continuity at every irrational point and it will 'pull flat' in a window centred on an irrational value of x, but not in a window centred on a rational.

What is happening here is that the graph is not formally continuous at *every* real number on an interval, so do not expect it to operate like a dynamically continuous *real* function.

The view expressed by Lakoff and Núñez in *Where Mathematics Comes From*[10] is that many concepts in formal mathematics fail to behave the way that they believe embodied mathematics should operate. They claim that 'romantic' mathematicians produce a form of mathematics that is 'counter-intuitive'. However, in formal mathematics, the mathematician *chooses* his axioms, and the consequences follow. By proving structure

[10] Lakoff & Núñez (2000).

theorems, mathematicians are able to give axiomatic systems new embodiments that are appropriate for their own prepared knowledge structure. The chosen axioms reveal crystalline formal structures whose consequences are secured by formal proof. These structures may then lead to structure theorems that give previously unimagined embodiments that, for the mathematician, now have a meaningful embodiment.

Different axiomatic systems give different crystalline structures. What is 'natural' depends on the experience of the learner. Learners who have experienced a locally straight introduction to the calculus would not be limited to thinking that 'most' curves are smooth with tangents 'almost everywhere'. They are more likely to *know* that a continuous function may be seriously wrinkled.

The development of axiomatic mathematics is not limited to 'natural' ways of thinking. A mathematician can formulate any consistent system of axioms and deduce theorems to develop a formal knowledge structure, which may then involve structure theorems that give entirely new ways of embodying mathematical structures to a prepared mathematical mind.

Every mathematician began life as a newborn child and has passed through a cognitive development to reach the heights of his mathematical imagination. It is *this* development that we should analyze, from child to mathematician, to find how the embodied brain *becomes* a mathematical mind. Top-down idea analysis from a highly theoretical viewpoint may give some insights, but it is the cognitive growth of the human individual that reveals the true development of human mathematical thinking.

5. New Organizational Principles

Mathematicians use definitions in a different way from everyday language. In particular, they often take a positive delight in seeing singular examples as part of a general pattern. For instance, the empty set is seen as a central example of a set in its role as a subset of every other set. This violates embodied conceptions where the empty set of apples is evidently different from the empty set of rational numbers. Yet in the axiomatic formal world they are precisely the *same* crystalline concept because they both have the same elements (namely, none).

The empty set is a particular favourite in mathematical formalism. For example, consider the notion of a subspace of a vector space. It is natural to say that the subset of a vector space V (over a field F) generated by a subset S consists of all sums $a_1\mathbf{v}_1 + \cdots + a_n\mathbf{v}_n$ where $a_1, \ldots, a_n$ are elements of F and $\mathbf{v}_1, \ldots, \mathbf{v}_n$ are any elements of S. If the elements $\mathbf{v}_1, \ldots, \mathbf{v}_n$ are linearly independent then the subspace is said to be n-dimensional. For $n = 1, 2, 3$ over the real numbers, these can be seen as one-dimensional, two-dimensional and three-dimensional space. But can the value of n be zero? If the generating subset is the empty set, then how can one have a sum of *no* elements?

This is where the careful use of definition comes into play. The subspace generated by any subset S of a vector space V is defined carefully to be 'the smallest subspace that includes all the elements of S.' This includes all the sums $a_1\mathbf{v}_1 + \cdots + a_n\mathbf{v}_n$ where $\mathbf{v}_1, \ldots, \mathbf{v}_n \in S$, but it must also contain the zero vector, because the rules for a vector space say so. This implies that if S is the empty set, the smallest subspace generated by S must consist of the zero vector alone. This means that a subset generated by n independent vectors has dimension n, and this now includes the case $n = 0$.

This subtle generality is the kind of thing that gives great pleasure to mathematicians, even if it seems bizarre in everyday conversation. It is an aesthetically beautiful notion that allows all cases to be included in a general pattern with no exceptions. I remember well as an undergraduate hearing exquisite lectures from the very reflective Oxford don, Ken Gravett. He told us that the empty set was the one that he felt most at home with, because he was absolutely certain what its elements are. If anyone asked, 'is x in the empty set?' (whatever x happened to be), he could always answer 'no.'

Another case of including a singular example as an instance of the general pattern arose when Chris Sangwin asked undergraduates and mathematicians to give examples of even and odd functions.[11] An even function satisfies $f(-x) = f(x)$ and includes functions such as x^2 or $\cos x$ and an odd function satisfies $f(-x) = -f(x)$ such as x^3 or $\sin x$. The students gave variants of 'typical examples' such as $x^2 + 1$ for even and $\sin 2x$ for odd. A possible response from professional mathematicians, however, was 'zero'. This singular case is both odd *and* even. For a mathematician it is a minimal example, requiring least effort: for a student it is a singular example that fails to be typical for either property.

The philosopher Paul Grice[12] formulated four maxims for cooperative dialogue, namely quality (truth), quantity (information), relation (relevance) and manner (clarity). The first involves only saying what you believe to be true, for which you have adequate evidence. The second involves making your contribution as informative as possible without giving excessive detail. The third requires what is said to be relevant, the

[11] Sangwin (2004).
[12] Grice (1989).

fourth requires the communication to be brief, avoiding obscurity and ambiguity.

Following Grice's maxims, in everyday language one says things in an informative and suitably clear manner. For instance, one might say 'five is bigger than four,' and never 'five is greater than or equal to four.' But formal mathematics seeks an economy of means – a parsimony where only what is absolutely necessary is highlighted. This leads to default cases being included in a pattern to minimize the complexity. Mathematicians usually abhor several choices and prefer binary decisions where the response is either yes or no.

For instance, the order property in its strong form $x > y$ requires the use of the trichotomy law: either $x > y$ or $y > x$ or $x = 0$, *and no two hold at the same time.* This follows the Gricean maxim of saying precisely what you know. When I formulated the axioms for order, I framed them using this axiom because I sensed that it would make more sense to readers who are not research mathematicians. It would be less 'natural' to use the order relation $x \geq y$ because in specific arithmetical examples we will always know whether the elements are the same or different.

In the search to reduce every decision as far as possible to a simple yes or no, the notion of order is often given in terms of the corresponding weak order relation $x \geq y$. The weak axioms for order on a set S are:

(WO1) Given $x, y \in S$ then either $x \geq y$ or $y \geq x$.
(WO2) If $x \geq y$ and $y \geq x$ then $x = y$.

These axioms avoid the three-way test of trichotomy and allow every decision to be binary. Now the definition says that either $x \geq y$ or $y \geq x$ and if both hold then $x = y$.

In mathematics, strong relations (where equality is excluded) are sometimes used in preference to weak relations (where equality is possible). For instance, the notion of parallel lines is a strong equivalence relation between two distinct lines and a line cannot be parallel to itself.

However, in the formal definition of equivalence, an element is always assumed to be equivalent to itself. This is simply a choice made to simplify decision-making. An equivalence relation $\sim$ on a set A is defined to satisfy three axioms:

(E1) $x \sim x$ for all $x \in A$.
(E2) If $x \sim y$ then $y \sim x$.
(E3) If $x \sim y$ and $y \sim z$ then $y \sim z$.

It is quite possible to define a corresponding 'strong equivalence relation' σ defined so that $a\,\sigma\,b$ *means* $a \sim b$ and $a \neq b$. This gives new axioms for a strong equivalence relation in the form:

> (SE1) The relation $a\,\sigma\,a$ does *not* hold.
> (SE2) If $a\,\sigma\,b$ then $b\,\sigma\,a$.
> (SE3) If $a\,\sigma\,b$, $b\,\sigma\,c$ and $a \neq c$ then $a\,\sigma\,c$.

These axioms lack the simplicity and elegance of (E1)–(E3), and so mathematicians do not use them. Aesthetic sense is part of the axiomatic formal world, choosing axioms and definitions in a form that is elegant and parsimonious, even if this involves different ways of operating from familiar everyday experience.

In some circumstances, changing the list of axioms may give the same underlying crystalline structure, for instance, replacing the axioms for a strong equivalence relation by the more elegant axioms for an equivalence relation, or replacing one version of the completeness axiom in an ordered field by another.

However, when a list of axioms is modified, perhaps by adding or removing an axiom, or making a change in one or more axioms, it often causes a radical change in the crystalline structure. This is not a problem: it is a rich source of freedom, to invent an axiomatic structure that the mathematician chooses for specific purposes. Having chosen a new list of axioms, the consequences of those axioms are not invented; they are discovered.

Often the crystalline structure is so beautiful that even the mathematician who invented the axioms and definitions in the first place is amazed by the sense of perfection that arises. It is no small wonder that a mathematician rich in the experience of discovering beautiful ideas in a given axiomatic system will believe that the crystalline structure is a Platonic entity with an existence beyond the confines of his or her own mind.

Structure theorems translate axiomatic systems and definitions within them into the possibility of new embodiments and new ways of operating symbolically. The power in mathematical thinking lies not just in formulating axioms to describe a familiar situation; it arises from blending together familiar ideas in new ways to solve new problems and, in doing so, to create new crystalline concepts and structure theorems that lead to new forms of embodiment and symbolism underpinned by formal proof.

13 Contemplating the Infinitely Large and Small

As mathematics evolves, meanings change. In the late nineteenth century, Weierstrass reformulated the visual and dynamic ideas of the calculus as the formal limit concept: 'Tell me how close you want the output (within epsilon) and I will tell you how close the input should be (within delta).' This offered a replacement for the concept of an actual infinitesimal, by a potentially infinite process of becoming as small as is required. In essence this reaffirmed the potential infinity of Aristotle, reinterpreted using the modern quantified formulation of mathematical analysis.

Meanwhile, Cantor and Dedekind introduced the idea of completeness to fill out the rational number line to become the real number line. This 'completeness' is often interpreted to mean that there is 'no room' on the line for infinitesimals. It is not possible for a positive real number x to be smaller than all other positive real numbers because $x/2$ would also be a positive real number even smaller than x.

Cantor also contemplated the infinitely large, extending the concept of number to infinite sets by saying that two sets have the same cardinal number if they can be put in one-to-one correspondence. The cardinal number of natural numbers $\mathbb{N}$ was named $\aleph_0$ (aleph zero). The sets $\mathbb{N}$, E, O of natural numbers, even numbers and odd numbers can be put in one-to-one correspondence by linking the natural number n to the even number $2n$ and the odd number $2n - 1$. This reveals that the set of even numbers and the set of odd numbers also have the same cardinal number $\aleph_0$.

Cantor added two cardinal numbers by putting together two separate sets (with no elements in common) to find its cardinal number. Putting together the odd numbers and the even numbers makes the set of natural numbers, and so $\aleph_0 + \aleph_0 = \aleph_0$.

He also defined multiplication of cardinal numbers by taking any two sets A and B and defining the product of their cardinal numbers to be the cardinal number of $A \times B$. He was then able to show that infinite cardinals satisfy the familiar commutative, associative and distributive properties that are shared by other number systems. In particular, the equation $\aleph_0 + \aleph_0 = \aleph_0$ can be written as $2\aleph_0 = \aleph_0$. Attempting to divide both sides by the non-zero number $\aleph_0$ would give $2 = 1$. He concluded that dividing by an infinite number to get an infinitesimal is not consistent with the rules of arithmetic. In two fundamentally different ways, using completeness and infinite cardinals, Cantor declared that the notion of infinitesimal is unacceptable.

However, we have seen this situation on many occasions before. In the evolution of mathematics in history and the maturation of a child's concept of number, we have encountered extensional blends in which ideas that are consistent at one stage become problematic in an extended system. This has happened every time number systems have been extended, from the natural numbers $\mathbb{N}$, to the integers $\mathbb{Z}$, the rational numbers $\mathbb{Q}$, the real numbers $\mathbb{R}$, and the complex numbers $\mathbb{C}$. In every case an extensional blend of a number system generalizes certain properties that are supportive (such as the commutativity, associativity, distributivity) while others become problematic. In every case, the smaller system retains its original properties but the broader system offers new ways of thinking mathematically.

The same phenomenon occurs again here. Cantor's idea that infinitesimals are unacceptable is absolutely correct – *in the system of real numbers*. But this does not mean that there cannot be an extensional blend of the real numbers that satisfies the supportive properties of arithmetic and order and includes elements that are infinitesimal.

In this chapter, after considering the differences of opinion that have arisen from ideas about infinitesimals that became problematic, I will use formal mathematics to reveal that *every* ordered field extension of the real numbers *must* contain infinitesimals. This involves a simple structure theorem that shows how infinitesimals may be manipulated algebraically using the symbolism of ordered fields and embodied visually as an extended number line. This uses the framework of three worlds of mathematics to relate high-level formal sophistication to its human sensori-motor origins. As a culmination of the chapter, I will reveal that an infinitesimal portion of a locally straight graph can be magnified to reveal a complete infinite real straight line that can be imagined in the mind and seen by the physical human eye.

My purpose is not to advocate that learners should be introduced to the calculus using non-standard analysis. Such an approach, as currently formulated, requires even greater subtlety in mathematical logic than standard analysis. This chapter continues the main theme of the whole book: that making sense of mathematics is a blending of human embodiment, operational symbolism and axiomatic formalism, generalizing supportive aspects and being aware of problematic met-befores that impede progress. In particular, the natural approach advocated in Chapter 11 – blending together dynamic human action and perception with algebraic symbolism – is not only suitable for the practical and theoretical needs of the wider population for their future role in society, but it also offers a natural foundation for the crystalline structure of the calculus as a powerful tool in applications, and as a formal theory in either standard analysis using the real numbers, or nonstandard analysis in an extensional blend that includes infinitesimals.

1. Contrasting Beliefs about Infinity and Infinitesimals

Cantor's theory of infinite cardinals proved results that seemed amazingly counterintuitive. For example, he proved that the integers and rationals had the same cardinal number but that the cardinal number of the real numbers $\mathbb{R}$ is strictly greater. More amazingly, the real interval between 0 and 1 has the same cardinality as a square in the real plane or a cube in $\mathbb{R}^3$ or the whole of n-dimensional space $\mathbb{R}^n$. Many mathematicians and philosophers felt uncomfortable and fiercely opposed his ideas, with comments such as the following:

> *Kronecker*: I don't know what predominates in Cantor's theory – philosophy or theology – but I am sure that there is no mathematics there.
>
> *Brouwer*: Cantor's theory as a whole is 'a pathological incident in history of mathematics from which future generations will be horrified'.
>
> *Wittgenstein*: Cantor's argument has no deductive content at all.
>
> *Weyl*: Axiomatic set theory is a 'house built on sand'.[1]

Paradoxes were found in the theory. For instance, it can be shown that for any set S, the set of subsets of S always has a larger cardinal number. This reveals a whole hierarchy of sets with successively larger cardinal numbers. Yet what is the cardinal number of the set of all sets? Clearly this must be

---

[1] Weyl made his comment in the introduction of his monograph *Das Continuum* (1918). This and other quotations given here arise often in the literature and online, though often without original references, for instance at http://en.wikipedia.org/wiki/Controversy_over_Cantor's_theory. (Accessed July 31, 2012.)

the largest cardinal of all because all other sets are subsets. Yet its set of subsets must have a cardinal that is even larger!

The harsh criticism that Cantor received was countered by praise from others. He was supported by Dedekind, who credited him as an inspiration in his construction of the real numbers using Dedekind cuts. Hilbert, the founder of formalism, defended the theory of infinite cardinals from its critics, declaring: 'No one shall expel us from the Paradise that Cantor has created.'[2]

As he grew older, Cantor continued to receive stinging criticism and suffered from continual bouts of depression, dying in a sanatorium where he spent the last year of his life, suffering from poverty and malnourishment.

But history has vindicated his theory of cardinal numbers. Since Aristotle, there had been but one infinity – the potential infinity of counting numbers. Now Cantor had shown that there were infinitely many cardinal infinities, growing ever larger in size.

His work has become the foundation of modern set theory and axiomatic mathematics. It is often encountered early in undergraduate courses in pure mathematics.

However, cardinal number theory and mathematical analysis seemed to spell the death of the infinitesimal. The widely read textbook of Courant, while acknowledging that Leibniz was 'capable of combining these vague mystical ideas with a thoroughly clear understanding of the limiting process'[3], set the tone for the attitude against infinitesimals, which he declared to be 'devoid of any clear meaning'[4] and 'incompatible with the clarity of ideas demanded in mathematics'.[5]

The concept of infinitesimal, although used regularly in applied mathematics, became an anti-goal to be avoided by many pure mathematicians who worked successfully in the epsilon-delta mode of mathematical analysis. By the mid-twentieth century, formal mathematics in general, and mathematical analysis in particular, was in the ascendant. In the real number system there is no room for infinitesimals. Then in the early sixties, something stirred.

In 1966, Abraham Robinson proposed a new theory that he believed was the solution of the age-old argument about infinities and infinitesimals.[6] He used mathematical logic to extend the real numbers $\mathbb{R}$ to a

---

[2] Hilbert (1926).
[3] Courant (2nd English edition, 1937), p. 101.
[4] Courant (1937), p. 88.
[5] Courant (1937), p.101.
[6] Robinson (1966).

larger ordered field that he called the *hyperreal numbers* $^*\mathbb{R}$. Infinitesimals were at last given a logical formulation.

But they did not set the world of mathematics alight. Though welcomed in some quarters, mathematicians in general remained attached to the well-established formulation of mathematical analysis.

My purpose here is to analyse what happened in terms of formalism, symbolism and embodiment (in that order), not only to understand the mathematical and cognitive nature of infinitesimals but also to analyse the continuing dispute over their use in terms of the three worlds of mathematics, and the supportive and problematic issues that affect personal conceptions and widely shared opinions.

2. Formal Ordered Fields with Infinitesimals

An ordered field F is simply a set with operations of addition, and multiplication and an order relation satisfying the required axioms given in Chapter 8. So far we have considered only well-known examples such as the rationals $\mathbb{Q}$ and the real numbers $\mathbb{R}$, but there are many others. For instance, in the later years of school we meet polynomials in a variable x and their quotients – called rational functions – of the form

$$\frac{a_0 + a_1 x + \cdots + a_n x^n}{b_0 + b_1 x + \cdots + b_m x^m}$$

where the coefficients a_r and b_s are all real numbers, with $b_m \neq 0$. These rational functions have the familiar algebraic properties of addition, subtraction, multiplication and division and satisfy all the axioms for a field that we denote by $\mathbb{R}(x)$. Moreover, any real number a can be written as $a/1$, so $\mathbb{R}$ is a subfield of $\mathbb{R}(x)$.

Initially rational functions are not ordered. However, to define an order on a field F only requires the definition of a subset F^+ satisfying the two order axioms:

(O1) For $x \in F$, precisely one of the following three properties holds:
      $x \in F^+$, or $-x \in F^+$, or $x = 0$.
(O2) If $x, y \in F^+$ then $x + y, xy \in F^+$.

As discussed in Chapter 8, an element x in F^+ is said to be *positive*, and its additive inverse $-x$ is *negative*. Axiom (O1) (the law of trichotomy) says that every element is either *positive*, or *negative* or *zero* and the three are mutually exclusive. Axiom (O2) says that the sum and product of two positive numbers are both positive.

Even though the field $\mathbb{R}(x)$ does not seem to be ordered in any obvious way, there is a natural way to define a subset $\mathbb{R}(x)^+$ of $\mathbb{R}(x)$ that satisfies (O1) and (O2) and gives a visual meaning to an order on $\mathbb{R}(x)$.

A rational function $f(x)$ is either the zero function, or the quotient of two nonzero polynomials, where each has only a finite number of zeros. A nonzero rational function therefore has only a finite number of points where it is zero or undefined. Choose a real interval $0 < x < k$ to the right of the origin that does not contain any of these points, then the rational function is neither zero nor infinite anywhere in $0 < x < k$. It cannot be negative somewhere and positive somewhere else in the interval; otherwise, being continuous, it would be zero in between. It must be either *strictly positive* or *strictly negative* in this interval to the right of the origin.

A rational function $f(x)$ is declared to belong to $\mathbb{R}(x)^+$ if there is a real number k such that $f(x) > 0$ for all real x in $0 < x < k$. Figure 13.1 shows three rational functions positive in this sense. The function $f(x) = x$ is positive in $0 < x < k$ for any positive k, $g(x) = x(1 - x)$ is positive for $0 < x < 1$, and $h(x) = 1/x$ is positive in any interval from 0 to k.

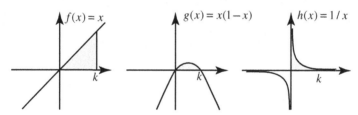

Figure 13.1. Examples of rational functions in the set P of 'positive' elements (positive in an interval $0 < x < k$ to the right of the origin).

This definition satisfies the axioms (O1) and (O2) and so the field of rational functions is an ordered field in a formal sense. The familiar order notations such as $f > g$ or $f \geq g$ can be defined in the usual way; for instance, $f > g$ means $f - g \in \mathbb{R}(x)^+$ and $f \geq g$ means that $f > g$ or $f = g$.

Viewing the elements of $\mathbb{R}(x)$ as graphs, the notation $f > g$ says that the graph of f is above the graph of g in some interval to the right of the origin. For instance, $f(x) = x$ satisfies $0 < x < k$ for any positive real number k because its graph lies above the x-axis and below the constant function $c(x) = k$ in the interval $0 < x < k$. The element $x \in \mathbb{R}(x)$ is positive and smaller than any positive real number. It is an *infinitesimal*.

At last we not only have an infinitesimal defined in a formal way, but we can also embody it visually as a graph. However, this may be problematic in several ways. The formal learner may be satisfied with the formal symbolic approach to the definition of the ordered field $\mathbb{R}(x)$ and have no need for a picture. The natural learner with a predisposition for thinking of an infinitesimal as a 'very small quantity' may have difficulty because the embodiment is a *graph*, not a *number*, or a *point* on a line.[7]

We will address this concern as soon as we have developed some formal properties that apply to *any* ordered field F that has $\mathbb{R}$ as an ordered subfield.

2.1 *A Structure Theorem for Ordered Extensions of* $\mathbb{R}$

Given an ordered field F that has $\mathbb{R}$ as an ordered subfield, we can define an infinitesimal to be a non-zero element $u \in F$ such that $-k < u < k$ for all positive $k \in \mathbb{R}$. An element u is *positive infinite* if $u > k$ for all $k \in \mathbb{R}$ and *negative infinite* if $u < k$ for all $k \in \mathbb{R}$. It is straightforward to prove that u is an infinitesimal if and only if $1/u$ is infinite.

If we make the assumption that F is a proper extension of $\mathbb{R}$, meaning that there is at least one element $u \in F$ where $u \notin \mathbb{R}$, then either u is infinite (positive or negative), in which case $1/u$ is infinitesimal, or u is finite and not real. In the latter case we can prove a structure theorem that describes a finite element in infinitesimal terms:

Structure theorem for any ordered extension of the real numbers:
A finite element x of an ordered field extension F of $\mathbb{R}$ is uniquely of the form $x = c + \varepsilon$ where $c \in \mathbb{R}$ and ε is infinitesimal or zero. The real number c is called the *standard part* of x and is written $c = \text{st}(x)$.

Proof: Because x is finite, we have $a < x < b$ for $a, b \in \mathbb{R}$. Apply the idea of a Dedekind cut to the real numbers to obtain the set L of real numbers less than x and the set R of real numbers greater than (or equal to) x. Let c be the real number given by this cut; then, in the real numbers $\mathbb{R}$, c is the least upper bound of L and the greatest lower bound of R.

Let $\varepsilon = x - c$. This expresses x as $c + \varepsilon$ where $c \in \mathbb{R}$.

For any positive real number k, $c + k > c$ so $c + k$ lies in the subset R and satisfies $c + k \geq x = c + \varepsilon$ in the field F, so $\varepsilon \leq k$. By a similar argument, $c - k < c$ lies in L and satisfies $c - k < x$ in F, so $c - k < c + \varepsilon$ and $-k < \varepsilon$. Hence $-k < \varepsilon \leq k$ for all positive real k, proving ε is either zero or infinitesimal.

---

[7] When I first suggested this meaning of an infinitesimal as a graph to Efraim Fischbein many years ago, he rejected it outright because he wished to *see* an infinitesimal as a small quantity. (See Tall, 1980b). I wonder if he would accept it if he were here now.

For finite numbers x, y it is straightforward to show that the standard parts satisfy

$$\text{st}(x \pm y) = \text{st}(x) \pm \text{st}(y), \quad \text{st}(xy) = \text{st}(x)\text{st}(y),$$
$$\text{and, for } \text{st}(y) \neq 0, \quad \text{st}(x/y) = \text{st}(x)/\text{st}(y).$$

The structure theorem implies that, surrounding every real number c, there is a whole cluster of elements in F of the form $c + \varepsilon$ where ε is a (positive or negative) infinitesimal. This cluster, together with the element c itself, is called the *monad* surrounding c, in honour of Leibniz, who formulated a theory of substances made up of monads.

The monads cover the whole finite part of F. One can start at the real number c and take any positive infinitesimal ε, then add it again and again, to get $c + \varepsilon, c + 2\varepsilon, \dots, c + n\varepsilon, \dots$ and still remain confined within the same monad. One can move in the opposite direction $c - \varepsilon, c - 2\varepsilon, \dots, c - n\varepsilon, \dots$ and the same phenomenon occurs. Taking such infinitesimal steps in either direction never reaches another real number. The monads extend around each real number as a universe of their own.

These monads are non-empty and bounded above by any bigger real number yet they cannot have a least upper bound $\ell \in F$. Any such ℓ would either be in the same monad and be exceeded by other elements in that monad, or it would be in a monad around a larger real number that would contain elements smaller than ℓ that would also be upper bounds. Both possibilities lead to contradictions. This confirms that F is not complete. In particular, the set of infinitesimals, which is the monad surrounding zero, has no least upper bound.

This structure theorem is extremely powerful. It tells us that *any* ordered field extension of the real numbers *must* contain infinitesimals. Far from being eliminated from mathematics as Cantor had declared, the formal world of Hilbert reveals that infinitesimals can be found in *every* ordered field extension of $\mathbb{R}$. In addition, the field extension does not satisfy the completeness axiom.

Now we have a formally defined ordered extension of the real numbers. The question that we now ask is whether there is any way that we can *see* these infinitesimals on a number line. The response to this challenge is a resounding *yes*.

2.2 *Embodying Infinitesimals as Points on a Visual Number Line*

Our human vision does not allow us to see arbitrarily small quantities, as the rods and cones in our eyes have a finite size that limits how small a quantity we can see with our unaided sight. To see smaller quantities in the physical world, we use a magnifying glass.

In the formal world of ordered fields, the notion of magnification is simply a linear map $m{:}F \to F$ with formula $m(x) = ax + b$ where a and b are elements of F. Writing this as

$$m(x) = \frac{x - c}{d} \quad \text{where } c, d \in F \text{ and } d > 0,$$

then the map m takes c to $m(c) = 0$ and $c + d$ to $m(c + d) = 1$. Using this map m we can take *any* two points, with one at c, and the other a distance d away so that that their images are a unit distance apart. This can be done whether c and d are finite, infinite or infinitesimal.

The map m is called the *d-lens* pointed at c. By taking c and d to have various values, we can distinguish any two elements in F, even if they differ by an infinitesimal or by an infinite quantity.

Looking through a d-lens pointed at c, the image of the point $c + e$ is indistinguishable from c if e/d is infinitesimal, it is visible and distinguishable from c if e/d is non-zero but not infinitesimal, and it is too far away to see if e/d is infinite.

Comparing any two non-zero elements $u, v \in F$, the element u is said to be of *higher order* than v if u/v is infinitesimal, it is the *same order* if u/v is finite and not infinitesimal, and it is of *lower order* if u/v is infinite. For example, if ε is an infinitesimal, then ε^2 is higher order than ε because $\varepsilon^2/\varepsilon$ is infinitesimal. Similarly, ε is lower order than ε^2.

If we take d to be an infinitesimal ε we call the map a *microscope* to allow us to separate points that differ by an infinitesimal, and if we take c to be infinite, we call the map a *telescope* to allow us to look at detail around the infinite point c.[8]

Using a microscope $m{:}F \to F$ given by

$$m(x) = \frac{x - c}{\varepsilon}$$

where $c \in \mathbb{R}$ and ε is a positive infinitesimal, we get the map in Figure 13.2. (If ε were negative, the map m would reverse the direction.)

The set of points x in the domain where $m(x)$ is finite is called *the field of view*. We can then define a map μ from the field of view to the real line $\mathbb{R}$ by taking the standard part of the image $\mu(x) = \mathrm{st}(m(x))$. I call such a map

---

[8] The notion of microscope and telescope were introduced by Stroyan (1972).

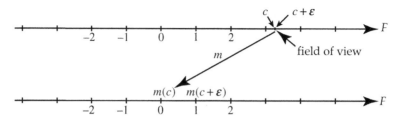

Figure 13.2. Using an ε-microscope pointed at c to separate c and $c + \varepsilon$ visually.

an *optical lens*.[9] If ε is infinitesimal, it is called an *optical microscope* and if c is infinite, it is called an *optical telescope*.

Figure 13.3 shows an optical microscope pointed at a real number c, with all but the field of view shaded in grey. The standard map-making convention is used to name the place on a map, such as 'New York', by the actual name of the place, so that the image $\mu(x)$ is also denoted by x. The optical microscope magnifies the field of view to see a real picture.

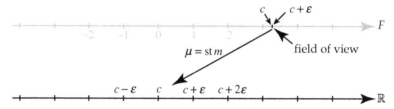

Figure 13.3. Using an optical microscope to see a real number picture of infinitesimal detail.

This is precisely what happens when we draw graphs as pictures of the real line. Our pencil line must be broad enough to see, and therefore a pencil mark will not distinguish between two close real numbers. For instance, drawing a line with a 0.1 mm pen, to a scale where a unit length is equal to one centimetre, gives a picture that cannot distinguish the marks for 0 and 0.001.

When a physical picture is drawn to represent the use of a d-lens pointed at c, the same phenomenon occurs, except that the accuracy is now measured not in terms of the thickness of a pencil, but in comparison with the size of the magnification factor d. Points on the original line that differ from c by a quantity of lower order than d are outside the field of view and

---

[9] The notion of optical lens was introduced in Tall (1980a).

too far away to be seen through the d-lens. Points in the field of view that differ from each other by quantities of higher order than d are mapped to the same real number by the optical lens.

When ε is infinitesimal, the field of view of an optical ε-microscope pointed at c is part of the monad around c. It need not be the whole of the monad. For instance, if we view $c + \varepsilon$ through a d-lens where $d = \varepsilon^2$, then ε is now of lower order than d, so $c + \varepsilon$ is outside the field of view.

In Figure 13.3 the field of view is infinitesimal in size. In the physical picture it is covered by the mark denoted by c and contains the infinitesimally close element $c + \varepsilon$.

However, for any $k \in \mathbb{R}$ we have

$$\mu(c + k\varepsilon) = \mathrm{st}\left(\frac{(c + k\varepsilon) - c}{\varepsilon} \right) = k,$$

so the optical microscope μ maps the field of view onto the whole real line $\mathbb{R}$ and we see the images of the quantities $\ldots, c - \varepsilon, c, c + \varepsilon, c + 2\varepsilon, \ldots$ visible in their expected places. This allows us to see infinitesimal detail of a chosen order, but we cannot distinguish differences of different orders in the same optical picture. Nevertheless, this is sufficient to imagine how infinitesimal quantities may be visualized and used in natural ways. To see infinitesimal detail of any chosen order, all we need is an optical microscope of that order of magnification.

2.3 *A Formal Example with Four Different Isomorphic Representations*

We now return to the earlier example of the field $\mathbb{R}(x)$ to see how it may be represented in several different ways as visualized in Figure 13.4. These are

(i) The symbolic system of rational expressions $\mathbb{R}(x)$ in an indeterminate x, including elements such as $k \in \mathbb{R}$, x, x^2, and the general term

$$\frac{a_n x^n + \cdots + a_0}{b_m x^m + \cdots + b_0} \quad \text{where } b_m \neq 0.$$

(ii) The set of graphs of rational expressions $\mathbb{R}(x)$ where the picture shows three graphs, $c(x) = k$ (a constant), $v(x) = x$ and $w(x) = x^2$ satisfying the order $k < x < x^2$.

(iii) The vertical line $x = v$ where v is a variable and $\mathbb{R}(v)$ are the points where a rational function meets the vertical line. The point k

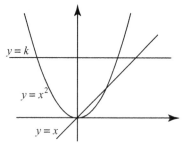

expressions including $k \in \mathbb{R}$, x, x^2,

with general term:

$$\frac{a_n x^n + \cdots + a_0}{b_m x^m + \cdots + b_0} \quad (b_0 \neq 0)$$

(i) elements of $\mathbb{R}(x)$ as algebraic expressions

(ii) elements of $\mathbb{R}(x)$ as graphs

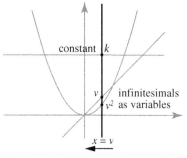

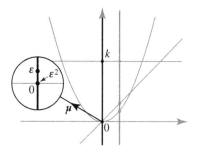

(iii) elements of $\mathbb{R}(v)$ as points on a line
with real numbers as constants and
infinitesimals as variables, such as v, v^2

(iv) elements of $\mathbb{R}(\varepsilon)$ as points on a line
with ε as a fixed infinitesimal,
visible under optical magnification μ

Figure 13.4. Four different isomorphic representations.

remains constant as v varies, and, as the line moves to the left, v is a variable point that moves below any fixed value k and v^2 moves down even faster.

(iv) The vertical y-axis, now considered as the number line representing the field $\mathbb{R}(\varepsilon)$ in a (fixed) infinitesimal ε.

These four representations are all isomorphic, with elements in (i) as algebraic symbols, in (ii) embodied as whole graphs, in (iii) as a variable quantities on a line, and in (iv) as fixed points on an enriched number line.

The framework of three worlds of mathematics unites all these four representations having very different cognitive and perceptual meanings, yet representing a single underlying crystalline concept.

Earlier in Chapter 3, Section 3.5, I referred to 'equivalence as a transition stage to flexible thinking'. This offers a choice to the individual to continue to maintain the difference between various equivalent representations or to recognize them as different ways to think about the single underlying crystalline concept. Although it may be advantageous to maintain a way of working that is stable and operates well, the evolution of mathematical thinking benefits from extensional blends that place the current system within a more powerful framework.

The first two representations as algebraic expressions and as graphs are familiar in school mathematics with the theoretical addition of a subtle definition of order. The third is evocative of the insights of Leibniz and Cauchy as the points representing the real numbers are *constant* quantities whereas others are *variables*, including infinitesimals and infinite quantities. The fourth is an extended vision of the number line using formally defined infinite magnification to reveal infinitesimal detail.

This is an extensional blend of the ideas of Leibniz, consistent with his vision that all infinitesimals have a specific order. The element ε is of order 1, its square is of order 2, its cube of order 3, and so on. All quantities in the extension field $\mathbb{R}(\varepsilon)$ have a specific order that is a signed integer, with those of positive order being infinitesimal and those of negative order being infinite.

The vision of Bishop Berkeley representing the perception of the plain man is supported by the fact that it is not possible to see an infinitesimal on a standard number line with human eyes, and higher orders of infinitesimal are beyond unaided human perception. Yet a mathematician experienced in formal mathematics can easily comprehend successive orders of smallness: in $\mathbb{R}(\varepsilon)$ it is not only clear that ε^2 is of order two, but also that ε^{1066} is an infinitesimal of order 1066.

The difference lies in the differing knowledge structures of the individuals concerned. A modern mathematician, steeped in the experience of formally defined axiomatic structures, has the appropriate mental equipment to imagine infinitesimals as formally defined objects. He or she also has the additional possibility of using the notion of isomorphism to contemplate not just equivalent concepts given by representations that may be blended together in various ways, but also to conceptualize equivalent structures in terms of underlying crystalline concepts that operate at a higher level.

Cantor's view can now be seen in a framework where his idea of the isomorphism between the real numbers and the geometric number line is supportive in standard analysis where infinitesimals are excluded as being problematic. However, they have their place in an extensional blend placing the complete ordered field of real numbers within a larger ordered field that must automatically include infinitesimals.

Mathematical analysis based on the completeness of the real numbers has stable and established methods of operation that continue to play a central role in mathematical research. However, there is substantial empirical and theoretical evidence that reveals the natural way in which humans think of quantities becoming 'arbitrarily small', in history, in modern applications of mathematics and in the development of modern student conceptions.

Personally, I have sympathies, as a mathematician, with formal mathematics at research level and, as a mathematics educator, with the theoretical idea of variable quantities that can be 'arbitrarily small'. Both can be based on the 'locally straight' approach blending dynamic visual perceptions and symbolic operations presented in Chapter 11.

3. Calculus Using Infinitesimals

In the remainder of this chapter, I will follow through the development of the use of infinitesimals to reveal the difficulties it poses and the amazing insights that it can offer.

Working in an appropriate extension field containing infinitesimals, we can perform calculus operations such as finding the derivative of x^2 by calculating

$$\frac{(x+\varepsilon)^2 - x^2}{\varepsilon} = \frac{2x\varepsilon + \varepsilon^2}{\varepsilon} = 2x + \varepsilon$$

and taking the standard part (for finite x and infinitesimal ε) to get the derivative as

$$\text{st}(2x + \varepsilon) = 2x.$$

In the field $\mathbb{R}(\varepsilon)$ of rational expressions in a single infinitesimal, such a technique can be used to obtain the symbolic derivatives of polynomials and rational functions.

But this technique is limited and does not work for more general functions. My first attempt at dealing with more general functions was to extend this field further to include power series in ε, including possibly a finite number of terms with negative powers that included multiplicative inverses of power series in the extension field $\mathbb{R}((\varepsilon))$) with elements

$$a_{-k}\varepsilon^{-k} + \cdots + a_{-1}\varepsilon^{-1} + a_0 + a_1\varepsilon + \cdots + a_n\varepsilon^n + \cdots$$

I termed this the field of *superreal numbers*.[10] This proved to be suitable to differentiate functions given by power series, including not only

---

[10] Tall (1980a).

polynomials and rational functions, but also trigonometric, exponential and logarithmic functions expressed as power series. Generalizing the method of taking the standard part of $((x + \varepsilon)^n - x^n)/\varepsilon$ to obtain nx^{n-1} allows power series to be differentiated and integrated term by term.

Such an approach had some success with students as part of an optional course after they had taken a standard analysis course, but it is limited because it fails to deal with more general functions.

To travel the full journey to deal with the general theory of analysis, it is necessary to consider *any* function $f : D \to \mathbb{R}$ where D is a subset of $\mathbb{R}$ and show how this can be extended to an appropriate extension field $*\mathbb{R}$ containing the necessary infinitesimals and infinite elements required for calculus. This is a massive challenge.

Abraham Robinson proposed a solution based on the logic of set-theoretic statements. Axioms use the quantifiers $\forall$ and $\exists$ which usually apply to elements belonging to sets, such as

- $\forall a \in S : a \sim a$ (symmetry in an equivalence relation S),
- $\forall a, b \in F : a + b = b + a$ (commutativity in a field F),
- $\exists e \in G \, \forall g \in G : g \circ e = e \circ g = g$ (existence of an identity in a group G).

Other axioms, however, quantify *sets* of objects. For instance, the completeness axiom states:

- $\forall S \subset \mathbb{R}$ if S is non-empty and bounded above, then S has a least upper bound.

Statements that quantify elements of specified sets are said to be *first-order* logic, and statements that quantify sets are said to be *second-order* logic. Higher-order logics quantify sets of sets, and more sophisticated levels of complexity.

Clearly the extension field desired needs to generalize properties such as the axioms for an ordered field, but we already know that the completeness axiom cannot hold in any ordered extension field of $\mathbb{R}$.

Robinson chose to develop a theory that generalized first-order logical statements but not higher-order statements (such as the completeness axiom).

He required a proper extension $*\mathbb{R}$ of $\mathbb{R}$ that allowed him to extend every subset D of $\mathbb{R}$ to a larger set $*D$ in $*\mathbb{R}$, so that every function $f : D \to \mathbb{R}$ could be extended to apply from $*D$ to $*\mathbb{R}$. Because the extended function agreed with f on the subset D, it may also be denoted by f to give an extended function $f \colon {}^*D \to {}^*\mathbb{R}$.

He hypothesized that the extension satisfied

The transfer principle: Every statement about the real numbers $\mathbb{R}$ expressed in first-order logic is true in the extended system ${}^*\mathbb{R}$.

Any field ${}^*\mathbb{R}$ satisfying the transfer principle is called a field of *hyperreal* numbers. Because the axioms for an ordered field are all first order statements in $\mathbb{R}$, by the transfer principle, they must also hold in the extension ${}^*\mathbb{R}$, which therefore must also be an ordered field. Because it is declared to be a *proper* extension, we know from the structure theorem for proper ordered field extensions that ${}^*\mathbb{R}$ contains infinite and infinitesimal elements and that any finite element is uniquely of the form $c + \varepsilon$ where c is real and ε is infinitesimal.

Because completeness is a second-order property, it need not hold and we have already shown that it does not because the set of infinitesimals is bounded above but does not have a least upper bound.

We already know that every real number x has natural numbers larger than x, which we can write

$$\forall x \in \mathbb{R} \quad \exists n \in \mathbb{N} : n > x.$$

By the transfer principle, this extends to the statement

$$\forall x \in {}^*\mathbb{R} \quad \exists n \in {}^*\mathbb{N} : n > x.$$

This says that for every hyperreal number x there is an infinite integer (an element in ${}^*\mathbb{N}$) that is larger. As we already know that ${}^*\mathbb{R}$ has infinite elements, then this proves that ${}^*\mathbb{N}$ has infinite elements. An infinite element in ${}^*\mathbb{N}$ is called a *hyperinteger*.

Many properties of the infinite hyperintegers follow by natural extension from the properties of the integers. For instance, as we know that there are no whole numbers between a whole number n and $n + 1$, so that the 'next' number after n is $n + 1$, we can deduce that the 'next' hyperinteger after a hyperinteger N is again $N + 1$, with no other hyperintegers in between.

Any sequence $a_1, a_2, \ldots, a_n, \ldots$ is a function $a \colon \mathbb{N} \to \mathbb{R}$ where $a(n) = a_n$ and therefore extends to a function $a \colon {}^*\mathbb{N} \to {}^*\mathbb{R}$ and for any positive hyperinteger N, we can write $a_N = a(N)$.

If the sequence is given by a known formula, such as

$$a_n = \frac{3n^2 + 2n}{4n^2}$$

then the term a_N is given by the same formula, which can be written:

$$a_N = \frac{3 + 2/N}{4}.$$

In general, a sequence (a_n) is defined to be convergent if $\mathrm{st}(a_N)$ is the same real number for all infinite N. For instance, in the given formula, when N is infinite, $1/N$ is infinitesimal and $\mathrm{st}(1/N) = 0$. Hence the limit of this sequence is

$$\mathrm{st}(a_N) = \frac{3 + \mathrm{st}(2/N)}{4} = \frac{3 + 0}{4} = \tfrac{3}{4}.$$

Likewise, a function $f : D \to \mathbb{R}$ is said to be differentiable at $x \in D$ if the standard part of $(f(x + \varepsilon) - f(x))/\varepsilon$ is the same real number for every infinitesimal ε (where $x + \varepsilon \in {}^*D$). For instance in the case of $f(x) = x^2$, the derivative is

$$f'(x) = \mathrm{st}\,\frac{(x + \varepsilon)^2 - x^2}{\varepsilon} = \mathrm{st}\,\frac{2x\varepsilon + \varepsilon^2}{\varepsilon} = \mathrm{st}(2x + \varepsilon) = 2x.$$

If $x, y \in {}^*\mathbb{R}$, we write $x \simeq y$ to say that $x - y$ is infinitesimal. A function $f : D \to \mathbb{R}$ can then be said to be *pointwise continuous* at $x \in D$ if, for all $y \in {}^*D$, $x \simeq y$ implies $f(x) \simeq f(y)$. The notion of *uniform continuity* over a domain D simply says that if $x, y \in {}^*D$, then $x \simeq y$ implies $f(x) \simeq f(y)$.

The integral of a continuous function f on an interval $a < x < b$ is found by calculating the finite sum $s_n = \Sigma_a^b f(x)\,dx$ where $dx = (b - a)/n$ and taking the standard part of s_N for infinite N. For instance, $f(x) = x$ has its integral determined by taking $dx = 1/n$. Then

$$\sum\nolimits_0^x f(x)\,dx = \frac{x}{n} \times \frac{x}{n} + \frac{2x}{n} \times \frac{x}{n} + \cdots + \frac{nx}{n} \times \frac{x}{n}$$

$$= \frac{\tfrac{1}{2} n(n+1)x}{n} \times \frac{x}{n} = \tfrac{1}{2}\left(1 + \frac{1}{n}\right)x^2.$$

For infinite N, the integral is

$$\int_0^x f(x)\,dx = \mathrm{st}\left(\sum\nolimits_0^x f(x)\,dx\right) \text{ for } dx = \tfrac{1}{N}$$

$$= \mathrm{st}\left(\tfrac{1}{2}\left(1 + \frac{1}{N}\right)x^2\right) = \tfrac{1}{2}x^2.$$

These techniques enable limits of sequences, derivatives and other concepts of the calculus to be determined in the ancient ways of operating with infinite numbers and infinitesimals and taking the standard part of the result, which means, in effect, 'neglecting the infinitesimal' or setting it to zero.

In one mighty stroke, Robinson had it all: the logical closure of a conundrum that had afflicted the mathematical mind of man for centuries. He was confident that this would be a new dawn. He sensed that he had the insight to resolve the problem of all problems.

But it didn't happen.

3.1 *Cultural Resistance to a New Theory*

Non-standard analysis was Robinson's vision of a brave new world that encompassed the ancient idea of infinitesimal. But it was presented to a world immersed in the epsilon-delta processes of mathematical analysis. Its first weak spot was that the theory did not seem to add any new results in standard mathematical analysis. Working with a colleague Allen Bernstein, Robinson proved a new theorem in mathematical analysis using the new infinitesimal methods.[11] Paul Halmos saw a pre-print and produced a standard proof that was published alongside the Robinson-Bernstein Theorem in the same journal.[12]

Second, the theory was initially published in the language of logic that was not a common specialism amongst research mathematicians. I well remember Abraham Robinson giving lectures on the subject when I was a student in the sixties in Oxford. As a young lecturer at Sussex University in Autumn 1966, I joined with the whole department in a term-long seminar as we read Robinson's book on nonstandard analysis together. However, although we developed a 'sense' of the ideas, many of us felt uneasy that we didn't really comprehend the logic.

Third, even later re-workings of the subject in a more familiar framework proved complicated to explain. Just search the Internet and look up the ideas in Wikipedia. You will find many articles, including 'nonstandard analysis', linked to topics such as 'hyperreal numbers', 'ultrafilters', 'Abraham Robinson'. The nonspecialist reader may sense some of the difficulties in attempting to grasp the content of these ideas.

Fourth, those mathematicians who insisted on making sure that mathematics is constructed in a finite human way criticized the assertion that the hyperreals exist without having any finite construction for them.

---

[11] Bernstein & Robinson (1966).
[12] Halmos (1966).

Fifth, and most practical, epsilon-delta analysis *worked* and was the common language of the mathematical community. If it ain't broke, don't fix it.

When I was a young researcher and took an interest in non-standard analysis, I was counseled by a senior professor that this would not be a sensible career path. I gave a final year optional course on 'infinitesimal calculus' to undergraduates. It was attended by more than a hundred students while other options had ten or twenty.

I was called in by the Head of Department and told I would not be allowed to offer the course as a mathematics option in the following year. His reasoning was that the regulations specified that students restricted to a pass degree need only take six courses, of which only three had to be in mathematics. He explained that 'one mathematics course was on the history of mathematics, and if students took this and infinitesimal calculus, they need only take *one* mathematics course to get a mathematics degree.' For him, and for several other members of the pure mathematics department, infinitesimal calculus was not 'proper' mathematics.

I gave the course the following year nominated as an 'education' option and still the vast majority of students attended. Fundamentally it 'made sense' to them in a way that clarified the standard analysis that they had studied and found difficult in their regular lectures.

Non-standard analysis continues as a bone of contention in the mathematics community. It remains a 'them and us' activity where it is accepted as a theoretically viable approach for experts in the subject but not followed by many mainstream mathematicians.

4. Constructing the Hyperreal Numbers

Basing non-standard analysis on the axioms of a complete ordered field and the hypothetical transfer principle allows the properties to be deduced, but it does not show how to *construct* the system.

This is analogous to the pre-Cantorian days when numbers were imagined as numbers on a line, including irrational numbers, which were used for calculations but were not formally constructed until Bolzano, Cantor and Dedekind saw the need to make sense of limiting processes that led to the idea of completeness.

Cantor's idea used Cauchy sequences of rational numbers to construct the real numbers and consequently to eliminate infinitesimals. It is poetic justice that a similar technique can be used to construct the hyperreals, which reinstates infinitesimals.

Cantor's construction of the reals from the rationals took the set of Cauchy sequences of rationals and defined an equivalence relation where two Cauchy sequences (a_n), (b_n) are equivalent if the sequence $(a_n - b_n)$ tends to zero. The real number system is the set of equivalence classes.

A similar technique, with more subtle logic, may be used to construct the hyperreals from the real numbers. This time the construction begins with the set of all sequences (a_n) of real numbers and an appropriate equivalence relation is defined so that the equivalence classes form an ordered field *$\mathbb{R}$.

The equivalence class containing the sequence (a_n) will be denoted by $[a_n]$ and, once we have decided precisely what the equivalence is, we will define arithmetic operations term by term (as in Cantor's construction of the real numbers):

$$[a_n] + [b_n] = [a_n + b_n], \quad [a_n] - [b_n] = [a_n - b_n]; \quad [a_n][b_n] = [a_n b_n].$$

Division presents a problem because defining the quotient $[a_n]/[b_n]$ as $[a_n/b_n]$ would not be appropriate if some terms b_n are zero.

If we insist that the relation includes the property:

$(a_n) \sim (b_n)$ if $a_n = b_n$ for all but a finite number of n,

then we could define $[a_n]/[b_n]$ when a finite number of terms b_n are zero, by replacing (b_n) by the equivalent sequence (b'_n) where $b'_n = b_n$ if $b_n \neq 0$ and $b'_n = 1$ if $b_n = 0$ and defining $[a_n] / [b_n] = [a_n / b'_n]$.

With such an equivalence, we can relate the real number k with the equivalence class $[a_n]$, where $a_n = k$ for all n. This carries over the arithmetic of $\mathbb{R}$ to see it as (isomorphic to) a subfield of *$\mathbb{R}$. Using the idea of a crystal-line concept allows us to think of $\mathbb{R}$ as an ordered subfield of *$\mathbb{R}$.

If we define $[a_n] > [b_n]$ to mean $a_n > b_n$ for all but a finite number of terms, then this reveals $\mathbb{R}$ as an ordered subfield of *$\mathbb{R}$.

The sequence of real numbers $(1, 2, 3, \ldots)$ gives the equivalence class $\omega = [1, 2, 3, \ldots]$ which satisfies $\omega > k$ for all real numbers k, because the nth term of $(1, 2, 3, \ldots)$ exceeds the real number k for all $n > k$.

The element $1/\omega$ given by $[1, \frac{1}{2}, \frac{1}{3}, \ldots, \frac{1}{n}, \ldots]$ is then a positive infinitesimal satisfying $0 < 1/\omega < k$ for any positive k, because its nth term $1/n$ is less than k for $n > 1/k$.

We can also see that $\omega + 1 > \omega$ because the corresponding sequences satisfy $n + 1 > n$, term by term. We can even add an infinitesimal $1/\omega$ to an infinite number to get $\omega + 1/\omega > \omega$.

Aha! We seem to be getting there.

Enjoy the moment.

On reflection, however, there is still a long way to go. We must assign *every* sequence (a_n) to an equivalence class $[a_n]$ so that the equivalence classes form an ordered field extending the real numbers.

A typical problem arises with a sequence such as

$$a_n = \begin{cases} \frac{1}{m} & \text{if } n \text{ is odd,} \quad n = 2m - 1 \\ m & \text{if } n \text{ is even,} \quad n = 2m. \end{cases}$$

This has odd terms, $1, \frac{1}{2}, \frac{1}{3}, \dots$ that tend to zero and even terms $1, 2, 3, \dots$ that tend to infinity. On the set O of odd numbers, it is infinitesimal and on the set E of even numbers, it is infinite. So what can we do in this case? The answer is: we must make a *choice*. If we make the decision based on what happens on the odd numbers O, then $[a_n]$ is declared to be infinitesimal and if we base our decision on E, it will be infinite. Depending on the choice we make, the extensions may be different.

In general, a sequence (a_n) has an infinite number of terms, so at least one of the following must hold:

(i) An infinite subsequence tends to $+\infty$.

(ii) An infinite subsequence tends to $-\infty$.

(iii) For some $A, B \in \mathbb{R}$, where $A < B$, an infinite number of terms lie between A and B.

All three possibilities may occur in one sequence. For instance, if

$$a_1 = 1, a_4 = 2, \dots, a_{3n-2} = n, \dots$$
$$a_2 = -1, a_5 = -2, \dots, a_{3n-1} = -n, \dots$$
$$a_3 = 1, a_6 = \frac{1}{2}, \dots, a_{3n} = \frac{1}{n}, \dots$$

then the subsequence (a_{3n-2}) tends to $+\infty$, (a_{3n-1}) tends to $-\infty$, and (a_{3n}) tends to zero.

The situation may be even more complicated. For instance in case (iii) all the terms may be between the two values A, B, but there may not be a unique limit.

However, we do know that in this case it can be proved that there is at least one subsequence that tends to a specific limit point. In general, therefore, there is at least one subsequence of a general sequence (a_n) that tends to $+\infty$, $-\infty$ or to a finite limit point c. The plan is then to choose a subsequence to determine the behaviour of the equivalence class $[a_n]$ as being either negative infinite, positive infinite or a finite value with standard part c.

The set of values of n for which the subsequence (a_n) is chosen to determine the behaviour of $[a_n]$ is called the *decision* set. The objective is to make a choice for every subset $S \subseteq \mathbb{N}$ so that just one of S and its complement $\mathbb{N} \backslash S$ is a decision set and to do this in a consistent way so that the equivalence classes form an ordered field $^*\mathbb{R}$.

Once such a choice is made, it will be simple to define the extension of any subset $D \subseteq \mathbb{R}$ by

$$^*D = \left\{ [x_n] \in {}^*\mathbb{R} \mid x_n \in D \right\}$$

and the extension of any function $f \colon D \to \mathbb{R}$ is given by

$$f([x_n]) = [f(x_n)].$$

This gives a beautiful *natural* definition of the extension of sets and functions from $\mathbb{R}$ to $^*\mathbb{R}$ that embeds the real numbers in a broader system including infinitesimals.

The final step in this construction of $^*\mathbb{R}$ to choose a consistent collection of decision sets involves an infinity of choices to be made. This is beyond our finite human capacity without some general principle to perform the task.[13]

One possible direction to take is to use the *axiom of choice* that says that given any collection of non-empty sets, then it is possible to choose *simultaneously* one element from each set. This provides all the machinery required to complete the proof.[14]

The use of the axiom of choice, however, continues to be a contentious issue between different kinds of mathematicians. Some insist that one can only 'prove' mathematical theorems that can be properly constructed in a finite number of steps. Others accept the use of the axiom of choice because it can be proved that if there is a contradiction when the axiom of choice is incorporated into set theory, then that contradiction already existed in the original theory. In other words, adding the axiom of choice gives more power of operation without introducing any new logical problems.

As in all extensional blends, old ideas remain and new ideas arise that are problematic yet, suitably interpreted, they offer more powerful ways forward. The original theory of mathematical analysis operating in a complete ordered field remains fully coherent and continues to be a significant topic of research. The choice between a standard approach through

---

[13] See, for example, Katz and Tall (2012) for an outline discussion.
[14] The construction requires the notion of 'ultrafilter' established by Tarski (1930).

mathematical analysis and a non-standard approach using infinitesimals remains open.

5. Consequences for Teaching and Local Straightness

The difficulties that students have with the notion of limit in standard analysis have been well documented. An undergraduate course using infinitesimal axioms was designed by Keisler[15] and there is evidence that students following this course had a better grasp of the intuitive ideas of the calculus.[16] However, the number of students taking such a course has always been a small percentage of those taking calculus in total and Keisler's book is now out of print, although it continues to be available as a free download from the Internet.[17] Even though the intuitive ideas resonate with many learners, the formulation requires a whole list of assumptions about the properties of numbers and infinitesimals that give rise to questions about its long-term value in teaching the calculus. Whatever 'proof' an educational study provided for the value of teaching students using non-standard analysis has not shaken the broad adherence to standard mathematical analysis.

My own view on the most appropriate initial introduction to the calculus for students is crystal clear. A formal approach based on the standard epsilon-delta definition of limit or on the formal definitions involving infinitesimals both belong in the formal world, whereas a locally straight approach is consistent with a learner's natural experience with graphs and operational use of algebraic symbolism. A blend of embodiment and symbolism provides a foundational base for the dynamic notion of continuity and the embodied notion of local straightness. It allows the derivative dy/dx to be conceived as a quotient of lengths (the components of the tangent vector). It leads naturally to the limit concept and can be used to develop the techniques of the calculus essential in applications or an appropriate basis for the formal mathematics of standard mathematical analysis or non-standard analysis, should either of these be desired.

The notion of local straightness does not require the introduction of the concept of infinitesimal, although it supports the intuitive idea of appropriately small quantities in good-enough arithmetic and limit concepts in regular calculus. Therefore, in a preliminary course on calculus,

---

[15] Keisler (1976).
[16] Sullivan (1976).
[17] www.math.wisc.edu/~keisler/calc.html (Accessed February 14, 2013.)

I would choose to use computer technology to experience the dynamic ideas of continuity and local straightness and introduce the limit once the learner has an insightful grasp of the relationship between the changing slope of a locally straight function and its symbolic derivative.

That being said, I cannot resist finishing this chapter with a picture in which the formal notion of infinitesimal, as found in any extension field of the real numbers, can be used to magnify a differentiable function to reveal the full formal property of local straightness in all its glory.

6. Magnifying a Differentiable Function

The idea of magnification given earlier operates just as simply in two or more dimensions, by magnifying each component. For instance, an $\varepsilon - \delta$ lens pointed at $(c, d) \in F^2$ is given by the map

$$m(x, y) = \left(\frac{x - c}{\varepsilon}, \frac{y - d}{\delta} \right)$$

and the corresponding optical lens $\mu : F^2 \to \mathbb{R}^2$ takes the standard part of each component:

$$\mu(x, y) = \text{st } m(x, y) = \text{st} \left(\frac{x - c}{\varepsilon}, \frac{y - d}{\delta} \right),$$

For any differentiable function $f(x)$, the derivative is given by

$$f'(x) = \text{st} \left(\frac{f(x + h) - f(x)}{h} \right) \quad \text{for any infinitesimal } h \neq 0.$$

Pointing an optical microscope μ at $(x, f(x))$ for an infinitesimal ε on both axes, and looking at a nearby point $(x + h, f(x + h))$ where h is the same order as ε, we get

$$\mu(x + h, f(x + h)) = \left(\text{st}\left(\frac{h}{\varepsilon} \right), \text{st}\left(\frac{f(x + h) - f(x)}{\varepsilon} \right) \right)$$

$$= \left(\text{st}\left(\frac{h}{\varepsilon} \right), \text{st}\left(\frac{f(x + h) - f(x)}{h} \frac{h}{\varepsilon} \right) \right)$$

$$= (\lambda, \lambda f'(x)) \quad \text{where } \lambda = \text{st}(h/\varepsilon).$$

This shows that the *field of view* – which consists precisely of the points $(x + h, f(x + h))$ where h is the same or higher order than ε – is mapped on the whole real line represented parametrically as $\lambda(1, f'(x))$ for any real number λ. Points with h of order higher than ε are mapped onto the same real point; points with h of the same order are mapped onto distinct real points; points with h of lower order are outside the field of view.

This shows us the remarkable fact that the infinitesimal detail of a given order on the graph is mapped into the plane as *a whole real line* of slope $f'(x)$. (Figure 13.5.)

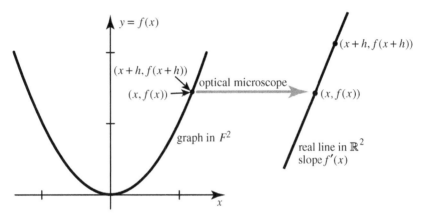

Figure 13.5. The infinitesimal detail of a differentiable graph is an infinite straight line when viewed through an optical microscope.

This view is *amazing*. It shows us that, when we magnify part of a locally straight graph by an infinite quantity, then *optically*, what we see visually and in our imagination is an *infinite* straight real line. Not just a computer-generated approximation, not only a rough 'good-enough' arithmetic calculation, not just a view limited by our own eyes as they take a fortieth of a second to make sense of an image, but a fully blended, formally defined crystalline concept, conceived in the axiomatic formal world, calculated using algebraic symbolism, visualized in the mind's eye as a thought experiment, and embodied using an optical microscope to produce a physical picture that can be seen, naturally, by the physical human eye.

14   Expanding the Frontiers through Mathematical Research

> We often hear that mathematics consists mainly in 'proving theorems'. Is a writer's job mainly that of 'writing sentences'? A mathematician's work is mostly a tangle of guesswork, analogy, wishful thinking and frustration, and proof, far from being the core of discovery, is more often than not a way of making sure that our minds are not playing tricks.
>
> (Gian-Carlo Rota)[1]

1. Solving Problems and Proving Theorems

We are now moving towards the frontiers of our journeys through three worlds of mathematics, as mathematicians build on their experience to develop new formal knowledge structures. Mathematicians who become successful in research have powerful integrated knowledge structures with crystalline concepts that blend together their previous experiences to produce new theories. Although the theories may be expressed in terms of formal definitions and proofs, their creation, in the words of Gian-Carlo Rota, is 'a tangle of guesswork, analogy, wishful thinking and frustration'.

As William Byers reveals in *How Mathematicians Think*[2], true creativity in mathematical research arises out of paradoxes, ambiguities and conflicts that occur when ideas from different contexts come into contact. It is the drive to solve problems that keeps mathematical research alive.

The wishful thinking of mathematicians considers possible new theorems, as yet unproven and yet supported by various kinds of evidence that

---

[1] Quoted from the preface to *The Mathematical Experience* by Davis and Hersh (1981), p. xviii.
[2] Byers (2007).

suggests to what extent the new theorem might be true. There may be evidence that give warrants for truth in a spectrum from doubtful, fairly likely, to highly likely. Until it is formally proved to be true, it remains a conjecture. At any given time, mathematicians around the world will be working on various conjectures to see if a proof can be provided. But until that happens, the intriguing possibilities are the lifeblood of the mathematical community. Some are well known and a few challenge successive generations, remaining unproven after years, even centuries, but beyond these are a whole host of conjectures of every kind, offering challenges to take forward the frontiers of mathematical knowledge.

To move forward, mathematicians must build on their existing knowledge structures, sharing ideas with others who may contribute differing viewpoints. Unlike the student in transition from embodiment and symbolism to formalism, the mathematical expert has crystalline knowledge structures underpinned by frameworks of formal definitions and proof to use when thinking about proposed conjectures.

Structure theorems enable axiomatic definitions to have an associated embodiment and symbolism. Research at the highest level therefore passes beyond formal definitions and shifts to a more sophisticated level of mental manipulation of crystalline concepts in various stages of development. At first a situation may be bizarre and confusing, but then new relationships may arise that give plausible new frameworks relating to established knowledge, thinking about possibilities, making conjectures and seeking formal proof (Figure 14.1).

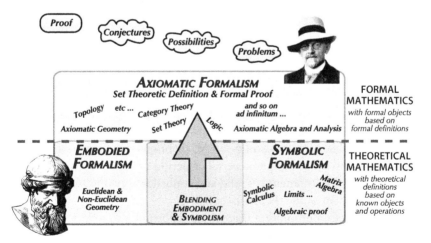

Figure 14.1. The widening boundaries of research mathematics.

This cycle of development, formulated in terms of *problems, possibilities, conjectures* and *proof,* has a format consistent with the broad van Hiele development through *recognition, description, definition* and *deduction* offered as a basis for the growth of mathematical thinking in Chapter 4 (Figure 4.9). There is an initial awareness and recognition of a problem, the description of various possibilities, moving on to formulating a conjecture as a possible definition that is amenable to the deduction of a proof. The four categories may be subdivided into two parts after the fashion of the earlier analysis: *exploring possibilities* and *proving theorems* (Figure 14.2).

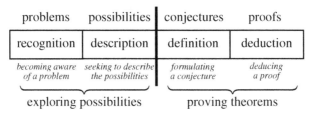

Figure 14.2. A structural analysis of the development of mathematical research.

The discussion on problem solving and proof in Chapter 8 now shifts from practical and theoretical problem solving to research in formal mathematics. Whereas the book on *Thinking Mathematically* nowhere mentions the word 'proof', in formal mathematics the eventual production of proof is the main objective. There will, of course, be initial stages of awareness of a problem, asking 'What do I want?', reflecting on 'What do I know?' in terms of the nature of the problem and formal theory already developed, to 'What can I introduce?' in terms of techniques and conjectures. Then there will also be phases of attacking the problem, seeking to formulate a proof, possibly leading to an 'Aha!' insight or the debilitating sense of being 'Stuck!'

If the researcher is unable to solve the problem, then it is necessary to think carefully about the solution so far, to consider other possible alternative ways of attack, or even to modify the original problem to produce a related conjecture that may be more amenable to a proof.

If the problem appears to be solved, there may be a sense of elation, even celebration. But then a more sober period of reflection is necessary, to check that the argument is sound and really does provide a proof of the precise statement of the theorem.

After a successful solution there is an opportunity to reflect further, to see if a simpler proof is possible and to see if the ideas can be extended to a wider class of problems, possibilities, conjectures and proofs.

The resulting formal mathematics may have theoretical and practical consequences in other areas such as computing, engineering, physics, astronomy, biology, economics, business and commerce. Applied mathematicians may use the results of formal proof as a foundation for different kinds of research and development. They may use structure theorems and the related embodiment and symbolism to develop novel ways to solve practical and theoretical problems.

Applications of mathematics lead to new insights and inventions that enhance our society. Mathematics is used on the Internet to formulate codes that protect our privacy, in the oil industry to predict the flows of oil and gas through permeable rocks, in meteorology to forecast the weather, in space travel to compute flights to other planets, in biology to handle DNA codes, and in many other applications in vital services and industries.

My objective is not to pursue this immensity of different directions, but to seek the essential underlying sense of *simplicity* of mathematical thinking that underpins all the creativity of the human brain. It lies in the crystalline structure of mathematical concepts that are chosen for study by the mathematician and integrated into tightly connected knowledge structures that go beyond mere formalism to blend with sophisticated forms of embodiment and symbolism. This leads to a widely diverse enterprise that has developed in mathematics, particularly in recent times.

2. The Diversity of Formal Mathematical Theories

The late nineteenth and twentieth centuries saw a huge diversity of growth in mathematical ideas. So many research papers are published every day that no individual can hope to keep in touch with every detail of mathematical endeavour. However, we may gain an overall grasp of the enterprise by reflecting on the fundamental processes of mathematical thinking that build through embodiment and symbolism from earlier times to modern formal theories.

The classical summit of mathematics in Greek times was the framework of Euclidean geometry. This grew out of embodiment and used language to formulate definitions and ways of building a coherent verbal theory of deduction of properties of geometric concepts.

Euclidean geometry had implicit properties that tied it to ruler and compass constructions in the plane and their generalizations to three-dimensional figures. It rose to the heights of Platonism with Platonic figures as crystalline concepts that have a beauty and perfection seemingly beyond the perceptions and actions of mere mortals.

However, subtle implicit properties such as the idea of a point on a line lying 'between' two other points on the line were not formulated in Euclidean geometry, and the notion of parallel lines was dependent on its context in the Euclidean plane. Seeing geometries on other surfaces and in other contexts, such as projective geometry, spherical geometry, and elliptic and hyperbolic geometries, all raised the awareness that geometry could have wider meanings. There were alternate geometries each with their own inevitable crystalline structures, with aspects that can be different from those of Euclid.

At the turn of the twentieth century, Hilbert recast Euclidean geometry into a set-theoretic form that retained the flavour of the original while addressing the logical gaps that had been noted in the theory. This essentially reorganized the classical theory and set the scene for new developments in mathematics that were arising at the time.

He also applied his new ideas to the whole of mathematics in formulating the new strategy of axiomatic formal mathematics in which the established mathematics was recast in terms of set-theoretic axiomatic systems and formal proof.

2.1 *Generalizing Embodied Geometry to Axiomatic Topology*

One of the first developments from an axiomatic approach to geometry arose in topology, often described as 'rubber sheet geometry'. This is a study of the properties of surfaces, solids and higher dimensional creations of human imagination that remain invariant as the objects are stretched and deformed. The eventual formalization of the concept of a 'topological space' is presented in an axiomatic form quite different from the formalization of algebraic structures based on the properties of the operations involved.

A topological space is defined to be a set S and a collection O of subsets of S satisfying the following axioms:

(T1) The whole set S and the empty set $\varnothing$ are in O.
(T1) If $U, V \in O$ then the intersection $U \cap V \in O$.
(T2) Given any collection of sets in O, their union is in O.

The sets in O are called *open sets*, and the axioms essentially say that a topological space is a set with a collection of open sets in which the whole set and the empty set are open, and the intersection of two open sets and the union of any collection of open sets are open. That's all.

In a given context, a topological space may have additional structure, for instance, in the usual context of sets on the number line, in the plane, or in three-dimensional space, the usual definition is:

> A set of points U is said to be *open* if, given any point $x \in U$, then there is a positive real number $\varepsilon > 0$ such that every other point within a distance ε of x is also in the set U.

An open set S on the line, on a surface, or in three-dimensional space, is simply a set with a little neighbourhood around any point that is all contained within the set. Essentially, a set is 'open' in this sense if there is room to move around near a point in S, while still remaining in S. These open sets satisfy properties (T1)–(T3) and so are the inspiration for ideas in general topology.

A function $f\colon A \to B$ is said to be continuous in $\mathbb{R}^n$ if it satisfies the formal epsilon-delta definition for every $x \in A$:

> Given $\varepsilon > 0$, there exists $\delta > 0$ such that whenever x and $x' \in A$ are within δ then $f(x)$ and $f(x')$ are within ε.

This starts with a desired closeness ε in the second set B and seeks a desired closeness δ in the first set A. This leads to working backwards from an open set U in the second space to consider the set of points denoted by $f^{-1}(U)$ of the form $x \in A$ where $f(x) \in U$. It can be shown that if U is open, then $f^{-1}(U)$ is open. A proof is not given here, as it is 'elementary' for the expert but convoluted for those with less experience.

What is important is that the notion of continuity can be generalized to a topological space in the following terms:

> A function from one topological space S to another T is said to be *continuous* if for any open set U in T, the pre-image $f^{-1}(U)$ – consisting of all elements $x \in S$ mapping into $f(x) \in U$ – is open in S.

Topology is the study of topological spaces and continuous maps between them. In particular, a continuous function $f\colon T \to S$ that is a bijection with a continuous inverse is called a *homeomorphism*. As in other axiomatic structures, this notion gives an equivalence relation between the structures involved, in this case between topological spaces. The theory of topology essentially focuses on those properties that remain invariant under homeomorphisms.

Topology allows us to imagine the deformation of one surface into another as a homeomorphism. For example, the surface of a cup with a handle can be continuously deformed into a torus. (Figure 14.3.)

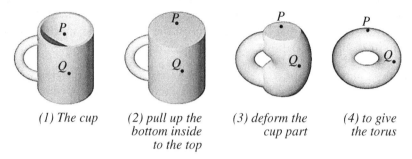

(1) The cup   (2) pull up the   (3) deform the   (4) to give
                 bottom inside   cup part   the torus
                 to the top

Figure 14.3. Deforming a cup into a torus.

At stage (1) we see the cup with two points P and Q marked on it. At stage (2) the inside base of the cup has been pulled up to the top and P is now on top, with Q in its original position. Stage (3) shows the body of the cup being deformed into the right half of the torus in stage (4) with P and Q moving to their final positions. The deformation at each stage is a homeomorphism in which the points P and Q represent the successive positions of the original points. The whole deformation can be imagined to shift smoothly in time, appealing to our dynamic human perception, with each successive position representing a homeomorphic image of the cup as it changes to a torus.

The theory of topology focuses on properties that are unchanged by this process. Points remain points and the deformations shift points continuously in space and time. But distances between points change, so distance is not an invariant.

Loops themselves, however, *are* invariant, in the sense that when a loop is deformed, it remains a loop. Indeed, topology studies not specific loops, but loops as they are deformed continuously on the surface.

We need only study loops on one of the equivalent spaces, so we do it on the torus. We consider loops which start and end at a particular point P. Figure 14.4 (1) and (2) shows a loop u going round the torus the short way and another loop v going round the torus the long way.

Because all loops start and end at P, we can follow one loop by another and call this 'the sum' of the two loops. Figure 14.4 (3) shows the sum $u + v$ of the loops u and v. We are interested not just in the specific loop itself but also in any other loop that can be continuously deformed from it. Figure 14.4 (4) shows an equivalent loop to $u + v$ that still starts and ends at P, but the middle part has been pulled away to give a loop that wraps round the torus once the short way and once the long way.

(1) *loop u starting and ending at P* (2) *loop v starting and ending at P* (3) *loop u + v following u by v* (4) *loop u + v moved continuously*

Figure 14.4. Loops on a torus.

2.2 *Relating Embodied Geometry to Symbolic Algebra*

Performing a thought experiment allows us to imagine that a general loop is specified by the number of times it loops round the short way and the number of times round the long way. A general loop can be written as $mu + nv$, where m and n are integers. The loops under addition form a group called the *fundamental group* of the surface, which is isomorphic to the Cartesian product of ordered pairs of integers $(m, n) \in \mathbb{Z} \times \mathbb{Z}$. The visual idea can be embodied in the creative human mind. The translation to symbolism needs to be described in a general form rather than writing explicit algebraic formulae for the loops. However, the translated relationships give algebra that is easily interpreted.

Equivalent topological spaces (having a homeomorphism between them) have isomorphic fundamental groups. Relationships in topology translate into corresponding symbolic relationships in group theory, giving a shift from mental objects in our imagination to computable operations in group theory. Theorems that we can only imagine in our minds can now be translated into algebraic form where a computable solution may possibly be found.

For instance, it is evident that no matter how we try, we cannot deform a sphere into a torus without at some time pushing a hole through it. But how can this be given a formal proof? Any picture of a deformation is only a *specific* picture of the process, so embodiment tells us what is likely to be true, but does not provide an acceptable proof.

The solution is to translate the problem into algebra. If we take the surface of a sphere, then any closed loop on it can be deformed to the trivial loop that stays at a point. So the fundamental group of the sphere has just one element (the identity), while the fundamental group of a torus is $\mathbb{Z} \times \mathbb{Z}$. A sphere therefore cannot be deformed continuously to a torus, as this would imply they must both have the *same* fundamental group.

This is typical of a marvelous range of theories linking the embodied world of geometry and various generalizations such as topology, to the symbolic world of groups. Geometry begins with pictures and dynamic embodiment and has the potential to realize corresponding properties in algebra that are amenable to calculation, with both the topology and the algebra being formulated in formal axiomatic ways.

3. Contrasting Developments in Geometry and Algebra

In recognition of the special nature of geometry, Christopher Zeeman began a course for second-year undergraduates with the clarion call:

> Geometry is that part of mathematics that relies on pictures, visual imag-
> ination and intuition to suggest the theorems, construct the proofs and
> inspire the conjectures.[3]

He saw his mission to encourage students to think geometrically to visualize good examples and only then to translate the mental pictures for algebraic study. His own research used dynamic thought experiments to imagine configurations not only in two and three dimensions, but also in higher dimensions. His experience suggested intuitions that – as the dimensions of space increased from a one-dimensional line to a two-dimensional surface to three-dimensional space – offered more and more space to move around. This enabled him to picture configurations in four dimensions and above in ways that were, for him, meaningful. It happens that in dimension five and above, there is so much more 'room' to move figures around that certain general theorems are more easily imagined and proved in higher dimensions. For instance, he was the first to prove a theorem describing the 'unknotting of spheres in five dimensions'.[4]

Meanwhile, the formal structures arising from the symbolism of algebra develop in a fundamentally different manner. In the opening of the book *Algebra*, Garrett Birkhoff and Saunders MacLane write:

> Algebra starts as the art of manipulating sums, products, and powers of
> numbers. The rules for these manipulations hold for all numbers, so the
> manipulations may be carried out with letters standing for the numbers. It
> then appears that the same rules hold for various different sorts of num-
> bers, rational, real, or complex, and that the rules for multiplication even

---

[3] From cyclostyled notes prepared for a second-year undergraduate course on Geometry given by Christopher Zeeman in 1977.

[4] Zeeman (1960).

apply to things such as transformations which are not numbers at all. An algebraic system, as we will study it, is thus a set of elements of any sort on which functions such as addition and multiplication operate, provided only that these operations satisfy certain basic rules. The rules for multiplication and inverse are the axioms for a 'group', those for addition, subtraction, and multiplication are the axioms for a 'ring', and the functions mapping one system to another are the 'morphisms'.[5]

These differences between ways of working in geometry and algebra were reported by MacLane from an insightful discussion he had with Sir Michael Atiyah, a geometer with wide interests in other areas:

> In the fall of 1982, Riyadh, Saudi Arabia … we all mounted to the roof … to sit at ease in the starlight. Atiyah and MacLane fell into a discussion, as suited the occasion, about how mathematical research is done. For MacLane it meant getting and understanding the needed definitions, working with them to see what could be calculated and what might be true, to finally come up with new 'structure' theorems. For Atiyah, it meant thinking hard about a somewhat vague and uncertain situation, trying to guess what might be found out, and only then finally reaching definitions and the definitive theorems and proofs. This story indicates the ways of doing mathematics can vary sharply, as in this case between the fields of algebra and geometry, while at the end there was full agreement on the final goal: theorems with proofs. Thus differently oriented mathematicians have sharply different ways of thought, but also common standards as to the result.[6]

It was this quotation that caused me to formulate the distinction between 'natural' and 'formal' thinking in cooperation with Marcia Pinto[7], taking the term 'natural' from Janet Duffin's description[8] of an individual who works by making personal sense of mathematics and the term 'formal' from one who works with formal definitions and logical proofs.

Atiyah is reported as speaking of development in terms of *thinking about a vague and uncertain situation, trying to guess what may be found out*, then finally reaching *definitions* and the *definitive theorems and proof*. This resonates with the long-term structural abstraction of mathematical thinking seen earlier in van Hiele's successive levels of development from

---

[5] From Birkhoff and MacLane (1999), p. 1.
[6] MacLane (1994), pp. 190–1.
[7] Pinto & Tall (2001).
[8] This refers to Janet Duffin's observation of her own 'natural learning', as opposed to her co-author Adrian Simpson who followed an 'alien' approach based on deductions from definitions, as in Duffin & Simpson (1993).

practical recognition and description to theoretical definition and deduction. (Figure 14.5.)

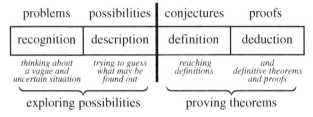

Figure 14.5. Research development: the structural abstraction of
van Hiele and Atiyah.

Meanwhile, MacLane speaks explicitly of *getting and understanding the needed definitions* (problems), working with them *to see what might be calculated* (possibilities), to *see what might be true* (conjectures), and then *come up with new structure theorems* (proofs). (Figure 14.6.)

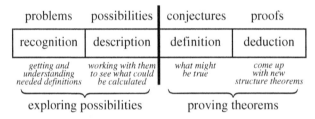

Figure 14.6. Research development: the structural abstraction of
van Hiele and MacLane.

Again we find the same overall framework. Of course these occur at a sophisticated level and the researchers are aware of the kind of strategies they follow, so they can imagine carrying out the whole sequence over time, moving from one stage to another as appropriate.

Moreover, mathematicians are much more varied in the ways that they form their personal conceptions of mathematical ideas. They do not in general think *only* in a natural way or only in a formal way, even if they express a preference for one mode of operation or another.

In an extensive study of seventy research mathematicians (with equal numbers of males and females), Leone Burton used grounded theory to study a range of aspects such as thinking styles, sociocultural relatedness, aesthetics, intuition and connectivities.[9] She initially hypothesized that she

---

[9] Burton (2002).

would find evidence of the two styles of thinking which she described as visual and analytic and that mathematicians would move flexibly between the two. Her data led her not to two, but to three categories, which she described as visual (thinking in pictures, often dynamic), analytic (thinking symbolically, formalistically) and conceptual (thinking in ideas, classifying). The majority of those interviewed (42/70) embraced two styles, a small number (3/70) used all three and the rest referred only to one (15 visual, 3 analytic and 7 conceptual).

However, this three-part analysis reflects the two developments from embodiment and symbolism and the longer-term development of formalism whose structure theorems take us back to embodiment and symbolism. The visual category is concerned with embodied proof in terms of 'thinking in pictures, often dynamic'. The analytic category specifically describes 'thinking symbolically, formalistically', which relates to the development from operational symbolism to axiomatic formalism, and includes a spectrum of performance from natural quantified symbolic thinking to fully formal set-theoretic thinking.

The conceptual category refers to 'thinking in ideas' relating to the exploratory phase of the research cycle, and 'classifying' structures that satisfy an appropriate definition. The definition may occur at various levels, from the theoretical mathematics of Euclidean geometry and algebraic proof to formal set-theoretic mathematics and the embodied and symbolic structures resulting from structure theorems. For instance, groups are defined formally, but when classified up to isomorphism to realize the specific crystalline concepts for each equivalence class, the classification may be performed using the results of structure theorems that return to the embodied and symbolic structure such as generators and relations rather than formal proof as a sequence of quantified statements. In mathematical research, mathematicians use a personal blend of various aspects dependent on their experience and personal conceptions that operate at sophisticated levels of formalism, embodiment and symbolism.

For example, MacLane and Atiyah had very different journeys in their conceptual developments. MacLane began his research with a thesis on logic and soon became interested in the relationships between different kinds of axiomatic structures with functions between them, such as topological spaces and continuous maps, or algebraic structures and homomorphisms. He created a new subject called 'category theory' which has 'objects' together with 'morphisms' between them, generalizing the idea of various kinds of mathematical structures where 'objects' satisfy specific axioms and 'morphisms' are functions between them that 'preserve the structure'.

He then considered transformations (called 'functors') between categories, which mapped objects in the first category to objects in the second and morphisms in the first to morphisms in the second. For instance, the theory of homotopy links the category of topological spaces and continuous maps to the category of groups and homomorphisms. Using category theory, problems in one area may be mirrored in another where there might be more appropriate structure to give a solution with a proof.

Atiyah preferred a broader natural approach that arose from his continuing love of geometry.

> I was always very attracted to geometry: I liked geometry because of its concrete nature, but I realized that you had to apply a variety of tools in order to make progress. That became the guiding thread through most of my subsequent life. I'm still doing geometry in the broad sense, but I discovered that to do geometry you had to do almost everything else as well: you get involved with topology, differential geometry, algebra, mathematical physics, you name it: but in some sense I still regard myself as a geometer.[10]

His preference for working on genuine problems that could be imagined geometrically was expressed whimsically in a comment:

> Algebra is the offer made by the devil to the mathematician. The devil says: 'I will give you this powerful machine; it will answer any question you like. All you need to do is give me your soul: give up geometry and you will have this marvelous machine.'[11]

His major activity focused on understanding important ideas from disparate sources that have something in common and developing a new framework that unifies the previously disconnected pieces. This strategy precisely fits the framework proposed here where complicated structures are seen to involve some kind of phenomena that can be named and compressed into thinkable concepts that in turn are connected together into new knowledge structures that lay the foundations for further progress. In this way the new crystalline ideas are more complex, yet simpler and less complicated. Ideas that seemed abstract for others were concrete for him,

---

[10] Quoted from http://www.ma.hw.ac.uk/~ndg/fom/atiyahqu.html. (Accessed June 11, 2012).
[11] Quoted from Atiyah (2004), p. 7.

in the sense suggested by Wilensky that concreteness relates to the quality of our relationship with the concept.[12]

Mathematicians develop a concrete relationship with abstract ideas in this sense and are able to manipulate the new ideas as thinkable concepts in their minds, enabling them to imagine new connections between them and to develop more sophisticated knowledge structures.

I had the privilege of studying for my doctorate in mathematics with Atiyah and saw his power of insight at first hand. He had ways of looking at things that suggested overall possibilities before even considering any details. For instance, to link different ideas in topology and algebra, he encouraged me by saying 'a vector bundle is a vector space varying continuously over a topological space, a module is an algebraic variation of a vector space, so they should have some things in common.'

His responses to questions were always insightful, but sometimes at a higher level than I expected. I remember trying to understand a theorem about the intersection of algebraic varieties in algebraic geometry (where an algebraic variety is a generalization of a curve or surface in space given by algebraic equations). I expected a simple answer, something like an example of the intersections of a hyperbola with an ellipse. He replied, 'consider the intersection of hyperplanes in complex projective *n*-space …'. I protested, saying, 'you call *that* simple?' He smiled and explained that it *is* simple, saying something like 'hyperplanes are linear, I choose complex space because it has all the required solutions of equations, and projective space because all the hyperplanes actually meet.' In mathematical terms, his explanation *is* simple, but it requires a sophisticated personal knowledge structure to grasp this simplicity. Mathematicians make progress by compressing ideas into new kinds of thinkable concepts that are, for them, simpler to think about, even if they seem highly abstract to others.

He suggested a problem for my thesis that related topology and algebra. He mentioned that it was a problem that he couldn't solve, so I asked him why he had given it to me. His reply was that I was fresh to the area and did not have the preconceptions that he had experienced. (An implicit understanding of the effect of problematic met-befores?) Over the weeks and months as I made painful progress and as we discussed ideas that took me weeks to think through to get a possible glimpse of a new pathway, when I spoke to him, the steps I took connected to his ideas in different

---

[12] Wilensky (1998), p. 58, discussed earlier in this book in Chapter 5, Section 3.3.

ways and with his mentoring I was able to complete the thesis. From out of a complicated situation, a new theorem grew.

Both MacLane and Atiyah have broad visions of mathematics. They have each developed new knowledge structures that connect and compress knowledge to form rich crystalline concepts as a basis for new theories. Despite their declared differences in operation, both have made giant strides, creating new knowledge structures that are simultaneously more general and more simple. As Atiyah explained in an interview on his interests in mathematics and physics:

> And the reason is of course because mathematics has this great propensity to unify. People find out lots of things, and then at the next stage they say, well all these are special cases of some one simple picture. We abstract out of them all. People object to that business abstracting, they say why don't you stay concrete. Well the whole point about it is if you stay concrete, you're always tied to tables and chairs, you can't see the bigger picture.
>
> So mathematicians constantly move up a level. As they go forward, they have all these examples of something, we'll see what's common, and give it a nice title and unify it. And with that under our belts, we can put it in a small textbook and move on.
>
> And for century after century, mathematicians have been building this big structure where we absorb what we've done before, put it together in a simple pattern, and I think that not only mathematics but science as a whole, only progresses if you can understand things. It isn't just a matter of, you know, getting a lot of results out of the computer. If science, all it did was to produce a string of numbers, we'd soon be terribly lost. Its aim is to produce ideas and explain things in simple terms. All science is like that.[13]

In a few sentences this insightful comment expresses the essence of what has taken me a whole book to formulate. It explains how ideas begin with concrete examples, but the essential aspects need to become the focus of attention to see the bigger picture. This focus leads to compressed thinkable concepts that shift to another level to build a new knowledge structure of relationships with the new concepts that are readily thinkable at the new level. The new level then becomes concrete in terms of the richness of meanings as perceived by the individual, with flexible connections and different ways of thinking about the underlying ideas.

---

[13] From an interview in which Sir Michael discusses the relationship between his mathematical research and the physics of string theory. Retrieved from: http://www.super-stringtheory.com/people/atiyah.html (Accessed June 9, 2012).

Mathematics develops through the researcher's struggle with the unknown, and progresses through putting ideas together in new ways to provide new understanding. This is crystallized as a new theorem with a formal proof.

As MacLane noted, mathematicians have different ways of working to create new knowledge but, at the highest level of pure mathematics, the one thing they have in common is the final goal of theorems and proofs.

However, while the 'final goal' of proof completes a full cycle of development, it is often a temporary stopping place, to enjoy the victory and to share the results through publication. At this point, new possibilities often appear, suggesting new ideas for further development. The scene is set once more for a new struggle to formulate conjectures and to seek new proofs to prove them.

Now we have attained the summit of the development of mathematical thinking where problems give rise to possibilities, on to hypotheses and the search for formal proof. The boundaries of mathematics are ever widening as the biological brain of *Homo sapiens* reflects on knowledge structures and blends together new possibilities that lead eventually to new and more powerful crystalline knowledge structures.

15 Reflections

Having developed an overall framework for the growth of mathematical thinking, it is time to ask the question 'Of what value is this general theory to individuals playing a particular role in the teaching and learning of mathematics?' What does it have to say to teachers of young children, to university mathematicians, to curriculum designers, to theorists in various communities of practice, or to learners themselves?

Learning to think mathematically is a cumulative experience that depends on what has already been experienced and current learning will affect what and how we learn in the future. Even though participants in the teaching, learning and using of mathematics are likely to focus on their particular area of responsibility and expertise, all our actions and effectiveness are part of a much bigger picture.

This chapter provides an overall summary of the whole framework and considers how it relates to other theories, not only in terms of similarities and differences, but also how apparently disparate theories may be blended together to evolve new insights.

1. Viewing the Whole Theory

The overall growth of mathematical thinking is outlined in Figure 15.1. It is based on the sensori-motor foundation of human thinking through *conceptual embodiment* and *operational symbolism* and the increasing sophistication of human reasoning that may later be transformed into the *axiomatic formalism* of set-theoretic definition and formal proof.

As a child matures, mathematical thinking develops in sophistication, beginning with *practical mathematics* exploring shape and space and encapsulating operations such as counting into concepts such as number, leading to *theoretical mathematics* involving definition of concepts and deduction of

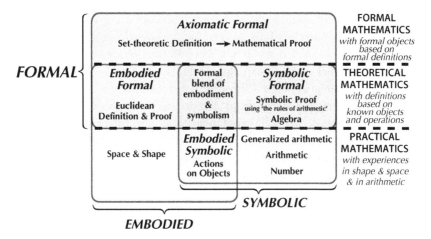

Figure 15.1. The three worlds of mathematics.

properties. As mathematical reasoning develops in both embodiment and symbolism, there is a further switch from the study of familiar objects and operations to *formal mathematics* whose consequences apply to any situation that satisfies the given axioms and definitions.

In the long term, individuals require differing kinds of mathematics to function as thinking individuals in society. Mathematical literacy requires practical mathematics with some insight into theoretical mathematics. Many trades and professions require relevant forms of practical mathematics, applications may require theoretical mathematics, while pure mathematicians create formal theories that may subsequently have practical and theoretical applications of value to the whole of society.

It is taken as a fundamental principle that every individual should be given encouragement and opportunity to make the best of his or her own mathematical learning, without any artificial ceiling placed on his or her development. As a consequence, teachers should be aware of supportive and problematic aspects that face learners as they seek to make sense of mathematics in ways that will affect their future development.

2. The Development of the Thinkable Concepts in Mathematics

The concepts that provide the basis for mathematical thinking are here classified as arising from three distinct forms of construction. In the embodied world the recognition and description of shapes arise through the practical *categorization* of figures based on exploring the properties of objects. In the symbolic world, concepts in arithmetic and algebra arise through the *encapsulation* of operations, such as counting and sharing, into symbolic concepts such as whole number and fraction. School mathematics blends together embodiment and symbolism to reveal complementary aspects of mathematical ideas. Theoretical refinements are based on *definition*, with properties deduced from definitions either through Euclidean proof in geometry or symbolic proof in arithmetic and algebra. Definitions take an even more essential role in the formal world where set-theoretic definitions are used to define the properties of formal concepts and all other properties are deduced as theorems.

Even though van Hiele saw his successive levels of mathematical thinking applying mainly to geometry and not to algebra, the surprise is that the succession of *recognition, description, definition, deduction* occurs not only in embodied geometry but also in symbolic arithmetic and algebra and later in axiomatic formalism, where the highest level of research involves *exploring possibilities* through recognition and description of possible new relationships, followed by *proving theorems* based on well-defined conjectures and the search for mathematical proof.

Mathematical proof is not the end of the story, for axiomatic formal theorems can lead to *structure theorems* that endow the theory with new forms of embodiment and symbolism, returning mathematical thinking to the fundamental sensori-motor mental world of thought experiments and the operational manipulation of symbols. This closes the circle to reveal the full integration of the three worlds of embodiment, symbolism and formalism and reinforces the need to have an overall theoretical framework for mathematical thinking that blends together all three. (Figure 15.2.)

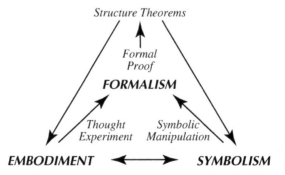

Figure 15.2. The full integration of the three worlds of mathematics.

Moreover, the overall view of the theory also reveals the universal idea of a *crystalline concept*, which enshrines the essential qualities of mathematical thinking. While humans initially *discover* mathematical properties through perception and action, they advance to *invent* definitions in given contexts that lead to crystalline concepts whose properties must then follow as a consequence of the definitions.

Crystalline concepts not only arise as the summit of mathematical thinking, but they are also sensed at an early stage by many young children as they realize flexible relationships between numbers and use them to simplify their understanding of arithmetic. In the long term, a sense of the underlying coherence of mathematical concepts has the potential to support the maturation of mathematical thinking at every stage.

Platonism is a natural outgrowth of human thinking, as reflective individuals focus on the essential properties while suppressing others (such as points that have position without size, and lines that have length and no breadth). This leads to the imagination of Platonic objects whose perfection can be shared in thought and word with others, even though this perfection cannot be realized in our physical world.

The formal mathematics of Hilbert requires an even greater leap in imagination, through realizing that it is possible to formulate *properties* of formal objects as definitions without needing to know what those objects are, only what may be proved from the definitions as formal theorems. This enables a research mathematician to explore a complicated situation and – inspired by various insights with varying warrants for truth – to formulate new theoretical frameworks that are necessarily linked tightly together through mathematical proof. There is no longer any need to be restricted by what may be observed perceptually or constructed physically. Now the mathematician is free to follow the consequences of his or her imagination and to share the results with others who have appropriate knowledge structures.

However, once choices have been made in a particular context, their consequences are no longer subject to the choice of the individual; they follow as a consequence of the crystalline mathematical structure proved from the axioms and definitions.

The long-term development of mathematical thinking at all levels is therefore enhanced by a sense of the crystalline structure of mathematics, in school, in the applications of mathematics to real-world situations, and on to the ever widening insight in formal mathematical research.

This leads to the important principle that learners should be continually encouraged to make sense of the mathematics that they encounter to develop their full potential for mathematical thinking in the longer term.

3. Individual Journeys through Three Worlds of Mathematics

The journeys that individuals take as they mature can be very different, depending on the individual's personal attributes as well as his or her developing experience. Within the overall picture of the growth of practical, theoretical and formal mathematics, those of us who participate as teachers, learners and researchers can focus on our own area of interest, yet keep an eye on what the learner has experienced before and how current teaching and learning may affect longer-term development.

The framework proposed here is intended to apply to the full range of aptitudes, from those who struggle with mathematics to the gifted, taking account of the possible developments of those who require practical mathematics in their everyday lives, theoretical mathematics in a wide range of applications, or formal mathematics at the frontiers of pure mathematical research. Though few may reach the heady heights of formalism, the products of those higher levels eventually feed back over the generations for the benefit of us all. It is therefore of great value for all who participate in the development of mathematical thinking to be aware of the wider vision.

As children go to school they may already be operating in very different ways. Our story began in Chapter 1 with two young children, one struggling, counting on his fingers, and the other already performing mental arithmetic with numbers in the millions. From a very early age, children think differently. It is not simply a case that some children learn faster than others: they learn to operate in very different ways.

Studies of children's methods of counting reveal the steady compression of counting procedures into number concepts. A closer analysis in Chapter 7 reveals the subtle distinction between *embodied compression* that enables the learner to *see* and *sense* fundamental relationships in arithmetic, as distinct from *symbolic compression* that focuses on practicing the step-by-step sequences of symbolic operation. Embodied compression offers the potential to sense general properties of arithmetic that can guide future development. However, some children remain limited to the physical act of counting with small numbers and fail to cope with more complicated problems. Others develop an overall sense of relationships that has the potential to guide a learner into more sophisticated ways of thinking. This can occur at many stages, such as the development of derived facts in arithmetic (Chapter 2), the solution of equations by 'doing the same thing to both sides' (Chapter 4) or the introduction to calculus through the dynamic visualization of 'local straightness' (Chapter 11). An awareness of the different conceptions that occur can enable the teacher as mentor to give appropriate guidance to encourage individuals to develop in ways that are appropriate, both at the time and as part of a more sophisticated longer-term development.

The three-world theory, integrated with the emotional responses to supportive and problematic developments, shows how embodiment, symbolism and more formal reasoning each play their part in the long-term maturation of mathematical thinking. Over the longer term, embodied strategies may give insightful meaning at various stages of development, but as the mathematics becomes more complicated, symbolic strategies offer greater power and precision. This requires a shift from making sense through perception of a physical situation to making sense of operational symbolism and increasingly sophisticated verbal reasoning.

While some continue to blend embodiment and symbolism in solving problems, others shift towards the verbal and symbolic. Not only is there a broadening spectrum of performance, but the manner in which learners succeed or fail in mathematics also broadens into a wider spectrum of approaches. This divergence arises not only from the cognitive growth of knowledge structures, but also from the emotional reactions to successive mathematical ideas and the consequent divergence in attitude that broadens the spectrum even further.

3. Supportive and Problematic Aspects and Related Emotions

As mathematical thinking demands greater sophistication, it presents new challenges that some find exciting and thought-provoking, but others find problematic and seek ways of coping, perhaps by learning *what* to do without worrying too much about the meaning or, when failing to cope, becoming disaffected and experiencing mathematical anxiety.

Cognitive theories usually focus mainly on what students know and how they develop, observing that learners go through various transition phases as they shift from one level of operation to another. Affective theories study the emotional spectrum of confidence and anxiety. The theory presented here blends together the cognitive and affective to reveal new insights.

Chapter 3 studies the cognitive development of mathematics as it passes through various stages of operational compression from step-by-step procedures to flexible thinkable concepts and also through structural compression, in which mathematical properties are recognized, described, defined and related by deduction.

Using the notion of met-before, Chapter 4 considers the supportive and problematic aspects of learning successive mathematical topics that have both cognitive and emotional consequences. Cognitively, supportive aspects enable generalization to new situations while problematic aspects impede development.

Chapter 5 considers the emotional reactions to mathematics that arise from a wide variety of sources, but most important, it focuses on the sources of pleasure and disaffection that arise from within mathematics itself, which may drastically affect future development.

Chapter 6 blends together the cognitive and affective to give the framework of three worlds of mathematics that offers emergent insight into the challenges faced by learners over the long term. As new contexts arise – in counting whole numbers, sharing using fractions, paying debts using signed numbers, measuring lengths that are not expressible as fractions, solving quadratic equations – new phenomena arise that are problematic. *Thus the very embodiment that gives perceptual support to making practical sense of specific mathematical operations may also involve aspects that become problematic in more sophisticated contexts.*

As mathematical ideas progress into more sophisticated levels, the balance between embodiment and symbolism changes. Chapter 7 reveals how visualizing numbers as lengths enables us to 'see' algebraic relationships, such as the difference between two squares in a physical picture and even the difference between two cubes in three dimensions, but the picture is more complicated for signed numbers, and goes beyond our physical experience in four dimensions and above, until a new form of simplicity arises as the symbolic factorization has a new embodiment as points equally spaced around the unit circle using complex numbers.

This shows that Bruner's framework of enactive, iconic and symbolic representations continues to have an overall validity, but that in specific areas of mathematics, increasingly sophisticated symbolic representations – using arithmetical calculation, algebraic manipulation and logical deduction – have a greater power and precision that goes beyond the resources of enactive and iconic modes of representation.

The precise relationship between various modes of representation therefore changes as mathematical ideas become more sophisticated. Practical mathematics usually benefits from a blend of embodiment and symbolism, but theoretical mathematics brings in theoretical definitions and sequential deductions that benefit from more verbal and symbolic forms of reasoning. Whereas some high achieving learners may maintain an embodied basis for their thinking – often blended with verbal and symbolic reasoning – others function well by shifting almost entirely to operational symbolism supported by verbal reasoning. Mathematical sense making develops long-term through individual blends of perception, operation and reason.

Mathematics as a whole benefits from different kinds of thinkers bringing together differing ways of conceptualizing ideas, even though debates continue over what approaches to mathematics are to be preferred. Society benefits from having individuals joining together in communities of practice with differing specializations and ways of working. However, the theories that evolve depend on the knowledge structures of the theoreticians themselves. As such the wide range of theories that have been developed may be supportive in some contexts yet problematic in others.

As we compare the relative aspects of differing theoretical approaches, it is important to realize that we are *all* subject to the met-befores in our knowledge structures that arise from our cumulative lifetime experiences.

4. Extensional Blends

One phenomenon that has recurred throughout personal development and in the historical evolution of mathematics is the notion of *extensional blend*. In one context a range of concepts and ways of working may operate coherently and supportively, yet in a broader context, some of these experiences may remain supportive while others become problematic.

Piagetian theory speaks of the need to *assimilate* new ideas and, at the same time, to *accommodate* mental schemas to take account of the changing situation. My doctoral supervisor, Richard Skemp, made a subtle distinction by asserting that there is a difference between the *expansion* of an existing schema by adding additional information and the *reconstruction* of an existing schema to take account of new data that no longer fit any current schemas.

The notion of *extensional blend* brings a new aspect to the development of knowledge structures. It is not only that new contexts may require a cognitive reconstruction of existing schemas, but also that the original mathematical structure remains coherent in itself, while lying within a larger structure that has a new form of coherence. This occurs both in personal development and historical evolution.

When working in a particular context, such as whole number arithmetic, a personal knowledge structure may be expanded by adding new facts and ways of deriving new facts from old. However, in shifting to an extensional blend, such as fractional arithmetic, new ideas arise – such as equivalence of fractions, new algorithms for addition and multiplication – that introduce both supportive and problematic aspects detailed in earlier chapters. The notion of extensional blend requires a reconstruction of knowledge and yet, the original structure of whole number arithmetic still retains all its original properties.

In the historical evolution of mathematics, such changes arise as observed by Thomas Kuhn in his *Structure of Scientific Revolutions*.[1] A stable scientific context that works well is affected by problematic aspects that lead to a period of instability, which later stabilizes to take account of the new data. These historical changes can be observed in Chapter 9, where it may take several generations for the resolution of problematic aspects to be grasped in a manner that becomes widely accepted.

Throughout history there has been an ongoing problematic conflict between the finite capabilities of human endeavor and the human capacity to imagine the infinite, which has been a major theme throughout this book. It continues to this day in the differences between formal analysis based on the potential infinity of epsilon-delta definitions and the human imagination of arbitrarily small variable quantities. The notion of supportive and problematic aspects of extensional blends allows us to see this debate in a rational light because there is a structure theorem that shows formally that any extension of the real number line must contain infinitesimals. The standard theory of mathematical analysis remains as a coherent theory in its own right while the alternative theory of infinitesimals exists as an extensional blend.

In the development of mathematical thinking, both historically and individually, extensional blends involve the same phenomenon. Working at a particular level – either in a community of mathematicians or as an individual learner operating with one number system prior to shifting to an extensional blend – the individual may feel comfortable at the current level yet the shift to another level may be a stimulating challenge for some while being problematic for others.

This phenomenon also applies to theory builders who are dedicated to a particular theoretical framework and encounter an alternative theoretical framework that does not fit their current way of thinking. The alternative framework may not be appropriate, it may even be faulty, but it may also happen that both frameworks are appropriate in their own context. Such alternative frameworks may benefit from a broader theory that is a blend of both, explicitly revealing the nature of aspects that are supportive in some contexts yet problematic in others, yet at the same time, these aspects may

---

[1] Kuhn (1962).

blend together so that an apparent dichotomy has the potential to offer new insights.

5. The Evolution of Theoretical Frameworks: Supportive and Problematic Aspects

Theoretical frameworks evolve according to the perceived needs in a given context and are constructed by theorists who have detailed experience that they may share with a particular community.

In Chapter 9 the historical evolution of mathematical concepts was seen in terms of the development of embodiment and symbolism and the relatively recent introduction of axiomatic formalism. As communities evolved, forms of mathematics developed that were appropriate for a particular context, but then, in the face of problematic aspects, new extensional blends arose.

Early civilizations developed highly sophisticated practical mathematics that enabled them to measure and trade, to build massive structures such as the pyramids, to predict the changing seasons and the movements of the heavens.

The Greeks developed subtle theoretical approaches to geometry and number that transcended the physical perception of figures drawn in sand, or pebbles placed in patterns, to reveal generic properties that intimated the perfection of Platonic concepts.

As time passed, some theories were shown to be highly plausible but were later in need of modification, such as the earth being the centre of the universe. Others were shown to be consistent in their own context, yet capable of being extended, such as the introduction of negative and complex numbers and the imaginative use of infinitesimals, each of which was considered to be problematic before being rationalized and integrated in an extensional blend.

Modern theories of mathematical thinking have proliferated to encompass a range of diverse aspects. These include mathematical, cognitive, affective, social, philosophical, technological, neurophysiological and a range of other aspects. No single framework can encompass the whole enterprise. Each has its own domain and validity that may prove to be supportive or problematic in other contexts. Yet our experience with supportive and problematic relationships between theories may suggest to us that we should seek new ways of blending differences to gain new insights.

All theoretical frameworks are formulated by individuals and communities that have their own experiences to build upon. As a mathematician who took an increasing interest in how individuals make sense of mathematics, I spent years comparing and analyzing the conflicting elements of different theoretical frameworks until I realized that greater progress can be made by seeing each alternative in a sympathetic light in its own appropriate context and seeking to blend together different viewpoints to evolve new insights.

My own development has strong links with theories that attempt to make sense of mathematical growth from the fundamental embodiment of human thought. It has aspects in common with the ideas in *Where Mathematics Comes From*[2], with its focus on grounding metaphors from human perception and action, building through definitional metaphors and linking metaphors and on to higher levels of mathematical thinking. However, it focuses on certain ingredients not emphasized in the embodied theory of Lakoff and Núñez, such as the roles of met-befores and their related emotional aspects, the long-term role of compression of ideas and the central notion of crystalline concept.

Their theory builds an insightful picture of 'natural mathematics' arising from the human body, employing ideas from linguistics and cognitive science, but has less sympathy with 'the romance of mathematics' as formulated by mathematicians, which they describe as a 'myth' of absolutism that fails to be in tune with natural human thinking.[3]

The three-world formulation sees mathematicians using the same underlying sensori-motor foundations as everyone else. They take practical and theoretical mathematics to greater heights by formulating axiomatic systems of their own choice. This reveals crystalline structures just as meaningful to them as the crystalline structures of arithmetic and geometry may be natural to others in the wider population. However, these axiomatic formal structures may be problematic to those who are familiar only with practical and theoretical mathematics.

By taking into account the possible met-befores of learners and theorists, the framework of three worlds of mathematics does not come to the conclusion that 'natural mathematics is good' but 'formal mathematics is a myth.' Instead it sees the 'tangle of guesswork, analogy, wishful thinking and frustration' that Gian-Carlo Rota highlighted as a prelude to formal proof as 'a way of making sure that our minds are not playing tricks'.[4]

---

[2] Lakoff & Núñez (2000).

[3] Lakoff & Núñez (2000), pp. 338–41.

[4] See the quotation at the opening of Chapter 14 (quoted from the preface to *The Mathematical Experience* by Davis and Hersh [1980], p. xviii).

By formulating mathematics axiomatically, researchers may refine their theoretical frameworks to prove structure theorems that enable them to return to natural forms of embodiment and symbolism. For example, the formal ideas of limit, continuity, differentiation and integration that are criticized as not being natural by Lakoff and Núñez can be introduced to students using the embodied and symbolic ideas of 'local straightness' that enable students to embody coherent ideas of continuity, differentiability and non-differentiability in a natural manner.

The three-world framework offers extensional blends of a range of theoretical frameworks. For example, van Hiele's structural theory of recognition, description, definition, deduction in geometry can be extended to all three worlds of mathematics. It also offers an extensional blend of the APOS theory of Dubinsky and the structural-operational duality of Sfard. Each of these remains a coherent contribution to the evolution of theoretical frameworks. However, the blending of van Hiele theory and the operational and structural framework of Sfard now extends to the full development of mathematical thinking through embodiment, symbolism and formalism.

There is a huge range of theories blending together various different representations from the American calculus reform movement proposing the pragmatic 'rule of three' that 'wherever possible topics should be taught graphically and numerically, as well as analytically'[5] to general theories of representation such as the semiotic theories of Peirce[6], Saussure[7], Duval[8] and many others. The three-world format offers a distinct blending of such theories with the individual cognitive and affective development through the full development of mathematical thinking. Aspects that are in common and aspects that are at variance should be considered in terms of the differing contexts where ideas that are problematic in one context may be supportive in another.

General theories of social constructivism focussing on the individual operating in society originated by Vygotsky[9] and developed in various forms by others[10] see learning as a social activity. A blend of cognitive, affective and social developments of mathematics offers the potential to evolve a broader theory.

---

[5] Hughes-Hallett (1991), p. 121.
[6] Peirce (ed. Hoopes) (1991).
[7] Saussure (1916).
[8] For example, Duval (1995).
[9] Vygotsky (1962, 1978).
[10] For example, Ernest (1998); Glasersfeld (1995).

The beautiful notion of situated cognition[11] shows a fundamentally meaningful way of enabling a novice to learn the practice of the expert through an apprenticeship. It is a profound method of learning to operate in a particular community of practice. However, the three-world conception of transition and problematic met-before reveals that, as the concepts of mathematics become sophisticated, there are significant problematic changes in meaning that must be addressed to move to another plane of mathematical thinking. Unlike an apprentice carpenter, who can observe the actions of an expert applying his trade, an apprentice mathematician cannot see what is going on inside an expert mathematician's head. However, a teacher with an insight into the possible problematic met-befores that impede a child's development can seek to develop new strategies to help learners make sense of new situations in new ways. In this way, a blend of the framework in this book and situated cognition offers richer insight than either theory operating on its own.

The continuing disputes in the 'Math Wars' in the United States contrasts traditional approaches 'learning the basics' as a foundation for more technical and theoretical mathematics with a constructivist approach in which children are encouraged to construct their own knowledge of mathematics. The three-world framework offers an extensional blend of both viewpoints, incorporating the crystalline concepts of mathematics and the personal struggle to construct mathematical ideas. It enhances the traditional approach by acknowledging the existence of problematic met-befores. At the same time it offers the constructivist approach a theory of compression of knowledge and an analysis of problematic met-befores that encourages teachers to act as mentors to guide children to grasp powerful mathematical ideas by making sense of personal constructions.

The Dutch project for 'realistic mathematics education' was introduced to build on the learner's experience and to replace an earlier mechanistic system of teaching routine procedures.[12] It provides the child with a realistic context in which to make sense of ideas that are often performed in a practical situation. Yet, as time passed, it was found that, at university level in the Netherlands, remedial classes needed to be introduced because more students lacked the necessary skills for advanced work in mathematics and its applications.[13]

---

[11] Lave & Wenger (1991).
[12] See lecture by Marja van den Heuvel-Panhuizen. Retrieved from http://www.fi.uu.nl/en/rme/ (Accessed February 14, 2013).
[13] Information supplied by my colleague Nellie Verhoef, based on articles in Dutch: Craats (2007); Tempelaar & Caspers (2008); Werkgroep 3TU (2006).

The Dutch translation of the verb 'to imagine' is 'zich ***realise***ren', emphasizing that what matters is not the real-world context but the realization of *the reality in the student's mind*, which Wilensky expressed as the personal quality of the mental relationship with the object under consideration.[14]

The three-world framework not only sees practical mathematics related to real-world problems, but it also offers a theoretical framework to realize ideas in conceptual embodiment that transcend specific examples and blend with flexible operational symbolism.

The Japanese development of lesson study involves carefully prepared lessons to encourage learners to interact with new ideas in personal ways that make sense. It is based on an aesthetic appreciation of mathematical ideas translated into supportive activities for developing children's conceptions. It may be further enhanced by blending lesson study with an appreciation of supportive and problematic aspects that arise in the long-term cognitive and affective development through embodiment, symbolism and increasingly sophisticated reason.

The three-world framework offers new insight to students making sense of the calculus, building on the dynamic embodiment of the changing slope of a locally straight graph blended with the operational symbolism using good-enough arithmetic and precise symbolism. Even though many approaches advocate real-world applications as a basis, they have many different physical meanings. For instance, in dynamic motion, distance varies with time, its derivative is a velocity, the second derivative is acceleration, and the third derivative is sometimes said to be a 'jerk'[15] as a (sudden) change in acceleration. Higher levels soon become even more complicated. The successive meanings can have unintended problematic meanings. For example, in simple harmonic motion, if the distance is $\sin t$, the velocity is $\cos t$, the acceleration $-\sin t$ and the derivative of acceleration is $-\cos t$. In what sense is this smooth acceleration a 'jerk'?

Local straightness is a natural embodied concept that allows a learner to conceptualize the difference between continuity, differentiability and what it means to be non-differentiable. When successive derivatives are locally straight, the same embodied process of finding the slope of the successive curves can be carried on leading to power series that relate all the

[14] Wilensky (1993), p. 58.
[15] See, for example, http://math.ucr.edu/home/baez/physics/General/jerk.html (Accessed March 6, 2011).

standard functions together in a single crystalline knowledge structure that generalizes naturally in higher dimensions.

More generally, the full range of embodied and symbolic mathematics in school may be seen as a foundation to natural and formal ideas in axiomatic formalism wherein structure theorems return to human embodiment and symbolism, uniting the whole of mathematical thinking into a single framework.

6. Implications for Teaching

The three-world framework offers a vision of the whole development of mathematical thinking taking into account the emotional effects of supportive and problematic met-befores that encourage or impede learning in more sophisticated contexts. This suggests the need to devise ways of teaching and learning that enable very different learners to make personal sense of the mathematics in coherent ways.

The empirical data detailed in this book emphasize that, throughout the development of the school curriculum, learners need to make appropriate sense of ideas and develop fluency in operation. The challenge for the curriculum designer and the teacher is how to manage the enterprise so that every learner can maximize his or her potential.

Various approaches are possible with different kinds of interaction between teacher and learner and different consequences for learning. At one end of the spectrum is traditional *transmission* of knowledge focusing on the teacher as the giver of knowledge to the learner. At the other is the *discovery* of knowledge focusing on the learner as the agent of learning with the teacher providing the management and working environment. However, this should not be seen as a dichotomy. A third approach is a *connectionist* blend in which the teacher works as a mentor to encourage the students to make connections that help them make sense of the mathematics.

In a practical study of the effectiveness of these three possibilities, a group of teachers was given a questionnaire designed to categorize them into one or more of the three approaches.[16] The results of their teaching were judged by the performance of their pupils on standardized national tests, classifying the teachers as moderately effective, effective and highly effective. Of the nine students having one main approach, the five connectionist teachers were all highly effective, while the two transmission and two discovery teachers were moderately effective. Of the seven teachers

[16] Askew et al. (1997).

Table 15.1. *The effectiveness of different teaching styles*

Teacher style	Highly effective	Effective	Moderately effective
Connectionist	5	–	–
Transmission	–	–	2
Discovery	–	–	2
Mixed	1	4	2

with no strong orientation, one was highly effective, four effective and two moderately effective. (Table 15.1.)[17]

This small study is consistent with the hypothesis that a strong orientation to connectionist teaching is likely to be more effective than a mixed variety of methods and this is in turn may be more effective than a focus only on transmission or only on discovery.

The three-world framework encourages a connectionist approach and provides a theoretical framework for the teacher to be aware of the specific cognitive and affective aspects involved in making sense of new mathematical ideas.

7. Thinking Rationally

It is clear that strong differences of opinion exist and disputes continue throughout the ages. However, the resolution of these disputes requires more than the triumph of one approach over another. We are all intent on improving mathematics teaching and learning, but we have different opinions as to what is important.

A learner may wish to understand the ideas, or at least to succeed in tests. A teacher may aspire to help learners understand the ideas. Faced with assessment from external examinations the goal may be to help them to perform well on the tests. Parents will want their children to do well, as will politicians whose aim is to produce visible success that will give them credit and lead to their re-election. A university mathematician seeking good students for undergraduate degrees will want those who can perform well in university mathematics courses and perhaps go on to mathematical research. But success in examinations requires more than learning techniques to obtain a good mark; in the longer term, it means developing the flexibility to conquer new challenges.

[17] Askew et al. (1997), p. 345.

The evolutionary framework of the three worlds of mathematics is based on the fundamentals of human thinking – how we make connections and build knowledge structures that grow in sophistication. As this happens, new ideas that prove to be useful are strengthened and old ideas that are superseded are lost. Sophisticated adults may no longer remember the details of their earlier development and may not appreciate the full needs of a learner.[18] Some who recall their struggles in mathematics may advocate the need to work hard 'to learn the basics', which may mean heavy doses of rote learning and practice without an initial appreciation of the need to make sense of the ideas as learning takes place. Others may enjoy solving problems and elevate problem solving above the mere learning of techniques. Professional mathematicians may focus on the essential role of definition and proof to formulate coherent mathematical theories.

There is a need for all of us involved in the learning of mathematics to be aware of the broader picture of mathematical growth, so that we can combine together for the greater good of each individual learner while taking account of the varied needs of different aspects of society.

Epilogue

In this book we have together climbed the mathematical mountain, from the thinking of the newborn child to the highest levels of mathematical research. The journey travels through a complex landscape with many possible routes, where some may follow paths that lead to powerful crystalline concepts and increasingly sophisticated knowledge structures, while others find their pathways difficult to climb. Compression of knowledge makes the baggage that we carry lighter to bear.

In school mathematics the framework offers a positive way forward, blending embodiment and symbolism, while being aware of the problematic aspects that require attention to enable the learner to make sense of new situations. The framework recognizes the need to balance embodied meaning with operational fluency to provide an emotionally positive sense of growth in mathematical thinking, building from practical experiences to theoretical ways of reasoning.

At more advanced levels it emphasizes the difference between applications of mathematics – which often needs only theoretical ideas blending embodiment with symbolism – and pure mathematics that leads on to

---

[18] See, for example, Johnson (1989, p. 219); Thurston (1994, p. 947); Freudenthal (1983, p. 469).

formal thinking and its greater generality. Structure theorems return the greater generality of formalism to the practical and theoretical bases of natural embodiment and symbolism.

The framework of three worlds of mathematics offers a broad picture of development of mathematical thinking from the newborn child to the frontiers of research through perception, operation and increasingly sophisticated forms of reason, taking account of supportive met-befores, that encourage generalization, and problematic met-befores, that impede progress. The theory formulates a framework for the long-term development of mathematical thinking that operates not only in the individual but also in the evolution of mathematics over the centuries. It also offers the possibility of blending with a range of other theoretical frameworks that encourage emerging insights that allow us to evolve more sophisticated insights.

It reveals how the sensori-motor and linguistic capabilities of a biological brain evolve into the creative thinking processes of a mathematical mind.

Appendix: Where It All Came From

The ideas in this book blend together a theoretical growth over many years. Here I trace the origins of the main ideas.

The early analysis of human thought in relation to mathematics includes the fundamental ideas of Aristotle and Plato with the human perception of potential infinity and the perfect existence of Platonic thought. Descartes shifted thinking to focus on the interaction between the physical brain and the spiritual mind. In his *Critique of Pure Reason*[1] Kant considered the way in which the brain contemplates the outside world and introduced the term 'schema' to describe the mental pattern that could delineate a general concept such as 'dog' as opposed to specific perceptions of individual dogs.

In the late nineteenth and early twentieth centuries two developments occurred, the first being the introduction of *The Principles of Psychology*[2] by William James and the second, the publication of occasional books in which mathematicians reflected on the nature of mathematical thinking, such as Poincaré's *Science and Hypothesis*[3]. In particular, Poincaré distinguished two kinds of mathematical thinking, one preoccupied by logic, advancing carefully step by step, the other guided by intuition, making quick but sometimes precarious advances. It was this that stirred my interest in the distinction between the ideas of formal and embodied ways of thinking.

In his *Psychology of Invention in the Mathematical Field*[4] of 1945, Hadamard noted that mathematical thinking had been studied previously either by

---

[1] Kant (1781).
[2] James (1890).
[3] Poincaré (1913) [quotation taken from page 210 of the University Press of America edition, 1982].
[4] Hadamard (1945).

specialists in psychology or by mathematicians and sought a new synthesis of mathematics and psychology.

In the 1960s, as I began my interest in mathematical thinking as a subject of study, few theoretical frameworks existed. The prominent figure in educational theory at the time was Piaget, who pioneered the simple strategy of talking to children and listening carefully as they responded to subtly designed questions. This led to two major developments. One was an overall stage theory from birth to adulthood, through stages called sensori-motor, preconceptual, concrete operational and formal operational. The other was a local development of concepts in which operations at one level became conceived as objects of thought at the next level. He also described three distinct forms of abstraction: *empirical abstraction* from abstracting the properties of objects, *pseudo-empirical abstraction* through focusing on the actions on those objects and *reflective abstraction* through reflection on mental actions on mental objects. Here, in embryo, is a possible starting point for the three worlds of mathematics, with empirical abstraction related to the categorization of shape and space, pseudo-empirical abstraction focusing on operations that become symbolized as numbers and generalized in algebra, and reflective abstraction leading to successively more sophisticated ways of thinking, culminating in the mathematics of formal definition and proof.

The other major pioneer at the time was Jerome Bruner, who in his 1966 book *Towards a Theory of Instruction*[5], formulated a theory of three different modes of representation: the *enactive*, through action, the *iconic* using visual and other sensory organization, and the *symbolic* through words or language. He also signaled two special forms of symbolism: number and logic. Here again we have forerunners of the embodied (enactive and iconic), the symbolic (this time focused on number and algebra) and the formal (focused on logic).

In geometry, Pierre Van Hiele (1959)[6] considered the stage theory of Piaget and decided he needed a theory of development in geometry that focused not only on learning but also on teaching, specifying his sequence of levels that is adopted in the three worlds framework. Over the years different authors modified the names of the levels and I chose to use the terms *recognition*, *description*, *definition* and *Euclidean deduction*, to fit with my own analysis, followed by a level of *rigor* in the axiomatic formal world.

---

[5] Bruner (1966).
[6] Van Hiele's theory as first announced in van Hiele (1959). A later version appeared in van Hiele (1986).

In algebra, Zoltan Dienes (1960)[7] saw the way in which actions are symbolized and thought of as mental objects, speaking of predicates in one sentence becoming subjects in another, so that the predicate in the sentence 'I am *adding 3 and 2*' becomes the subject in the sentence '*adding 3 and 2* gives 5.' In the seventies, when I came across this idea, I was very taken by it, but could not get beyond the idea that 'adding' becomes 'sum' and 'repeated adding' gives 'multiplication' that becomes 'product' and repeated multiplication becomes 'power'.

In the late seventies and early eighties I took to studying undergraduate thinking in mathematics and found the phenomenon that most students (and teachers in secondary schools) believed that the infinite decimal 0.999… is 'just less than one'. At first I was bewildered by this, but then began to realize it may relate to the view of the infinite decimal as an ongoing approximation (which never reached 1 in a finite time) rather than the limiting value 1 itself.

By 1980, I had a huge collection of data revealing intriguing student responses in the calculus and mathematical analysis but lacked a coherent theory to make sense of it. Then Shlomo Vinner visited with a paper he had written with Rina Hershkowitz on concept image and concept definition in geometry.[8] Immediately I saw the students' problems were related not to the definitions they were using but to their concept image. The joint paper with Shlomo was written on *Concept definition and concept image with particular reference to limits and continuity.*[9]

At this point, I learnt of the work of Bernard Cornu (1981),[10] who had studied students working on limits and the calculus and concluded that they were thinking of quantities that were 'arbitrarily small but not zero'. He introduced me to the earlier work of Bachelard (1938)[11] on 'epistemological obstacles', which are ideas that worked in an earlier context but no longer work in a new context. He focused on 'spontaneous conceptions' that arose when students interpreted new ideas based on their intuitive knowledge that remained with them and could cause significant problems later on.

At the time, I was teaching a course on development of mathematical concepts and had focused on the idea of infinitesimals. David Pimm, then an undergraduate, pressed me to give a course on infinitesimal calculus and

---

[7] Dienes (1960).
[8] Vinner & Hershkowitz (1980).
[9] Tall & Vinner (1981).
[10] Cornu (1981).
[11] Bachelard (1938).

I realized that, under infinite magnification, the graph of a differentiable function would reveal an infinite straight line. This gave me the confidence to begin a 'locally straight' approach to the calculus and by 1982, desktop computers arrived with decent colour graphics and I programmed *Graphic Calculus* software to enable the ideas of calculus to be investigated visually.

In 1986 I completed a second doctorate with Richard Skemp on *Building and testing a locally straight approach to the calculus.* This included concepts such as 'generic limits' and 'generic tangents' that formulated how human beings think of limiting concepts as being 'typical of the process of getting close' rather than the strict mathematical definition. My ideas here built heavily on Leibniz's principle of continuity, that the limit object had the same properties as the objects in the limiting process.

At this time I met Ed Dubinsky. whose APOS theory approach to learning mathematics based on Piaget's notion of encapsulation of process to object unlocked my earlier blockage with Dienes' ideas turning addition to sum, multiplication to product, repeated multiplication to power. Now I began to see encapsulation everywhere. However, Dubinsky did not trust visualization and his approach focused on performing processes that were programmed on a computer and encapsulated as objects by turning them into functions that could be used as inputs to other functions.

A range of researchers were by this time turning their attention to university mathematics, and Gontran Ervynck formed a working group that he termed 'advanced mathematical thinking' that eventually produced a book that I edited entitled *Advanced Mathematical Thinking.*[12]

I also met Anna Sfard, who was working on her own PhD thesis combining an operational approach through performing calculations to a structural approach with mental objects. In 1990 she stayed at my home for several weeks on sabbatical leave and we attempted to put together our ideas, combining her operational and structural thinking with my research on the transition from secondary school to university where I had studied the transition to formal mathematical thinking. Anna had given an example of structural thinking from a book I had written with Ian Stewart, *Complex Analysis,*[13] and I believed that she used the term 'structural' to refer to the structural mathematics of axioms and definitions. She declared that this was different from her use of the term 'structural', which referred more to the properties of the structure of objects. A further discussion of her use of the term 'condensation' to refer to a sequence of steps being conceived as an

[12] Tall (1991c).
[13] Stewart & Tall (1983).

overall process led me to suggesting the term 'crystallization' to represent the compression of a process into a manipulable concept. There was already a question of whether to use the terms 'encapsulation' or 'reification' at the time, so a further suggestion was not welcomed. The term 'crystallization' lay dormant in my mind for nearly twenty years before it was used in the current theory.

At the same time, Eddie Gray, already an experienced teacher of children in primary and secondary schools, was completing his PhD on how young children performed calculations in arithmetic. If they were asked a simple question such as 13 − 9, if they did not know the answer, how did they do it? Did they use some method of counting or relating the problem to other facts such as knowing 9 is one less than 10, so the difference is 4? Now we saw that this represented two quite different ways of thinking, one using counting processes, and the other manipulating number concepts. The idea of 'procept' suddenly occurred. It linked dramatically with all my earlier experiences of processes encapsulated as concepts through the ideas of Dienes, Dubinsky and Sfard. Procept theory was born.

Meanwhile, I met a young Rafael Núñez who had produced an amazing analysis of limiting concepts in his own PhD thesis, and we talked about generic limits and the Leibniz principle of continuity that was later generalized into the Basic Metaphor of Infinity.

In 1991, the book *Advanced Mathematical Thinking*[14] was published and in its final chapter I returned to the question of two distinct forms of mathematical thinking, one represented by Shlomo Vinner and others on concept images leading to definitions and proofs, another represented by Ed Dubinsky and others on encapsulation of process as object.

In 1992, I met John Pegg at a conference in Australia. He was deeply involved in the SOLO taxonomy of Biggs and Collis and in the Van Hiele theory of development in geometry. This enlivened my interest in these theories. In particular, SOLO taxonomy, designed as a way of classifying observed learning outcomes, was another example of the combination of global and local theories. The global theory considered the long-term cognitive development of the child, based on a combination of Piaget and Bruner, with successive modes of operation called sensori-motor, ikonic, concrete-symbolic, formal and post-formal. This theory saw successive modes incorporating earlier forms, so that the ikonic mode would include the sensori-motor and allow a more sophisticated mode incorporating both. The lines between different modes had minor differences from those

[14] Tall (1991c).

of Piaget (for example, Biggs and Collis noted that the first part of Piaget's formal mode had more in common with the latter part of the concrete-operational mode, so the concrete-operational mode was extended to include it). There was also an extra 'post-formal' mode that was hypothesized to occur later. This encouraged the idea of the categorization of the three worlds. The sensori-motor and ikonic modes were extended by verbal definition and deduction through to Euclidean proof. The concrete-symbolic corresponded to a mode focusing on the manipulation of symbols as process and concept. The later formalism and post-formalism corresponded to the higher levels of definition and deduction in embodiment and symbolism and later to the axiomatic formal world, which grows in sophistication from formal deduction to more sophisticated knowledge structures based on structure theorems.

The local structure of SOLO taxonomy saw a cycle of development in each mode of operation, from unistructural, through multistructural, relational and on to extended abstract that becomes the unistructural level of the next cycle. John Pegg saw more than one local cycle in individual modes and together we worked towards the local cycles being related to the formation of individual thinkable concepts rather than to the whole mode of operation.[15]

In 1992 I contracted an illness that kept me off work for more than a year and I returned to take study leave and, after giving my inaugural lecture in 1994, I was unable to maintain a full day's work and retired to work for one-third of the time as a professor. This involved a little undergraduate teaching and a full range of PhD supervisions. Many of these PhD studies provided extra data for the developing theory in this text.

In 1997 I worked with a group including Michael Thomas, Gary Davis and Adrian Simpson on the question: *What is the object of a mathematical process?* This separated out the structural mode of Sfard from the axiomatic thinking in formal mathematics and gave at least three distinct ways of forming mathematical concepts.[16] In 2001, Eddie Gray and I published a paper identifying such mathematical concepts in the following terms:

> One is the *embodied object*, as in geometry and graphs that begin with physical foundations and steadily develop more abstract mental pictures through the subtle hierarchical use of language. Another is the *symbolic procept* which acts seamlessly to switch from a 'mental concept to manipulate' to an often unconscious 'process to carry out' using an appropriate cognitive algorithm.

---

[15] See, for example, Pegg & Tall (2005).
[16] See Tall, Davis & Thomas (1997) and Tall, Davis, Thomas, et al. (2000).

The third is an *axiomatic concept* in advanced mathematical thinking where verbal/symbolical axioms are used as a basis for a logically constructed theory. (Here the fourth type of concept might occur by distinguishing between those concepts evolving from embodied objects and those from encapsulated processes.)[17]

These three (or four) modes of forming mathematical concepts were in the air for several years, being discussed in seminars with graduate students at Warwick. Then, working with Anna Poynter on her PhD, studying students learning about vectors, we were speaking about the distinctions between vectors as arrows with magnitude and direction and vectors as symbolic coordinates operating with matrices. I also had in mind the knowledge that axiomatic vectors were defined formally without any structure of magnitude and direction with linear functions that need not be formulated as matrices. Suddenly I saw that there were *three different worlds of mathematics*: the *embodied*, the *symbolic* and the *formal*.

Anna and I worked on these ideas for several years. A major breakthrough came when she told me of the work of one of her students, Joshua, who looked at the embodied representation of a free vector and said that 'the sum of two vectors is the single vector that has the same effect.' In other words, if a free vector is represented by the translation of an object on a flat surface, the sum of two translations has the same effect as a single translation from the starting position of the first to the final position of the second. This chance remark had an enormous theoretical consequence. It offered an *embodied* way of encapsulating the sum of two vectors into a single entity by focusing not on the steps of the process, but on the embodied effect. This unified operations in embodiment and symbolism to provide a form of *embodied compression* where previously APOS theory focused mainly on *symbolic compression*.

However, the idea of 'three worlds of mathematics' required far more detailed working before it was released to the world. There were so many other interpretations of the nature of mathematical thinking: the embodied theory of Lakoff where the term 'embodied' meant something different, the semiotics of Peirce where the term 'symbolic' has a different meaning, and the theory of Piaget where 'formal' has a different meaning. In Peirce's theory of semiotics, a symbol is one of three kinds of sign used by human beings: an *icon*, which serves to convey ideas of the things they represent simply by imitating them; an *index* that indicates a connection,

---

[17] Gray & Tall (2005).

such as a signpost or an exclamation such as 'hi there' that alerts attention; and a *symbol* or general sign that becomes associated with their meanings by usage, such as words, phrases, speeches, books and libraries.[18] Likewise there are rich theories of *representations* and the *registers* of Duval,[19] which relate to a range of modes of operation, be they gestural, written, spoken, graphic, numeric, algebraic or involve different forms of language, be it everyday language or a more precise use of logical or formal language. These have many points of contact with the framework of three worlds of mathematics with embodiment, symbolism and formalism. What I have attempted to do is to use a small number of categories to produce a viable framework for the growth of mathematical thinking. It is here presented as building from three fundamental set-befores of recognition, repetition and language that lead to three distinct forms of cognitive growth. As I worked on these ideas, I realized the fundamental nature of what I now termed 'the sensori-motor language of mathematics' that united all three into a single theory in which language is used to express sophisticated ideas building out of human perception and action.

In the last two decades, modern neurophysiology has steadily produced more scientific evidence of the mind as the workings of the biological brain. I took great inspiration from popular books of recent years, particularly Gerald Edelman's Darwinian view expressed in *Bright Air, Brilliant Fire* (1992)[20], Francis Crick's fundamental assertion that the mind and soul arise from the workings of the biological brain in *The Astonishing Hypothesis* (1994)[21], Terence Deacon's *Symbolic Species* (1997)[22], and Merlin Donald's seminal analysis of human consciousness from selective binding through dynamic local awareness to extended awareness over a longer time in *A Mind So Rare* (2001)[23]. Meanwhile over two decades, George Lakoff developed a focus on metaphor as a fundamental basis of human thought in *Metaphors We Live By* (Lakoff and Johnson, 1980)[24] and *Women, Fire and Dangerous Things* (1987)[25], *Philosophy in the Flesh* (Lakoff and Johnson 1999)[26], and *Where Mathematics Comes From* (Lakoff and Núñez, 2000)[27].

---

[18] From the writings of Charles Sanders Peirce, 1895. Retrieved from: http://www.marxists.org/reference/subject/philosophy/works/us/peirce1.htm (Accessed August 1, 2010).
[19] Duval (1995).
[20] Edelman (1992).
[21] Crick (1994).
[22] Deacon (1997).
[23] Donald (2001).
[24] Lakoff & Johnson (1980).
[25] Lakoff (1987).
[26] Lakoff & Johnson (1999).
[27] Lakoff & Núñez (2000).

Lakoff and Núñez saw thoughts being built on grounded metaphors from interaction with the outside world, definitional metaphors that formulated these ideas in mathematical terms and linking metaphors that connected together metaphors in the mind. However, there was no emphasis on the notion of *compression* of knowledge that plays such an important part in mathematical thinking where operations performed in time are symbolized and compressed into thinkable concepts. The first combination of compression and blending that I encountered came in the book of Fauconnier and Turner, *The Way We Think: Conceptual Blending and the Mind's Hidden Complexities* (2002)[28].

A range of theories were now available, including APOS theory that focused more on symbolic and formal compression than on embodiment, and operational-structural theory that would benefit from a refinement to distinguish the role of structure both in embodiment and in formalism. The result was the production of three categories that cover the development of mathematical thinking from the birth of a child through personal routes that lead in many directions, including journeys to the boundaries of mathematical research. The 'three worlds of mathematics' were formulated to take account of the three distinct long-term developments of mathematical thinking through embodiment, symbolism and formalism.

I used the term 'met-before' for several years informally, noting how it seemed to 'make sense' to a range of others before setting it down in print. The term 'set-before' was also used in a general sense to represent aspects that are essentially 'set before' our birth and blossom naturally in the early years. It was only early in 2008 that I realized that the set-befores of *recognition* and *repetition* were fundamental to mathematical thinking, using *language* to give rise to *categorization* of recognized phenomena, *encapsulation* of actions as thinkable concepts and *definition* in embodiment, symbolism and axiomatic formalism.

The notion of *crystalline concept* came in mid-2009 after discussions about parsimony with Boris Koichu and a remark by Walter Whiteley about the interdependence of the properties of an isosceles triangle, where any one of a range of *equivalent* properties defined the concept. This led to the sudden realization that the three worlds of mathematics all followed the same basic development from the complication of multi-structural phenomena, through the relational structure of various properties, the equivalence of certain properties and the inevitable crystalline structure of Platonic figures in geometry, procepts in arithmetic and algebra and defined concepts

---

[28] Fauconnier & Turner (2002).

in axiomatic mathematics. Honor is due to Kevin Collis and John Pegg for their work on SOLO taxonomy with its sequence of compression from unistructural responses, through multistructural, relational and extended abstract that I now see in terms of the crystalline concepts at the highest levels of mathematical thinking.

Additional consolidation of the theory arose even later, with the realization that the idea of three (or four) ways of forming mathematical concepts originally published with Eddie Gray in 2001 could be reorganized to give a fourth kind of abstraction that I called 'Platonic abstraction' that extended Piaget's three forms of abstraction to give a bigger picture, which could then be re-categorized as two longer-term developments in the structural abstraction of properties of objects and the operational abstraction of actions becoming proceptual symbolism. The reflective abstraction of formal theories could then be re-categorized as formal abstraction through specifying systems of axioms and definitions from which other properties could be deduced by formal proof.

It was only in 2011, when Pierre van Hiele passed away at the grand old age of 100, that I explicitly realized something that I had 'known' all along: that the structural abstraction through *recognition*, *description*, *definition* and *deduction* applied successively to the three worlds as concepts in geometry, arithmetic and algebra, and formal mathematics were recognized, described, defined and deduced using appropriate forms of proof.

An even more recent significant insight has been the notion of supportive and problematic conceptions where each can contain both supportive and problematic aspects, formulated by my doctoral student Kin Eng Chin. This resonated so strongly with long-standing ideas from my own doctoral supervisor Richard Skemp, whose theory of goals and anti-goals offers enormous insight into the spectrum of confidence and anxiety that arise in individual attitudes to mathematics. Now I could truly integrate the cognitive and affective in our human construction of mathematical ideas. Even the most sophisticated mathematicians with highly supportive knowledge structures that enable them to perform expertly in mathematics have problematic aspects in their thinking. These may be suppressed because other supportive aspects enable them to operate effectively, or they may be reflected upon to develop new ideas in mathematical research. Meanwhile, those who are deeply anxious about mathematics have some supportive aspects that they may cling to, even if it is only counting on fingers. Differing communities of practice develop their own ways of working but they may benefit from realizing aspects of other theories that can be blended together to give new insight.

In this way, the evolution of our understanding of how humans learn to think mathematically continues, from generation to generation, into the future.

References

Akkoc, H., & Tall, D. O. (2002). The simplicity, complexity and complication of the function concept. In Anne D. Cockburn & Elena Nardi (Eds.), *Proceedings of the 26th Conference of the International Group for the Psychology of Mathematics Education*, 2, 25–32. Norwich, UK.

Alcock, L. J., & Simpson, A. P. (2004). Convergence of sequences and series: Interactions between visual reasoning and the learner's beliefs about their own role. *Educational Studies in Mathematics*, 57, 1–32.

  (2005). Convergence of sequences and series 2: Interactions between non-visual reasoning and the learner's beliefs about their own role. *Educational Studies in Mathematics*, 58, 77–110.

Alcock, L., & Weber, K. (2004). Semantic and syntactic proof productions. *Educational Studies in Mathematics*, 56, 209–34.

Alexander, L., & Martray, C. (1989). The development of an abbreviated version of the Mathematics Anxiety Rating Scale. *Measurement and Evaluation in Counseling and Development*, 22, 143–50.

Argand, R. (1806). *Essai sur une manière de représenter les quantités imaginaires dans les constructions géométriques*. 1st ed., Paris. 2nd ed. reprinted, Paris: Albert Blanchard, 1971.

Ashcraft, M. H., & Kirk, E. P. (2001). The relationships among working memory, math anxiety, and performance. *Journal of Experimental Psychology*, 130(2), 224–37.

Asiala, M., Brown, A., DeVries, D., Dubinsky, E., Mathews, D., & Thomas, K. (1996). A framework for research and curriculum development in undergraduate mathematics education. *Research in Collegiate Mathematics Education II*, *CBMS Issues in Mathematics Education*, 6, 1–32.

Askew, M., Brown, M., Rhodes, V., Johnson, D., & Wiliam, D. (1997). *Effective Teachers of Numeracy, Final Report of a Study Carried Out for the Teacher Training Agency 1995–96 by the School of Education*, King's College, London.

Atiyah, M. F. (2004). *Collected Works*. Vol. 6. Oxford: Clarendon Press.

Ausubel, D. P., Novak, J., & Hanesian, H. (1978). *Educational Psychology: A Cognitive View* (2nd ed.). New York: Holt, Rinehart & Winston.

Bachelard, G. (1938, reprinted 1983). *La formation de l'esprit scientifique*. Paris: J. Vrin.

Bakar, M. N., & Tall, D. O. (1992). Students' mental prototypes for functions and graphs. *International Journal of Mathematics Education in Science & Technology*, 23(1), 39–50.

Baron, R., Earhard, B., & Ozier, M. (1995). *Psychology* (Canadian edition). Scarborough, ON: Allyn & Bacon.

Baroody, A. J., & Costlick, R. T. (1998). *Fostering Children's Mathematical power: An Investigative Approach to K–8 Mathematics Instruction*. Mahwah, NJ: Lawrence Erlbaum.

Barrow, I. (1670). *Lectiones Geometricae*, translated by Child (1916). *The Geometrical Lectures of Isaac Barrow*. Chicago and London: OpenCourt.

Bartlett, F. C. (1932). *Remembering*. Cambridge: Cambridge University Press.

Bayazit, I. (2006). *The Relationship between Teaching and Learning the Function Concept*. PhD thesis, University of Warwick.

Berkeley, G. (1734). *The Analyst* (ed. D. R. Wilkins, 2002). Retrieved from www.maths.tcd.ie/pub/HistMath/People/Berkeley/Analyst/Analyst.pdf (Accessed April 21, 2012).

Bernstein, A., & Robinson, A. (1966). Solution of an invariant subspace problem of K. T. Smith and P. R. Halmos. *Pacific Journal of Mathematics*, 16(3), 421–31.

Beth, E. W., & Piaget, J. (1966). *Mathematical Epistemology and Psychology*, trans. by W. Mays. Dordrecht, The Netherlands: Reidel.

Betz, N. (1978). Prevalence, distribution, and correlates of math anxiety in college students. *Journal of Counseling Psychology*, 25(5), 441–8.

Biggs, J., & Collis, K. (1982). *Evaluating the Quality of Learning: The SOLO Taxonomy*. New York: Academic Press.

Birkhoff, G., & MacLane, S. (1999). *Algebra* (3rd ed.). Providence RI: Chelsea Publishing Co., American Mathematical Society.

Bitner, J., Austin, S., & Wadlington, E. (1994). A comparison of math anxiety in traditional and nontraditional developmental college students. *Research and Teaching in Developmental Education*, 10(2), 35–43.

Blokland, P., & Giessen, C. (2000). *Graphic Calculus for Windows*. Retrieved from: http://www.vusoft2.nl (Accessed February 19, 2013).

Boyer, C. B. (1923/1939). *The History of the Calculus and Its Conceptual Development*. Reprinted by Dover, New York.

Breidenbach, D., Dubinsky, E., Hawks, J., & Nichols, D. (1992). Development of the process conception of function. *Educational Studies in Mathematics*, 23, 247–85.

Bruner, J. S. (1966). *Towards a Theory of Instruction*. Cambridge, MA: Harvard University Press.
  (1977). *The Process of Education* (2nd ed.). Cambridge, MA: Harvard University Press.

Burn, R. P. (1992). *Numbers and Functions: Steps into Analysis*. Cambridge: Cambridge University Press.

Burns, M. (1998). *Math: Facing an American Phobia*. Sausalito, CA: Math Solutions Publications.

Burton, L. (2002). Recognising commonalities and reconciling differences in mathematics education. *Educational Studies in Mathematics*, 50(2), 157–75.

Byers, W. (2007). *How Mathematicians Think*. Princeton, NJ: Princeton University Press.

Campbell, K., & Evans, C. (1997). Gender issues in the classroom: A comparison of mathematics anxiety. *Education*, 117(3), 332–9.

Cantor, G. (1872). Uber die Ausdehnung eines Satzes aus der Theorie der trigonometrischen Reihen. *Mathematische Annalen*, 5, 123–32. Reproduced in G. Cantor, *Gesammelte Abhandlungen mathematischen und philosophischen Inhalts*, ed. E. Zermelo. Berlin: J. Springer, 1932, pp. 92–102. Reprinted Hildesheim: Olms.

Cardano, G. (1545). *Ars magna*. Translated and published as *Ars Magna or The Rules of Algebra* (1993). New York: Dover.

Chace, A. B. (1927–1929). *The Rhind Mathematical Papyrus: Free Translation and Commentary with Selected Photographs, Translations, Transliterations and Literal Translations.* Classics in Mathematics Education 8. 2 vols. Oberlin: Mathematical Association of America. (Reprinted Reston: National Council of Teachers of Mathematics, 1979).

Challenger, M. (2009). *From Triangles to a Concept: A Phenomenographic Study of A–level Students' Development of the Concept of Trigonometry*. PhD thesis, University of Warwick.

Chin, E. T. (2002). *Building and Using Concepts of Equivalence Class and Partition*. PhD thesis, University of Warwick.

Chin, E. T., & Tall, D. O. (2001). Developing formal mathematical concepts over time. In M. van den Heuvel-Panhuizen (Ed.), *Proceedings of the 25th Conference of the International Group for the Psychology of Mathematics Education*, 2, 241–8. Norwich, UK.

   (2002). University students embodiment of quantifier. In Anne D. Cockburn & Elena Nardi (Eds.), *Proceedings of the 26th Conference of the International Group for the Psychology of Mathematics Education*, 4, 273–80. Norwich, UK.

Chin, K. E., & Tall, D. O. (2012). Making sense of mathematics through perception, operation and reason: The case of trigonometric functions. *Proceedings of the 36th Conference of the International Group for the Psychology of Mathematics Education*, 4, 264. Full paper http://homepages.warwick.ac.uk/staff/David. Tall/pdfs/dot2012c-chin-making-sense.pdf (Accessed February 18, 2013).

Clement, J., Lochhead, J., & Monk, G. S. (1981). Translation difficulties in learning mathematics. *American Mathematics Monthly*, 4, 286–90.

Clements, D. H., & Battista, M. T. (1992). Geometry and spatial reasoning. In D. Grouws (Ed.) *Handbook of Research on Teaching and Learning Mathematics* (pp. 420–64). New York: Macmillan.

Collis, K. F. (1978). Operational thinking in elementary mathematics. In J. A. Keats, K. F. Collis, & G. S. Halford (Eds.), *Cognitive Development: Research Based on a Neo-Piagetian approach*. New York: John Wiley & Sons.

Cornu, B. (1981). Apprentissage de la notion de limite: Modèles spontanées et modèles propres, *Actes du Cinquième Colloque du Groupe Internationale PME*, Grenoble, France, 322–6.

   (1991). Limits. In D. O. Tall (Ed.), *Advanced Mathematical Thinking* (pp. 153–66). Dordrecht, The Netherlands: Kluwer.

Cottrill, J., Dubinsky, E., Nichols, D., Schwingendorf, K., Thomas, K., & Vidakovic, D. (1996). Understanding the limit concept: Beginning with a coordinated process scheme. *Journal of Mathematical Behavior*, 15(2), 167–92.

Courant, R. (1937). *Differential and Integral Calculus*. Vol. I. Translated from the German by E. J. McShane. Reprint of the second edition (1988). Wiley Classics Library. New York: Wiley-Interscience.

Craats, J. van de (2007). Contexten en eindexamens. *Euclides* 82(7), 261–6.

Crick, F. (1994). *The Astonishing Hypothesis*. London: Simon & Schuster.

Davis, P. J., & Hersh, R. (1981). *The Mathematical Experience*. Boston: Houghton Mifflin.

Davis, R. B. (1984). *Learning Mathematics: The Cognitive Science Approach to Mathematics Education*. Norwood, NJ: Ablex.

Deacon, T. (1997). *The Symbolic Species: The Co-evolution of Language and the Human Brain*. London: Penguin.

Dedekind, R. (1872). *Stetigkeit und irrationale Zahlen*. Braunschweig: Vieweg. Reproduced in R. Dedekind, *Gesammelte mathematische Werke*, eds. R. Fricke, E. Noether, & O. Ore. Braunschweig: Vieweg, 1930–1932.

DeMarois, P. (1998). *Facets and Layers of the Function Concept: The Case of College Algebra*. PhD thesis, University of Warwick.

De Morgan, A. (1831). *On the Study and Difficulties of Mathematics*. London: Society for the Diffusion of Useful Knowledge.

Descartes, R. (1641). *Meditations on First Philosophy* In *The Philosophical Writings of René Descartes*, trans. by J. Cottingham, R. Stoothoff, & D. Murdoch, Cambridge: Cambridge University Press, 1984.

  (1954). *The Geometry of René Descartes*, trans. by D. E. Smith & M. L. Latham. New York: Dover.

Dienes, Z. P. (1960). *Building Up Mathematics*. London: Hutchinson.

Donald, M. (2001). *A Mind So Rare*. New York: W. W. Norton.

Duffin, J. M., & Simpson, A. P. (1993). Natural, conflicting and alien. *Journal of Mathematical Behaviour*, 12(4), 313–28.

Duval, R. (1995). *Sémiosis et pensée humaine*. Bern, Switzerland: Peter Lang.

Edelman, G. M. (1992). *Bright air, brilliant fire*. New York: Basic Books.

Ernest, P. (1998). *Social Constructivism as a Philosophy of Mathematics*. Albany, NY: State University of New York Press.

Fauconnier, G., & Turner, M. (2002). *The Way We Think: Conceptual Blending and the Mind's Hidden Complexities*. New York: Basic Books.

Feynman, R. (1985). *Surely You're joking Mr Feynman*. New York: W. W. Norton. Reprinted 1992, London: Vintage.

Filloy, E., & Rojano, T. (1989). Solving equations: The transition from arithmetic to algebra. *For the Learning of Mathematics*, 9(2), 19–25.

Fischbein, E. (1987). *Intuition in Science and Mathematics: An Educational Approach*. Dordrecht, The Netherlands: Kluwer.

Foster, R. (2001). *Children's Use of Apparatus in the Development of the Concept of Number*. PhD thesis, University of Warwick.

Freudenthal, H. (1983). *Didactic Phenomenology of Mathematical Structures*. Dordrecht, The Netherlands: Reidel.

Furner, J. M., & Berman, B. T. (2003). Math anxiety: Overcoming a major obstacle to the improvement of student math performance. *Childhood Education*, Spring, 170–4.

Gauss, K. (1831). Theory of biquadratic residues, part 2. lecture presented to the Royal Society, Gottingen, April 23, 1831.

Glasersfeld, E. von (1995). *Radical Constructivism*. London: Routledge Falmer.

Gleason, A. M., & Hughes-Hallett, D. (1994). *Calculus*. New York: John Wiley & Sons.

Gödel, K. (1931). Über formal unentscheidbare Sätze der Principia Mathematica und verwandter Systeme, *Monatshefte für Mathematik und Physik*. Vol. 38. Available in English at http://home.ddc.net/ygg/etext/godel/ (Accessed February 19, 2013).

Gray, E. M. (1993). *Qualitatively Different Approaches to Simple Arithmetic*. PhD thesis, University of Warwick.

Gray, E. M., Pitta, D., Pinto, M. M. F., & Tall, D. O. (1999). Knowledge construction and diverging thinking in elementary and advanced mathematics. *Educational Studies in Mathematics*, 38(1–3), 111–33.

Gray, E. M., & Tall, D. O. (1991). Duality, ambiguity & flexibility in successful mathematical thinking In *Proceedings of the 15th Conference for the International Group for the Psychology of Mathematics Education*, 2, 72–9, Assisi, Italy.

(1994). Duality, ambiguity and flexibility: A proceptual view of simple arithmetic. *Journal for Research in Mathematics Education*, 26(2), 115–41.

(2001). Relationships between embodied objects and symbolic procepts: An explanatory theory of success and failure in mathematics. In Marja van den Heuvel-Panhuizen (Ed.), *Proceedings of the 25th Conference of the International Group for the Psychology of Mathematics Education*, 3, 65–72. Utrecht, The Netherlands.

Grice, H. P. (1989). *Studies in the Way of Words*. Cambridge, MA: Harvard University Press.

Gutiérrez, A., Jaime, A., & Fortuny, J. (1991). An alternative paradigm to evaluate the acquisition of the Van Hiele levels. *Journal for Research in Mathematics Education*, 22(3), 237–51.

Hadamard, J. (1945). *The Psychology of Invention in the Mathematical Field*. Princeton, NJ: Princeton University Press. Dover edition, New York, 1954.

Halmos, P. (1966). Invariant subspaces for polynomially compact operators. *Pacific Journal of Mathematics*, 16(3), 433–7.

Hart, K. M., Johnson, D. C., Brown, M., Dickson, L., & Clarkson, R. (1989). *Children's Mathematical Frameworks 8–13: A Study of Classroom Teaching*. London: Routledge (formerly NFER Nelson).

Heath, T. L. (1921). *History of Greek Mathematics*. Vol. 1. Oxford: Oxford University Press. Reprinted Dover Publications, New York, 1963.

Hembree, R. (1990). The nature, effects, and relief of mathematics anxiety. *Journal for Research in Mathematics Education*, 21(1), 33–46.

Herrmann, E., Call, J., Hernàndez-Lloreda, M. V., Hare, B., & Tomasello, M. (2007). Humans have evolved specialized skills of social cognition: The cultural intelligence hypothesis. *Science*, September 7, 2007, 317, 1360–6. Retrieved from:

http://www.sciencemag.org/cgi/reprint/317/5843/1360.pdf (Accessed April 6, 2012).

Heuvel-Panhuizen, M. van den (1998). Realistic Mathematics Education. Work in progress, Text based on the NORMA-lecture held in Kristiansand, Norway on June 5–9, 1998, Freudenthal Institute. Retrieved frpm: http://www.fi.uu.nl/en/rme/ (Accessed July 13, 2012).

Hiebert, J., & Lefevre, P. (1986). Procedural and conceptual knowledge. In J. Hiebert (Ed.), *Conceptual and Procedural Knowledge: The Case of Mathematics* (pp. 1–27). Hillsdale, NJ: Lawrence Erlbaum.

Hilbert, D. (1900). *Mathematische Probleme*. Göttingen Nachrichten, 253–97.

(1926). Über das Unendliche. *Mathematische Annalen* (95), 161–90.

Hoffer, A. (1981). Geometry is more than proof. *Mathematics Teacher*, 74, 11–18.

Horgan, J. (1994). Profile: Andre Weill, great French-born mathematician, *Scientific American*, 270 (6), June 1994, 33–34.

Howat, H. (2006). *Participation in Elementary Mathematics: An Analysis of Engagement, Attainment and Intervention*. PhD thesis, University of Warwick.

Howson, G. C. (1982). *A History of Mathematics Education in England*. Cambridge: Cambridge University Press.

Hughes-Hallett, D. (1991). Visualization and Calculus Reform. In W. Zimmermann & S. Cunningham (eds.), *Visualization in Teaching and Learning Mathematics*, MAA Notes No. 19, 121–126.

Inglis, M., Mejia-Ramos, J. P., & Simpson, A. P. (2007). Modelling mathematical argumentation: The importance of qualification. *Educational Studies in Mathematics*, 66(7), 3–21.

Inoue, S., & Matsuzawa, T. (2007). Working memory of numerals in chimpanzees. *Current Biology*, 17(23), R1004–R1005.

Jackson, C., & Leffingwell, R. (1999). The role of instructors in creating math anxiety in students from kindergarten through college. *Mathematics Teacher*, 92(7), 583–7.

James, W. (1890). *The Principles of Psychology*. Vols. I & II. New York: Henry Holt.

Johnson, D. C. (Ed.) (1989): *Children's Mathematical Frameworks 8–13: A Study of Classroom Teaching*. Windsor, UK: NFER-Nelson.

Jones, W. (2001). Applying psychology to the teaching of basic math: A case study. *Inquiry*, 6(2), 60–5.

Jowett, B. (1871). *Plato's The Republic*. New York: Scribner's Sons.

Joyce, D. E. (1998). *Euclid's Elements*. Retrieved from http://aleph0.clarku.edu/~djoyce/java/elements/elements.html on 26th March 2012.

Kant, E. (1781). *Kritik der reinen Vernunft* (Critique of Pure Reason). Königsberg, Germany.

Katz, M., & Tall, D. O. (2012). The tension between intuitive infinitesimals and formal analysis. In Bharath Sriraman (Ed.), *Crossroads in the History of Mathematics and Mathematics Education* (pp. 71–90). The Montana Mathematics Enthusiast Monographs in Mathematics Education 12. Charlotte, NC: Information Age Publishing.

Keisler, H. J. (1976). *Foundations of Infinitesimal Calculus*. Boston: Prindle, Weber & Schmidt.

Kerslake, D. (1986). *Fractions: Children's Strategies and Errors*. London: NFER-Nelson.

Koichu, B. (2008). On considerations of parsimony in mathematical problem solving. In O. Figueras, J. L. Cortina, S. Alatorre, T. Rojano, & A. Sepulova (Eds.), *Proceedings of the 32nd Conference of the International Group for the Psychology of Mathematics Education*. Vol. 3 (pp. 273–80), Morelia, Mexico.

Koichu, B., & Berman, A. (2005). When do gifted high school students use geometry to solve geometry problems? *The Journal of Secondary Gifted Education*, 16(4), 168–79.

Kollar, D. (2000). Article in the *Sacramento Bee* (California), December 11, 2000.

Krutetskii, V. A. (1976). *The Psychology of Mathematical Abilities in Schoolchildren*. Chicago: University of Chicago Press.

Kuhn, T. (1962). *The Structure of Scientific Revolutions*. Chicago: University of Chicago Press.

Lakoff, G. (1987). *Women, Fire, and Dangerous Things: What Categories Reveal About the Mind*. Chicago: University of Chicago Press.

Lakoff, G., & Johnson, M. (1980). *Metaphors We Live By*. Chicago: University of Chicago Press.

(1999). *Philosophy in the Flesh: The Embodied Mind and Its Challenge to Western Thought*. New York: Basic Books.

Lakoff, G. & Nùñez, R. (2000). *Where Mathematics Comes From: How the Embodied Mind Brings Mathematics into Being*. New York: Basic Books.

Lave, J., & Wenger, E. (1991). *Situated Learning: Legitimate Peripheral Participation*. Cambridge: Cambridge University Press.

Lean, G., & Clements, K. (1981). Spatial ability, visual imagery, and mathematical performance. *Educational Studies in Mathematics*, 12(3), 267–99.

Leibniz, G. W. (1920). *The Early Mathematical Manuscripts of Leibniz*, ed. and trans. by J. M. Child. Chicago: University of Chicago Press.

Li, L., & Tall, D. O. (1993). Constructing different concept images of sequences and limits by programming. In *Proceedings of PME* 17, Japan, 2, 41–8.

Lima, R. N. de, & Tall, D. O. (2006). The concept of equation: What have students met before? In *Proceedings of the 30th Conference of the International Group for the Psychology of Mathematics Education*, Prague, Czech Republic, 4, 233–41.

(2008). Procedural embodiment and magic in linear equations. *Educational Studies in Mathematics*, 67(1), 3–18.

Ma, L. (1999a). A meta-analysis of the relationship between anxiety toward mathematics and achievement in mathematics. *Journal for Research in Mathematics Education*, 30(5), 520–40.

(1999b). *Knowing and Teaching Elementary Mathematics*. Mahwah, NJ: Lawrence Erlbaum.

MacLane, S. (1994). Responses to theoretical mathematics. *Bulletin (new series) of the American Mathematical Society*, 30(2), 190–1.

Mason, J. (1989). Mathematical abstraction as the result of a delicate shift of attention. *For the Learning of Mathematics*, 9(2), 2–8.

(2002). *Researching Your Own Practice: The Discipline of Noticing*. London: Routledge Falmer.

Mason, J., Burton, L., & Stacey, K. (1982). *Thinking Mathematically*. London: Addison-Wesley.

Matthews, G. (1964). *Calculus*. London: John Murray.

McGowen, M. A. (1998). *Cognitive Units, Concept Images, and Cognitive Collages: An Examination of the Process of Knowledge Construction*. PhD thesis, University of Warwick.

McGowen, M. A., & Tall, D. O. (2013). Flexible Thinking and Met-befores: Impact on Learning Mathematics, with Particular Reference to the Minus Sign. Retrieved from: http://homepages.warwick.ac.uk/staff/David.Tall/downloads.html (Accessed February 19, 2013).

Md Ali, R. (2006). *Teachers' Indications and Pupils' Construal and Knowledge of Fractions: The Case of Malaysia*. PhD thesis, University of Warwick.

Mejia-Ramos, J. P. (2008). *The Construction and Evaluation of Arguments in Undergraduate Mathematics*. PhD thesis, University of Warwick.

Miller, G. A. (1956). The magic number seven plus or minus two: Some limits on our capacity for processing information. *Psychological Review*, 63, 81–97.

Monaghan, J. D. (1986). *Adolescent's Understanding of Limits and Infinity*. PhD thesis, University of Warwick.

National Council of Teachers of Mathematics. (1989). *Curriculum and Evaluation Standards for School Mathematics*. Reston, VA: National Council of Teachers of Mathematics.

Neill, H., & Shuard, H. (1982). *Teaching Calculus*. London: Blackie & Son.

Neugebauer, O. (1969). *The Exact Sciences in Antiquity* (2nd ed.). Reprinted by Dover, New York.

Núñez, R., Edwards, L. D., & Matos, J. P. (1999). Embodied cognition as grounding for situatedness and context in mathematics education. *Educational Studies in Mathematics*, 39(1–3), 45–65.

Nunokawa, K. (2005). Mathematical problem solving and learning mathematics: What we expect students to obtain. *Journal of Mathematical Behavior*, 24, 325–40.

Pegg, J. (1991). Editorial. *Australian Senior Mathematics Journal*, 5(2), 70.

Pegg, J., & Tall, D. O. (2005). The fundamental cycle of concept construction underlying various theoretical frameworks. *International Reviews on Mathematical Education* (ZDM), 37(6), 468–75.

Peirce, C. S. (1991). *Peirce on Signs: Writings on Semiotic* (ed. Hoopes, J.). University of North Carolina Press.

Piaget, J. (1926). *The Language and Thought of the Child*. New York: Harcourt, Brace, Jovanovich.

   (1952). *The Child's Conception of Number*. London: Routledge & Kegan Paul.

Piaget, J., & Inhelder, B. (1958). *Growth of Logical Thinking*. London: Routledge & Kegan Paul.

Pinto, M. M. F. (1998). *Students' Understanding of Real Analysis*. PhD thesis, University of Warwick.

Pinto, M. M. F., & Tall, D. O. (1999). Student constructions of formal theory: Giving and extracting meaning. In O. Zaslavsky (Ed.), *Proceedings of the 23rd Conference of PME*, Haifa, Israel, 4, 65–73.

   (2001). Following students' development in a traditional university classroom. In Marja van den Heuvel-Panhuizen (Ed.), *Proceedings of the 25th Conference of the International Group for the Psychology of Mathematics Education* 4, 57–64. Utrecht, The Netherlands.

——— (2002). Building formal mathematics on visual imagery: A theory and a case study. *For the Learning of Mathematics*, 22(1), 2–10.

Pitta, D. (1998). *Beyond the Obvious: Mental Representations and Elementary Arithmetic.* PhD thesis, University of Warwick.

Pitta, D., & Gray, E. M. (1997). In the mind: What can imagery tell us about success and failure in arithmetic? In G. A. Makrides (Ed.), *Proceedings of the First Mediterranean Conference on Mathematics*, Nicosia: Cyprus, 29–41.

——— (1999). Changing Emily's images. In A. Pinel (Ed.), *Teaching, Learning and Primary Mathematics* (pp. 56–60). Derby, UK: Association of Teachers of Mathematics.

Plake, B. S., & Parker, C. S. (1982). The development and validation of a revised version of the Mathematics Anxiety Rating Scale. *Educational and Psychological Measurement*, 42(2), 551–7.

Plato (360 BC). *The Republic.* Book VII, trans. by Benjamin Jowett (1871). New York : Scribner's Sons. Reprinted 1941, New York: The Modern Library.

Playfair, J. (1860). *Elements of geometry; containing the first six books of Euclid, with two books on the geometry of solids. To which are added, elements of plane and spherical trigonometry*, Philadelphia: J. B. Lippincott & Co.

Poincaré, H. (1913). *The Foundations of Science*, trans. by G. B. Halsted. New York: The Science Press.

Pólya, G. (1945). *How to Solve It.* Princeton, NJ: Princeton University Press. Reprinted 1957, Garden City, NY: Doubleday.

Poynter, A. (2004). *Effect as a Pivot between Actions and Symbols: The case of Vector.* PhD thesis, University of Warwick.

Presmeg, N. C. (1986). Visualisation and mathematical giftedness. *Educational Studies in Mathematics*, 17(3), 297–311.

Reid, C. (1996). *Hilbert.* New York: Springer.

Richardson, F. C., & Suinn, R. M. (1972). The Mathematics Anxiety Rating Scale: Psychometric data. *Journal of Counseling Psychology*, 19(6), 551–4.

Robinson, A. (1966). *Non-Standard Analysis.* Amsterdam: North Holland.

Rodd, M. M. (2000). On mathematical warrants. *Mathematical Thinking and Learning*, 2 (3), 221–44.

Rosch, E., Mervis, C. B., Gray, W. D., Johnson, D. M., & Boyes-Barem, P. (1976). Basic objects in natural categories. *Cognitive Psychology*, 8, 382–439.

Rosnick, P. (1981). Some misconceptions concerning the concept of variable. Are you careful about defining your variables? *Mathematics Teacher*, 74(6), 418–20, 450.

Sangwin, C. J. (2004). Assessing mathematics automatically using computer algebra and the internet. *Teaching Mathematics and Its Applications*, 23(1), 1–14.

Saussure, F. (1916). *Cours de linguistique génerale* (ed. Bally, C. & Séchehaye, A.). Paris: Payot.

Schools Mathematics Project (1982). *Advanced Mathematics* Book 1. Cambridge: Cambridge University Press.

Schwarzenberger, R. L. E., & Tall, D. O. (1978). Conflicts in the learning of real numbers and limits. *Mathematics Teaching*, 82, 44–9.

Sfard, A. (1991). On the dual nature of mathematical conceptions: Reflections on processes and objects as different sides of the same coin. *Educational Studies in Mathematics*, 22, 1–36.

(1992). Operational origins of mathematical objects and the quandary of reification – the case of function. In Guershon Harel & Ed Dubinsky (Eds.), *The Concept of Function: Aspects of Epistemology and Pedagogy*, MAA Notes 25 (pp. 59–84). Washington, DC: Mathematical Association of America.

(2008). *Thinking as Communicating*. New York: Cambridge University Press.

Sheffield, D., & Hunt, T. (2006). How does anxiety influence maths performance and what can we do about it? *MSOR Connections*, 6(4), 19–23.

Skemp, R. R. (1971). *The Psychology of Learning Mathematics*. London: Penguin.

(1976). Relational understanding and instrumental understanding. *Mathematics Teaching*, 77, 20–6.

(1979). *Intelligence, Learning, and Action*. London: John Wiley & Sons.

Snapper, E. (1979). The three crises in mathematics: Logicism, intuitionism and formalism. *Mathematics Magazine*, 52(4), 207–16.

Steele, E., & Arth, A. (1998). Lowering anxiety in the math curriculum. *Education Digest*, 63(7), 18–24.

Stewart, I. N., & Tall, D. O. (1983). *Complex Analysis*. Cambridge: Cambridge University Press.

(2000). *Algebraic Number Theory and Fermat's Last Theorem* (3rd ed.). Natick, MA: A. K. Peters.

Strauss, A., & Corbin, J. (1990). *Basics of Qualitative Research: Grounded Theory Procedures and Techniques*. London: SAGE.

Stroyan, K. D. (1972). Uniform continuity and rates of growth of meromorphic functions. In W. J. Luxemburg & A. Robinson (Eds.), *Contributions to Non-Standard Analysis* (pp. 47–64). Amsterdam: North-Holland.

Struik, D. J. (1969). *A Source Book in Mathematics, 1200–1800*. Cambridge, MA: Harvard University Press.

Sullivan, K. (1976). The teaching of elementary calculus: An approach using infinitesimals, *American Mathematical Monthly*, 83, 370–5.

Tall, D. O. (1977). Cognitive conflict in the learning of mathematics. Presented at the first meeting of the *International Group for the Psychology of Learning Mathematics*, Utrecht, The Netherlands. Retrieved from: http://homepages.warwick.ac.uk/staff/David.Tall/pdfs/dot1977a-cog-confl-pme.pdf (Accessed February 19, 2013).

(1979). Cognitive aspects of proof, with special reference to the irrationality of $\sqrt{2}$. In *Proceedings of the Third International Conference for the Psychology of Mathematics Education*, Warwick, 206–7.

(1980a). Looking at graphs through infinitesimal microscopes, windows and telescopes. *Mathematical Gazette*, 64, 22–49.

(1980b). The anatomy of a discovery in mathematical research. *For the Learning of Mathematics*, 1(2), 25–30.

(1980c). Intuitive infinitesimals in the calculus. *Abstracts of Short Communications, Fourth International Congress on Mathematical Education*, Berkeley, p. C5. Full paper available from http://www.warwick.ac.uk/staff/David.Tall/pdfs/dot1980c-intuitive-infls.pdf (Accessed February 19, 2013).

(1985). Understanding the calculus. *Mathematics Teaching*, 10, 49–53.

(1986a). *Building and Testing a Cognitive Approach to the Calculus Using Interactive Computer Graphics*. PhD thesis, University of Warwick.

(1986b). Constructing the concept image of a tangent. In *Proceedings of the Eleventh International Conference of PME*, Montreal, III, 69–75.

(1986c). Talking about fractions. *Micromath*, 2(2), 8–10.

(1986d). A graphical approach to integration and the fundamental theorem. *Mathematics Teaching*, 113, 48–51.

(1991a). Recent developments in the use of the computer to visualize and symbolize calculus concepts. In *The Laboratory Approach to Teaching Calculus*, M.A.A. Notes 20. (pp. 15–25). Washington, DC: Mathematical Association of America.

(1991b). *Real Functions and Graphs* (for the BBC computer and Nimbus PC). Cambridge: Cambridge University Press.

(1991c). *Advanced Mathematical Thinking*. Dordrecht, The Netherlands: Kluwer.

(1992). Visualizing differentials in two and three dimensions. *Teaching Mathematics and Its Applications*, 11(1), 1–7.

(2001). A child thinking about infinity. *Journal of Mathematical Behavior*, 20, 7–19.

(2004). Thinking through three worlds of mathematics. In *Proceedings of the 28th Conference of the International Group for the Psychology of Mathematics Education*, Bergen, Norway, 4, 281–8.

(2009). Dynamic mathematics and the blending of knowledge structures in the calculus. *ZDM – The International Journal on Mathematics Education*, 41(4), 481–92.

Tall, D. O., Davis, G. E., & Thomas, M. O. J. (1997). What is the object of the encapsulation of a process? In F. Biddulph & K. Carr (Eds.), *People in Mathematics Education, MERGA 20, Aotearoa*, Rotarua, New Zealand, 2, 132–9.

Tall, D. O., Lima, R. N. de, & Healy, L. (2013). Evolving a three-world framework for solving algebraic equations in the light of what a student has met before. Available from http://homepages.warwick.ac.uk/staff/David.Tall/downloads. html (Accessed February 19, 2013.)

Tall, D. O., Thomas, M. O. J., Davis, G. E., Gray, E. M., & Simpson, A. P. (2000). What is the object of the encapsulation of a process? *Journal of Mathematical Behavior*, 18(2), 1–19.

Tall, D. O., & Vinner, S. (1981). Concept image and concept definition in mathematics, with special reference to limits and continuity. *Educational Studies in Mathematics*, 12, 151–69.

Tall, D. O., Yevdokimov, O., Koichu, B., Whiteley, W., Kondratieva, M., & Cheng, Ying-Hao (2012). Cognitive development of proof. In G. Hanna & M. De Villiers (Eds.), *ICMI 19: Proof and Proving in Mathematics Education*.

Tarski, A. (1930). Une contribution á la théorie de la mesure. *Fundamenta Mathematicae*. 15, 42–50.

Tempelaar, D., & Caspers, W. (2008). De rol van de instaptoets. *Nieuw Archief voor Wiskunde*, 5/9(1), 66–71.

Thurston, W. P. (1990). Mathematical education. *Notices of the American Mathematical Society*, 37(7), 844–50.

(1994). On proof and progress in mathematics. *Bulletin of the American Mathematical Society*, 30(2), 161–77.

Tobias, S. (1990). Mathematics anxiety: An update. *NACADA Journal, 10*, 47–50.

Tomasello, M. (1999). *The Cultural Origins of Human Cognition*. Cambridge, MA: Harvard University Press.

Toulmin, S. E. (1958). *The Uses of Argument*. Cambridge: Cambridge University Press.

Van der Waerden, B. L. (1980). *A History of Algebra: From al Khwarizmi to Emmy Noether*. New York: Springer-Verlag.

Van Hiele, P. M. (1957). The child's thought and geometry, trans. into English and reproduced in T. P. Carpenter, J. A. Dossey, & J. L. Koehler (Eds.), *Classics in Mathematics Education* (pp. 61–55). Reston, VA: National Council of Teachers of Mathematics.

(1959). Development and the learning process. *Acta Paedagogica Ultrajectina* (pp. 1–31). Gröningen: J. B. Wolters.

(1986). *Structure and Insight*. Orlando, FL: Academic Press.

(2002). Similarities and differences between the theory of learning and teaching of Skemp and the Van Hiele levels of thinking. In D. O. Tall & M. O. J. Thomas (Eds.), *Intelligence, Learning and Understanding – A Tribute to Richard Skemp* (pp. 27–47). Flaxton, Australia: Post Pressed.

Van Hiele-Geldof, D. (1984). The didactics of geometry in the lowest class of secondary school. In D. Fuys, D. Geddes, & R. Tischler (Eds.), *English Translation of Selected Writings of Dina van Hiele-Geldof and Pierre M. van Hiele* (pp. 1–214). Brooklyn, NY: Brooklyn College.

Vinner, S., & Hershkowitz R. (1980). Concept images and some common cognitive paths in the development of some simple geometric concepts. In *Proceedings of the Fourth International Conference of PME*, Berkeley, 177–84.

Vlassis, J. (2002). The balance model: Hindrance or support for the solving of linear equations with one unknown. *Educational Studies in Mathematics*, 49, 341–59.

Watson, A. (subsequently Poynter, A.), Spyrou, P., & Tall, D. O. (2003). The relationship between physical embodiment and mathematical symbolism: The concept of vector. *The Mediterranean Journal of Mathematics Education*, 1(2), 73–97.

Weber, H. (1893). Leopold Kronecker. *Mathematische Annalen*, 43, 1–25.

Weber, K. (2001). Student difficulty in constructing proofs: The need for strategic knowledge. *Educational Studies in Mathematics*, 48(1), 101–19.

(2004). Traditional instruction in advanced mathematics courses: A case study of one professor's lectures and proofs in an introductory real analysis course. *Journal of Mathematical Behavior*, 23, 115–33.

Werkgroep 3TU. (2006). Aansluiting vwo en technische univrsiteiten. *Euclides*, 81(5), 242–7.

Wessel, C. (1799). Om directionens analytiske betegning, et forsøg, anvendt fornemmelig til plane og sphaeriske polygoners opløsning, *Nye samling af det Kongelige Danske Videnskabernes Selskabs Skrifter*, 5, 496–518.

Weyl, H. (1918). *Das Continuum*. trans. by Pollard, S. & Hole, T. (1987) as *The Continuum: A Critical Examination of the Foundation of Analysis*. New York: Dover.

Wilensky, U. (1993). *Connected Mathematics: Building Concrete Relationships with Mathematical Knowledge*. PhD thesis, M.I.T. Retrieved from: http://ccl.north-western.edu/papers/download/Wilensky-thesis.pdf (Accessed July 11, 2012).

(1998). What is normal anyway? Therapy for epistemological anxiety. *Educational Studies in Mathematics*, 33(2), 171–202.

Wilkins, D. R. (2002). *The Analyst by George Berkeley*. Retrieved from www.maths.tcd.ie/pub/HistMath/People/Berkeley/Analyst/Analyst.pdf (Accessed April 21, 2012).

Wood, N. G. (1992). *Mathematical Analysis: A Comparison of student development and historical development*. PhD thesis, Cambridge University.

Woodard, T. (2004). The effects of math anxiety on post-secondary developmental students as related to achievement, gender, and age. *Virginia Mathematics Teacher*, Fall, 7–9.

Zeeman, E. C. (1960). Unknotting spheres in five dimensions. *Bulletin of the American Mathematical Society*, 66, 198.

(1977). *Catastrophe Theory*. London: Addison-Wesley.

Index

The Learning in Doing series was founded in 1987 by Roy Pea and John Seely Brown.

Lightning Source UK Ltd.
Milton Keynes UK
UKOW01f1220080817

306901UK00021B/554/P